ABLE TO PROCURE AN ARTIFICIAL PHALLUS

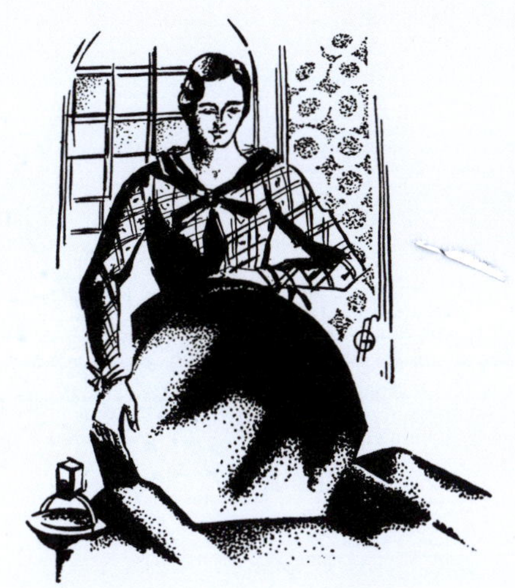

MILLIE WILSON *The Museum of Lesbian Dreams*

ARRIVE AFTER DARK IN CLOSED GONDOLAS

Edited by David Evans Frantz
and Amy L. Powell

With contributions by
Jill H. Casid
Beatriz Cortez
David Evans Frantz
Richard Hawkins
Kang Seung Lee
Jess Rath

Exhibition curated by
David Evans Frantz

Krannert Art Museum, University of Illinois Urbana-Champaign Inventory Press

CONTENTS

FOREWORD

KRANNERT ART MUSEUM (KAM) is honored to present the first retrospective exhibition and publication devoted to Millie Wilson's astonishing body of work. *The Museum of Lesbian Dreams* exemplifies our long-standing commitment to cutting-edge, interdisciplinary research, especially on understudied contemporary artists from positions marginalized in the history of art. Wilson taught at our university for two years in the 1980s, so hosting the exhibition also extends our ongoing project to illuminate artists connected to, and shaped by, Illinois.

A deeply influential professor at the California Institute of the Arts who is beloved by her fellow artists, Wilson has yet to receive due recognition. This may stem in part from the remarkably varied character of her practice, which evades succinct description, and the fact that she has often operated outside the gallery system. Wilson explores feminist and queer subjects with incisiveness and humor, often through institutional critique that examines the conditions in which art institutions have diminished or effaced these positions.

We are immensely grateful to guest curator David Evans Frantz, who has been developing this exhibition and publication since 2019, in close rapport with the artist. David's intellectual brio, passionate advocacy, and groundbreaking research have been at the core of this project. KAM's Curator of Modern and Contemporary Art and Curator of Campus Arts Research Amy L. Powell has organized the exhibition for the museum with characteristic rigor, intellect, and clarity.

It is impossible to adequately convey our gratitude to Millie Wilson for opening up her significant body of work for reassessment. Her collaboration and commitment have been the bedrock of the project. We admire her dedication to creating such cerebral and affecting work and for the surprising, beautiful, and often amusing ways she has interrogated so many histories.

In addition to many loans directly from the artist in Austin, Texas, the exhibition includes significant loans from institutions and private collectors. We are indebted to all the lenders.

An initiative of this scale demands substantial external support, and we are profoundly grateful to the Terra Foundation for American Art, the Henry Luce Foundation, and The Andy Warhol Foundation for the Visual Arts, as well as the Michael Asher Foundation, the Eileen Harris Norton Foundation, the Richard M. and Rosann Gelvin Noel Krannert Art Museum Fund, and additional support from Jerry Carden and Tim Temple, Nancy Davidson and Greg Drasler, Brice Hutchcraft, Tim Hutchison and Michael Lambert, Steven Incontro and David Joselit, Dirk Mol and Jerry Wray, Ingrid Nyeboe/President of the Louise Fishman Foundation, Mary Parker, Julie Rundell, and an anonymous donor. The project is also supported by a grant from the Illinois Arts Council Agency.

JON L. SEYDL
Director
Krannert Art Museum

MILLIE WILSON: MISS WORLD

David Evans Frantz

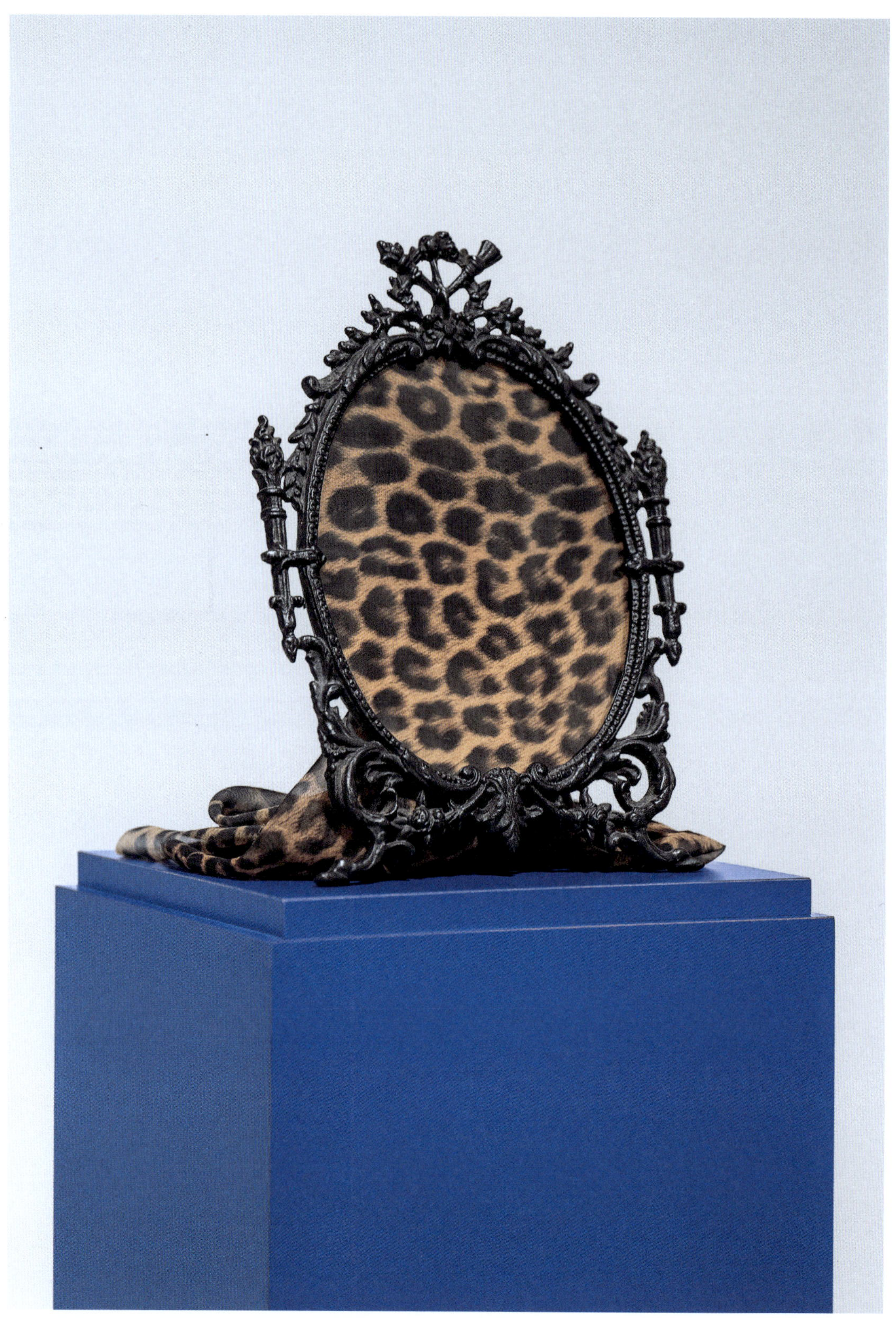

OPPOSITE *Miss Meret*, 1991. Iron frame, mirror, chiffon, plexiglass, and Formica-veneer pedestal, 66 × 13 × 20 in. (167.6 × 33 × 50.8 cm). Collection of Gwen and Peter Norton, New York

Founded in 1989, the *Museum of Lesbian Dreams* is a projection, a proposition, and a provocation.[1] While museums are most often associated with institutional power, donor largesse, and ideas of collective enterprise and the public good, this museum is, in fact, the singular project of artist Millie Wilson, a vehicle for her examination of histories of queer deviance and for her idiosyncratic riffs on modern and contemporary art history. Wilson's project builds on the legacies of artists who have similarly grappled with the role of museums and their political and social authority, at the same time as it playfully and queerly engages the museological enterprise. As Wilson describes it:

> The [Museum of Lesbian Dreams] will provide a kind of natural science of transgressing lesbian stereotypes and inventing signs for her subjectivity, desire and presence by decolonizing the oppressive ones. Along with elegant signage, didactic brochures and panels, the individual pieces will function together to cross-reference each other. In the numerous exchanges of information, a complexity of discourses and a multiplicity of pleasures will be proposed.[2]

Wilson's museum has no permanent location but instead takes physical form sporadically through the artist's installations in galleries and museums. Its collection accumulates through objects she makes for shows, yet she does not insist that the collection remain together; Wilson has sold works to collectors, and works have found their way into museum holdings throughout the United States via purchase and donation. As the artist teased soon after initiating the project, "The Museum of Lesbian Dreams can be anywhere. This is making a lot of people very nervous!"[3]

Wilson inaugurated her *Museum of Lesbian Dreams* at a pivotal moment in queer culture in the United States. The decade that followed witnessed the continued influence of activist groups such as the AIDS Coalition to Unleash Power (ACT UP) in combating misinformation about and erasure of the AIDS crisis. Foundational texts in what would come to be known as queer theory also appeared, such as Judith Butler's *Gender Trouble* and Eve Kosofsky Sedgwick's *Epistemology of the Closet*, both published in 1990. Wilson's work anticipated the decade's theoretical discourses; as she observed in the late 1980s, lesbians were absent from the theorization of postmodernism, which prompted her to more directly examine queer history and identities in her practice.[4] Indeed, Wilson has consistently drawn attention to the absence of women and gender-nonconforming people in contemporary art. In one of her most oft-quoted assertions, Wilson argued that to be a painter and contend with the legacy of the male-dominated canon, a woman artist must engage in "aesthetic cross-dressing."[5] Her conception of queerness and lesbian identity emerged from an unruly context on the West Coast, and her work provocatively contends with questions of gender and sexuality, respectability politics, and the significance of artistic production in turbulent times.

Millie Wilson: The Museum of Lesbian Dreams is the first retrospective exhibition of this influential artist's work. Alongside peers such as Nayland Blake, Felix Gonzalez-Torres, and Lorna Simpson, Wilson joined 1980s postmodernism with the personally and politically charged conceptualism of the 1990s. In a 1992 *New York Times* article about how AIDS had affected queer artistic production, writer Michael Cunningham identified Wilson as the most prominent American artist exploring lesbian identity.[6] Between 1989 and 2000 Wilson realized eleven major installations, and her work appeared in era-defining exhibitions on gender and sexuality, including the dueling iterations of *Bad Girls* at the New Museum of Contemporary Art in New York and UCLA's Frederick S. Wight Art Gallery in 1994, and *In a Different Light*, the first museum show on queer art history, mounted in 1995 at the University Art Museum and Pacific Film Archive, University of California, Berkeley.[7]

Wilson was an influential faculty member at the esteemed California Institute of the Arts (CalArts) for twenty-nine years, from 1985 to 2014. Before that, she taught for two years at the University of Illinois Urbana-Champaign. Through her roles as teacher and mentor, she profoundly impacted generations of artists, many of whom have since achieved considerable art-world acclaim.[8] As a pedagogue, Wilson was creative, curious, and fearless, organizing courses on topics that excited both her and her students, including seminars on drag, femme fatales, male hysteria, teen films, and vampires. As a mentor, Wilson was, according to her students, generous and steadfast in her support. While this publication and the exhibition it accompanies focuses primarily on Wilson's artistic contributions, the book also includes a conversation among four of Wilson's former students (see pp. 165–74) that seeks to illuminate her efficacy as an educator, particularly in supporting discussions around queerness on campus and its role in artistic production.[9]

Wilson's work is as intellectually robust as it is aesthetically pleasurable. As the art itself and this essay demonstrate, Wilson revels in the (often unexpected) visually sublime; by her own admission, she is a "surface freak."[10] Throughout her career, Wilson has deftly examined issues of gender politics, queerness, and historical erasure, always with a critical yet mischievous eye toward the art-historical canon and art institutions. Wilson's friend, artist Robert Blanchon, remarked in an interview with her, that rather than creating an artistic niche by uniting seemingly disparate interests—such as Surrealist art and 1960s lesbian pulp—Wilson creates a conceptual space of possibility in her work. To this, Wilson agreed, "I try to make an intersection that hasn't existed before."[11] This is the space of potential within the *Museum of Lesbian Dreams*.

She Was Framed

In 1980 Wilson enrolled in the MFA program at the University of Houston to study painting. Surrealism, feminist politics, and attention to the body as a contested site guided her artistic inquiries at the time. In the decade prior to her enrollment, Wilson completed her BA in English at the University of Texas at Austin, got married, got divorced, came out, educated herself in the women's movement, and (in her words) "got a studio and a haircut."[12] The work she made in the MFA program often broke from the two-dimensional plane by incorporating scavenged objects onto the canvas's painted surface in sculptural assemblages recalling paintings by Jasper Johns and Robert Rauschenberg. Many of these works demonstrate

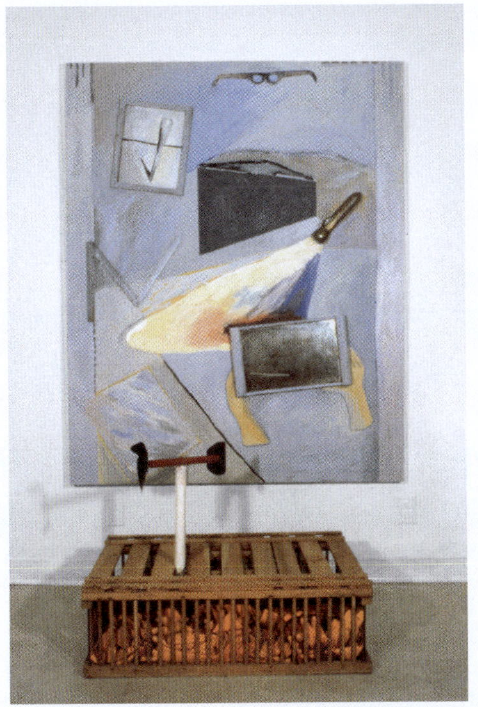

FIG. 1 *Classical Reverie*, 1982. Acrylic on canvas with mixed media, 90 × 50 × 36 in. (228.6 × 127 × 91.4 cm)

Wilson's affinity for art-historical quotation, already active at this early stage in her career. For example, *Classical Reverie* (1982; fig. 1) positions a patinaed metal flashlight on the canvas, an artful allusion to Johns's bronze-case *Flashlight* series from the late 1950s and early 1960s.[13]

For the written component of her master's thesis, Wilson addressed the work of five artists she identified as having "emotional power": Laurie Anderson, Louise Bourgeois, Mary Beth Edelson, Eve Hesse, and Ree Morton. According to Wilson, their work contains "an implicit refusal of what is given as appropriate to the behavior of art, especially the strictly formal and cerebral. In their seemingly regressive preoccupation with negative and dimly sensed feelings, there is an unwillingness to reinforce the false clarity of any 'objective' cultural rationale."[14] The affinities identified in this quotation would also animate Wilson's paintings of the later 1980s. In such works, Wilson rendered the ghostly outlines of bodies in various shades and finishes of black and dark gray, sometimes emphasizing them with an expressive white or red outline or by creating a painterly texture within a body's frame. These shadowy configurations are based on images the artist sourced from newspapers, reflecting her fascination with recasting ubiquitous and mundane imagery as uncanny and unsettling while also engaging postmodern debates around appropriation. For instance, *The Body You Want* (1986; fig. 2) is a large, eight-panel painting on paper of various corporeal silhouettes suspended in darkness. Although photographs of the work reveal subtle differences in the black tones and surface textures of its acrylic paint, when experienced in person such details become more readily apparent through simple shifts of position in relation to the work. This three-dimensional activation anticipates Wilson's subsequent foray into sculpture. Similarly, her humorous and surreal drawings of rooms and otherworldly spaces from this period in her career could be easily mistaken for rough sketches of objects or installations, given their attention to dramatic spatial dynamics (p. 49).

After Wilson earned her MFA, the School of Art and Design at the University of Illinois Urbana-Champaign recruited her to teach painting. She arrived to find an artistic program so dominated by men (with a few significant exceptions, including photographers Bea Nettles and Barbara DeGenevieve) that, as she later quipped, her presence as the department's only out lesbian "inspired some of her male colleagues to uncover the Amazon Conspiracy."[15] Three semesters later, after meeting Wilson while delivering a lecture and critiquing student work at Urbana-Champaign, John Baldessari recruited Wilson to CalArts in Valencia, California.

Newly situated in Southern California, Wilson made a body of work that examined conventions of media representation by establishing a set of conceptual parameters and systems. This choice constituted a significant shift in her painting practice. In *The Los Angeles Times Series* (1988–89; pp. 54–55), Wilson reconceived her artistic

FIG. 2 *The Body You Want*, 1986. Acrylic on paper, eight sheets, 64 × 124 in. (162.6 × 315 cm). ONE National Gay & Lesbian Archives at the USC Libraries

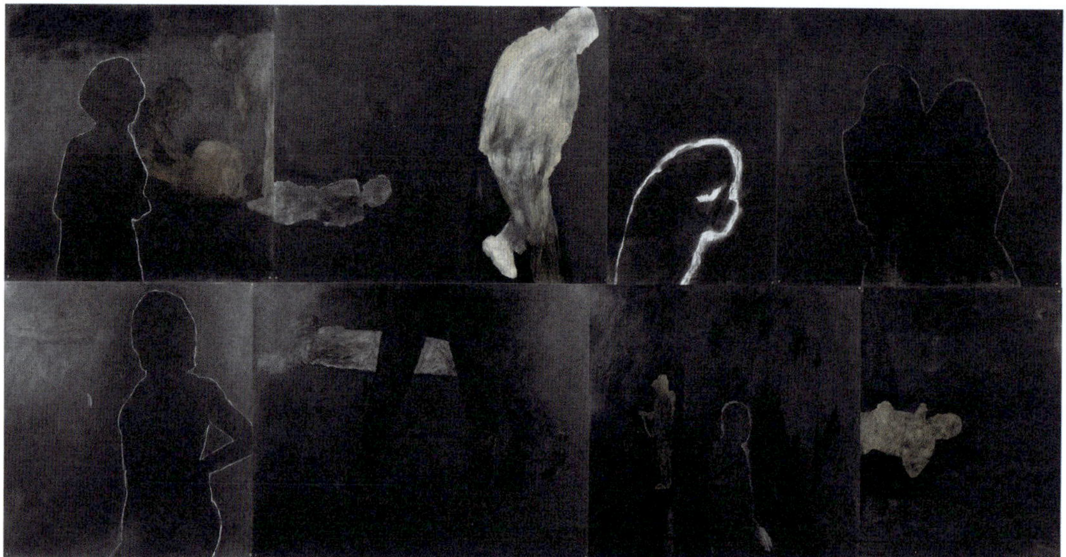

authorship as a matter of "mechanical reproduction rather than . . . expressionism and aesthetic decisions."[16] Each work in the series comprises three to six canvases of varying sizes arranged systematically. All include a canvas matching the dimensions of an unfolded newspaper; these canvases are various tones of gray, light brown, off-white, and yellow. The newspaper dictates each piece's structure, with blocks of black signaling the placement of an image on the page, and sections of white demarcating a detail Wilson has enlarged on a separate canvas or canvases. On a smaller, horizontal canvas, she silkscreened identifying details, including the newspaper section, page number, date, day of the week, related caption(s), and headline(s).

The Los Angeles Times Series focuses on depictions of women and gender-nonconforming individuals selected from news and sports sections where non-cis-male gender presentation was rare. Many of Wilson's headlines and images reflect ingrained assumptions and stereotypes about feminine roles and archetypes. A young girl signifies virtue and innocence; a screaming Palestinian woman denotes violence and victimization; a North Korean terrorist communicates danger and allure. In one composition about the eruption of the volcano Kīlauea on the island of Hawai'i, Wilson paints a smoldering caldera to reference the Hawaiian goddess Pele. In another work, two small accompanying panels present a horizontally bisected portrait of jazz musician and family man Billy Tipton, who lived a quiet life in Spokane, Washington, but after his death was outed as a transman and continually misgendered in sensational media coverage.[17] Wilson's arrangement of canvases in *The Los Angeles Times Series* offers a fragmented view of text and images that circulate, often frictionlessly, in contemporary society while holding up a mirror to underlying ideologies. Wilson quoted artist Martha Rosler to describe her intention with the series as "the appropriation of elements from the dustbin of official historiography . . . to destroy the credibility of those reigning historical accounts in favor of the point of view of that history's designated losers."[18] Her next project continued to follow Rosler's injunction to excavate history and elevate the absent and the under-recognized.

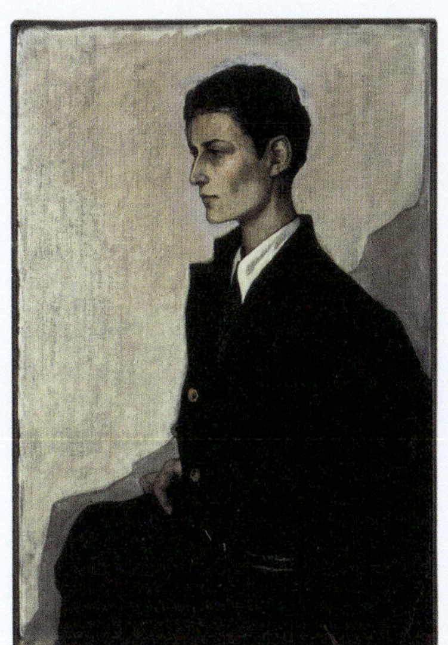

FIG. 3 Romaine Brooks, *Peter (A Young English Girl)*, 1923–24. Oil on canvas, 36⅛ × 24½ in. (91.9 × 62.3 cm). Smithsonian American Art Museum, Washington, DC, Gift of the artist, 1970.70

Fauve Semblant

Wilson's installation *Fauve Semblant: Peter (A Young English Girl)*, which purported to present a rediscovered early twentieth-century lesbian artist named Peter, comprised a pivotal development in her artistic trajectory of spirited institutional critique and queer world-making (pp. 62–84). First presented in 1989 at the dynamic alternative art space LACE (Los Angeles Contemporary Exhibitions), the installation's subtitle and central character's name adopted the title of Romaine Brooks's 1923–24 portrait of the artist Gluck (born Hannah Gluckstein; fig. 3). Both artists' biographies informed Wilson's construction of Peter. Brooks was a wealthy American artist who lived in Paris's Left Bank during the 1920s and was known for painting stylized portraits, mostly of women, in muted tones of gray, lavender, and blue. Gluck was a British painter of landscapes and flowers who circulated in the same bohemian circles as Brooks and was widely known for her lifelong insistence on wearing men's attire. Although Peter shares certain affinities with Brooks and Gluck (for example, her interest in cross-dressing), Wilson took liberties in crafting this character. For instance, Peter is described in the installation's introductory text as coming from a working-class background more closely resembling Wilson's own than Brooks's and Gluck's extravagantly privileged lives. As she devised the installation, Wilson was prompted by the posthumous outing of Billy Tipton to research the history of cross-dressing among women and other people assigned female at birth.[19] The lives of American Civil War soldier, nurse, and spy Franklin Thompson (née Sarah Edmonds); French artist Rosa Bonheur, best known for her paintings of animals; and English vaudeville male impersonator Vesta Tilley all attested to a hidden legacy of masculine presentation and gender transgression preceding the equally unrecognized legacy of Brooks and Gluck.[20]

The title of Wilson's installation, *Fauve Semblant*, positions Peter in relation to the early twentieth-century artists' group known as *les Fauves* (French for "wild beasts"). Neither Brooks nor Gluck aligned with this movement's boldly colored canvases and fondness for the exotic. Rather, Wilson chose the reference because of the Fauves' penchant for the bestial and the untamable, which echoed the salacious pathologization of lesbian sexuality found in contemporaneous sexology studies. Wilson casts Peter as arousing, menacing, confounding, and inconceivable:

> Peter, the artist I have constructed, is a counterfeit feline. She gives the appearance of a wild beast, a semblance of bestiality, whether in reference to The Fauves, that paradigm of masculinity and colonialism

> from which she would have been excluded, or to the sphinx, which symbolized nineteenth-century feminine evil and decadence, as well as the Surrealist androgyne whose riddle was conflated with the question of sexuality. However, by cross-dressing, she does change her spots, so to speak; she demonstrates that gender is constructed. She is a fake several times over. She is a fiction, and, had she actually lived, she would have been an imposter, a woman in men's clothing, a lesbian painter, a lesbian engaged in aesthetic cross-dressing.[21]

Wilson's interest in mimicking the exhibition form was partially inspired by the elaborate presentation of *Mata Mua*, an 1892 painting by Paul Gauguin (at one point a Fauve) at the Museo Nacional Centro de Arte Reina Sofía, Madrid, in 1989.[22] The work was accompanied by a large, aggrandizing photographic portrait of the artist, as well as other images contextualizing Gauguin's life in Tahiti and the Marquesas Islands that, as Wilson observed, epitomized the tendency of museums to uncritically heroize the (male) artist while ignoring the savagery of white imperialism.

Fauve Semblant documents Peter's life and work through the museological display of fictitious objects and documents. The installation includes an introductory wall featuring an enlarged photograph of Wilson dressed dapperly as Peter before a painter's easel. The image was taken by Catherine Opie, then a recent graduate of CalArts, where she had studied with Wilson. Text panels throughout resemble the appearance of museum labels yet provide only fragmentary anecdotes (some contradictory) about Peter's practice and biography. Life-size images of Peter's bowtie, cane, eyeglasses, shoes, and smoking jacket, and vintage photographs of a baby on a tractor and two women in sharply tailored men's suits flesh out the imagined historical context for this artistic, gender, and sexual renegade. A brass plaque under an ornately framed photograph of a painter's palette identifies it as Peter's last, though it appears unused. The triptych *Leotard, Cheater, Painter* is a witty reflection on the work of art in the age of mechanical reproduction and consists of three parts: a mass-produced, cheetah-print leotard stretched over a canvas; a framed black-and-white photograph of cheetah fur; and a painting of cheetah print with numerous miniature silhouettes of a gender-ambiguous figure scattered among the spots.[23] Peter's only surviving painting, *We Two in Solitude Were Wandering There (Sphinx and Wild Lilies)*, is safeguarded behind plexiglass. Taking its title from a poem by Sappho, the canvas alludes to the supposed exoticism of lesbian sexuality, depicting a prowling leopard alongside a bouquet of blooming lilies against a dark background reminiscent of Gluck's sumptuous canvas *Lords and Ladies* (1936; fig. 4).[24]

By concocting the character of Peter as a lesbian and gender-transgressive artistic forebear, Wilson herself became an artistic forerunner for subsequent feminist and queer artists

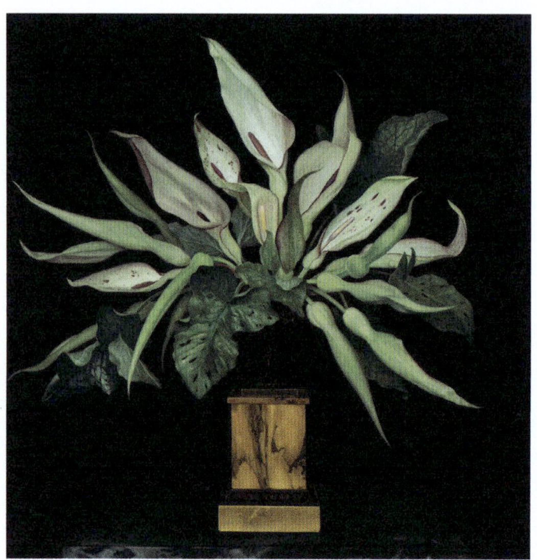

FIG. 4 Gluck, *Lords and Ladies*, 1936. Oil on canvas, 29½ × 29½ in. (75 × 75 cm). Private collection

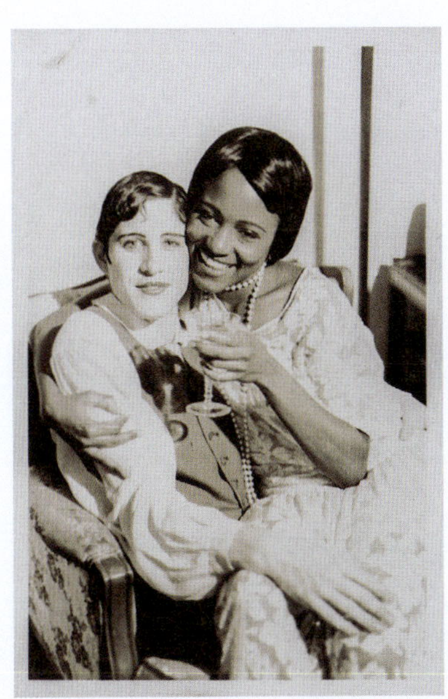

FIG. 5 Zoe Leonard, *The Fae Richards Photo Archive* (detail), 1993–96. Seventy-eight black-and-white photographs, four color photographs, six pages of typed text on typewriter paper, dimensions variable. Created for Cheryl Dunye's film *The Watermelon Woman* (1996)

who investigate the past to imagine liberatory futures. Her imaginative world-making anticipates queer projects that excavate the past to propel new ways of envisioning desire, gender, sexuality. Take, for example, Zoe Leonard's production of an elaborate photo archive of a fictional Black lesbian actress named Fae Richards that is "rediscovered" in Cheryl Dunye's feature film *The Watermelon Woman* (1996; fig. 5); or Chris E. Vargas's Museum of Trans Hirstory & Art (MOTHA; 2010–present), which appropriates the institutional authority of museums—through exhibitions, posters, and a book, among other forms—to (often playfully) investigate the history of trans people and their assimilation into the mainstream.[25]

For Wilson, *Fauve Semblant* marked a significant transformation in her practice, from painting to sculpture and installation. Poetically, Peter's "only surviving painting" is one of Wilson's last significant canvases.[26] The installation also deepened Wilson's engagement with queer politics and history and inaugurated her ongoing project of queer museological play, the *Museum of Lesbian Dreams*.

Living in Someone Else's Paradise

Like many artists of her generation, Wilson found an art historical antecedent in Marcel Duchamp's expansive oeuvre. Numerous works in the *Museum of Lesbian Dreams* take as their point of departure for mischievous experimentation Duchamp's investigation of authorship and authenticity, play with personae and gender conventions, and subversion of seemingly everyday objects. As scholar Amelia Jones has argued, art criticism and production in the United States have addressed the French artist repeatedly as an "obsessive object (and subject) of desire," producing a myriad of Duchamps as the generative patriarch of postwar artistic movements.[27] Wilson and her peers followed in the footsteps of American artists of the 1960s and 1970s who similarly championed Duchamp as a forerunner of pop art, Fluxus, minimalism, happenings, performance art, and conceptualism. For queer artists of the 1990s who engaged appropriation, institutional critique, and identity politics, Duchamp provided a roadmap for producing work about queerness independent of representational frameworks during the escalating culture wars. In their essay about organizing the landmark 1995 exhibition on queer art and culture, *In a Different Light*, artist Nayland Blake reflected on Duchamp's resurgent importance:

> By stepping to one side of aesthetic culture, Duchamp managed to produce works that prefigured many of the experiences and strategies of queers when confronted with straight culture. His works play with gender, twist language into arch double entendres, and (in the form of the three stoppages) question the notion of straightness as the measure of all things.[28]

FIG. 6 Marcel Duchamp, Poster after *Self-Portrait in Profile*, for an exhibition at the Librairie La Hune, Paris, 1959. Silkscreen, 25⅝ × 19¹¹⁄₁₆ in. (65 × 50 cm)

FIG. 7 Cover of Ann Bannon's *Women in the Shadows*, 1959. Published by Gold Medal Book

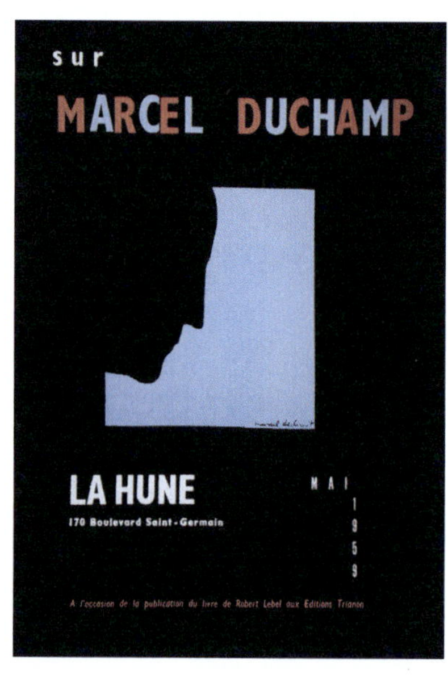

Wilson toyed with Duchampian trickery, made use of the readymade for queer devices, and ran with Duchamp's linguistic cunning. Many works in her 1992 exhibition *Living in Someone Else's Paradise*, presented at San Francisco's venerable alternative art space New Langton Arts, demonstrate her play with his legacy. Wilson's fold-out poster for the show (1992; fig. 8) announces this engagement. It presents the red silhouette of a face in profile interjecting into a block of white, a visual quotation of Duchamp's 1957 multiple *Self-Portrait in Profile*, a torn-paper silhouette mounted on velvet paper, which Duchamp adapted to promote an exhibition of his work at the Librarie La Hune in Paris in 1959 (fig. 6). Where Duchamp's profile faces right, Wilson's silhouette faces left, suggesting a conversation between two elusive figures. Yet Wilson's poster offers another trick. Where Duchamp teases the viewer with an evasive self-portrait, Wilson models her profile after Brooks's depiction of Gluck's square-jawed profile in *Peter (A Young English Girl)*. Wilson's poster thus calls back to suppressed queer histories of art and continues her purposeful muddling of her image and identity with these histories.

The silhouette has an illustrious history as a vernacular medium in Europe and the United States (among other contexts), and both Duchamp and Wilson play with the ability of this simple form to hold contradictory impulses simultaneously. The silhouette is flat yet corporal, anonymous yet particular, suggestive yet silent.[29] Wilson's *Red Top* (1992; p. 107) is a flocked, red silhouette attached to a cardboard easel, reminiscent of a velvety jewelry display stand, presented atop a modular wall shelf recalling the work of minimalist artist Donald Judd. *Red Top* takes its name from post-World War II slang for a lesbian who only dates blondes, while the androgynous silhouette is based on the cover of the 1959 novel *Women in the Shadows* (fig. 7) by Ann Bannon, the "Queen of Lesbian Pulp Fiction."[30] With *Red Top*, Wilson "place[d] a sign for deviant femininity on top of something that looks like a well-behaved Minimalist statement," a gesture typifying her numerous artistic subversions of mainstream (and male-dominated) art history.[31] However, given the artist's own vivid auburn-colored hair and her predilection for flirting with autobiography, the work is also a restrained self-portrait of the artist as both Duchamp and dyke.[32]

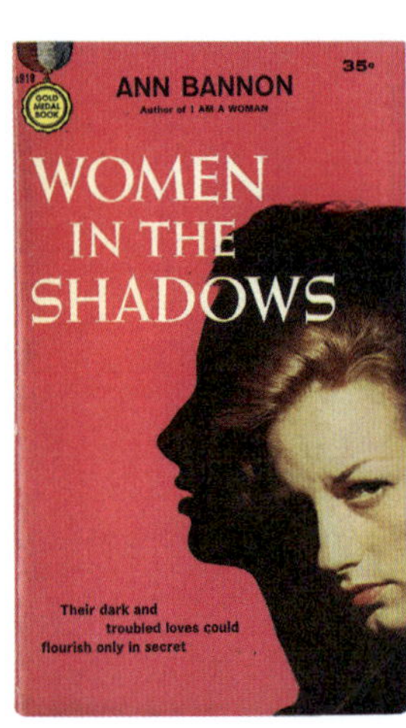

Other works by Wilson also riff on the modernist canon and outmoded terms for queer women. Wilson's *Lace Curtain Window* (1991; p. 123) is both an oversized replica of Duchamp's *Fresh Widow* (1920) and a visual pun on "lace curtain," a 1950s term for a femme lesbian. Similarly, *La folle* is derogatory French slang for both a crazy girl and a lesbian, and Wilson's 1991 work of this name (p. 117) presents a color photocopy of René Magritte's *The Rape* (1934), which depicts a headless, naked female torso onto which Wilson has drawn a mustache that visually remakes her

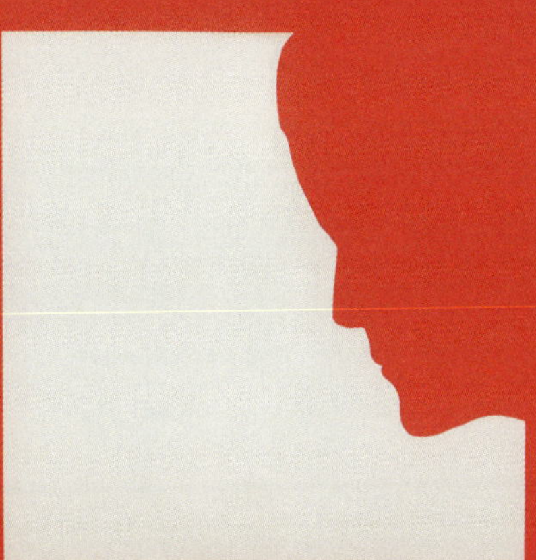

FIG. 8 Poster for Millie Wilson's exhibition *Living in Someone Else's Paradise* at New Langton Arts, San Francisco, 1992. Offset lithograph, 17 × 11 in. (43.2 × 27.9 cm)

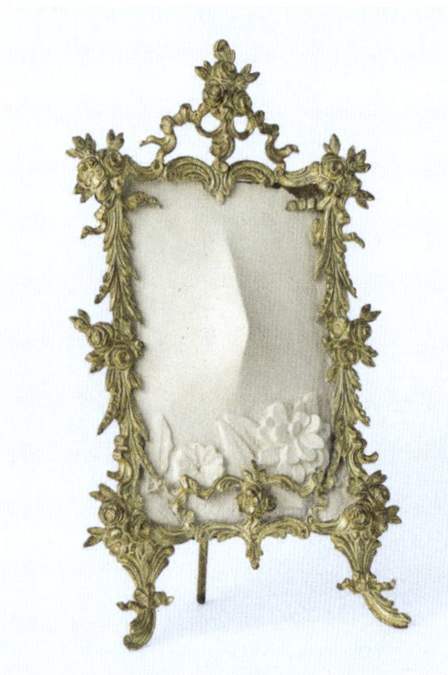

FIG. 9 Meret Oppenheim, *Miss Gardenia*, 1962. Plaster in metal frame with metallic paint, 10⅝ × 6½ × 4¼ in. (27 × 16.5 × 10.8 cm). San Francisco Museum of Modern Art. Helen Crocker Russell Memorial Fund purchase

pubic hair into a goatee; she has also written the title below. This intervention invokes Duchamp's addition of a mustache, goatee, and letters to a postcard of the *Mona Lisa* in the work *L.H.O.O.Q.* (1919).[33] Duchamp's title is a gramogram that, when pronounced in French, sounds like the statement "She has a hot ass." Wilson disrupts Duchamp's sexist gag while calling attention to equations of pathology, queerness, and sexual violence through a similar use of language and art-historical juxtaposition.

Many of Wilson's works quote canonical male artists to ruminate on gendered power, but *Miss Meret* (1991; p. 8) is an evocative homage to the pioneering work of the iconoclastic Swiss Surrealist Meret Oppenheim. While the work of women Surrealists in Europe, Latin America, and the United States, such as Oppenheim, Leonora Carrington, or Dorothea Tanning, have recently received increased art historical attention, in the 1990s they were still wildly under-recognized; as Wilson stated in 1998, when she first learned about the Surrealists in the 1970s, she didn't even know Oppenheim was a woman.[34] Wilson first encountered Oppenheim's work *Miss Gardenia* (1962; fig. 9) at the San Francisco Museum of Modern Art while installing an exhibition of her own work in 1992. Oppenheim's intimately sized sculpture consists of a decorative gold frame augmented with a plaster relief of flowers and an evocative, convex curve. *Miss Meret* utilizes a similarly ornamental frame (now of black iron) inset with a mirror covered by a piece of opaque, leopard-print chiffon that "allows the viewer an exoticized reflection."[35] The excess chiffon is tied with a ribbon behind the mirror as if it were a woman's hair, and the object is displayed behind a plexiglass bonnet on a handsome royal-blue Formica-veneer pedestal.

Errors of Nature

Another crucial area of investigation for Wilson in her *Museum of Lesbian Dreams* has been pathologizing queer stereotypes and sensational depictions of sexual deviance that originated in the early to mid-twentieth century. She examined scientific research (including psychoanalysis, sexology, and dream interpretation) as well as lesbian pulp novels and pseudo-scientific studies to uncover suppressed histories of queer desire and gender transgression before the advent of the feminist and gay liberation movements of the 1970s, when alternative sexual norms and identities became more publicly visible. Wilson subverted the scientific and cultural discourses of illness and aberration used against queer people so that, in her words, "we [could] speak for ourselves."[36]

Sex Variants: A Study of Homosexual Patterns, written by the American psychiatrist George W. Henry, became a fount of inspiration for numerous works in Wilson's museum. Initially published as two volumes in 1941, and later as a combined edition in 1948, this scientific study was overseen by the Committee for the Study of Sex Variants, formed in 1935 to further "the prevention as well as the treatment of sexual maladjustment."[37] *Sex Variants* grew from the life's work of Jan Gay, a German-born American amateur researcher of human sexuality who visited Magnus Hirschfeld's Institute for Sexual Science in Berlin to learn Hirschfeld's interview methodologies.

FIG. 10 Robert Latou Dickinson, figure seven in "The Gynecology of Homosexuality," in the single volume edition of George W. Henry's *Sex Variants: A Study of Homosexual Patterns*, 1948. Published by Paul B. Hoeber

Seeking to illuminate the lives of queer women like herself, beginning in the 1920s she amassed a trove of case-study interviews with lesbians in Europe and New York City; but, lacking scientific credentials, was unable to secure ongoing support for her research. Henry devised the Committee for the Study of Sex Variants so that Gay could continue her work under his oversight. However, Gay eventually lost control of her work to Henry. When Wilson first stumbled upon a 1948 edition of *Sex Variants* at a used bookstore in Los Angeles, Gay's pivotal role in the research was not widely known.[38] Yet what Wilson found in the case studies, between Henry's homophobic conjectures, were captivating and intimate stories of hardship, loss, love, and persistence that Gay secured from participants by winning their trust.

Wilson's *Trophy* (1990; pp. 90–91) takes inspiration from the *Sex Variants* case study of "Nora M.," a thirty-year-old business executive whom Henry repeatedly characterized as man-hating, rebellious, and resentful. According to the study, Nora "claimed no hesitancy in acknowledging homosexual interests," and by her own estimation was "neither masculine nor feminine."[39] *Trophy* is a classic bronze chalice on a wood base that reproduces as a bronze plaque the familial diagram devised about Nora in *Sex Variants*. In this coded diagram, shapes convey the gender of relatives, while shading within these forms communicates the individual's supposed proportion of aggressive or submissive personal traits. Additional abbreviations on the diagram highlight other information about family members, including alcoholism, artistic aptitude, promiscuity, and psychopathy. The interior of the chalice is lined with rabbit fur, another homage to Oppenheim through reference to her most recognized work, *Object* (1936), a teacup, saucer, and spoon covered in gazelle fur.[40] Henry's assessment of Nora concluded that a "heterosexual adjustment" was unlikely for her. Jesting about *Trophy* in an interview with *The Advocate*, Wilson quipped, "Rather than blaming her, I'm giving her an award [for this diagnosis]."[41]

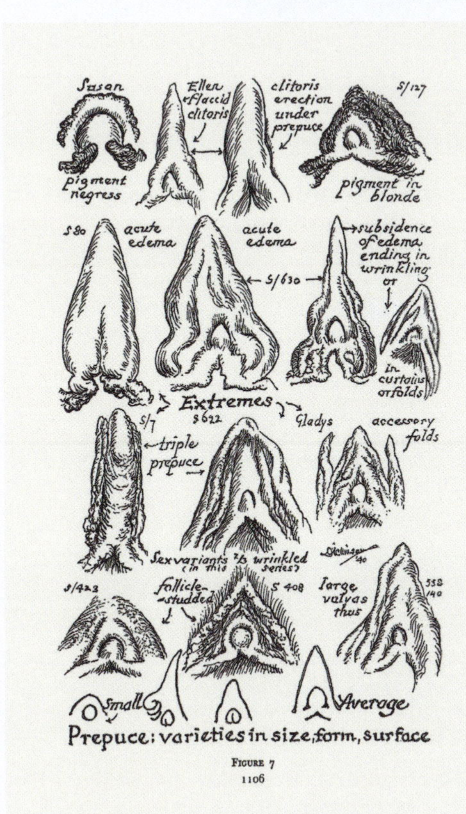

The combined edition of *Sex Variants* included extensive appendices of charts, diagrams, and tables about the study's volunteers, reflecting a belief in the field of eugenics that sexual deviance (like other qualities deemed undesirable) could be detected through physical examination of the body. "The Gynecology of Homosexuality," a report by Robert Latou Dickinson focusing exclusively on the anatomy of the forty female subjects in *Sex Variants*, provided a detailed, if often subjective, review of the appearance of each participant's genitals. A medical illustrator as well as a gynecologist, Dickinson accompanied his study with diagrams drawn from life or made from measurements of the women's vulvas, including a page of clustered genitals drawn with flourishing linework, each identified by the subject's first name (fig. 10). As Wilson has noted, "Museums can often generate dubious meanings based

FIG. 11 *Wig/Cunt*, 1990. Synthetic hair wig, mahogany and glass case, chrome and steel wig stand, gelatin silver prints, and mahogany frames, 78 × 75 × 30 in. (198.1 × 190.5 × 76.2 cm). The Frances Young Tang Teaching Museum and Art Gallery, Skidmore College, Gift of a private collection. Installation view from *Scientia Sexualis* at the Institute of Contemporary Art, Los Angeles, 2024

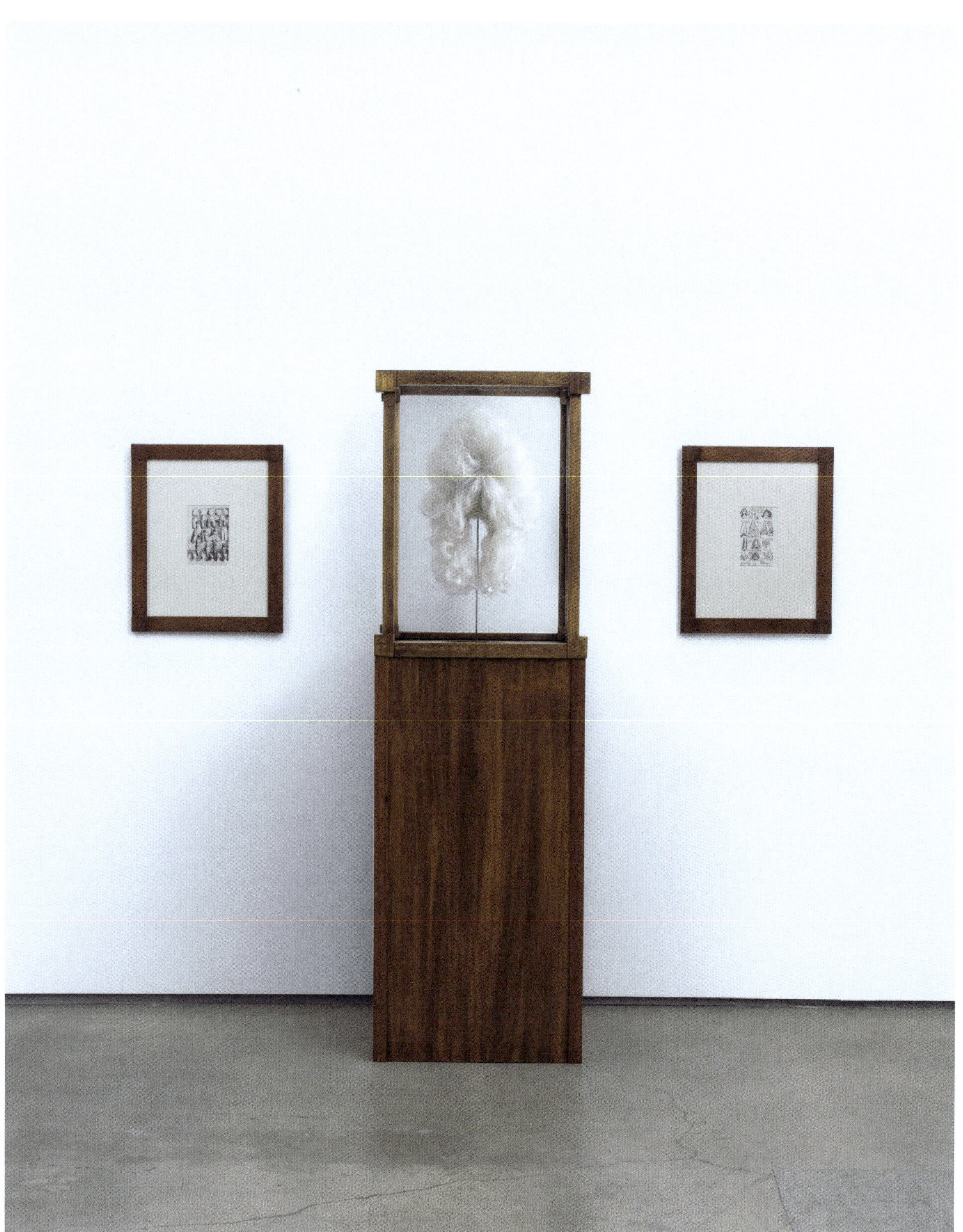

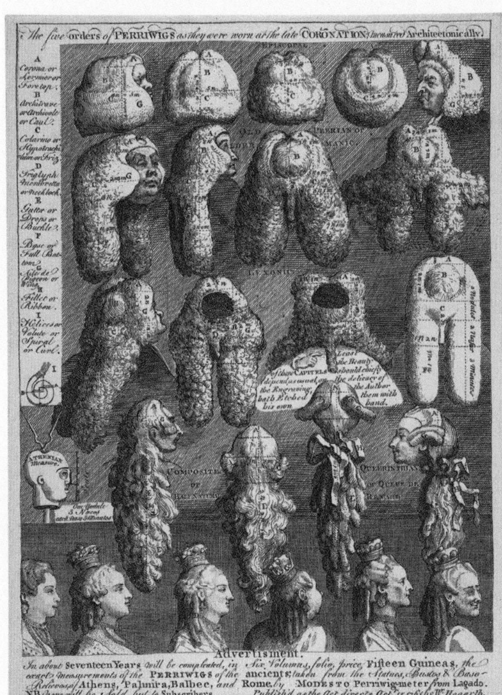

FIG. 12 William Hogarth, *The Five Orders of Periwigs*, 1761. Etching; 11⅞ × 8⅝ in. (30.2 × 21.9 cm). The Metropolitan Museum of Art, Harris Brisbane Dick Fund, 1932, 32.35(116)

solely on formal semblance," and in the installation *Wig/Cunt* (1990; fig. 11), she does just that, juxtaposing reproductions of Dickinson's invasive drawings and William Hogarth's satirical engraving *The Five Orders of Periwigs* (1761; fig. 12).[42] Wilson wickedly aligns Dickinson's diagram of "varieties in size, form, [and] surface" with Hogarth's typology of hairpieces for aristocratic British men, linking eighteenth-century European systems of social classification and hierarchy with the violence of twentieth-century pseudoscientific examination and pathologization. Both images are displayed in mahogany frames, between which is positioned a handsome display case with a fanciful, vulva-shaped white hairpiece.

Dickinson's illustration similarly inspired Wilson's series *Merkins* (1992; pp. 95–97), named for the pubic wigs often worn by sex workers in fifteenth-century Europe. Each work in the series features a fantastical, genital-inspired hair form identified by a name taken from Dickinson's drawing and engraved on a brass plaque: Ellen, Gladys, Kathleen, Patricia, Susan, and Virginia. An inconspicuous stand holds each merkin on a simple, black square shelf that juts off the wall without visible hardware; displayed in a row, the presentation recalls nothing so much as a Donald Judd sculpture hijacked by a drag queen for displaying her wigs. While each of the *Merkins* is distinct, all are made from the same red hair reminiscent of the artist's own. Throughout the 1990s, Wilson realized numerous works that use hair, turning this sensual yet everyday material into a medium for fantastical sculptures that highlight its gendered, sexualized, and racialized connotations.

Wilson also found inspiration in pseudoscientific books about homosexuality and pulp novels from the 1950s and 1960s that sought to entice and arouse through scandalous details and conjecture. A prodigious maker of lists, Wilson began collecting some of the most beguiling, evocative, and telling statements about queer women found in these mid-century publications and compiled them in a small artist's book, *Errors of Nature* (1992; p. 86). Assertions that lesbians "arrive after dark in closed gondolas" and are "given to excessive puns" are as playful as they are absurd, a reflection of cultural stereotypes and ingrained associations (though Wilson's work certainly reflects a predilection for punning). Other citations, such as "increasingly found among suburban housewives" and "more prevalent among other races and classes," unveil the cultural paranoia that positioned homosexuality as a threat to the white, middle-class political order of the mid-century United States.[43]

Following the psychoanalytic frameworks around dream interpretation established by Sigmund Freud as a window into the unconscious, researchers in the early twentieth century often emphasized dreams in studies on homosexuality, particularly pseudoscientific reports that gained attention in popular print. Wilson produced multiple works that make the simultaneously uncanny and silly nature

FIG. 13 René Magritte, *La condition humaine*, 1933. Oil on canvas, 39⅜ × 31⅞ × ⅝ in. (100 × 81 × 1.6 cm). National Gallery of Art, Washington, DC, Gift of the Collectors Committee, 1987.55.1

of these dream interpretations physically present within the gallery. For example, *Turnip/Potato* (1991; pp. 92–93) makes a tabletop monument from a passage in Robert C. Robertiello's 1959 study *Voyage from Lesbos: The Psychoanalysis of a Female Homosexual* in which a patient, "Connie," equates consuming turnips with homosexuality and eating potatoes with heterosexuality. The work features a cast bronze turnip and potato alongside a plaque bearing the passage in which Robertiello summarizes and analyzes Connie's dream. According to Robertiello, Connie came to realize through her dream that eating potatoes (heterosexuality) "leads to having children and getting fat," while eating turnips (homosexuality) "leads to frustration, but there is no physical disfigurement."[44] Held within a finely crafted wood vitrine, Wilson lampoons medical authority and museological display.

Wilson's *Easel/Mirrors* (1990; pp. 100–01) draws on a passage from volume seven of the French-English sexologist Havelock Ellis's *Studies in the Psychology of Sex* (1928). Appearing in a section of Ellis's text "about aesthetic inversion confined to dreams," it deals with an individual identified simply as "the Welshwoman" and her dream of a frightening, hovering violin. In the passage, the Welshwoman shares her affinities for masculinity and her belief that she "must have been a boy once."[45] Just as Wilson used direct quotation in *Turnip/Potato*, here she has sandblasted the account of the patient's dream into a mirror propped up on a painter's easel. Another mirror hangs on the wall behind. In the dream, the Welshwoman sees herself in a mirror wearing a man's suit and finds herself fond of a young woman in a crowd; a surreal scene unfolds of the "loathsome violin" flying into position under her hand and on her shoulder as if she were about to play it, then emitting a melody before dropping from her hands. Ellis interprets the patient's dream as symptomatic of sexual delusion and narcissism and as an "aesthetic inversion carried to a point which is not possible in real life except during insanity."[46] In response to the passage, Wilson positions viewers before multiple mirrored surfaces. The installation's arrangement is also a clever visual quotation of René Magritte's *The Human Condition* (1933; fig. 13), in which an easel set before a window displays a completed canvas that appears to correspond seamlessly with the window's view. Through her work examining sexological studies, Wilson provides an opportunity to encounter distressing histories of queer pathologization while celebrating, with considerable panache, the tenacity of individuals subjected to the disciplinary structures of a medical examination.

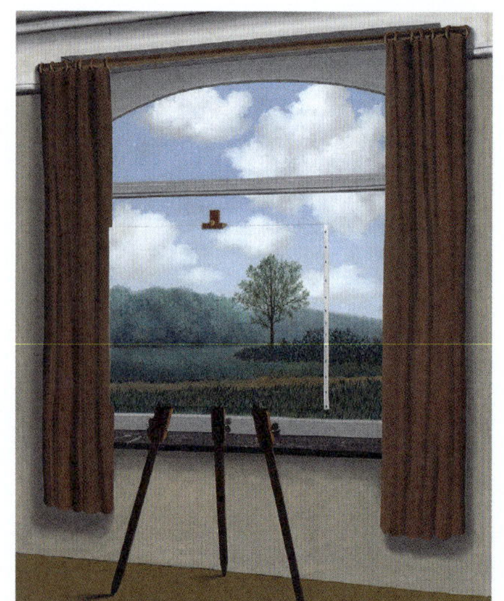

Dressed as a Girl

In her work, Wilson has consistently and purposefully obscured visual semblances of the human form. Nonetheless, the body as a site of contestation and mutability has been a through line in her practice, which thus participates in a legacy of bodily abstraction championed by pioneering lesbian artist Harmony Hammond, who describes her practice as follows:

> I have long been interested in the potential of erotic abstraction in which the body part or sexual act is not depicted but rather referenced from a combination of abstract form, and the associations and physical manipulations of the materials themselves. For instance, human hair off the body always has sexual overtones, and a material like latex rubber usually suggests skin or body fluids. Since materials can reflect marginalization and minimal forms can evoke emotional states, abstraction offers the possibility of an erotic art that bypasses the problematics of figuration.[47]

While Wilson has not always foregrounded an erotic relation to her medium, she is similarly invested in using materials—including hair, fur (natural and synthetic), rubber, leather, and flocked paper and cloth—to arouse bodily associations. Wilson often juxtaposes these organic substances with industrial and everyday materials such as brass, laminate, metal, plastic, plexiglass, and wood to throw their differences into relief or prompt unexpected associations. Wilson's *Deviant Cyborg F* (1992; pp. 114–15), for instance, is an homage to theorist Donna J. Haraway's influential 1985 essay "A Cyborg Manifesto"; the sculpture lays out a speculative toolkit for the would-be female cyborg, uplifted on a Formica-veneer pedestal. Wilson's assemblage offers a range of small objects shelved in a glass display case: a tuft of golden hair, red fingerless driving gloves, and a plaster cast of the artist's teeth allude to the corporeal, while metal tools, medical trauma shears, and flashlights hint at implements that augment the human body.

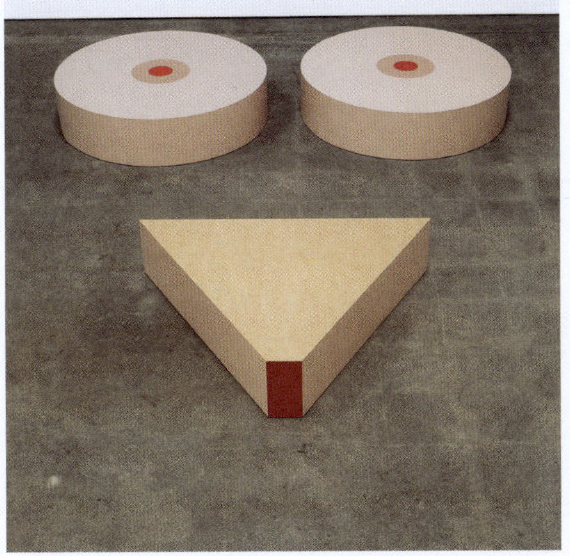

FIG. 14 *Dressed as a Girl*, 1992–93. Formica veneer on wood forms, 120 × 82 × 12 in. (304.8 × 208.3 × 30.5 cm)

As Wilson has explained, minimalism has been a fruitful foil in her practice: "In some ways Minimalism is an easy target, because it stands for High Modernism. But the seeming 'blankness' of Minimalism makes it a convenient site of projection. There's a lot of open space in those pieces."[48] Wilson looked to these and other art histories with mischievous attention and reverence, much like her peer and friend Felix Gonzalez-Torres. In the sculpture *Dressed as a Girl* (1992–93; fig. 14), Wilson presents three Formica-covered forms reminiscent of Richard Artschwager's sculptures referencing banal, everyday items such as chairs or tables. In Wilson's installation, three platform-like objects (two circular and one triangular) positioned on the gallery floor become surrogates for breasts and a pelvis. A rosy pink suggests a white skin tone, while a faux-burlwood pattern on the pelvic triangle stands in for pubic hair. With *Dressed as a Girl*, Wilson puts minimalism in drag. In line with the phenomenological underpinnings of that artistic movement, this work's corporeal references only come into view when encountered from particular vantage points; from other angles, the components only loosely register a bodily resemblance. Critic Michael Fried famously bemoaned this reliance on the viewer's subjective experience of an object in his oft-cited essay, "Art and Objecthood." In his published writing, Fried abhorred what he perceived as a certain "theatricality" in minimal art; in an unpublished letter, he derided this phenomenon as a "faggot sensibility."[49] Fried's statement reflects both the homophobia of the late 1960s art world and a latent queerness within minimalism that Wilson and numerous others have variously identified, critiqued, and appropriated.

Wilson's most directly corporeal work may be *Monster Girls* (1994–95; pp. 120–21), a collection of clothes bearing an array of animal patterns sourced from thrift stores, sewn shut at the openings, and stuffed with polyfill. The installation features over fifty articles of clothing including blouses, bodysuits, pantyhose, trousers, and other items in cheetah, giraffe, leopard, zebra, and other prints, some wildly colored. Piled haphazardly on the gallery floor, the orgiastic mound of canoodling parts indirectly registers the female body as unruly and seductive. Animal print is a persistent interest for Wilson, first explored in *Fauve Semblant* in 1989. That same year an article in *Time* magazine (saved by the artist in her papers) heralded the arrival of "vulgar chic" animal print in women's fashion, noting that while these garish patterns had previously been associated with Hollywood (the article mentions actress Zsa Zsa Gabor), they were now firmly in the mainstream.[50] These prints' other associations, with the queerness of drag pageantry and the faux opulence of lower-class taste, remain unstated by *Time*, but these associations resonate with Wilson's employment of these wild motifs.

Monster Girls reiterates Wilson's fascination with fashion and clothing. In 1993 she speculated that "the increasing prevalence of artists (myself included) using clothing abstracted from the body" arose as "a strategy for avoiding literal, illustrative readings, [and from] a revived interest in surrealism, and the influence of fashion layouts in print media."[51] Cross-dressing, drag, and other forms of gender transgressive presentation have been both critical tools and subject matter for Wilson's *Museum of Lesbian Dreams*. In *Trousers (for Tony)* (1992; pp. 162–63), the artist considered how her own interests in masculine attire intersected with the unfolding AIDS crisis. The work is a tribute to the late painter Tony Greene, a student of Wilson's at CalArts and a close friend, who died in 1990 from AIDS-related complications.[52] Two bronze plaques installed on a brilliant blue wall present differing reflections on memory and death. On the left is a personal narrative of devastating generational loss told through the story of a woman (a figure like the artist herself) who scoured the men's section of a thrift store run by an AIDS service organization to achieve "the look of a privileged dandy."[53] As "beautifully tailored jackets, shirts, and trousers" began to appear with regularity, she understood "that her shopping was an archeology of thousands of lost lives." The work's second panel, on the right, lists nine evocative eighteenth- and nineteenth-century terms for trousers: indescribable, ineffable, inexpressible, indomitable, inexplicable, unthinkable, unmentionables, unspeakable, unutterable. Deploying these outdated terms in the context of the AIDS epidemic, Wilson alluded to the silence and stigma around the disease—an echo of the cultural silence around homosexuality—as well as the inability of language to adequately express anguish. *Trousers* also engages with debates about AIDS and representation while also functioning as a conceptual memento mori to both a particular individual and a generation of gay men.[54]

Not A Serial Killer

In May 1994, Wilson presented a body of work titled *Not a Serial Killer* at José Freire Fine Art in New York which concerned the media representation of purported serial killer and tabloid sensation Aileen Wuornos. In 1989 and 1990, Wuornos murdered seven men while supporting herself as a sex worker along highways in northern Florida. Though she claimed she acted in self-defense after or to prevent sexual assault, Wuornos was convicted of multiple murders, sentenced to death in 1992, and eventually executed by the state of Florida in 2002. Wuornos was depicted in the media and at trial as a predatory, aggressive, and man-hating lesbian—a "demon-dyke."[55] Her case was a lightning rod for debates about gender roles, sexuality, and the definition of sexual harassment and assault. Although for some feminists Wuornos became a symbol of resistance to male sexual violence, Wilson's installation did not seek to celebrate or exonerate Wuornos, nor did it convey any details about her life or the case against her. Rather, as critic Elizabeth Hess observed, Wilson kept her subject at a distance, observing that "the show's nine artworks form[ed] a chilly nonnarrative that [was] the antithesis of the media's coverage of this sex- and bloodbath."[56] In a letter to Freire, Wilson rejected a didactic framing of her work as merely calling attention to Wuornos's story. Wilson asserted instead that the exhibition was "playing rather savagely with postmodernism," seeking to offer the viewer "a series of complex, pleasing, and uncomfortable positions, not unlike what [John] Waters manages in [the film] *Serial Mom*" (released shortly before Wilson's exhibition opened).[57]

In the ambitious installation, Wilson eschewed direct representation by presenting fabricated objects and tableaux that exuded equal parts camp exuberance and macabre humor. Seven wall-mounted metal boxes—minimalist surrogates for each man Wuornos killed—each feature a delicate, lace-lined, heart-shaped chest hair-piece that has been bolted into the support. Similarly, seven automobile bucket seats in various animal print patterns stood throughout the gallery in a work called *Autopsies* (1994; pp. 142–43). Per scholar Miriam Basilio, by displaying these anthropomorphized seats as "interchangeable, replaceable objects," the work presents a "reversal of the usual positioning of a prostitute as a disposable commodity within the heterosexual economy."[58] Arranged on the gallery floor, the seats place many viewers in an imaginary space of power over an empty seat.

Wilson used Harley-Davidson motorcycle accessories to allude to The Last Resort, a biker bar Wuornos frequented and where she was arrested, as well as to the associations of biker culture with working-class aesthetics, outlaw criminality, and rugged masculinity—not unlike the associations the media projected on Wuornos as a poor, queer woman.[59] These works also call up queer associations with biker cultures, ranging from the group Dykes on Bikes to the many gay men's motorcycle clubs that have

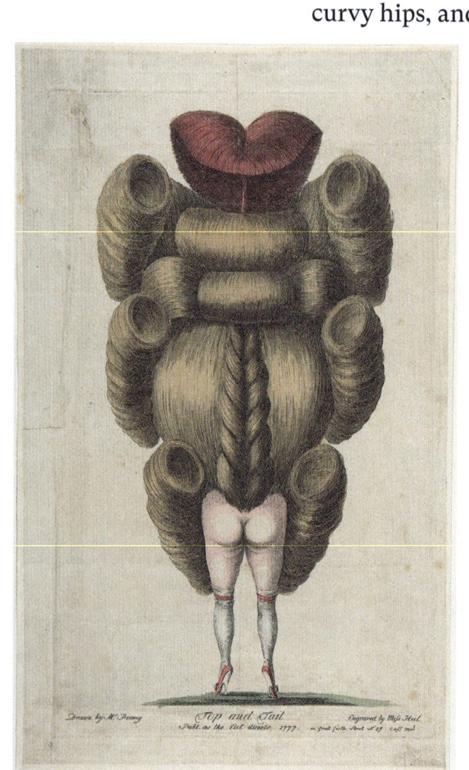

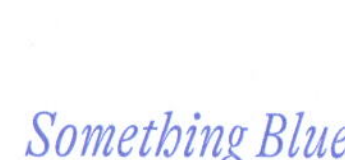

FIG. 15 Anonymous, after Mr. Perwig, *Top and Tail*, 1777. Hand-colored etching with stipple, 14 1/16 × 8 9/16 in. (35.7 × 21.8 cm). The Metropolitan Museum of Art, The Elisha Whittelsey Collection, The Elisha Whittelsey Fund, 1959, 59.533.5

existed in the United States since the 1950s. Wilson's tableau *Family Room* (1994; p. 141) places two "nuzzling" black leather Harley motorcycle seats on a patterned rug; a section of faux wood paneling recalls a mid-century basement while a blue-toned photograph of two quietly distraught women invokes the melancholic undercurrents of lesbian pulp. Hess identifies this image as the aesthetic sentiment of Radclyffe Hall's prototypical lesbian novel, *The Well of Loneliness* (1928); however, the image is actually lifted from the back cover of a mid-century pulp, *The Odd World*.[60]

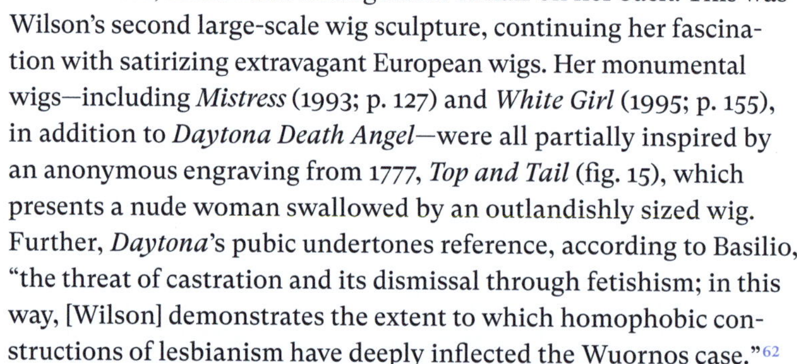

Daytona Death Angel (1994; pp. 135–37), Wilson's most direct invocation of Wuornos, is a "coiffed abstraction" of hair roughly the same height as its subject.[61] Standing on a vintage dress form, this angel features tendril-like braids on her bust, curvy hips, and an elaborate, mullet-like arrangement of hair on her back. This was Wilson's second large-scale wig sculpture, continuing her fascination with satirizing extravagant European wigs. Her monumental wigs—including *Mistress* (1993; p. 127) and *White Girl* (1995; p. 155), in addition to *Daytona Death Angel*—were all partially inspired by an anonymous engraving from 1777, *Top and Tail* (fig. 15), which presents a nude woman swallowed by an outlandishly sized wig. Further, *Daytona*'s pubic undertones reference, according to Basilio, "the threat of castration and its dismissal through fetishism; in this way, [Wilson] demonstrates the extent to which homophobic constructions of lesbianism have deeply inflected the Wuornos case."[62]

Two months after the New York exhibition, Wilson realized *Lee's Locker (M.D./M.O./M.W.)* (1994; pp. 129–33).[63] The artist took inspiration from the storage locker Wuornos maintained, in which investigators found items belonging to some of the slain men. Wilson's installation is a long, blue-painted corridor that imagines "the contents of the locker as objects produced by myself, Marcel Duchamp and Meret Oppenheim."[64] The storage unit is brimming with art-historical allusions. Wilson's leopard-print *Sneakers* are reminiscent of Oppenheim's pair of boots conjoined at the toe. *For Any Job*, a set of rubber gloves with elegant fur-trimmed cuffs, plays off Oppenheim's *Pelzhandschuhe* (Fur Gloves with Wooden Fingers; 1936). Wilson's version of Duchamp's readymade *Trap* (1917)—a coat hanger nailed to the floor—is made even more useless as a circular piece of wood. *Bride* contains a chessboard made of rawhide leather, alluding to Duchamp's lifelong fascination with chess as both a game and an artistic theme in his work; the squares on Wilson's board feature tufts of fur in the form of the letter *L*, placing lesbianism within the crosshairs of Duchamp's beloved pastime.

Something Blue

Something Blue (1998–2000; pp. 156–61) is a tableau of objects, paintings, and photographs that together present "an anecdotal history of the color blue," encompassing the many cultural references and emotional experiences associated with this color.[65] Taking for its title a line from a nineteenth-century English rhyme advising brides to wear blue for good luck on their wedding day, Wilson's installation invokes a rite of heterosexual (and, more recently, homosexual) normativity, a day associated with celebration and love and a context in which the color blue has been related historically with female chastity, fidelity, and virtue.[66] However, Wilson had other associations in mind: "The twilight hour is blue, as is the blue chamber of the fairy tale ["Bluebeard"]. Blue is the color of ambiguous depth, of the shadow side, the tint of the inexplicable, of desire, knowledge, and of the rare."[67] Blue has also been a significant color in modern art, from Pablo Picasso's Blue Period and Yves Klein's eponymous blue to, more recently, British filmmaker Derek Jarman's final feature, *Blue* (1993), produced after Jarman had become partially blind from AIDS-related complications and could only see tones of blue.

Foremost for Wilson in devising *Something Blue* were the connections between this color and a range of feelings associated with "the blues." In the artist's own words, the installation is "about having a whole other realm of experience that I want to articulate that has to do with clinical depression . . . and wanting to actually look at what it's like to experience that sensory, intellectual, and motor dysfunction."[68] Having previously produced work that examined so-called sexual deviance, Wilson was well-versed in wittily deconstructing subject matter associated with medical diagnosis, pathologization, and negative emotions. She describes the installation's numerous objects as akin to clues in an unfolding mystery, and by bringing together a range of disparate objects in unconventional arrangements, the work recalls the fantastical accumulations of seventeenth-century European Wunderkammers. In seeking to communicate depression's broad sway, the installation's objects ask viewers to consider equally the corporeal and cerebral implications of the tableau. For *Scuba*, Wilson filled a set of comically large plastic clown shoes with sand, invoking a sense of weight and lethargy. Multiple display cases and containers also allude to restraint or confinement, even as their contents produce humorous juxtapositions: for instance, in *Model*, light-blue feather boas coil within a glass display case like caged snakes. In the diminutive assemblage *Deceit*, a decorative column is capped by a gloved hand that clasps a small toy brain. The installation also features a handful of objects that cite earlier works by the artist: a wood painter's palette and a blue plexiglass cutout of the same form leaning against the wall recalls the photograph of Peter's unused last palette in *Fauve Semblant*; another piece of blue acrylic in the shape of the island of Lesbos placed neatly on a wood table mimics the polished aluminum form in *Puddle* (1993; fig. 6, p. 44).

Looks Bad

Like any respectable dandy, Wilson is an avid collector and connoisseur. When she became fascinated with tawdry mid-century pulps, vintage bookstores became a site of research and discovery. Thrift stores have been another source of both personal and artistic inspiration, as well as literal artistic material, as in *Trousers (for Tony)* and *Monster Girls*. Wilson has also lovingly assembled for her personal enjoyment collections of jewelry boxes, Art Deco ceramics, sentimental Victorian brooches of women's names, and vintage scarves. In 2001, the artist began a project of playfully reconstructing her family albums, which led her to begin assembling digital files of vernacular photographs of American life that were then making their way onto the internet. Her digital archive quickly grew to some 20,000 images, many of them depicting mid-twentieth-century domesticity and family. A large portion of the collection came from enterprising eBay sellers looking to unload actual prints for which they had no context, either about the circumstances under which they were made and preserved or the pictured individuals.

In three installations between 2010 and 2013, Wilson enlarged and reproduced images from this archive as lightboxes, allowing viewers a window into the "liminal spaces of hybridity and flux" in these images of the ordinary and the uncanny.[69] Wilson's selections establish a conversation about gender roles and presentation, particularly for white women. A smiling woman stands beside a futuristic car; a pair of delicate white hands gesture evocatively before a black background; a young girl poses outside wearing a collar that resembles enlarged pink flower petals; a nude young woman in a stereotypically mid-century, middle-class domestic space looking over her shoulder at the camera (pp. 148–50). Describing the project, Wilson has said, "I think of my installations as unfinished inventories of fragments: objects, photographs, and other inventions; as improvisational sites where the constructed and the readymade are used to question our making of the world through language and knowledge."[70] While this work expanded the artist's practice into a new medium, with it Wilson persisted in asking questions about history and identity while still rewarding visitors with aesthetic pleasure.

Through objects and installations rich with aesthetic and historical allusions, Wilson proposes in her *Museum of Lesbian Dreams* a "secret history of modernity informed by queer sexuality, femininity, race, and class."[71] The artist revels in making work that is witty, playful, pleasurable, and seductive, all while participating in rigorous debates about history, identity, the museum, the body, and the mind. Indeed, there is as much intellectual pleasure in Wilson's work as there is artistic gratification. As her friend and fellow artist Robert Blanchon has observed, in her work, rather than "chipping away at aesthetics and the language of formalism to [construct] meaning, it's like they dance together. . . . Nothing's hidden—not the visual pleasure, not the topical subject matter. It's all dancing on the surface."[72] This spirited dance of form and meaning reflects an inherent generosity in Wilson's work. Although the *Museum of Lesbian Dreams* is a solo project, by its very nature as a museum, it opens its metaphorical doors to others to investigate its holdings, to imagine themselves in its parameters, or to take up its strategies to perform their own critiques and transformations.

The title for this essay is borrowed from the second track on the band Hole's album Live Through This *(1994), in part for its association (in my mind) with Wilson's work* Miss Meret *(1991; p. 8), which is itself an homage to Meret Oppenheim's* Miss Gardenia *(1962; fig. 9), both discussed in this essay. While Wilson was not deeply connected to or impacted by the dissonant sonic cultures of the 1990s, I like to imagine a through line among these intergenerational Misses.*

1. Millie Wilson's *Museum of Lesbian Dreams* shares many conceptual affinities and strategies with Chris E. Vargas's Museum of Trans Hirstory & Art (MOTHA; 2010–present). In my opening sentence, I echo a sentiment expressed by curator and educator Christina Linden: "I've heard MOTHA described as virtual, faux, fictional, and fake. In fact, I would say that it is none of these. Not a hoax but a possibility and a projection. It is, in fact, a small organization, sometimes just the size of one artist's imagination and action." See Christina Linden, "Museum/Trans/Hirstory/Art," in *Trans Hirstory in 99 Objects*, ed. David Evans Frantz, Christina Linden, and Chris E. Vargas (Pasadena, CA: Museum of Trans Hirstory & Art; Munich: Hirmer, 2023), 18.

2. Millie Wilson, "Museum of Lesbian Dreams: Objects and Tableaux," 1990, unpublished notes, archive of the artist. Wilson's institutional critique grew from the conceptually potent contributions of artists such as Michael Asher, Marcel Broodthaers, and Hans Haacke in the 1960s and 1970s. Wilson and her contemporaries, including Andrea Fraser, James Luna, and Fred Wilson, among many others, brought attention to the intersections of gender, sexuality, race, and class within institutional critique in the 1990s. For more on artists practicing institutional critique, see Johanna Burton and Anne Ellegood, eds., *Take It or Leave It: Institution, Image, Ideology* (Los Angeles: Hammer Museum; New York: DelMonico Books; Munich: Prestel, 2014); John C. Welchman, ed., *Institutional Critique and After* (Zurich: JRP | Ringier, 2006); and Alexander Alberro and Blake Stimson, eds., *Institutional Critique: An Anthology of Artists' Writings* (Cambridge, MA: MIT Press, 2009). Wilson's absence from these publications is notable, and this publication and the exhibition it accompanies seek to redress this omission.

3. Millie Wilson quoted in Ross Bleckner, "Independents: Emerging Artists," *Out Magazine*, no. 2 (Fall 1992), 46.

4. Millie Wilson, artist statement in the brochure for *Fauve Semblant: Peter (A Young English Girl)*, (Los Angeles: LACE [Los Angeles Contemporary Exhibitions], 1989), n.p.

5. Millie Wilson quoted in Terry Wolverton, "Thoroughly Postmodern Millie," *The Advocate*, no. 564 (November 20, 1990), 71.

6. Cunningham mentioned Wilson in an aside about the overall dearth of contemporary lesbian artists, following the statement, "Real attention has also been paid to artists like David Wojnarowicz, Donald Moffett, Robert Gober and others. But if you ask dealers and curators to name some interesting gay women artists, you'll probably get an embarrassed silence." See Michael Cunningham, "After AIDS, Gay Art Aims for a New Reality," *New York Times*, April 26, 1992.

7. *Bad Girls* was curated by Marcia Tucker and presented in two consecutive parts at the New Museum of Contemporary Art in New York from January 14 to April 10, 1994. A companion show, *Bad Girls West*, was curated by Marcia Tanner at UCLA's Frederick S. Wight Gallery from January 25 to March 20, 1994. Wilson had work in both shows. *In a Different Light* was curated by Nayland Blake and Lawrence Rinder at the University Art Museum and Pacific Film Archive (today the Berkeley Art Museum and Pacific Film Archive) from January 11 to April 9, 1995.

8. Among these students are Andrea Bowers, Mark Bradford, Cassils, Beatriz Cortez, Zackary Drucker, Sam Durant, Tony Greene, Richard Hawkins, Steven Hull, Doug Ischar, Denise S. Johnson, Kang Seung Lee, Catherine Opie, Vincent Ramos, Jess Rath, Marcos Rosales, and Dean Sameshima. As Wilson's impact has been wide-reaching, this constitutes only a partial list. Moreover, many of her students may not be widely known today in the art world, yet this does not diminish the significance of Wilson's impact on them, nor the significance of their education at CalArts and the quality of their work, given the vagaries of artistic recognition.

9. In 1991, Wilson noted the burgeoning queer community and pedagogy at CalArts, and the need to defend its legitimacy and importance: "One of the things that happened [at CalArts] is that a space opened up—and I don't know how long it will remain open—for gay artists, both students and teachers, to declare themselves and explore their practices." Wilson stated, "It takes people in significant positions in institutions, whether they're schools, alternative spaces, or film groups, to stake out some territory and insist that certain kinds of programming go on." Millie Wilson quoted in Terry Wolverton, "Portraying Sexuality," *The Advocate*, no. 574 (April 9, 1991), 73.

10. Millie Wilson quoted in *Millie Wilson: An Interview*, directed by Robert Blanchon (Chicago: Video Data Bank, 1998), Hi8 video, 41 min. 16 sec.

11. Wilson quoted in Blanchon, *Millie Wilson: An Interview*.

12. Millie Wilson, artist statement in the brochure for *Fauve Semblant*.

13. Wilson cites as influential, along with her education in various legacies of women's and feminist art, John Baldessari's traveling retrospective at the Contemporary Arts Museum Houston. The exhibition *John Baldessari: Work 1966–1980* was organized by the New Museum of Contemporary Art and was presented at the Contemporary Arts Museum Houston from March 6 to April 18, 1982.

14. Millie Wilson, "Master's Thesis" (master's thesis, University of Houston, 1983), 2.

15. Wilson, artist statement in the brochure for *Fauve Semblant*.

16. Millie Wilson, "The *Los Angeles Times* Series," *Exposure* 27, no. 1 (1989): 17.

17. Wilson registers the misgendering of Tipton by reproducing the headline "Death Reveals Musician Who Lived as Man to Be Woman." While Wilson described *The Los Angeles Times Series* as focusing on depictions of women, Tipton's appearance in the series reflects the artist's interest in exploring who was identified (even mistakenly) as a woman at the time, as well as her expansive conception of gender and interest in gender transgression. For more on Tipton, see Diane Wood Middlebrook, *Suits Me: The Double Life of Billy Tipton* (New York: Houghton Mifflin, 1998) and the documentary *No Ordinary Man*, directed by Aisling Chin-Yee and Chase Joynt (Montreal: Parabola Films, 2020).

18. Martha Rosler, "Notes on Quotes," *Wedge: An Aesthetic Inquiry*, no. 2 (Fall 1982): 68–69.

19. In this essay I use the terms preferred at the time of writing by trans and gender-nonconforming individuals and communities even though these words either

did not exist or were not widely used when Wilson produced her work, on the grounds that the current terms reflect the spirit of Wilson's practice and research interests. For Wilson and many other thinkers in the late 1980s and early 1990s, the identities of "woman" and "lesbian" were capacious, anticipating the ever-evolving trajectory of queer and trans identity and terminology in the next century.

20. In her research on female-to-male cross-dressers, gender-nonconforming individuals, transmen, and other masc figures, Wilson's interests prefigure such projects as the exceptional research and loving portraits of artist Ria Brodell in their series *Butch Heroes*. See Ria Brodell, *Butch Heroes* (Cambridge, MA: MIT Press, 2018).

21. Millie Wilson, "1991 Talk," unpublished notes, archive of the artist.

22. *Mata Mua: Paul Gauguin (1848–1903)* was presented at the Museo Nacional Centro de Arte Reina Sofía from June 28 to July 24, 1989. Simultaneously, a major exhibition of Gauguin's work, *The Art of Paul Gauguin*, appeared at the National Gallery of Art, Washington, DC; the Art Institute of Chicago; and the Galeries Nationales du Grand Palais, Paris.

23. The use of a leotard in the work and its title is also meant to call to mind the name of French philosopher and theorist Jean-François Lyotard. Wilson, "1991 Talk."

24. The title comes from the concluding lines of a poem by Sappho relating her heartbreak over Atthis, a young woman who recently left Lesbos to be married. See Sappho, "To Atthis," in *Greek Lyric Poetry*, trans. Willis Barnstone (New York: Bantam, 1962), 68–69. During the 1930s Gluck took as a recurring subject flower arrangements by Constance Spry, a high-society florist and Gluck's lover.

25. The photographs produced for *The Watermelon Woman* are compiled in Zoe Leonard, *The Fae Richards Photo Archive* (San Francisco: ArtSpace Books, 1996). For more on Chris E. Vargas's Museum of Trans Hirstory & Art (MOTHA), see https://www.motha.net/.

26. On occasion Wilson has made paintings as components of her installations. For her gallery exhibition *Sweet Thursday* (1991), Wilson produced monochrome paintings inspired by Aleksandr Rodchenko's triptych *Pure Red Color, Pure Yellow Color, and Pure Blue Color* (1921). In her exhibition *Wolf in a Garden* (1993), she painted another monochrome inspired by René Magritte's *The Palace of Curtains, III* (1928).

27. Amelia Jones, *Postmodernism and the En-Gendering of Marcel Duchamp* (Cambridge, UK: Cambridge University Press, 1995), xii.

28. Nayland Blake, "Curating *In a Different Light*," in *In a Different Light: Visual Culture, Sexual Identity, Queer Practice*, ed. Nayland Blake, Lawrence Rinder, and Amy Scholder (San Francisco: City Lights, 1995), 14–15.

29. For more on the history of the silhouette in American art, see Asma Naeem, ed., *Black Out: Silhouettes Then and Now* (Washington, DC: Smithsonian Institution, 2018).

30. *Women in the Shadows* was Bannon's third novel in what would eventually be referred to as *The Beebo Brinker Chronicles*, published between 1957 and 1962. Attesting to the continuing appeal of the silhouette, editions of these novels published in the 1980s featured sexy silhouette covers designed by artist Tee Corinne. Wilson utilized editions of the flocked silhouette devised for *Red Top* in two other works: *Little Maids* (1993) presents ten red profiles on the floor in a corner, while *Les Garconnes* (1991) places twelve black silhouettes on white shelves in various groupings.

31. Millie Wilson quoted in David Hirsch, "Lesbian Dreams," *New York Native* 11, no. 19 (April 20, 1992), 45.

32. *Red Top* appears as the flocked cover decal of the present book, a sensual invitation to touch the printed object that recalls Duchamp's similarly tactile cover design for *Le Surréalisme en 1947*: a foam-rubber breast mounted on velvet. Wilson identified this connection to Kimberly Varella's design. David Evans Frantz, conversation with the artist, June 18, 2024.

33. The original work was a color photocopy of a reproduction of *Le viol*. Wilson has since remade the work twice using museum gift shop postcards of Magritte's painting.

34. Wilson quoted in Blanchon, *Millie Wilson: An Interview*, 1998.

35. Millie Wilson, "1992 Talk," unpublished notes, archive of the artist.

36. Wilson quoted in Terry Wolverton, "Thoroughly Postmodern Millie," 71.

37. Eugen Kahn, foreword to *Sex Variants: A Study of Homosexual Patterns*, by George W. Henry (New York: Paul B. Hoeber, 1948), v.

38. The history behind *Sex Variants* was only recovered over the last decade and features prominently in Justin Torres's *Blackouts: A Novel*. Torres's semi-fictional novel reproduces numerous pages of the study, which he has reworked via erasure, blacking out select words, phrases, and sections. Not only do Torres and Wilson share an interest in *Sex Variants* as an understudied record of queer history, but Torres's conceptual investment in concealing parts of this source material for artistic reimagining finds a visual parallel in Wilson's strategies in *The Los Angeles Time Series* and *The Painter Who Is Not One*. See Justin Torres, *Blackouts: A Novel* (New York: Farrar, Straus and Giroux, 2023).

39. Henry, *Sex Variants*, 842.

40. The same year Wilson made *Trophy*, artist Jenny Holzer, similarly recognizing *Object*'s madcap boldness, called the work "sinister" and "a cup that could fight back." See Jenny Holzer, "A Cup of Words," in *Contemporary Art in Context*, ed. Christopher Lyon (New York: Museum of Modern Art, 1990), 55.

41. Millie Wilson quoted in Terry Wolverton, "Thoroughly Postmodern Millie," 71. Multiple works by Wilson quote from case studies in *Sex Variants*. A framed print in her multipart work *Disturbances* (1990; pp. 146–47) reproduces a text from the case study for "Sadie S.," who, according to Henry, has the "attitudes and behavior" of a "young boy," with a "quick and strong" handshake and a gait that "is firm, almost a strut." Henry, *Sex Variants*, 818. A passage from *Sex Variants* also appears on a panel mimicking a museum label in Wilson's *The Painter Who is Not One: Millie Wilson/Romaine Brooks* (1990; pp. 56–59).

42. Millie Wilson, "SMMOA Panel 1994," unpublished notes, archive of the artist.

43. The statements compiled in *Errors of Nature* have been tucked vertically into the gutters of the present book.

44. Robert C. Robertiello, *Voyage from Lesbos: The Psychoanalysis of a Female Homosexual* (New York: Citadel, 1959), 51.

45. While the Welshwoman's masculine inclinations suggest she might today identify as transgender, I have chosen to retain the feminine pronouns used in Ellis's text, as there is no indication the subject used (or later used) masculine pronouns. The passage that inspired

Wilson's *Easel/Mirrors* appears in Havelock Ellis, *Studies in the Psychology of Sex*, vol. 7 (Philadelphia: F. A. Davis, 1928), 39.

46. Ellis, *Studies in the Psychology of Sex*, vol. 7, 40.

47. Harmony Hammond, "A Space of Infinite and Pleasurable Possibilities: Lesbian Self-Representation in Visual Art," in *New Feminist Criticism: Art, Identity, Action*, ed. Joanna Frueh, Cassanova Langer, and Arlene Raven (New York: Icon, 1994), 122. For a significant analysis of queer abstraction and the meanings of artists' impulses against figuration, see Lex Morgan Lancaster, *Dragging Away: Queer Abstraction in Contemporary Art* (Durham, NC: Duke University Press, 2022).

48. Wilson quoted in David Hirsch, "Lesbian Dreams," 45.

49. See Michael Fried, "Art and Objecthood," *Artforum* 5, no. 10 (June 1967), 12–23. For more on Fried's homophobic statement, uncovered by art historian Christa Noel Robbins in Philip Leider's papers at the Smithsonian Institution's Archives of American Art, see Robbins, "The Sensibility of Michael Fried," *Criticism* 60, no. 4 (Fall 2018): 429–54.

50. J. D. Reed, "On the Prowl with Vulgar Chic," *Time* 134, no. 16 (October 16, 1989), 92.

51. Millie Wilson quoted in Nina Felshin, *Empty Dress: Clothing as Surrogate in Recent Art* (New York: Independent Curators Incorporated, 1993), 68.

52. Just as Wilson has used plaques, labels, and other museological devices, Greene produced linguistic artworks on plaques.

53. All quotes are from Wilson's *Trousers (for Tony)* (1992). The text on *Trousers* was also published in the anthology *The New Fuck You: Adventures in Lesbian Reading*, ed. Liz Kotz and Eileen Myles (New York: Semiotext(e), 1995), 283–84.

54. Numerous artists making works about the AIDS crisis in the late 1980s and 1990s refused to depict the AIDS-affected body, offering various alternatives to media depictions of individuals dying from the disease. This tactic aligned with activists' and scholars' critiques of both sensationalized media coverage of AIDS-related deaths and depictions of people with AIDS, even if from a sympathetic viewpoint, that showed the disease's ravages without social or political context. See Simon Watney, "The Spectacle of AIDS," in "AIDS: Cultural Analysis/Cultural Activism," special issue, *October* 43 (Winter 1987): 71–86.

55. The tabloids often described Wuornos using the term "demon-dyke." It appears, for example, in Karen Avenoso's "Is the Abuse Defense Getting Roughed Up?" *Daily News*, February 6, 1994. Lesbianism had long aroused fear and titillation in twentieth-century American popular culture, so it is unsurprising that the phrase also served as the title of a lesbian pulp novel published in 1968. See Tracy Lane, *The Demon Dyke* (San Diego: Greenleaf Classics, 1968).

56. Elizabeth Hess, "Flat Cracker Love," *Village Voice*, May 31, 1994.

57. Millie Wilson to José Freire, April 23, 1994, copy of letter, archive of the artist. Wilson also cited the 1992 documentary *Aileen Wuornos: The Selling of a Serial Killer*, which highlighted the intense media interest in Wuornos and how individuals close to the case profited from their associations. *Aileen Wuornos: The Selling of a Serial Killer*, directed by Nick Broomfield (Culver City, CA: Strand Releasing, 1992).

58. Miriam Basilio, "Corporal Evidence: Representations of Aileen Wuornos," *Art Journal* 55, no. 4 (Winter 1996): 57.

59. At The Last Resort, Wuornos was known to be a "flat cracker," a term used to refer to lesbians. The phrase inspired Wilson's vinyl banner *Flat Cracker Love* (1994; p. 145). Cannonball, The Last Resort's bartender, shares this idiosyncratic term in Mark MacNamara, "Kiss and Kill," *Vanity Fair* 54, no. 9 (September 1991), 90–106.

60. Hess, "Flat Cracker Love." See also Donna Richards, *The Odd World* (New York: Domino, 1965).

61. Hess, "Flat Cracker Love."

62. Basilio, "Corporal Evidence," 58.

63. *Lee's Locker (M.D./M.O./M.W.)* was realized as part of the group exhibition *Altered Egos*, curated by Karen Moss at the Santa Monica Museum of Art (today the Institute of Contemporary Art, Los Angeles) and on view from July 9 to September 4, 1994.

64. Millie Wilson to Karen Moss, Proposal for *Lee's Locker: M.D./M.O./M.W.*, April 27, 1994, copy of letter, archive of the artist.

65. Millie Wilson, installation description for *Something Blue in COLA 2000* at the Hammer Museum, 2000, archive of the artist.

66. The title also connects to *Something Borrowed*, the installation devised by Wilson and Catherine Lord for SITE Santa Fe in 1995. The installation similarly evoked aspects of the Wunderkammer by assembling various objects collected from lesbians across the state of New Mexico. For more on this work, see "The 'Erotics of Lesbian Looking': Revisiting Millie Wilson and Catherine Lord's Installation, *Something Borrowed*," in Genevieve Flavelle, "Once Upon a Queer Time: A Study of Reparative and Speculative Histories in the Work of 2SLGBTQ+ Contemporary Artists" (PhD diss., Queen's University, Toronto, 2023).

67. Millie Wilson, installation description for *Something Blue* in *COLA 2000*. "Bluebeard" is a French folktale about a man who had many wives and murdered each of them, and the attempts of his present wife to avoid this fate. The fable has been historically interpreted as a cautionary tale against female curiosity and, conversely, as a tale encouraging women not to unquestioningly follow patriarchal authority. In her description of the installation, Wilson quotes Marina Warner, "Bluebeard's Brides: The Dream of the Blue Chamber," *Grand Street* 9, no. 1 (Autumn 1989): 121–30.

68. Wilson quoted in Blanchon, *Millie Wilson: An Interview*, 1998.

69. Millie Wilson quoted in Denise Johnson, "Millie Wilson: On Both Sides and in Between," *Make/Shift*, no. 14 (Fall/Winter 2013–14), 11.

70. Millie Wilson, "Statement," in *Looks Bad* (Chicago: Iceberg Projects, 2011), 5.

71. Wilson, "Statement," in *Looks Bad*.

72. Robert Blanchon quoted in Blanchon, *Millie Wilson: An Interview*, 1998.

LESBIAN AS METHOD

Jill H. Casid

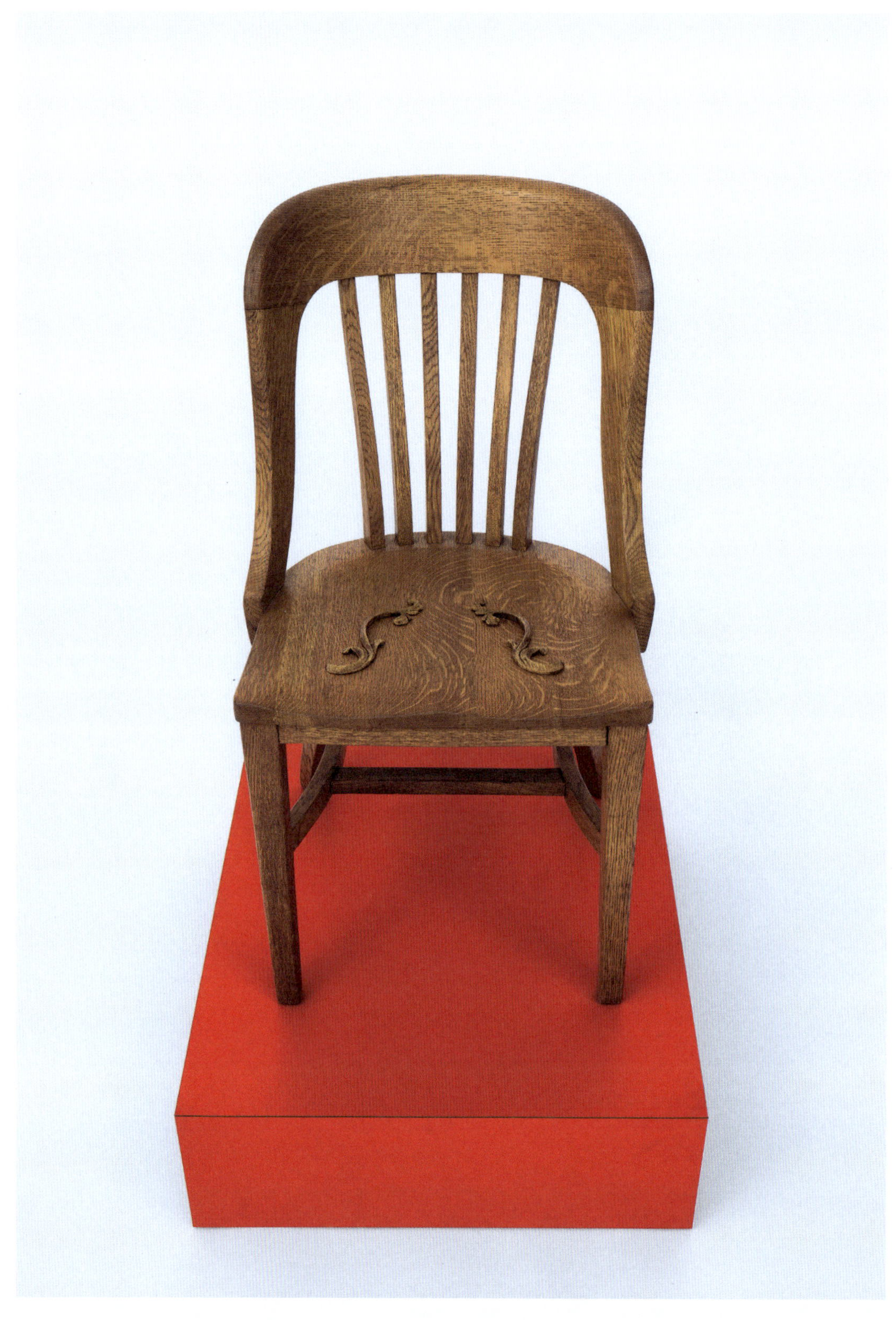

OPPOSITE *Teacher*, 1991. Oak chair, wood motifs, and Formica-veneer base, 41½ × 24 × 28 in. (105.4 × 61 × 71.1 cm)

FIG. 1 *Rorschach Pillow*, 1991 (remade 2024). Vinyl, screenprint, and upholstery filling, 17¼ × 15½ × 2½ in. (43.8 × 39.4 × 6.4 cm)

Camp, burlesque, tragicomedy, bump, grind, assemble, juxtapose, cut, cut up, crack, drape, slip through: Millie Wilson's art of material trespass brazens the bad beauty of the unrepentant aesthete-as-criminal who dumpster dives into the trashing wrought by global heteropatriarchal racial capitalism to re-set the scenes of our trouble. Along the way, Wilson keeps showing us how to make the swerve of perversion a tactical practice of sculptural fabulation and material speculation. In encountering the arguably inaugurating glam, crip-queer conceptualism of Wilson from before the letter of what became known as "queer theory," make no mistake about the role played by the thinking with and connections made in what follows to Eve Kosofsky Sedgwick, Judith Butler, Luce Irigaray, and Monique Wittig, among others. What I call Wilson's practice of "lesbian as method" is no mere translation of concepts worked out elsewhere. Rather, Wilson's method shows us what happens when a deconstructive queer feminist art practice offers its speculative and critical propositions through the risks of a kind of sculptural slapstick. Via material instantiations of a version of the gag of literalism that is not merely rhetorical, Wilson gives us something uncannily familiar as, at once, materialized object and its re-setting—that is, as a scene into which we are lured and in which we are situated to see and feel otherwise. To flesh out Wilson's way of showing us how to work with and through the junk of the given, the rebuked, and the thrown away, let us take the junket of the altering force of thirteen key aspects of Wilson's queer feminist practice, which I call "lesbian as method" and diagram through its counter-schoolings, scene-settings, table turnings, and calls to the materializing force of desire and the play of fantasy.

One: invite. Take a seat, if you dare, invites Millie Wilson's red *Rorschach Pillow* (1992; fig. 1).[1] Its inkblot mirror-image of lesbian pulp and pin-up serves hot girl-on-girl coupling at least doubled—with a side for each ass cheek. The blazened image is appropriated from the cover of the 1970 pulp paperback *Lesbian Wives*, a pseudo-sexology book published as part of a series titled *Barclay House Psycho-Sex Study*.[2] The weight of histories of fantasy and actual pathologization at the hands of what is not exclusive to sexology and psychoanalysis might be more than enough to make us need the kind of hemorrhoid-easing support-pillow meets (what it is tempting to invoke as a sort of) "making-whoopee" cushion. Even if not actually hollow, it makes a teasingly erotic bottom prop out of the projective identification tests that measure our fates out of "what you see is what you are" diagnostic evidence.[3]

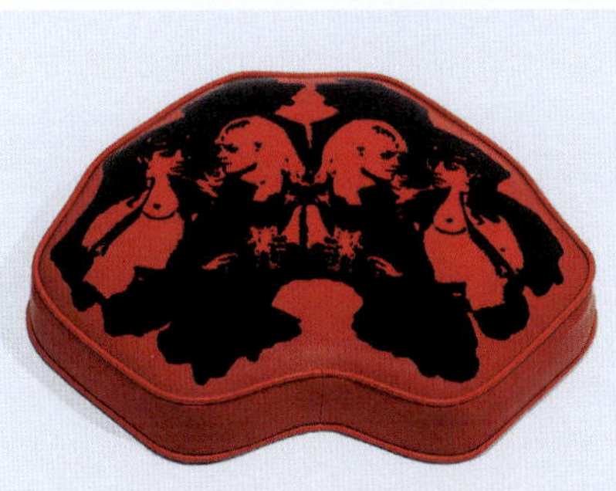

However, in inviting us to take a seat—or even just to contemplate one—Wilson's sculptural propositions also school us. Take Wilson's *Teacher* (1991; p. 32), which props a classic oak wood institutional chair on a platform covered in hot-red Formica laminate. To set up the minima required for the little machine of instruction, it reminds us sometimes all you need is a chair. The base raises this minimal apparatus of the scene of pedagogy closer to eye level. But the tricked-out seat induces us to bend over to see our projective desires reflected back. Here the erotics of pedagogy meet the high-stakes political theater of the wild potentials and no less ferocious restrictions on the schoolroom of our lives. To take up Wilson's invitation to take a seat schools us in what that little machine of instruction can do to us in terms of what we may be or become. And yet we may also feel the tables turn.

Two: instruct. The scenes of instruction that Wilson re-sets in taking us from the schoolroom to the museum (as its own classroom in which the violences of sorting colonial classification endeavor to rule) do more than just flip the dominating scripts. They also call on the disavowed magic of objects as devices of material contact and confrontation with the power to transport and transform. *Odd Glove* (1990; p. 119) takes its title from the odd euphemism for ascribed sexual and gendered deviance used especially in the nineteenth century for the unsorted, uncoupled, unmarried woman, the figure of trouble with whom, Elaine Showalter wrote, "sexual anarchy begins."[4] That is, "odd glove" also marks what remains or is left behind after all the ostensible matches have been culled. Looking at it now, it calls up for me those scenes of sorting selection—which is to say, ordinary humiliation and not at all extraordinary danger—from the dance or gym class floor to the bar or police lineup, where it can be just as devastating to be singled out, ranked, and divided from the others as to be passed over.

Odd Glove is inspired by a passage in Surrealist writer and artist André Breton's 1928 novel *Nadja* that focuses on the threat of the possible donation to the Centrale Surréaliste (Bureau of Surrealist Research or Enquiries) of a lady's single "sky-blue glove." The brass plaques that flank the table issue their own counter-instruction regarding the threat to cisheteropatriarchy issued by what gloves and the hands they sheathe (or sheave) are capable: "he was afraid of her glove / because she had / a certain success / with the women he wanted."[5] While featuring a finely made blue cotton one with flourishes, *Odd Glove* is, nonetheless, ghosted by its less refined though no less threatening kin, the disposable blue latex gloves of the fingerings and fistings of physical examination as well as of safer sex practices. The blue glove is set on an oak table pedestal support stand that assumes the height and dimensions of the sort used to prop an object to be not just seen but also judged. Set on a mirror laid on the floor, the table's legs lead us down to the institutional-style brass-plate signage which has been shifted from the expected placement on the tabletop or nearby wall to the floor underneath. In place of an identifying name, the italics of emphasis seem to wink and wave as they spell *well*, calling up the devastating reflecting pools in which we're meant to drown, from Ovid's tale of Narcissus (and its key role in Sigmund Freud's articulation of homosexuality) to Radclyffe Hall's 1928 novel *The Well of Loneliness*. The "well" of *Odd Glove* negotiates the toxic scenography that plays across the fictions become pretend sciences of the social that position sex and gender deviance from a naturalized norm as, at best, the not-at-all "well" of an ostensible lack of solid ground.[6] But to thus move from table to the ground underfoot is not just to feel the tables turn. Wilson's sculptural propositions serve us the often invisibilized and otherwise taken-for-granted infrastructurings by which knowledge and value are produced by sorting separation, classification, framing, and labeling in the apprehensible, and thus contestable, material—with an excess of winking wit.

Three: school. To encounter Wilson's seductive sculptural propositions and their re-setting of the scenes of instruction and desire is also to be schooled in another way. In a version, that is, of "How To Bring Your Kids Up Gay."[7] This is not the title of the how-to book I never found in the school library of policed books in Texas that became for me both refuge and training ground in the queer, nonbinary, and trans survival skills of working against the punishing grain—though the actual one of my childhood was perhaps not unlike the school library (also in Texas) where Wilson recounts reading the case studies of Sigmund Freud that were kept from other children (but to which, thanks to a beloved librarian, she was granted special access).[8] Rather, "How to Bring Your Kids Up Gay" is the reparative turnabout title of the 1991 essay by Eve Kosofsky Sedgwick that expects and demands more. Insinuated into the instructional language of the burgeoning how-to genre, "How to Bring Your Kids Up Gay" does not just mimic but also endeavors to counter the brutal reality of how "it's always open season on gay kids." "How to Bring Your Kids Up Gay" calls up as it calls out for the seemingly impossible curricular project: not merely participation in a gay- and trans-affirmative tutelage that would merit the name but even more so a political pedagogy that would set thriving queer and trans childhoods as the kind of social achievement worthy of our dedicated cultivation.[9]

That was 1991. The exterminating force of anti-gay and anti-trans projection still sees in queer and trans life the threatening shape of its own killing predation. This scene of exterminating projection is an apparatus of anti-femme, anti-gay, anti-trans pedagogy on repeat.[10] And it never seems to get old. One need not be a conspiracy theorist to see in the "Don't Say Gay" legislation (from Florida's HB 1557, which passed in 2022, to the copycat laws passed in North Carolina, Iowa, Indiana, and Arkansas in 2023) the organized displacement of white cisheteropatriarchy's own violences.[11] Were it not that the viabilities of queer and trans lives are still at stake it would be tempting to liken the disavowed brutalities of white cisheteropatriarchy's stalking imagination to the tricks of a compulsory carnival ride—this one lined with a hall of warping mirrors. How do any of us get out of this un-fun-house alive?

Four: wink the way. Let's follow the winking signs. For the signs in and of Wilson's sculptural solicitations do not just school us. They also beckon and light the way for those of us who were never supposed to survive the more-than-bullying of the schoolyards of everyday life. The neon signage of Wilson's *Student in Lesbos* (1992; p. 164) spells out the terms of its cast light in the lurid yellow lettering of the title, poached from the cover of a 1967 lesbian pulp novel that warns of "adult reading" while promising to take us on a trip to where "primeval passions lured them to lust's outlands."[12] Wilson's lifting of the title may be to taunt and tease in withholding any direct representation of the cover's lurid fleshing out of the already curvaceous font. But Wilson's neon recasting of *Student in Lesbos* offers us not suppression but rather the kind of voluptuous material restraint that invites us along to work with and through the persistence of the question of the materializing consequences of what and how we imagine, of how we participate in the making and unmaking of signs in not just the textual but also the textural literal.[13]

FIG. 2 *Diva*, 1991–92. Chair and ottoman, oak frame, cotton and upholstery materials, 48 × 56 × 24 in. (121.9 × 142.2 × 61 cm). Collection of Ruth and Jake Bloom, Los Angeles

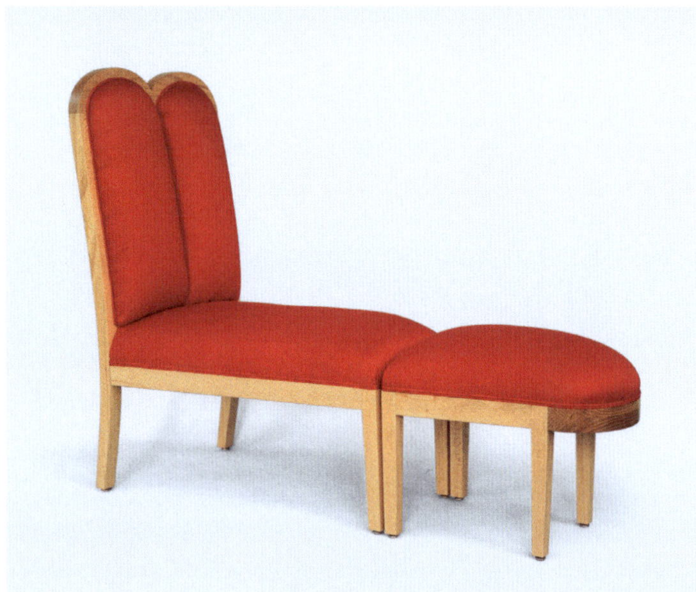

Five: lie back. Wilson's art of material trespass might seem to instruct us to lie back in more than one sense. To take in the sly assemblage of *Diva* (1991–92; fig. 2) is to be presented by this red upholstery version of a divan, or not-so-therapeutic couch, with the problem of the visual lie, or the real material effects of what is not just illusion. Jokes not at all aside about the ostensibly passive pillow queen, what exactly are we made to see and feel via this furniture of and for sex, fantasy, and dreaming? Constructed in parts, *Diva* is composed out of a chaise made especially "longue" by the augmentation of an ottoman as added tip abutting an already ample chair. In the outlines of its punch lines, the forms of *Diva*'s ghosting articulation tease us to go ahead and read penis in the padding—and yet also that member's, or dis-member's, ready disarticulation, transference, and plasticity. *Diva* as monumental not exactly strap-on and, more, lie back also sports a high back, doubled or divided into two. As if an outsized version of Wittgenstein's duck-rabbit philosophical lesson on how seeing is always haunted by an irresolvable "seeing as," *Diva*'s recliner teasingly tests us with an unsettling morphism that flickers: *Diva*'s furnished affordance as dildo from one aspect, erect fingers from another.[14]

Six: unsee, fail to see, make us feel it anyway. Now try and unsee either, both, neither. And yet whether or not you see or unsee, the double or triple entendre of *Diva* lies not merely in the deliciously ambivalent delirium of its form. *Diva*'s play on the cishetero fantasy furniture that props the anatomy of its version of the real gives the plush lie to the truth claims of its regime of visual evidence. *Diva*'s triple entendre lays down its lesson about the tyranny of the visual to serve up another kind of truth about not just being and having but also doing a version of what Judith Butler famously called the "lesbian phallus." Butler's teasing term for the real erotogenic but also morphogenic power of what is consigned to the imaginary, the "lesbian phallus" makes its appearance as a deconstructive conceit in their audacious 1992 article of that title, which became a key chapter in their 1993 book *Bodies that Matter: On the Discursive Limits of "Sex"* (the follow-up to their 1990 classic *Gender Trouble*).[15] With their 2024 book *Who's Afraid of Gender*, about how we make up and do the mattering of sex, gender, and sexuality, Butler has returned to confront the ways in which the "phantasm of gender" is mobilized by authoritarian regimes to collect and displace anxieties about the not-at-all-natural routes to world-ending destruction to which the rise of fascism is actually leading.[16]

FIG. 3 *Fauve Semblant: Peter (A Young English Girl)*, 1989. Installation view at SF Camerawork, 1990

Seven: lie back to tell another truth (a.k.a. the lesbian phallus). In their essay "The Lesbian Phallus and the Morphological Imaginary," Butler immediately follows the seductive promise of the title with a notoriously retractive punch line: "After such a promising title, I knew that I could not possibly give a satisfying paper, but perhaps the promise of the Phallus is always dissatisfying in some way."[17] The "lesbian phallus" is hinged by Butler to not the lie back but, rather, the letdown. For the deconstructive lesson of "The Lesbian Phallus and the Morphological Imaginary" schools us that the lesbian phallus is not an economy of substitution, not a new body part, not a visible thing at all, but a plastic, erotogenic practice, a way of being and doing that "offers the occasion" for scripts in excess of the cisheteropatriarchal. In other words, we may not see it. However, while the lesbian phallus may be a joke at the expense of the visual field altogether, we are, nonetheless, made to feel it at work anyway.[18] Ultimately, what is at stake amid the slapstick is a queer theory—or call it a lesbian phallus at work with a capacity for insight, a way to see that is also a way to feel beyond the dominant formations of the given-to-see. *Diva's* morphological conjuring makes the plushly upholstered occasion of the powers of the lesbian phallus firmly material. In other words, things get more complicated and more implicating chez Wilson's aesthetic tactics of puncturing decorum and its illicit adventures in a literalism that risks the seemingly tacky, taking the lofting abstractions of what might be deemed high theory (from Freudian school psychoanalysis to French feminist theory) lying down with and on the diva's couch. In giving material form to what is supposed to remain in the domain of the unreal and the unrealizable, Wilson's practice of the lie back to tell another truth about the erotogenic and materializing force of what is not just fantasy makes an art of material trespass in, out of, and even through the white cisheteropatriarchal structurings it casts as not at all immutable or inevitable.

Eight: discover the lesbian (as the conspicuous absence). In their artist bio-cum-artist statement that is also a text-based art piece, Wilson launched the winking lure, "Discovered the lesbian to be the conspicuous absence in postmodern theory." But not only there. The noticeable absence of any subject whatsoever in the sentence itself announces as it performs a version of the audacious cunning of the material punning that is everywhere in Wilson's work.[19] Gauntlet thrown. Let's try to catch it. We might start with the fabulation of Wilson's most famous and signature work, the installation *Fauve Semblant: Peter (A Young English Girl)* (1989; fig. 3)—first exhibited at LACE (Los Angeles Contemporary Exhibitions) in 1989 and then at SF Camerawork in 1990.[20] Wilson's

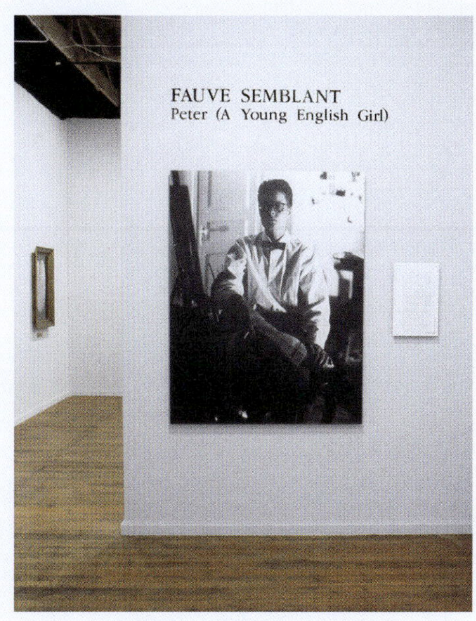

strategic use of the past tense and the spatial device of the invented retrospective still exerts a strangely magnetic, even materializing, power, as if the conspicuous absence called "the lesbian" once summoned might do more than stand out—might rock the not merely "theoretical closet" and unhinge the master's house of the museum display, opening its relation to the asylums, attics, workhouses, and dustbins that line its operations.[21] For the not entirely faux retrospective (in which the display apparatus of the life of the invented lesbian painter is made up out of the culling of discursive and material actualities), Wilson had herself photographed (by Catherine Opie) seated at an easel. Sporting a bowtie and cuffed trousers from her own wardrobe and with legs crossed wide and open, the artist takes up space. "Aesthetic cross-dressing," Wilson called it.[22] Placed prominently at the entrance, the photograph positions the artist looking up and out through spectacles that accentuate the unabashed directness of the look as dare. Seaming together the French *fauve* of a modernist art movement, wild cats, and the uninhibited, with the *semblant* or seeming of what is already a gender-binary-destabilizing title taken from Romaine Brooks's portrait of the artist Gluck (fig. 3, p. 13), juxtaposition is more than just a positioning. A blue-green wall that places plexiglass plaques emblazoned with the word "painter" in the same field as "bulldagger," but with bulldagger featured at high center and painter relegated to the bottom right corner is to play seriously with the persistence of the question of what it would take to do justice to a history and a present of corrosive forms of discounting and disposal. A darkly framed mirror set next to what is labeled, with a certain longing, "Her Last Palette," does more than play with the ends of erasure and the force of disappearance. These devices stage a museological raid to propose that sometimes it seems you have to DIY. Or nearly die. And not just laughing. Like so much of Wilson's larger project pursued under the pointed and precarious umbrella of the *Museum of Lesbian Dreams* (1989–present), the wild seeming of the "fauve semblant" and the not entirely invented persona of "Peter" are also already after the end and, thus, under the ruse of the retrospective look back. But *Fauve Semblant* is nonetheless necessarily iterative and even ongoing, if in fits and starts and with long gaps between the 1990s and the late 2000s. In the context of the 2019 exhibition *Millie Wilson: Errors of Nature* (curated by David Evans Frantz for Reading Ours in Los Angeles), for example, Wilson displayed her poster *Wanted* (1997), which reprints the photograph taken by Opie and sets it beside the main part of the introductory text for *Fauve Semblant*, thus juxtaposing the eponymous "Peter"—who is also a persona—with the frame text that makes an art of the exposure of forms of underestimation and erasure.[23] To "discover the lesbian" is to leave a trail of cunning clues made up, in *Fauve Semblant*, of crossing the modernist canon with its cast-offs as at once evidence, lure, and space of and for a pleasure that is not without its punctures. Wilson's practice of lesbian as method works with and through a form of fabulation that refuses to merely fill in the blanks—insisting, instead, on the play of negation and its capacities for summoning speculation to call up an address to the future, to the will have been and the not yet that also offers a playful erotics in and of the meanwhile.[24]

Nine: play the not. To pursue the play of the "not" in Wilson's practice takes us to the installation *The Painter Who is Not One: Millie Wilson/Romaine Brooks* (1990; pp. 56–59), which riffs on the refutation of lack and the speculative rewriting of the body and desire beyond phallocentric organizations of sex and sexuality in French feminist philosopher Luce Irigaray's *This Sex Which Is Not One.*[25] As Irigaray famously puts the "not it," "And her sexual organ, which is not one organ, is counted as none. The negative, the underside, the reverse of the only visible and morphologically designatable organ . . . the penis." [26] The "not one" of Wilson's wielding of negation interrupts that narrative of modernist painting that would have none of us by taking up modernist painter Romaine Brooks as a kind of occasion for the resignifying play of what Irigaray's nots would seem to rule out, not least the top-hatted painter's lesbian phallus. Not far away would be not the negations of Irigaray's not one of "When Our Lips Speak Together," but, rather, the nots of lesbian feminist Monique Wittig's "The Straight Mind" (1978) in which Wittig offers "lesbian" not as identifying noun but rather as interference verb, as a radically altering change of perspective, a shift, an operation inside the mattering, deformative force of language: "It would be incorrect to say that lesbians associate, make love, live with women, for woman has meaning only in heterosexual systems of thought and heterosexual economic systems. Lesbians are not women."[27] To say that the not of Wilson's negations is more Wittig than Irigaray is not to choose sides within a false binary. It is to follow Wilson's lesbian as method at play in the way that Wilson's *The Painter Who is Not One* defies the binarizations that structure to uphold the modernist canon's exclusions, juxtaposing in defiance the minimalist and the decorative, and the abstract and the figurative to lead us into another field altogether, occupying extravagantly the outsider gutter made glamorous of the reproductive, the ostensibly derivative, and the faux.

This outsider, rogue interference operation of the "not" of lesbian as method is perhaps unleashed most ferociously in Wilson's installation *Lee's Locker (M.D./M.O./M.W.)* (1994; pp. 129–33) and the exhibition *Not a Serial Killer* (1994). Both projects elaborate their gorgeous vengeance on the violences of cisheteropatriarchy through a working of revenge on a history of the object in modern art from Surrealism to pop. Replaying the fetish object and the series via the castration threat and revenge-fantasy lure of Aileen Wuornos, Wilson takes seriously Wuornos's statement on the consequential distinction between the serial and the series which Wilson takes as her own last word in the article "*History Lessons* from *The Museum of Lesbian Dreams*": "I'm not a serial killer. I only killed a series of men."[28] Wilson transformed the serial into, among other series, *Autopsies* (1994; pp. 142–43), an array of plush faux-fur bucket seats (one for each of the seven dead "johns") that enact their own hilarious wilding of the unnatural history of the violences and violations of collection.[29] The figure of Wuornos, spectacularized in the media as a lesbian man-killer and executed as "America's first female serial killer," becomes in Wilson's deviantly devoted dive into the animations of the charged object (also known as the fetish) the spatial occasion for occupying what is not the no-man's land of indistinction between the museum, the prison, and the scenes of sex work.

Ten: take it, make it literally. Controversies regarding the "not" that is the deviation or "lesbian" in the "straight mind" and its language systems might be said to swirl even around the use of the adverb "literally" as an intensifier that betrays rather than shores up the policed boundary between the figurative and the actual. That troubled and troubling shore between the figurative, the fantasized, the fabulated, the hard to see, and the actual might be another way to describe that strange terrain of the Freudian unconscious and the efforts of the Freudian school to subject whatever access to the unconscious dreams may open to interpretative excavation. In *The Interpretation of Dreams*, Freud famously writes of how any interpretation is challenged by the "alterations the dream-material itself undergoes for the purposes of dream-formation"—not least compression, displacement, and other forms of transvaluation.[30] If it is already hard enough to distinguish whether attention to the study of dreams exaggerates the elusively figurative, reveals the latent actual in or beneath the manifested figurative, or exacerbates the ways that the figurative, the fantasized, and the fabulated matter, the take it and make it literal of lesbian as method as practiced by Wilson across her meta-project of the *Museum of Lesbian Dreams* might be said to make the intensifying force of literalism a way to set the Freudian cigar on fire—literally. Consider especially Wilson's sculptural setup as send-up and set it off in the sculptural mise-en-scènes from *Easel/Mirror* (1990; pp. 100–01) and *Turnip/Potato* (1991; pp. 92–93) to *The Language of Dreams* (1991; pp. 98–99) and *faute de mieux (for lack of anything better)* (1991; fig. 5) that use the furniture of museum display to bring to the demonstration surface the historical violences of the administration of dream interpretation as a trapping "gotcha" apparatus of pathologization and punishment (especially in its abetting of the development of aversion and conversion therapies that ranged from the use of nausea-inducing drugs to electroshock). In the fabrication of each of these little literalization machines, Wilson's operative device is to take the ostensible transcriptions of dreams as recounted by "lesbian subjects" from postwar studies in the new *scientia sexualis* of sexology that claimed to turn dreams into diagnostic evidence for the medical ascription of criminalized deviance or perversion—a crime for which some studies offered the punishment of rehabilitative cure.

As Wilson's method of taking literally involves a process of material making, we are confronted by these little machines with what Freud called the "dream-material" reconstituted as three-dimensional material objects with their own weight and, therefore, a version of still life—at once presented within the display apparatus of their attempted confinement and reduction and yet charged and animate, still. Take what Wilson makes with and out of *The Language of Dreams* that takes the elements of a dream as recounted in the chapter on "The Dream Life of Lesbians" in Frank S. Caprio's 1954 study, *Female Homosexuality: A Psychodynamic Study of Lesbianism*, positioned as the first medical book on lesbianism. In it, Caprio claims that lesbians are unstable and neurotic but curable. The passage that Wilson takes and makes literal is worth quoting in full, as sometimes to make things is not at all the same as making things up: "Dream: 'Esther needed a ruler (penis). I said I have one right in my desk drawer (panties) and gave it to her with a feeling of satisfaction (insertion followed by orgasm).'"[31]

FIG. 4 Sketch for *The Language of Dreams* and *Faute de mieux (for lack of anything better)*, ca. 1991. Ink on paper, 11 × 8½ in. (27.9 × 21.6 cm)

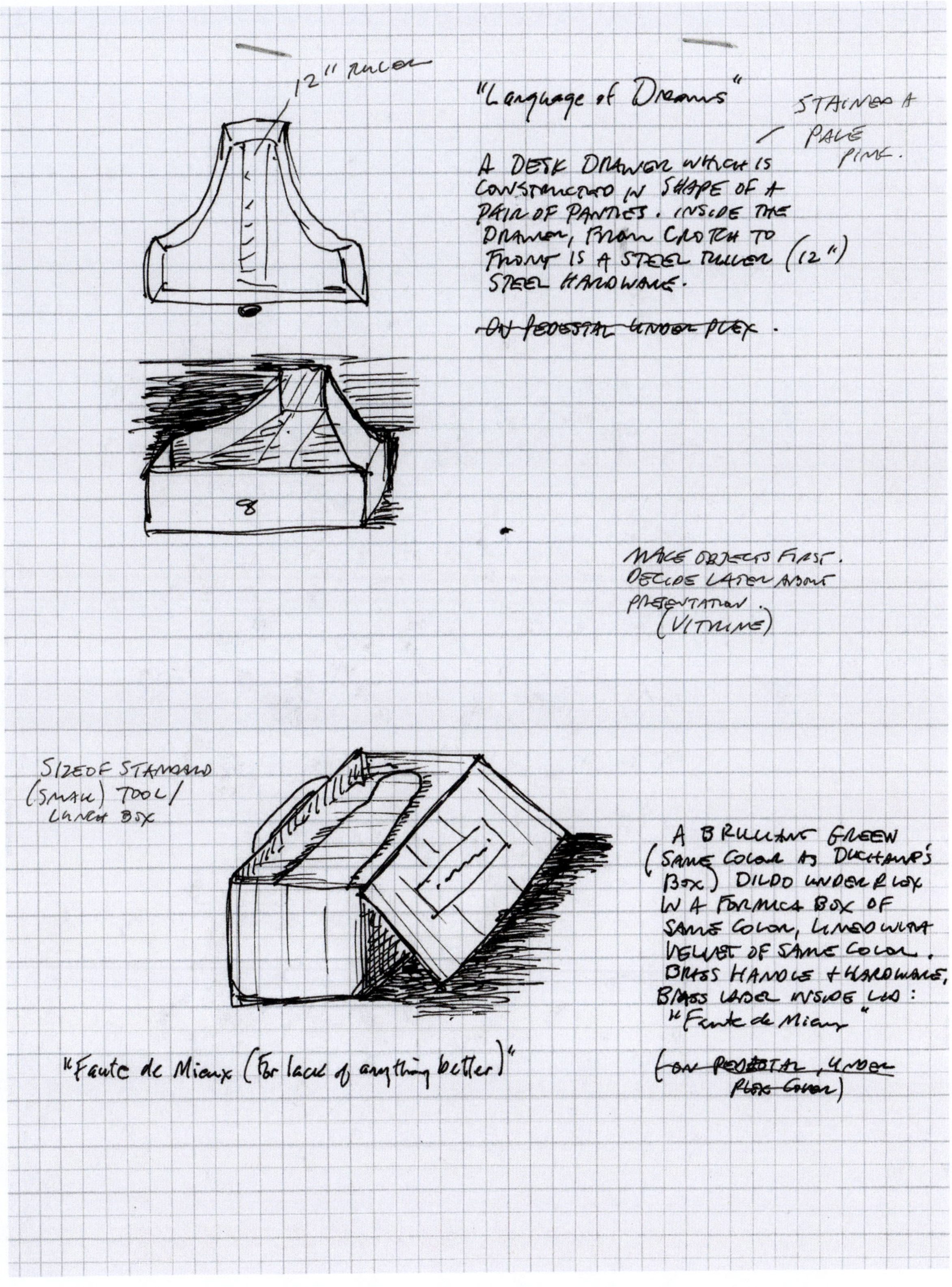

FIG. 5 *Faute de mieux (for lack of anything better)*, 1991. Quartz, wood, plexiglass, Formica veneer, brass hardware and label, and wood table, 42 × 28 × 25 in. (106.7 × 71.1 × 63.5 cm). Private collection

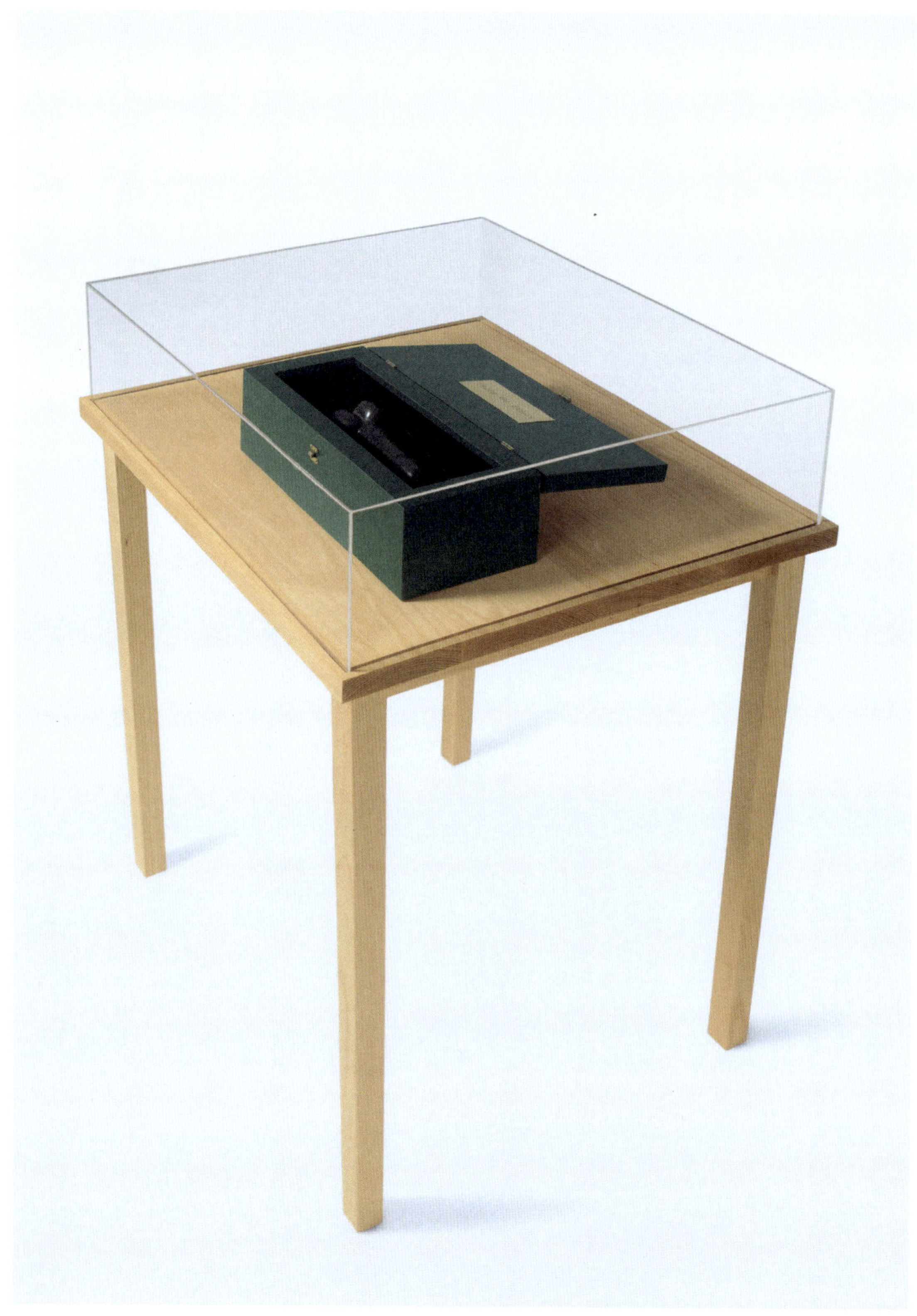

Thus recounted and then subjected to analysis by Caprio ("Had a penis and was on top of Esther") as if manifest evidence of "penis envy" and "penis aggression" (defined as "desire to penetrate the vagina"), it's hard not to read the dream text as presented by Caprio as the unintended occasion for showing the not nothing that it would already be tempting to call "lesbian phallus envy" were it not that Wilson's *The Language of Dreams* uses the force of literalization as at once figuration, actualization, and intensification. "Drawers" is already another name for the panties that here lend their morphological shape to a single pale pink-tinted drawer set on top of a desk (as propping table of discipline, display, and desire) at a height that allows us to bend over to see a twelve-inch steel ruler positioned to span the drawer's interior, as Wilson's diagramming notes describe it, "from crotch to front."

In a related little machine of literalization (diagrammed out on the same ruled page as *The Language of Dreams*; fig. 4) titled *faute de mieux* (French for "for lack of anything better"), Wilson presents a brilliant green stone dildo in a green, velvet-lined wood box of the shape and dimensions of a standard toolbox or lunchbox with brass hardware. Thus set into scenes, the ruler in the drawer taken and made literal and the dildo that we might say eats its rivals for lunch, do not just implicate our viewing. To take and make literally as part of the *Museum of Lesbian Dreams* is to resituate the not dream but, rather, indicting social and historical material from its forced roles in what it is hard not to see as part of at least one of the longer-running serial medical crime scenes in history into the ironized and unstable frame of the "museum" not just *of* but, with this turnabout re-setting, perhaps now even *for* the working through of our own dream work. At the same time, any implied jokes about detumescence and size that might hover are not just taken and made literal but are also intensified by the obdurate objecthood of Wilson's literalization machines that, in withdrawing the rules of straightening decorum, insinuate with material deadpan that the lesbian phallus might just last longer.

Eleven: blow it up. The play of scale is crucial to the way Wilson's sculptural propositions might be said to not just set the Freudian cigar alight but, in scaling the scene up, take on the house (the house of taste, the house of the museum, the house of the history of modern art—which is to say, a history of what is aggregated and extracted to shore up the house of faux reason and its claimed avant-garde of a disavowed history of Western violence, violation, and possessive appropriation) by blowing it up. Take the many hair pieces from *Ponies (Light)* and *Ponies (Dark)* (both 1992; pp. 112–13) made from actual human hair to the *Merkins* (1992; pp. 95–97) each a styled synthetic wig on a shelf inscribed with a feminine first name—Ellen, Virginia, Gladys, Kathleen, Patricia, and Susan. They oscillate necessarily uncomfortably between trophy, fetish, pelt, and Rorschach blot made not scratch and sniff but stroke, fondle, and pet. Here the tactic of take and make literally is scaled up to wax outsized and impeccable in not just their hirsute refusal of the clean wax or shave. They also offer an extravagantly shaggy demonstration of a having, being, and doing of a version of the lesbian phallus as occasion gone not just hairy but also long. Such blowing it up mobilizes lesbian as estrangingly active verb that it's also hard not to think in relation to other historical nots—not least to the strange etymology of the word itself that classicist and writer Daniel Mendelsohn mines in an essay on the elusive poet Sappho who may or may not have leapt off a cliff to her death but did bequeath us the word "lesbian," derived in part from the island where she lived. Blowing it up, as it turns out, takes us to the scene—literally and in all its exacerbation—of blowing it or, as Mendelsohn puts it, "when we hear the word today we think of love between women, but when the ancient Greeks heard the word they thought of blow jobs. In classical Greek, the verb *lesbiazein*—'to act like someone from Lesbos'—meant performing fellatio."[32] In Wilson's the *Museum of Lesbian Dreams*, to "lesbian" does not just suck, it is also to make the mutable matter of sex and gender blow in all the difficulty and deliciousness of the uncontrollably non-reproductive yet roving and recruiting proliferation we are supposed to refuse. Or, as Wilson's 1992 *Errors of Nature* (p. 86) (the accompanying chapbook to *Living in Someone Else's Paradise*) puts it in its found text set against a background of morphogenic and erotogenic woodgrain patterns: "hide their heads beneath each other's skirts . . . increasingly found among suburban housewives . . . prefer islands to continents."[33]

Twelve: dis- and relocate Lesbos; confront to refuse white supremacy. To practice lesbian as method by mobilizing lesbian as an active verb is to intensify what is already the performative of a strange estrangement in which the term of ostensible identification enacts in and by its naming a "you're not from around here" topological exile from heteropatriarchal formations of family and home and a geographic displacement to a floating island that is and is not the actuality of Lesbos. This vertiginous unbelonging is exacerbated by such seemingly slight but no less slicing machines of dislocating literalization as Wilson's *Puddle* (1993; fig. 6), which serves up or, rather, down the aerial topographic outlines of the island as not reflecting pool but, rather, sad puddle of an aluminum slice on a low, teal-blue-Formica-clad platform that, in its intensifying making of "lesbian" an estranging verb, performs the thud of a dislocation of lesbian from that fantasy Lesbos of a falsely enwhitened Greece. Making literal by rendering the coastal outline of Lesbos in aluminum, a common industrial material that is also used for, among other utilitarian objects, storage cans and waste containers, calls back in the disavowed material realities of that island that is also at the epicenter of the Black Mediterranean.[34] Looking at the mapped shape of Lesbos now, in the wake of the so-called migrant crisis in which it has loomed large, it is hard not to see reflected back the Lesbos of the debt crisis of global capitalism and the Lesbos of the necropolitics of the endless war and induced migration of the insecurity state.[35] Then as

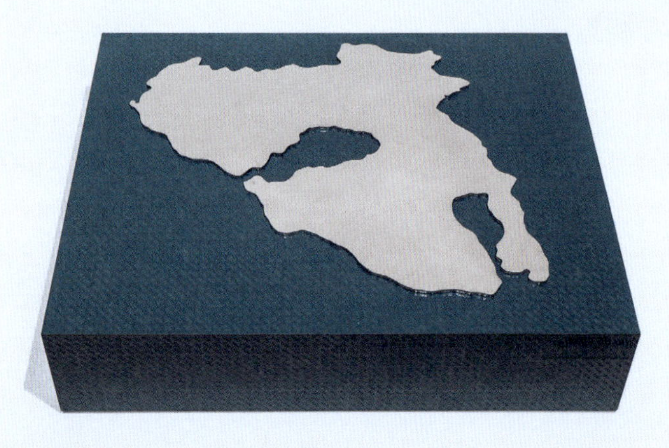

FIG. 6 *Puddle*, 1993. Aluminum and Formica-veneer base, 22 × 28 × 6½ in. (55.9 × 71.1 × 16.5 cm)

now Wilson's practice of lesbian as method sets loose the powers of taking and making it literal to confront to refuse the ruse of white supremacy that positions itself as if an extremity over there to show it up as instead an everyday and intimate force woven into the materializing construction of a toxic femininity that is blown up in the wig formations of *White Girl* (1995; p. 155) and *Daytona Death Angel* (1994; pp. 135–37), and laid down in *Dressed as a Girl* (1992–93; fig. 14, p. 23), in ways that, rather than proffer the false feeling of resolution, necessarily intensify and exacerbate to discomfit, leaving us to do the requisite work of structural change.

Thirteen: go down. To lesbian as method is also to go down in that no less material sense of depression—from the ascribed hollows of lack to severe depression as a sign of the "nothing deep" of disavowed, unnamable feeling in Freud's article "Psychogenesis of a Case of Female Homosexuality."[36] In Wilson's installation *Something Blue* (1998–2000; pp. 156–61), first presented at Matthew Marks Gallery in New York and later at the Hammer Museum in Los Angeles, her taking and making literal as a mode of exacerbating intensification binds that tradition of the cisheteropatriarchal formation of the wedding ceremony in which the bride wears something blue to the blue of that other side of the color codings of enforced gender binarization and the so-called gender inversion by which the lesbian was described and diagnosed to the downbeat of the blues. A restrained palette of literalized blues permeates an arrangement of objects that, even when they don't go down to the floor, are hung low to give sluggish weight and drag to Wilson's re-scenarization of what, in many cases, revisit objects such as a palette (now leaning against, rather than hung on, the wall). That what now is called a crip aesthetics (a strategy that turns the questions of care and support back onto the institutions of their structural retraction) is anticipatorily here makes this no scene of triumph but another way in which *The Museum of Lesbian Dreams* was already not just haunted by failure but also by losses that the powers of creative rhapsodizing in the blues of the triple entendre may at most only ramify.

In the *Museum of Lesbian Dreams* again, I can't help but remember the electric charge of my first encounter with the audacity of Wilson's making material of the powers of the exclamatory fabulous, making it up—at once large, louche, lush, and yet meta-reflectively winking and conceptually cool—out of the residue of these things (discourse, material culture, art) that, as we say, colloquially and in mock disbelief, you can't make up. What happens to the working of the work of the art of making and making up a life out of what may seem like less than nothing when that inaugurating labor begins in and with the inventive conceit of the past tense? "Chose to speak of thievery by the disenfranchised," Wilson writes.[37] As if the—call it an unruly, untamed queerness, a perversity not yet here—had already become museum, had already passed into history. What happens when the work of that artist known (if known at all—even as they are a legend to many of us) for seductively volatilizing the conceit of the museum exhibition becomes a career-spanning museum exhibition that takes its title, the *Museum of Lesbian Dreams*, from a project that Wilson unhinged from the institution as an incessant dare to steal pleasure? How to look back when the work was already seeming to look back? To enter the exhibition space of the proposition to discover, rediscover, even recover the work of Wilson is to be tipped, clued in, and yet tripped up by the work's persistent troubling of the act of discovery.

To respond to its invitation is to be danced close to the violences and violations of possessive mastery and yet veered to where the museum meets the gutter and the cliff and the salon the lock-up. But it is also to be taken into what is not just a ruse of presence and a bid on what may still happen here and now. It is ultimately to make the life of art—and art as a life we were never meant to live or have. Make your own museum. Confront as you slice your way through while taking up space with your pathologization as deviant, as porn trope, as a figure somehow always already clinically depressed, if we take the hollow of absence (of affect, energy, capacity for movement) as not, or not only, metaphor. Create the storage locker of the killer you might have been, end up with your work in a storage locker anyway, keep teaching, shape the field of what we might now call crip queer critical and trans feminist art practice in outlines just beginning to be recognized. Refuse recognition. Keep troubling. Make us feel the frisson of the jokes for which we are for once not just the butt, not entirely taking the fall. And, yet, in reencountering the work of Wilson, I find myself taking the fall anyway by taking in what still pierces in the extraordinary endurance exercise of voluptuous wit it takes to make out of the absence that is its own perversely barbed and often punishing presence the exercise of its own art of losing. All the while admiring the bravado of the ways that Wilson's "lesbian as method" still and yet shows us how to slip, fall, lose our balance, our capacities, and even our minds—with a generous excess of breathtaking style.

1. The image on the cushion also appears on the cover of Millie Wilson's chapbook *Errors of Nature* (San Francisco: New Langton Arts, 1992).

2. Lisa A. Robbins, *Lesbian Wives* (North Hollywood, CA: Barclay House, 1970).

3. For a history of the development and long afterlife of the inkblot test, see Damion Searls, *The Inkblots: Hermann Rorschach, the Iconic Test, and the Power of Seeing* (New York: Crown, 2017).

4. In the chapter "Odd Women," literary critic Elaine Showalter writes, "Writing to a friend about his novel *The Odd Women* (1891), George Gissing explained, 'the title means "Les Femmes Superflues"—the women who are odd in the sense that they do not make a match; as we say 'an odd glove.'" Showalter, *Sexual Anarchy: Gender and Culture at the Fin-de-Siècle* (New York: Viking, 1990), 19.

5. The text of the act of donating a single sky-blue glove that lies at the center of the vignette of what is to stay in the unrealized of recollection and which Wilson, instead, materializes, reads in full: "I also remember the apparently jocular proposition once made in my presence to a lady, asking that she present to the 'Centrale Surréaliste' one of the remarkable sky-blue gloves she was carrying on a visit to us at this 'Centrale,' my sudden fear when I saw that she was about to consent, and my supplications that she do nothing of the kind." André Breton, *Nadja*, trans. Richard Howard (New York: Grove, 1960), 55–56.

6. Radclyffe Hall, *The Well of Loneliness* (London: Jonathan Cape, 1928); Sigmund Freud, "On Narcissism" (1914) in *The Standard Edition of the Complete Psychological Works of Sigmund Freud, Volume XIV (1914–1916): On the History of the Psycho-Analytic Movement, Papers on Metapsychology and Other Works* (London: Hogarth, 1957), 67–102.

7. Eve Kosofsky Sedgwick, "How To Bring Your Kids Up Gay," *Social Text* 29 (1991): 18–27.

8. Millie Wilson quoted in *Millie Wilson: An Interview*, directed by Robert Blanchon (Chicago: Video Data Bank, 2998), Hi8 video, 41 min. 16 sec.

9. See also Jill H. Casid, "The Cut-Away Method," *Satanic Panic: Catalina Schliebener Muñoz* (Buenos Aires: Letra Viva S. A., 2023).

10. Jill H. Casid, *Scenes of Projection: Recasting the Enlightenment Subject* (Minneapolis: University of Minnesota Press, 2015); and Casid, *Escenas de proyección: Reenvíos del sujeto iluminista*, trans. Fermín Rodriguez and Paola Cortes-Rocca (Santiago, Chile: Ediciones Metales Pesados, 2023).

11. According to PEN America, an organization dedicated to free speech, "educational gag orders" constituting variants of the "Don't Say Gay" bill have been introduced in twenty-three states. See Samantha LaFrance, "It's Not Just Florida: 4 New 'Don't Say Gay' Laws Passed in 2023," Pen America, https://pen.org/4-new-dont-say-gay-laws-passed-in-2023/.

12. Saxon Craig, *Student in Lesbos* (New York: Leisure, 1967).

13. Wilson's schooling is explicit in her writing about the projective and displacing violence of the bullying and rape culture her work navigates. For example, she juxtaposes the neon work with a quote from the pulp paperback: "Lynn had been an innocent when they sent her to the third floor of the dormitory. She wanted to be a nurse, but now she was a student in Lesbos. . . . a captive of twisted women who sought and demanded their own sinful kind. Then the boys arrived with a cruel final lesson . . . (1960s pulp fiction)." See Millie Wilson, "*History Lessons* from *The Museum of Lesbian Dreams*," *Artweek* 25, no. 7 (April 7, 1994), 18–22.

14. Ludwig Wittgenstein, *Philosophical Investigations*, trans. G. E. M. Anscombe (New York: Macmillan, 1953). Wittgenstein criticizes the use made of this image in the psychological account of perception by Joseph Jastrow. See Jastrow, *Fact and Fable in Psychology* (New York: Houghton Mifflin, 1900), 276.

15. Judith Butler, *Bodies that Matter: On the Discursive Limits of "Sex"* (New York: Routledge, 1993).

16. Judith Butler, *Who's Afraid of Gender?* (New York: Farrar, Straus and Giroux, 2024).

17. Judith Butler, "The Lesbian Phallus and the Morphological Imaginary," *differences: A Journal of Feminist Cultural Studies* 4, no. 1 (1992): 133; Butler, "The Lesbian Phallus and the Morphological Imaginary," in *Bodies That Matter*, 57.

18. Jordy Rosenberg, "Butler's 'Lesbian Phallus'; or, What Can Deconstruction Feel?," *GLQ: A Journal of Lesbian and Gay Studies* 9, no. 3 (2003): 393.

19. Millie Wilson, artist biography in the brochure for *Fauve Semblant: Peter (A Young English Girl)* (Los Angeles: LACE [Los Angeles Contemporary Exhibitions], 1989), n.p.

20. Select images from Wilson's installation, *Fauve Semblant: Peter (A Young English Girl)*, first presented at LACE (Los Angeles Contemporary Exhibitions) in 1989, are reproduced in "Counts Would Not Acknowledge," a special issue dedicated to fabulation in and with the archive of JUF projects, an artistic project curated by Beatriz Ortega Botas and Leto Ybarra. See Millie Wilson in "Counts Would Not Acknowledge," *JUF projects*, September 5, 2022, https://jufjuf.org/en/post/counts-would-not-acknowledge.

21. Millie Wilson, "The Theoretical Closet," in *All But the Obvious*, ed. Pam Gregg and Catherine Lord (Los Angeles: LACE [Los Angeles Contemporary Exhibitions], 1990), 16. The text incorporates as its own form of evidence telling elements of the reception of *Fauve Semblant* at LACE in 1989.

22. In *Lesbian Art in America*, Harmony Hammond quotes Wilson's wry assertion that "any woman who undertakes the historically male act of painting is forced to engage in 'aesthetic cross dressing.'" Hammond elaborates that "this statement, made in connection with her 1989 installation *Fauve Semblant*, a museum retrospective for a fictional lesbian painter, a young English girl named Peter who worked in Paris at the turn of the century, reminds us of the noticeable absence of women from museum spaces and histories of art." Harmony Hammond, *Lesbian Art in America: A Contemporary History* (New York: Rizzoli, 2000), 106.

23. *Millie Wilson: Errors of Nature*, Reading Ours, Los Angeles, curated by David Evans Frantz, 2019, https://davidevansfrantz.com/Millie-Wilson-Errors-of-Nature. *Wanted* was printed by Us Girls Editions, New York.

24. Millie Wilson, "The *Los Angeles Times* Series," *Exposure* 27, no. 1 (1989): 23.

25. Luce Irigaray, *This Sex Which Is Not One*, trans. Catherine Porter (Ithaca, New York: Cornell University Press, 1985).

26. Irigaray, *This Sex Which Is Not One*, 26.

27. Luce Irigaray, "When Our Lips Speak Together," trans. Carolyn Burke, *Signs* 6, no. 1 (1980): 69–79. Monique Wittig, "The Straight Mind," *Feminist Issues* 1 (1980): 103–11.

28. Wilson, "*History Lessons* from *The Museum of Lesbian Dreams*," 19.

29. On Wilson's interest in Wuornos and especially *Not a Serial Killer*, see also Miriam Basilio, "Corporal Evidence: Representations of Aileen Wuornos," *Art Journal* 55, no. 4 (Winter 1996): 56–61.

30. Sigmund Freud, "The Dream-Work" (1900), chap. 6 in *The Interpretation of Dreams*, trans. James Strachey (New York: Avon, 1965), 311.

31. Frank S. Caprio, *Female Homosexuality: A Psychodynamic Study of Lesbianism* (New York: Citadel, 1954), 276.

32. Daniel Mendelsohn, "Girl, Interrupted: Who Was Sappho?," *New Yorker*, March 9, 2015.

33. Wilson, *Errors of Nature*.

34. Jill H. Casid, "Necropolitics at Sea," in *Migration and the Contemporary Mediterranean: Shifting Cultures in Twenty-First-Century Italy and Beyond*, ed. Claudia Gualtieri (Oxford: Peter Lang, 2018), 193–214.

35. Edgar Córdova Morales, "The Black Holes of Lesbos: Life and Death at Moria Camp, Border Violence, Asylum, and Racisms at the Edge of Postcolonial Europe," *Intersections* 7, no. 2 (2021): 73–87.

36. Sigmund Freud, "The Psychogenesis of a Case of Homosexuality in a Woman" (1920) in *The Standard Edition of the Complete Psychological Works of Sigmund Freud, Volume XVIII (1920–1922): On the History of the Psycho-Analytic Movement, Papers on Metapsychology and Other Works* (London: Hogarth Press, 1957), 145–72.

37. Wilson, artist's statement in the brochure for *Fauve Semblant: Peter (A Young English Girl)*, n.p.

MUSEUM OF LESBIAN DREAMS

Following the configuration of the exhibition at Krannert Art Museum, the plates in this publication are organized into seven sections that overlap chronologically and conceptually. The themes are derived from titles of works and exhibitions by Millie Wilson.

LEFT Untitled drawings, ca. late 1980s. Ink on paper in bound sketchbook

RIGHT Cover of *Millie Wilson: The Los Angeles Times Series*, 1989. Published by the University Art Museum, State University of New York at Binghamton

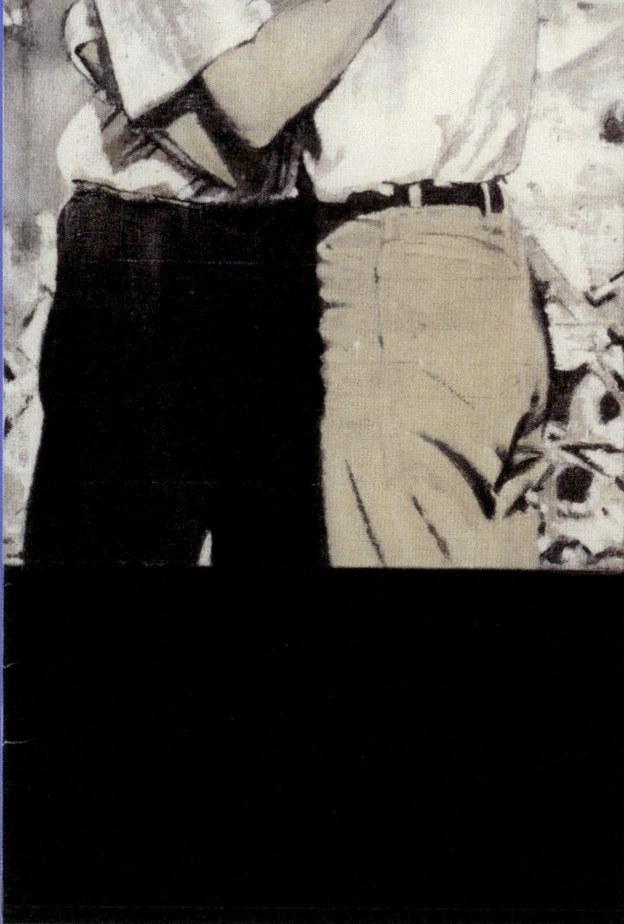

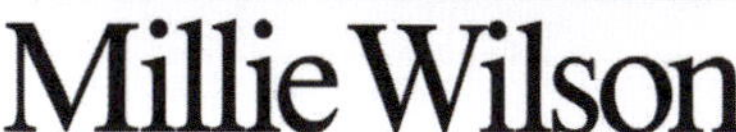

The Los Angeles Times Series

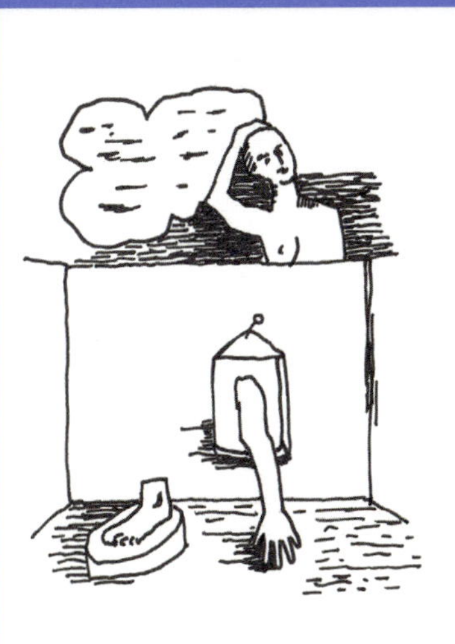

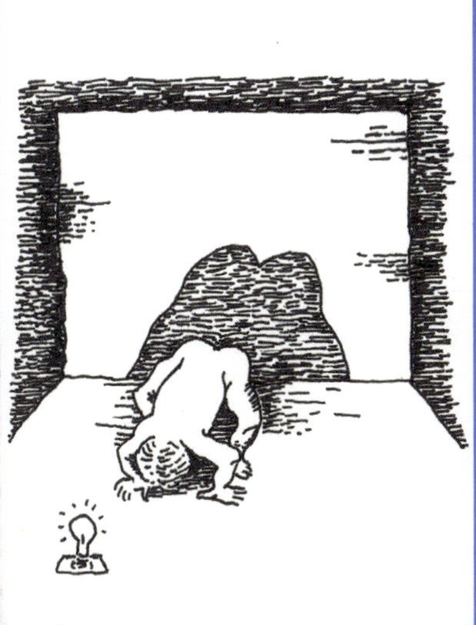

CLOCKWISE FROM BOTTOM LEFT Catalogue for *Situation: Perspectives on Work by Lesbian and Gay Artists*, 1991. Published by New Langton Arts, San Francisco; Catalogue for *Post-Boys & Girls: Nine Painters*, 1990. Published by Artists Space, New York; Brochure for *Fauve Semblant: Peter (A Young English Girl)*, 1989. Published by LACE (Los Angeles Contemporary Exhibitions); Millie Wilson's faculty ID at CalArts, 1990

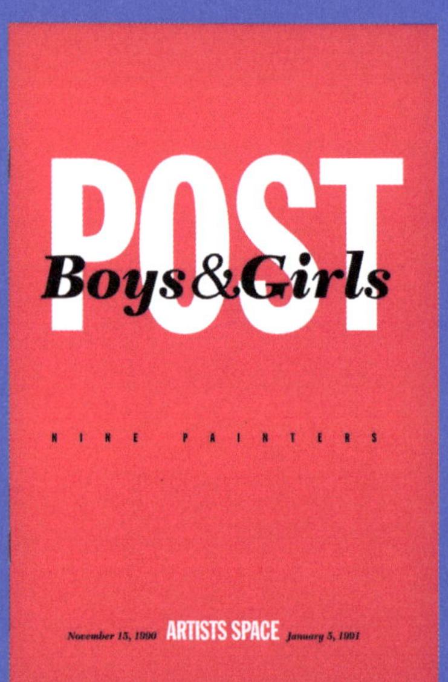

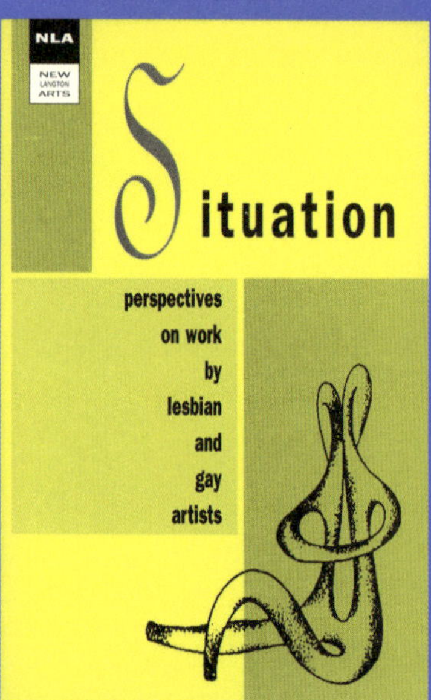

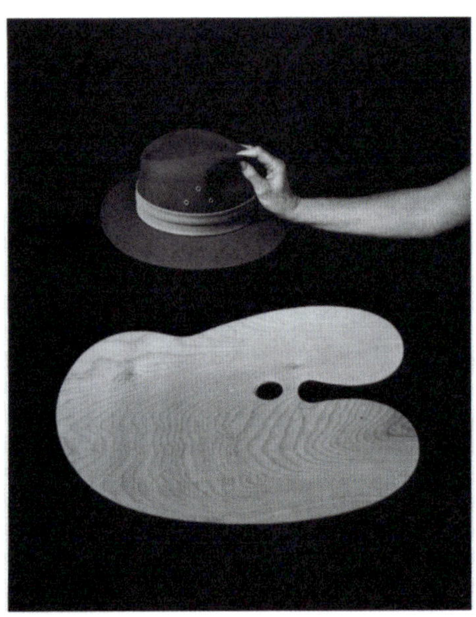

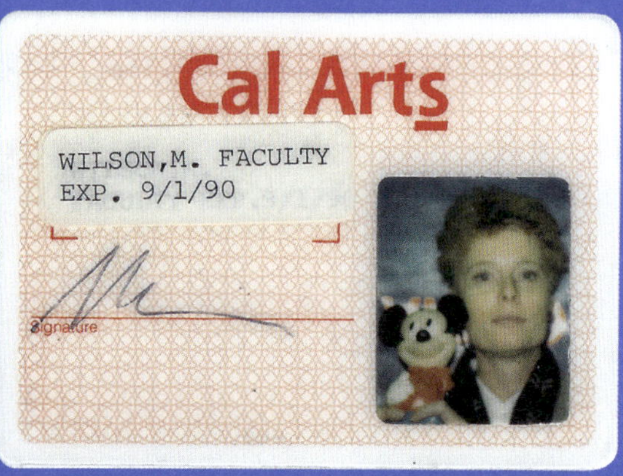

ARTISTS

Thoroughly Postmodern Millie

Artist Millie Wilson Invents a Lesbian Painter and Exhibits Her Work

BY TERRY WOLVERTON

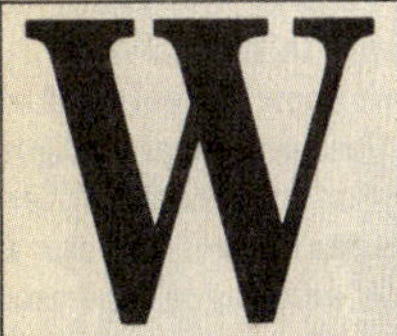

What would you put in a Museum of Lesbian Dreams? If you're like most lesbians, probably a life-size color photo of Jodie Foster. But if you ask Millie Wilson, lesbian artist and director of the Program in Art at the California Institute of the Arts in Valencia, you discover she has something else in mind.

A wig styled to resemble women's genitalia? A fur-lined trophy for personal pathology? A plaque boasting a bronzed turnip and potato? What's she trying to do?

"The Museum of Lesbian Dreams" is Wilson's latest art project, and the objects and tableaux she's producing abound with references to psychoanalysis, art history, contemporary French philosophers, and early sexology manuals. Not content to simply reproduce images of lesbians for popular consumption, Wilson is out to make us aware of the social messages that work to construct the image of the lesbian in our culture.

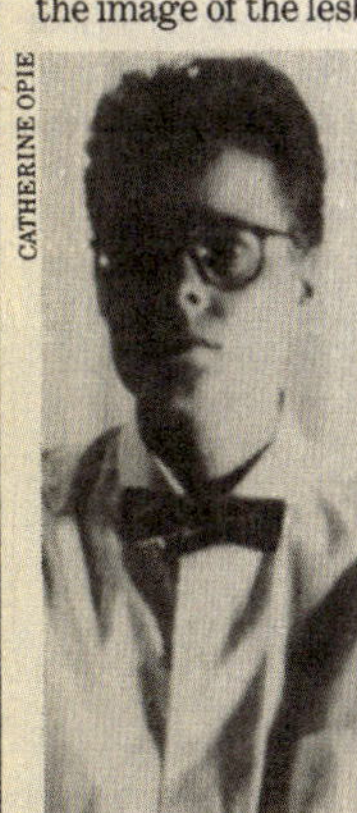
CATHERINE OPIE

Millie Wilson as Peter

Wilson operates in the heady world of postmodern art, where the function of art is not merely to provide visual pleasure to the viewer but to call into question the way we think about reality. Postmodern theory insists that the meaning of anything is not inherent but rather is culturally created. Wilson maintains that the cultural image of the lesbian cannot be divorced from how she has been defined and pathologized in the "pseudoscientific" sexology texts from the first half of the 20th century.

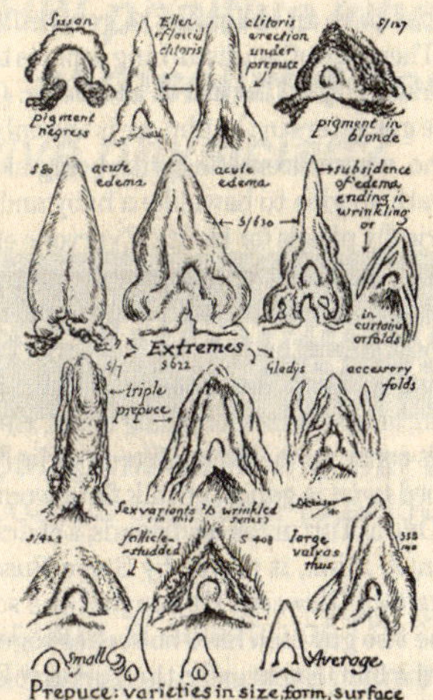

Deviant genitalia
Images from a 1948 sexology text

"I have an enormous collection of these out-of-print books about homosexuality and lesbianism," Wilson says. In one of these books, published in 1948, she discovered a drawing of the genitalia of homosexual women. Sometime later she happened to be flipping through a book on the history of costumes and came across a 1761 Hogarth engraving of periwigs for men.

"I was riveted," Wilson explains, "because it looked so much like the images of 'deviant' genitalia. It is one of those formal resemblances; there are the same number of rows and everything." Drawing from the two black-and-white images, Wilson produced an artfully styled object that looks like a synthesis of a periwig and genitalia, which she keeps in a tall mahogany case in her office.

"I'm not telling the viewer what to see," Wilson continues. "I'm making a set of connections that may not be chatty and informative – it's almost twisted. I'm interested in doing things that can't automatically be identified as 'Oh, that's just a lesbian trying to make one more case for herself.' "

When asked if she believes it's possible to make lesbian art that is not a reaction to lesbian oppression, Wilson responds, "There's the question of how much to respond to how we've been constructed and how much to speculate wildly. But we're in this setting, and we can't pretend it doesn't exist. Rather than idealizing the stereotypes, let's take them and reverse them, take power over them."

Wilson is a tall, handsome strawberry blonde. Born in Hot Springs, Ark., in 1948, she expressed her aptitude for art early on. "A lot of things were hell about my childhood," she recounts, "but the one thing that was always pleasurable, that I always got praise for, was the fact that I could draw."

She studied literature, photography, and painting, earning a bachelor's degree from the University of Texas at Austin and a

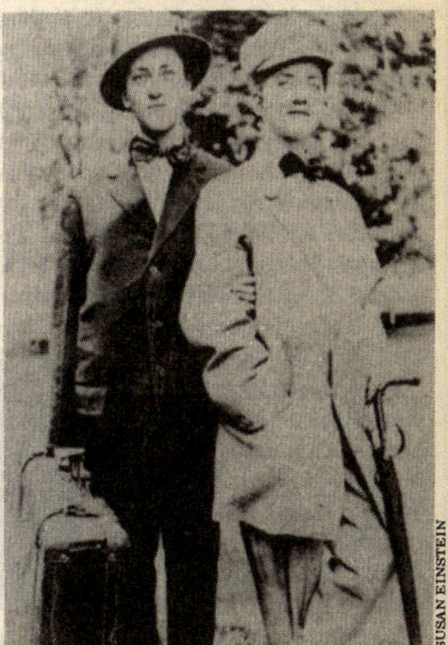
SUSAN EINSTEIN

Cross-dressed women
Postcard image from "Fauve Semblant"

70

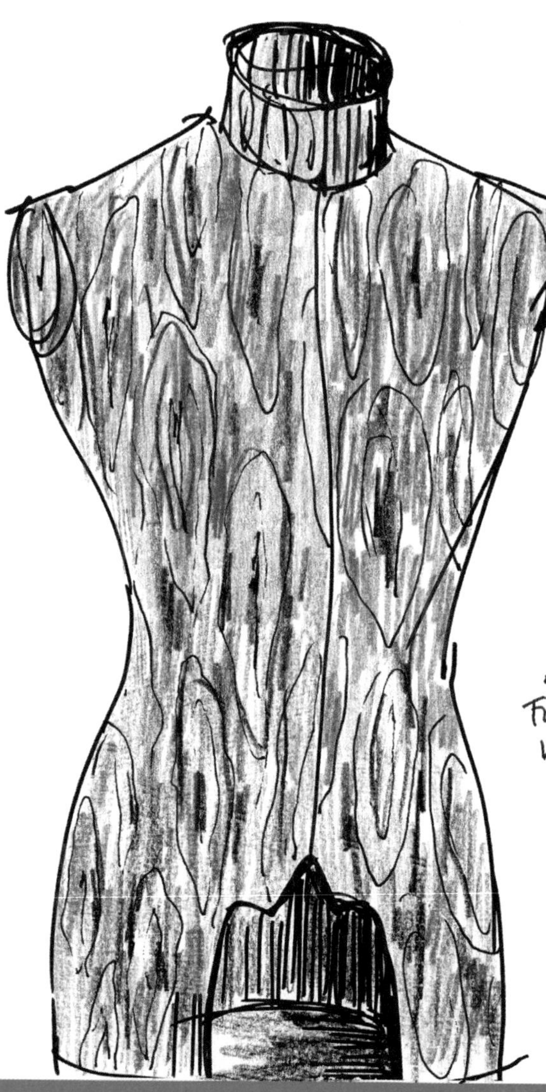

Sketch for *Elektra*, 1991. Ink and colored pencil on paper

Elektra, 1991. Upholstered torso and head forms and two Formica-veneer pedestals

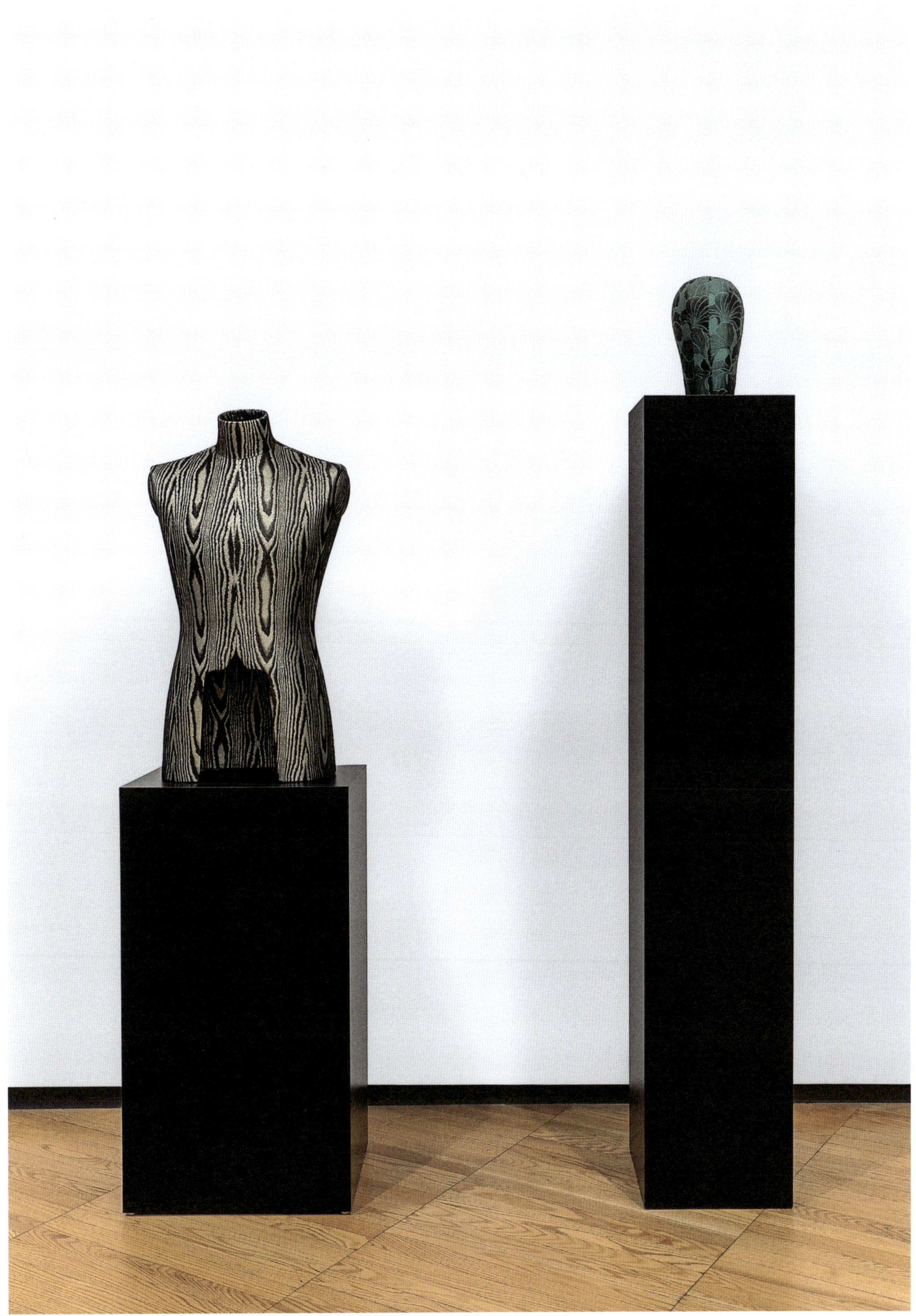

The Los Angeles Times Series, 1988–89. *Part 1, page 26, Thursday, February 2, 1989, "Musician Billy Tipton shown in the 1950s."* DEATH REVEALS MUSICIAN WHO LIVED AS MAN TO BE WOMAN. *High rates. No anxiety.* Acrylic on canvas

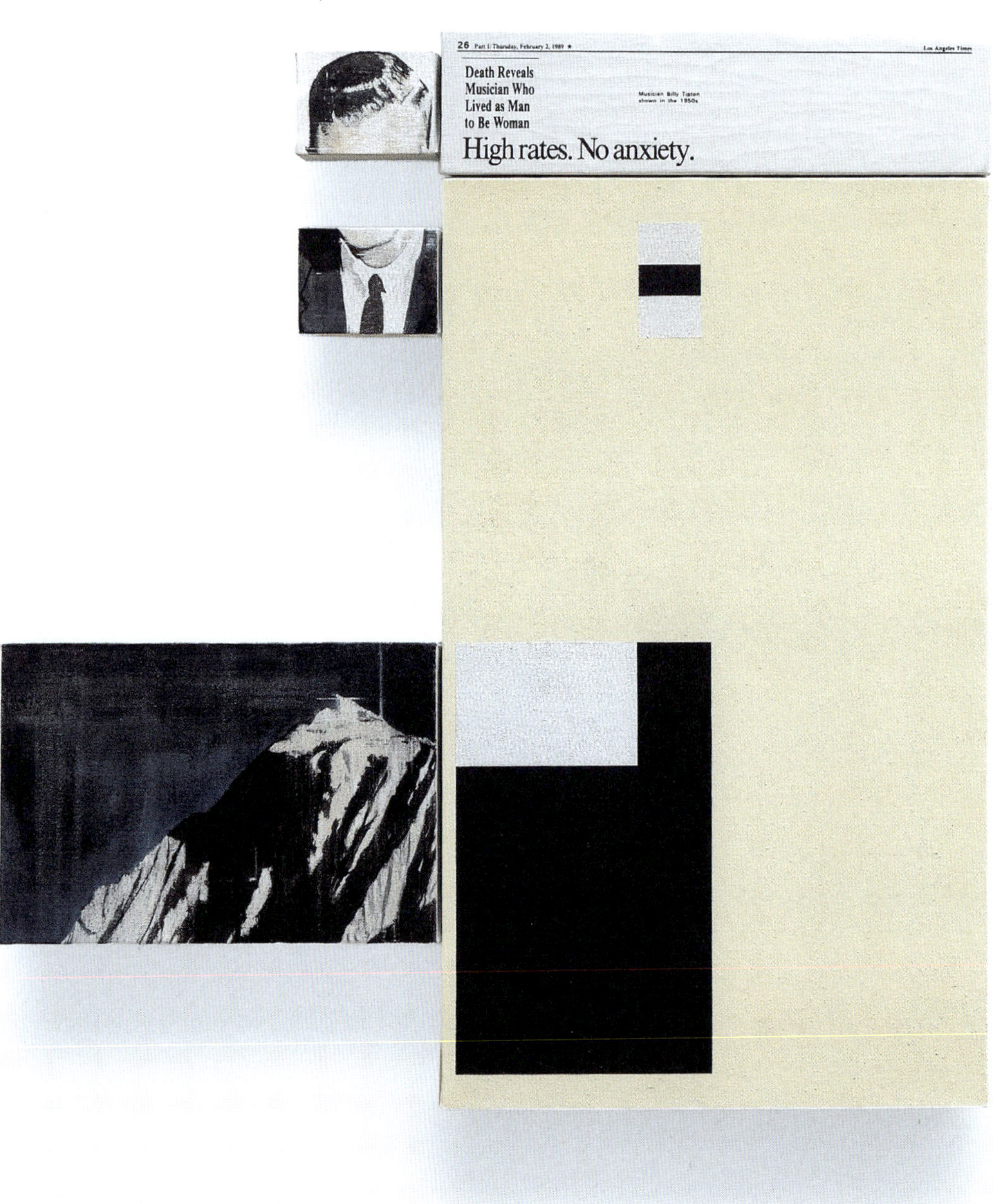

The Los Angeles Times Series, 1988–89. *Part 1, page 12, Sunday, January 31, 1988, "Carolina Garcia Salas displays giant molar of a mammoth that her son found in their yard."* BONES: OFFICIALS ARE SHOWING SCANT INTEREST IN TOWN'S NEW 'TREASURE' BALI SUPPORT BRAS, 30% OFF. *Lowest prices this season! Plus, meet a Bali fitting specialist at a May Company listed below.* Acrylic on canvas

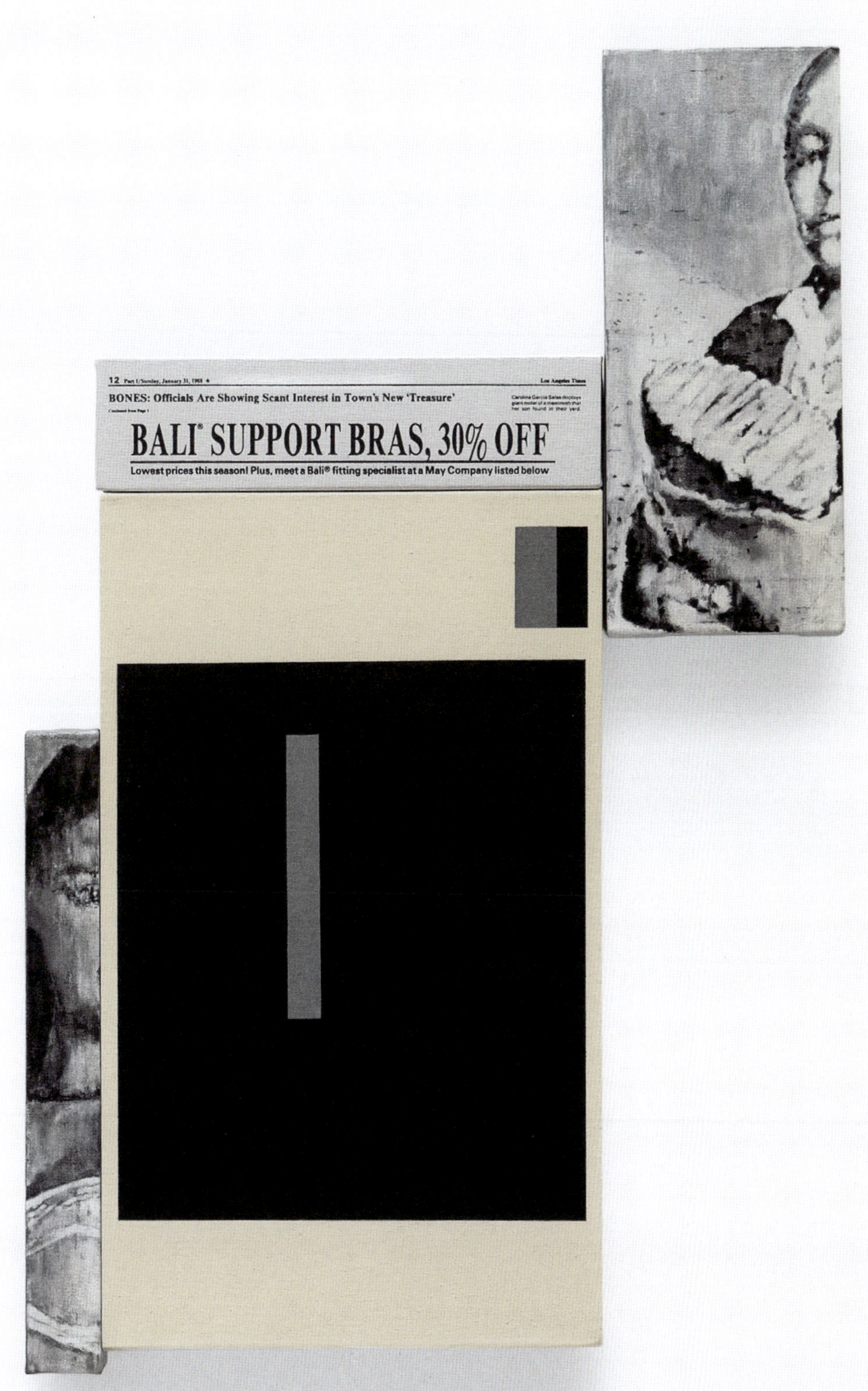

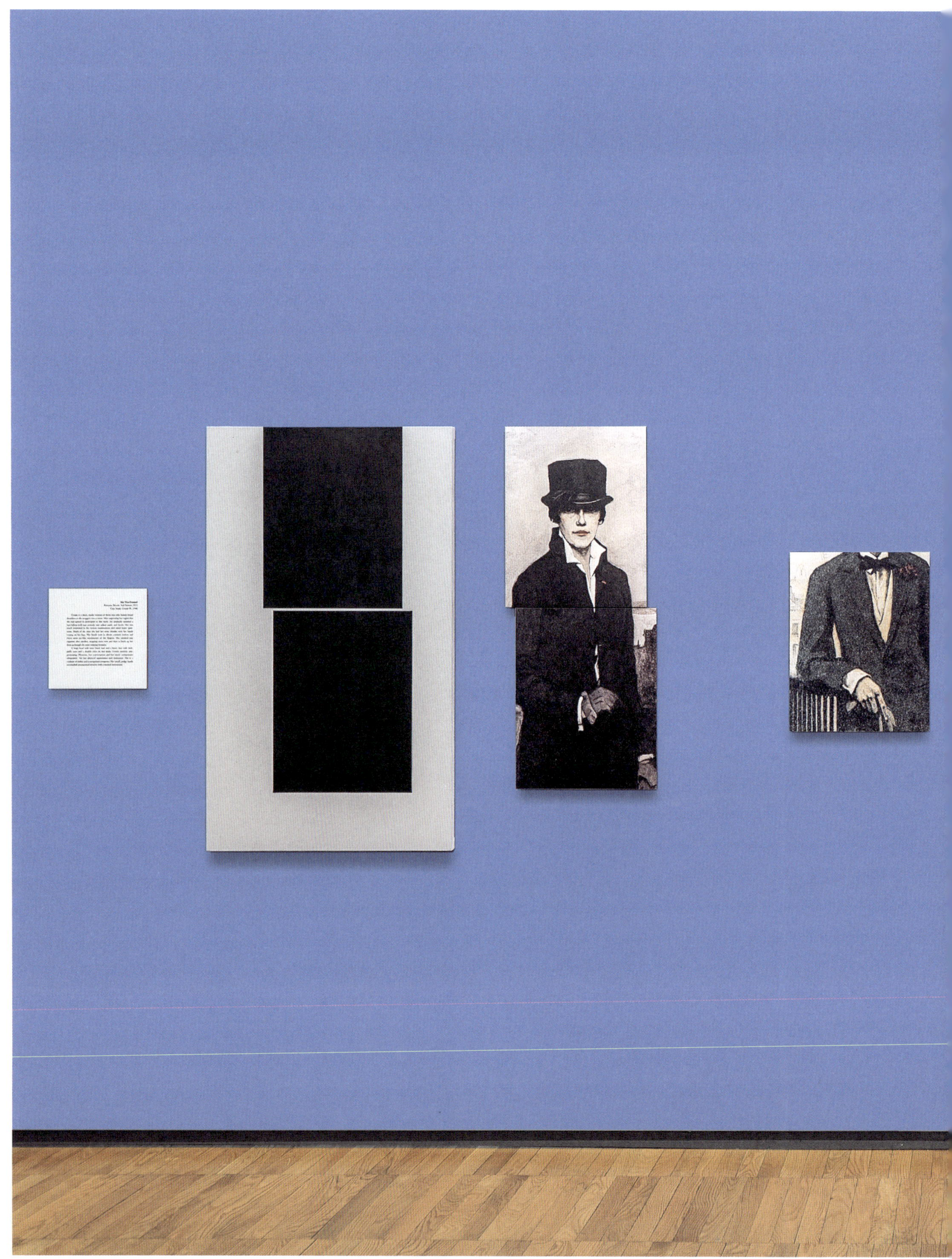

PAGES 56–59 *The Painter Who Is Not One: Millie Wilson/ Romaine Brooks*, 1990. Acrylic on canvas, periwinkle wall paint, color photographs, and text panels

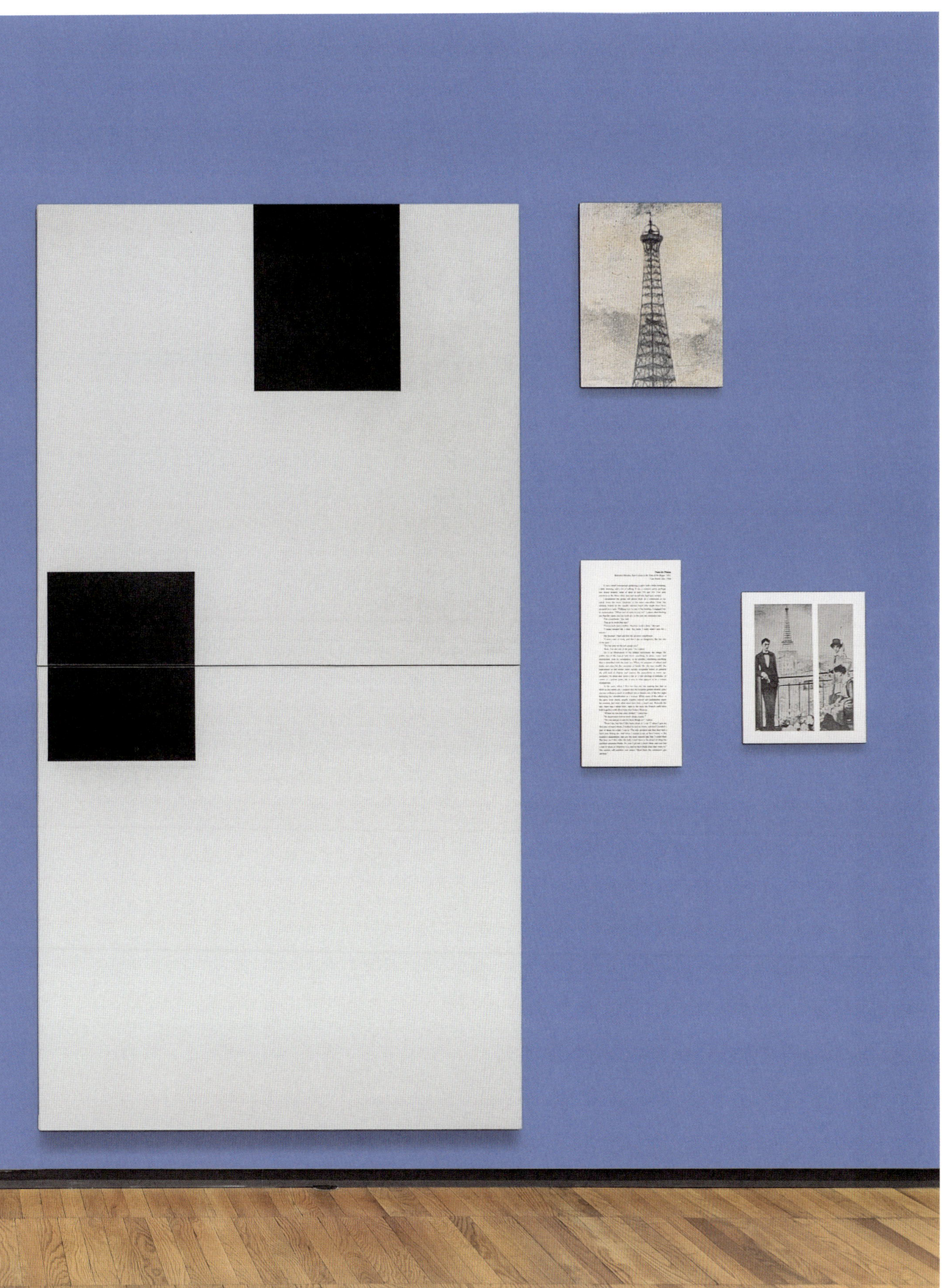

She Was Framed

Romaine Brooks: *Self Portrait*, 1923
Case Study: Ursula W., 1948

Ursula is a short, stocky woman of thirty-two who heaves broad shoulders as she swaggers into a room. After expressing her regret that she had agreed to participate in this study, she gradually assumed a hail-fellow-well-met attitude and talked easily and freely. She was much interested in the various examinations and asked many questions. Much of the time she had her arms akimbo with her hands resting on her hips. Her hands were in almost constant motion and there were tic-like movements of the fingers. She smoked one cigarette after another, stopping every now and then to hitch up her dress as though she were wearing trousers.

A large head with wavy black hair and a heavy face with dark, puffy eyes and a double chin do not make Ursula entirely prepossessing. However, her conversation and her music compensate adequately for her physical appearance and demeanor. She is a violinist of ability and a recognized composer. Her small, pudgy hands accomplish unsuspected miracles with a musical instrument.

Nom de Plume

Romaine Brooks: *Jean Cocteau in the Time of the Rogue*, 1912

Case Study: Joe, 1964

It was a small homosexual gathering, a party with a little drinking, a little dancing, and a lot of talking. It was a women's party, perhaps two dozen women, most of them in their 20's and 30's. Few paid attention to the three other men and myself who had been invited.

I scrutinized the group and placed them on a continuum in my mind, from the most feminine to the most masculine, from the extreme femme to the equally extreme butch who might have been accepted as a male. Walking over to one of the butches, I engaged her in conversation. "What sort of work do you do?" I asked, after finding out that her name was Joe (with an *e* at the end, she reminded me).

"I'm a machinist," Joe said.

"You go to work this way?"

"Not in such fancy clothes. Machine work is dirty," she said.

"I mean dressed like a man. You know, I really wasn't sure for a minute."

She beamed. I had paid her the greatest compliment.

"I wear a suit to work, and then I put on dungarees, like the rest of the guys."

"Do the men on the job accept you?"

"Sure, I'm just one of the guys," Joe replied.

Joe is an illustration of the lesbian stereotype, the image the public has of the typical lady-lover: searching, by dress, voice, and mannerism, even by occupation, to be manlike, emulating anything that is identified with the male sex. While, for purposes of school and work, and even for the amenities of family life, she may modify the masculinity to fall within more socially acceptable limits, in general she will seek to display and express this masculinity at every opportunity. So when one enters a bar or a club catering to lesbians, or comes to a private party, she is seen in what appears to be a virtual masquerade.

At the party where I first met Joe, she was wearing her hair as short as any man's; yet, I suspect that the beautiful golden blonde color was not without a touch of artificial tint or bleach, one of the few signs betraying her identification as a woman. While some of the others at the party wore slacks, usually brightly colored and indubitably made for women, Joe wore what must have been a man's suit. Beneath the suit, there was a white shirt, open at the neck; the French cuffs were held together with silver links that looked Mexican.

"Where do you buy your clothes?" I asked her.

"In department stores–men's shops, mainly."

"Do you just go in and try these things on?" I asked.

"Now I do, but first I felt funny about it. I was 17 when I got my first pair of men's shoes. I walked in and sat down, and said I needed a pair of shoes for a play I was in. The only problem was that they had a hard time fitting me. And when I wanted a suit, at first I went to the women's department, and got the most tailored one that I could find. But later on I felt, what the hell, I don't have to be afraid of what the goddam salesman thinks. So, now I go into a men's shop, and just buy a suit or shoes or whatever it is, and let them think what they want to." She smiled, self-satisfied, and added, "Most likely the salesman's gay, anyway."

Kang Seung Lee in collaboration with Millie Wilson, *Millie* from the series *Untitled (Artspeak?)*, 2014–15. Ink, watercolor, colored pencil, acrylic, gouache, pen, pencil, and collage on paper

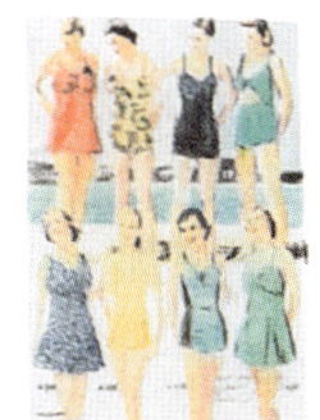

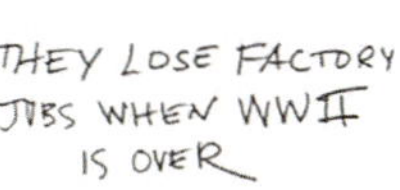

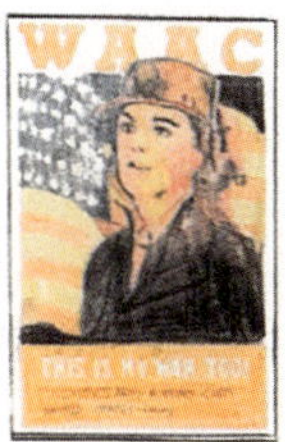

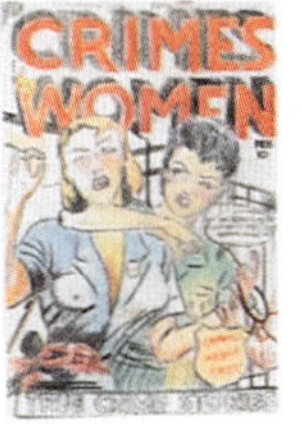

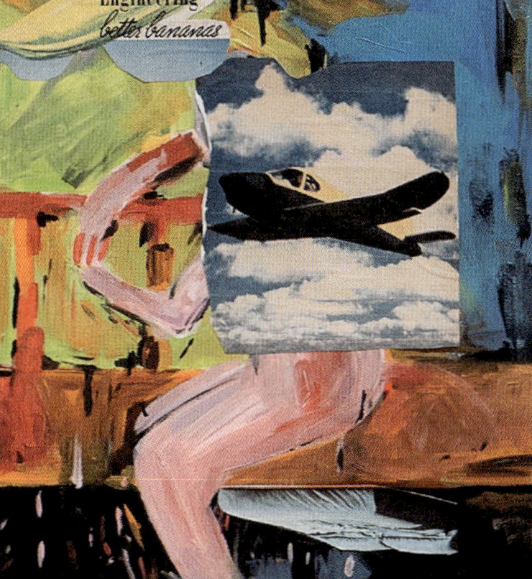

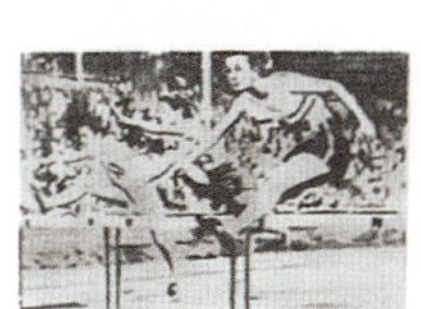

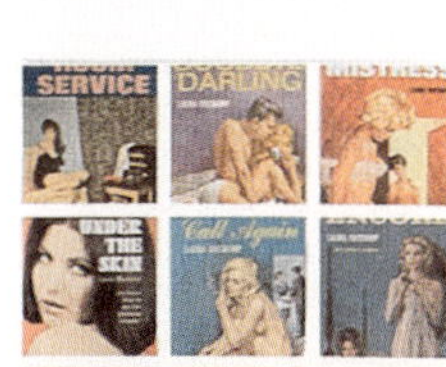

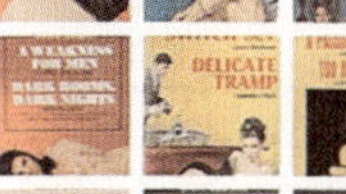

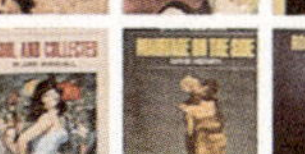

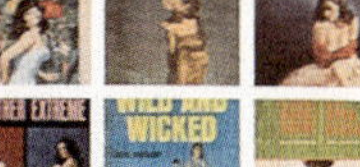

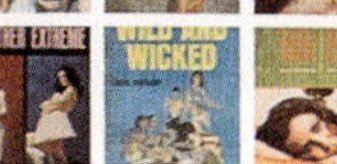

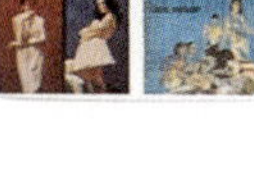

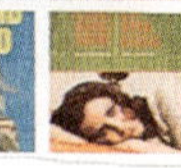

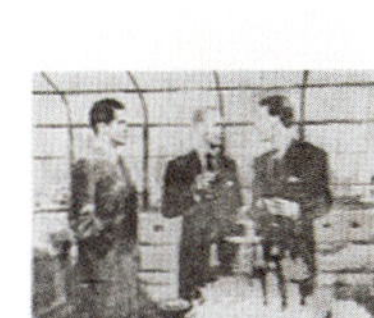

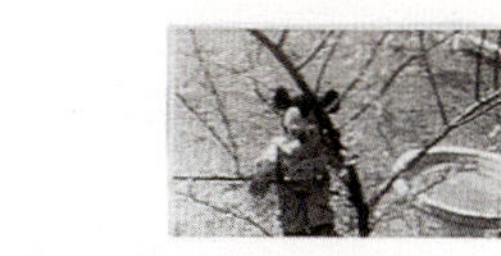

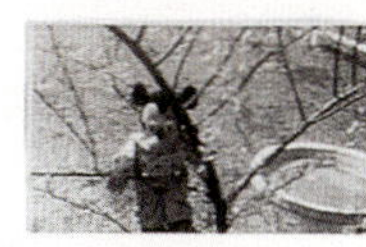

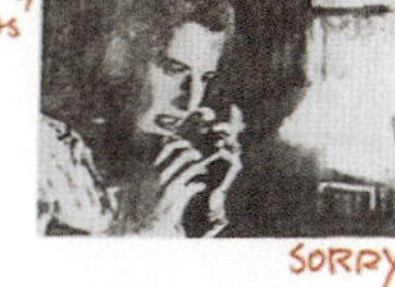

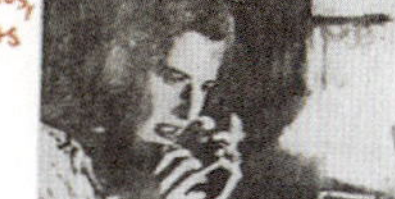

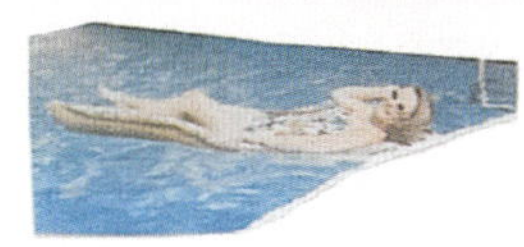

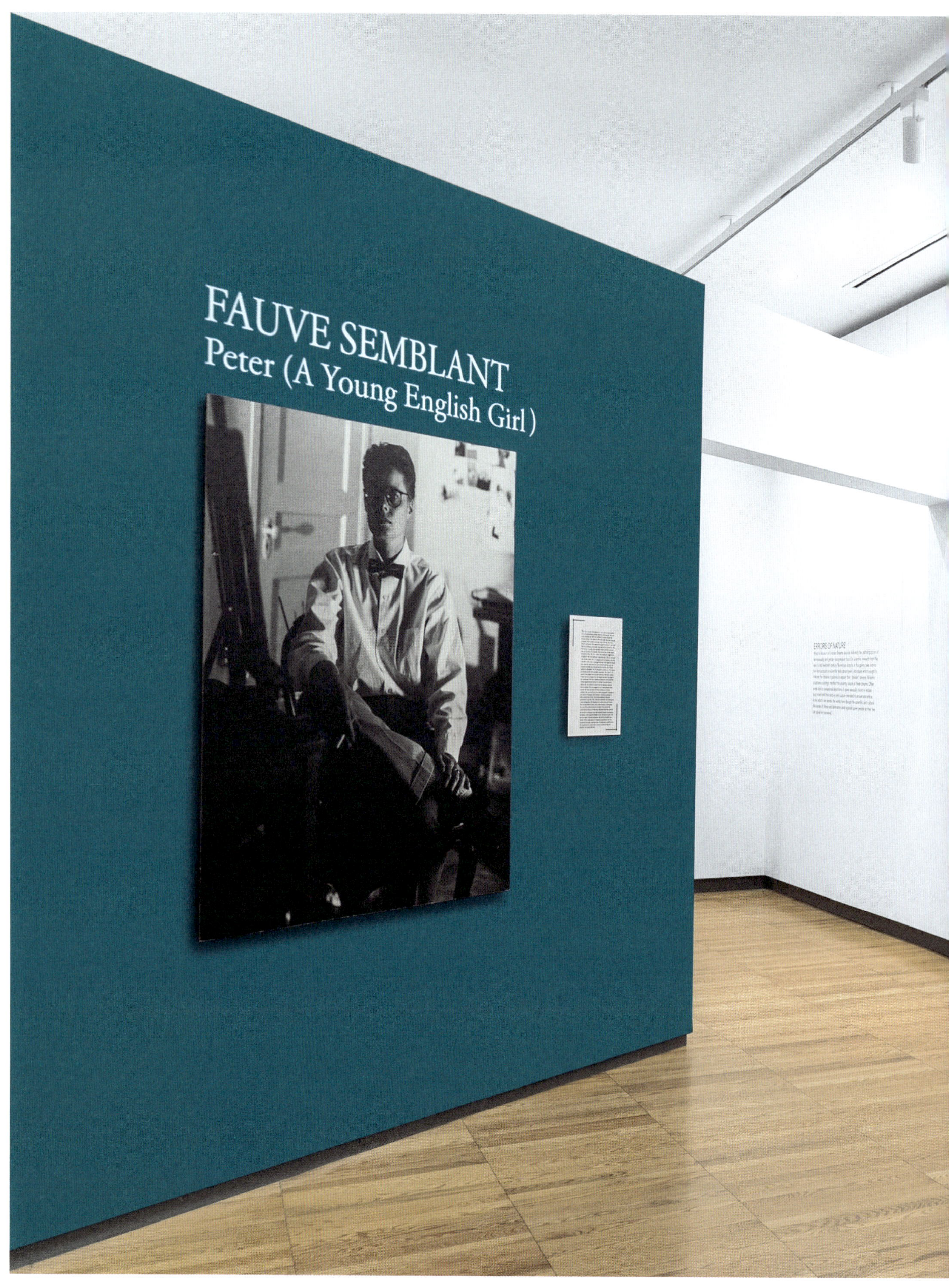
FAUVE SEMBLANT
Peter (A Young English Girl)

Fauve Semblant: Peter (A Young English Girl), 1989.
Installation view at Krannert Art Museum, 2024

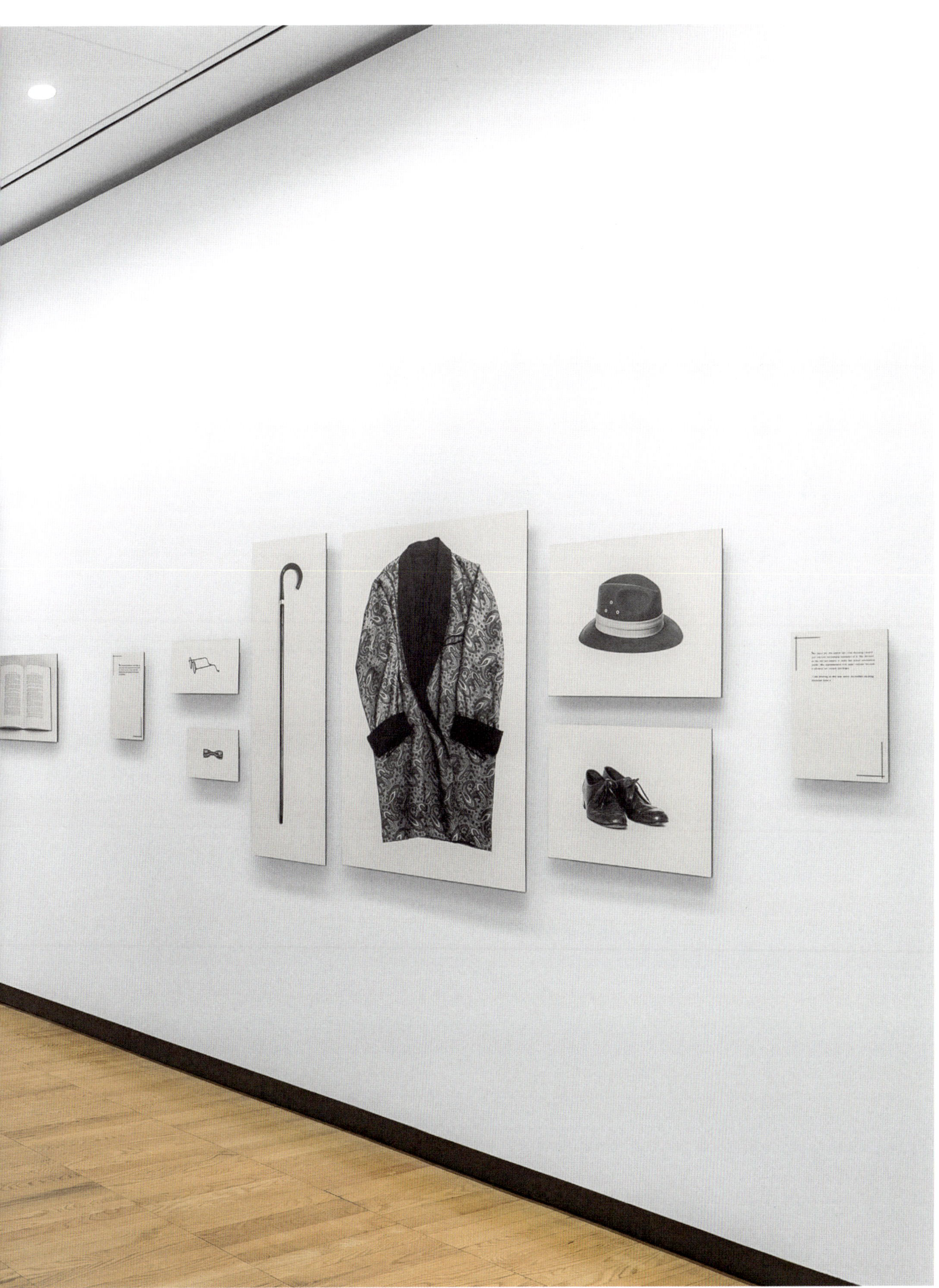

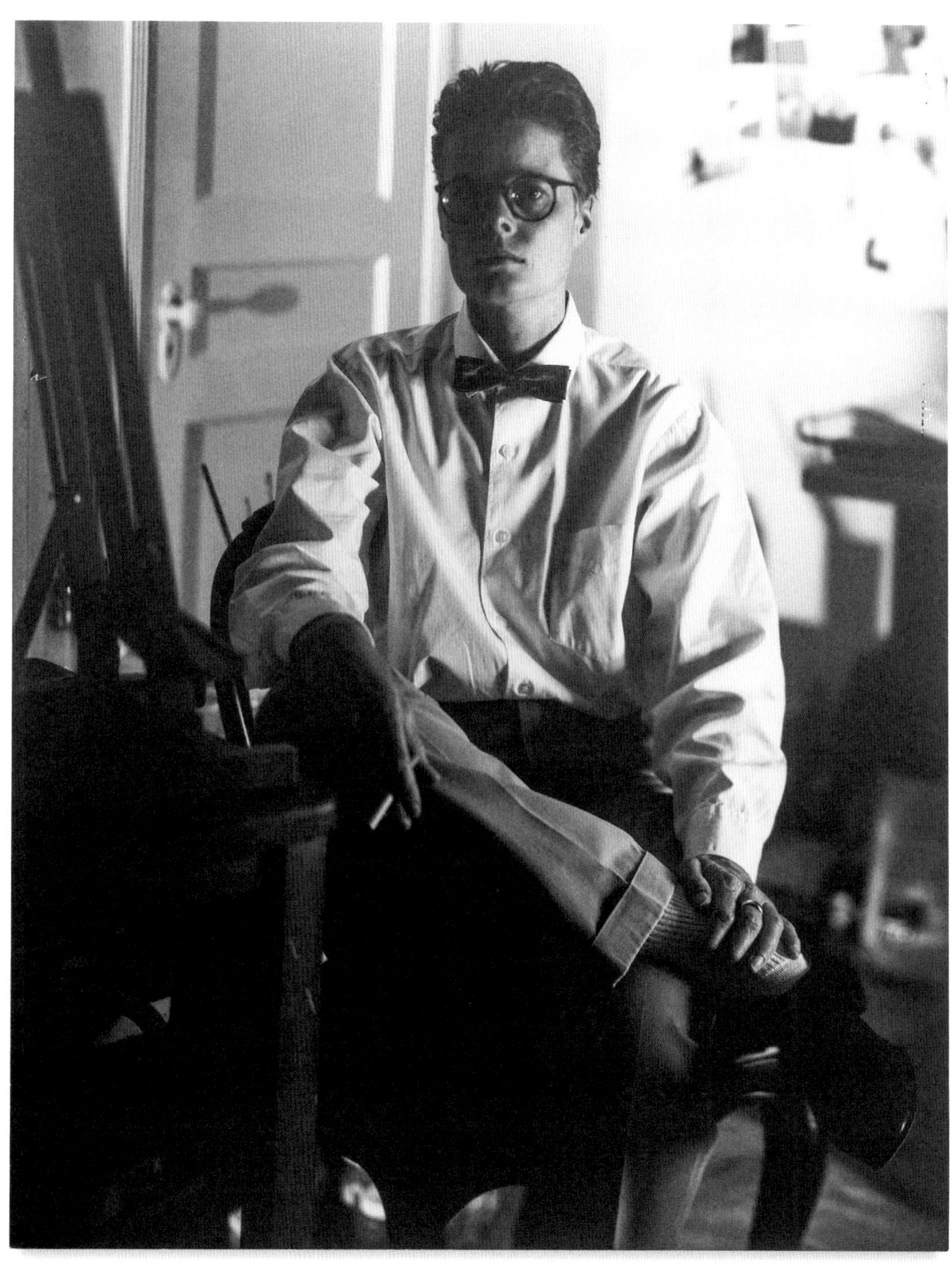

She was a woman. She dressed as a man. She was authoritative and uncompromising. She was romantic and domestic. She was born working class. She was acclaimed in stylish circles. She became famous. She withdrew from the public. She was a mannish renegade. She wanted to marry the love of her life. She was a flawless technician. She neglected to paint for years at a time. She risked everything to be an artist. She gave up her art for love. She flaunted her sexuality. She accepted various inversion theories. She was scornful of art schools. She was generous in her support of genuine talent. She was a misfit. She continually sought to be recognized. She was indifferent to material gain. She was obsessed with worldly details. She was dangerous in her intentions. She was a favorite of the wives of distinguished men. She longed for nature. She could live only in the city. She wanted autonomy. She was haunted by family ties. She generated excitement. She secretly wished for tranquility. She was flagrantly promiscuous. She insisted on integrity in the most mundane transactions. She worked very quickly. She painted with exquisite precision. She had a reckless temper and was arrogant. She was deeply moved by the plight of the unfortunate. She was a disaffected expatriate. She found that certain neighborhoods allowed for refuge in unconventional salons. She was subject to anxiety that her alienation from art history instilled. She was engaged by the central debates of the period. She was concerned with the invention of a lesbian aesthetic. She was irrelevant to the male avant-garde's nostalgia for the women of antiquity. She endured a loneliness particular to those erased from history. She devised aesthetic strategies grounded in mutuality. She could never match the devastating wit of the intelligentsia. She displayed on occasion the gift of retort. She was described by male critics as the heroine of modernism. She was all but absent from the accounts of the period. She espoused the rhetoric of collectivity. She demanded that each of her lovers be all things to her. She escaped abroad to anonymous adventures. She longed for delight in love and perfect union. She was the target of sexual speculation. She did not resemble case studies of the consequences of unnatural attachments. She was accused by her male contemporaries of displaying a morbid desire. She found that the courts of law would not acknowledge the existence of a desire like hers.

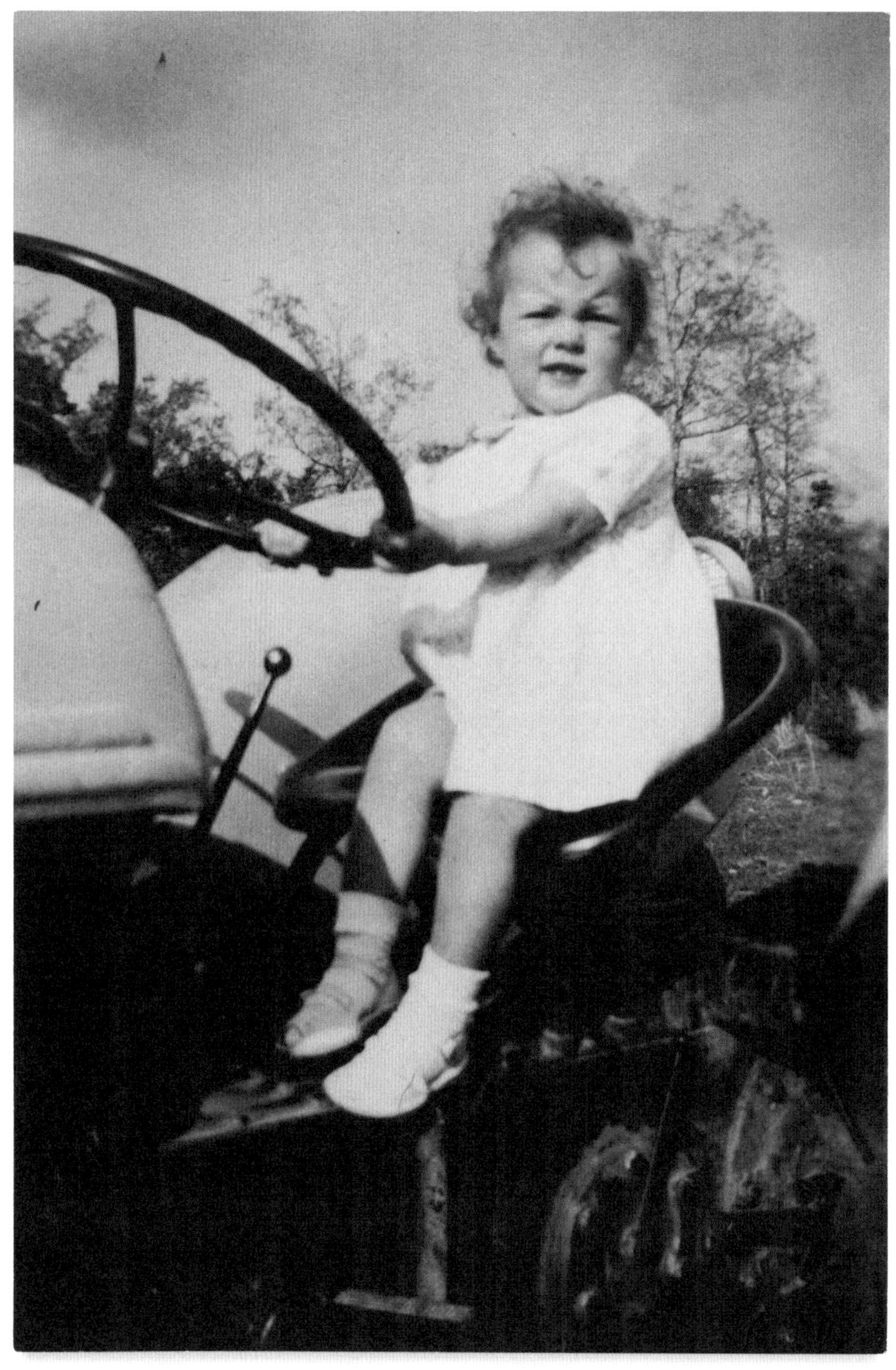

Baby on Tractor, 1989. Gelatin silver print and text panel mounted on Dibond

She came to believe that lesbianism could be detected in a baby's physical characteristics, and preserved only those photographs which confirmed her theories.

Two Women, 1989. Gelatin silver print panel mounted on Dibond

OPPOSITE *Bulldagger/Painter*, 1989. Teal wallpaint and plexiglass panels with vinyl text

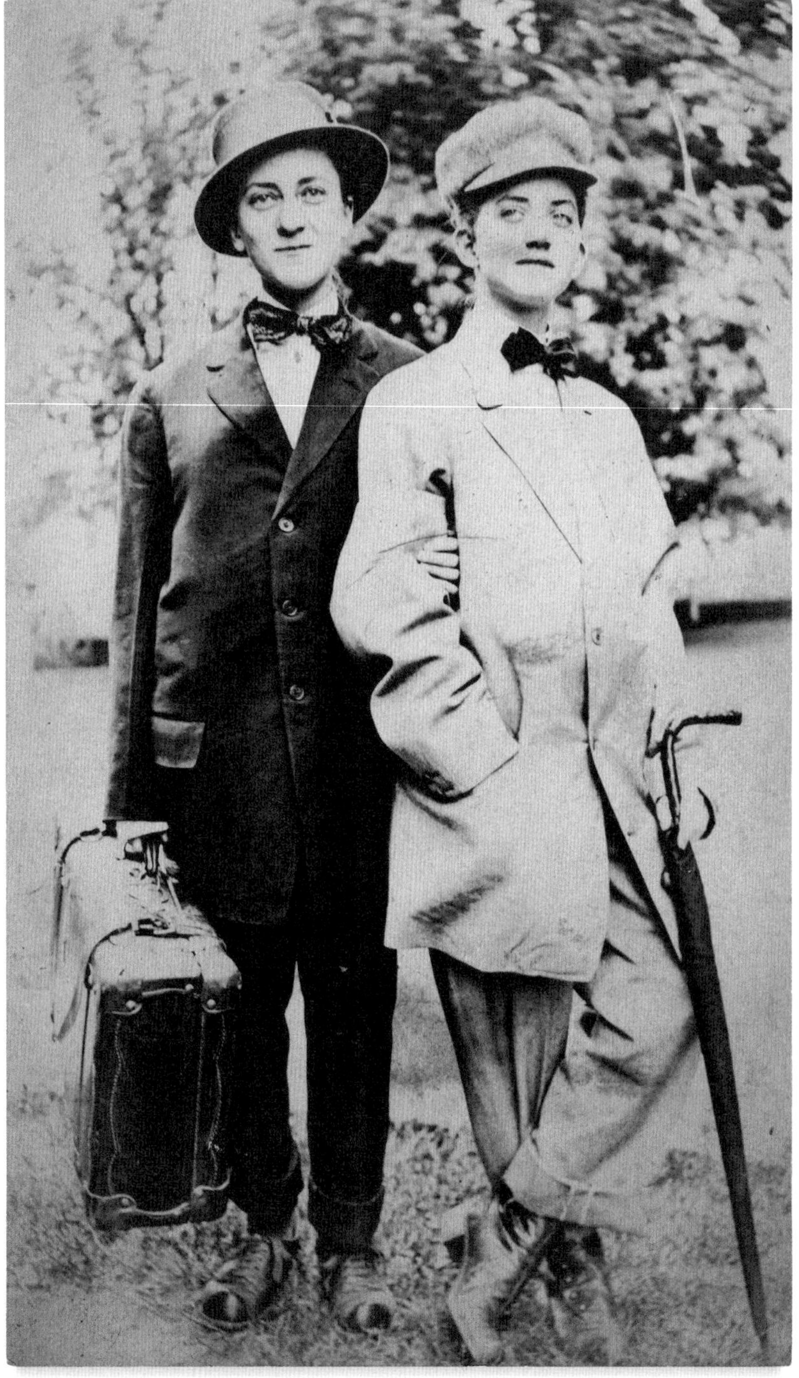

bulldagger

painter

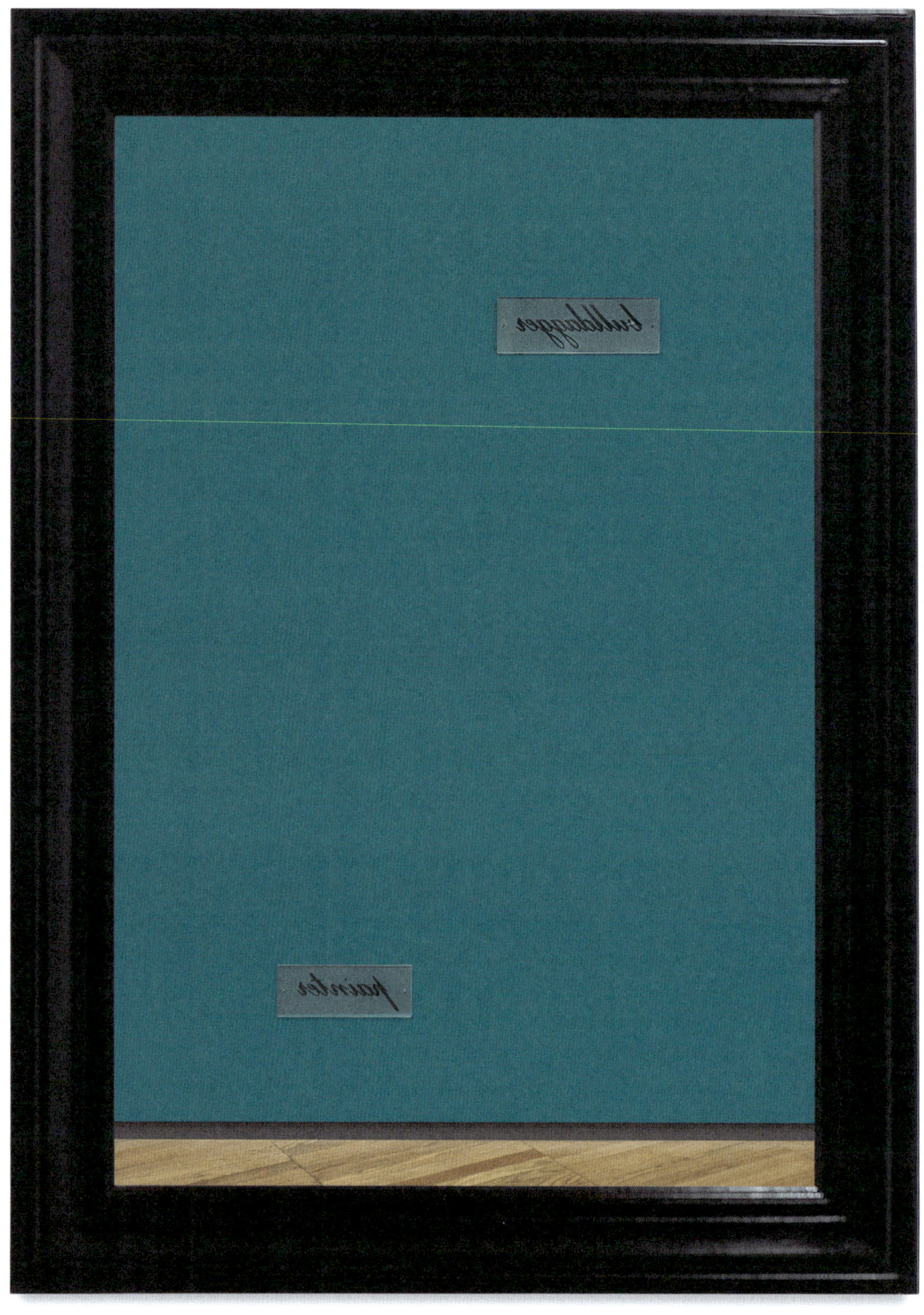

She was known primarily for her portraits of women and politicians.

We Two in Solitude Were Wandering There (Sphinx and Wild Lilies), 1989. Acrylic on linen, frame, wood, plexiglass, burlap, and brass label

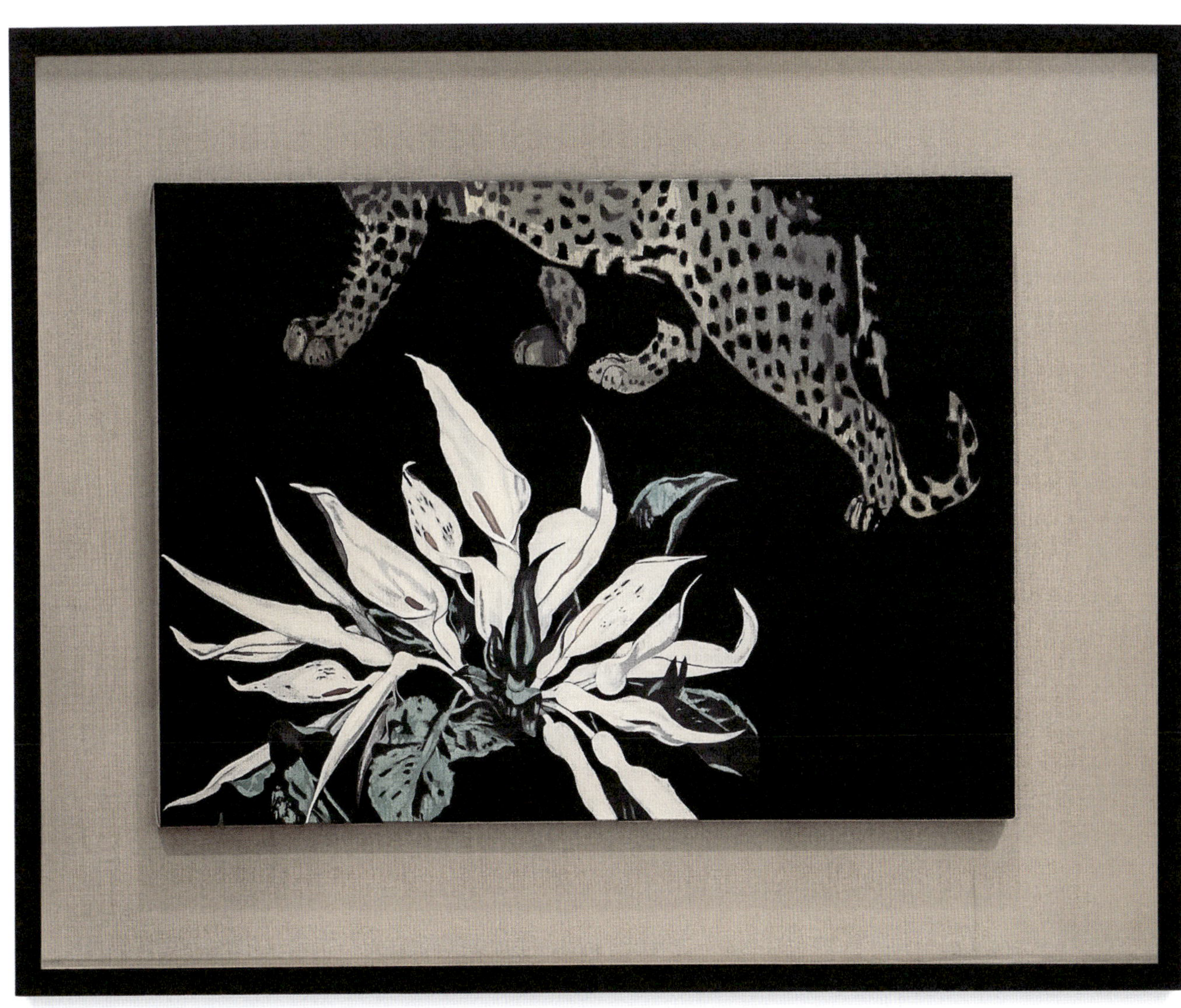

PAGES 74–77 *Leotard, Cheater, Painter*, 1989. Stretched fabric, gelatin silver print, acrylic on canvas, vinyl type, and text panel mounted on Dibond

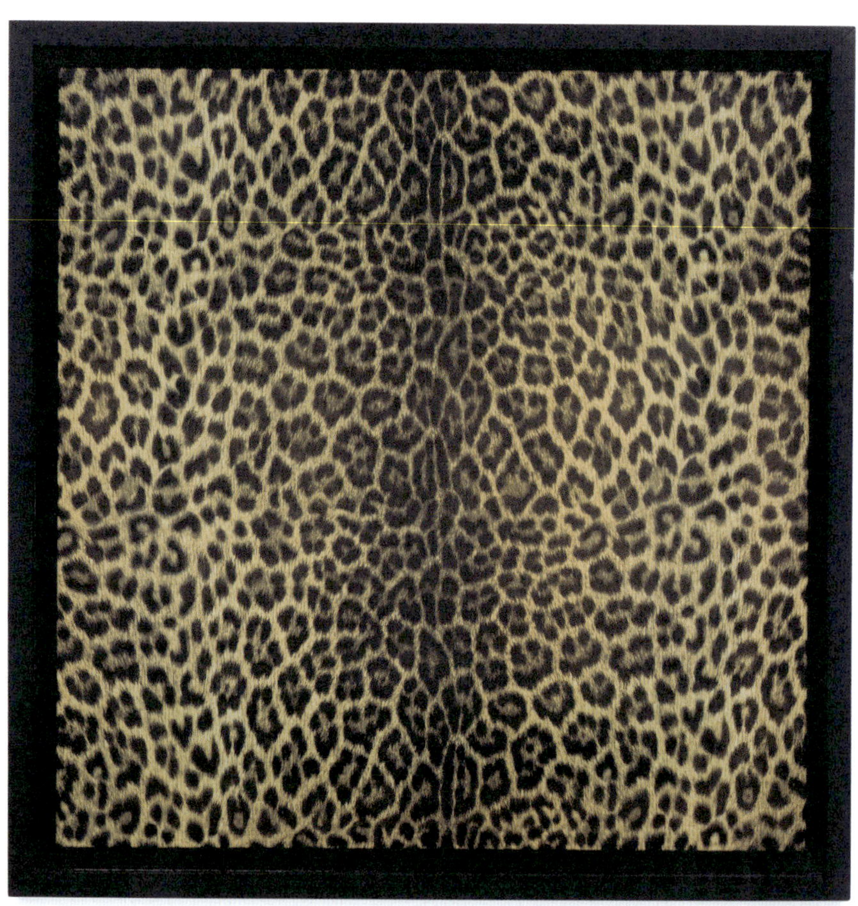

LEOTARD

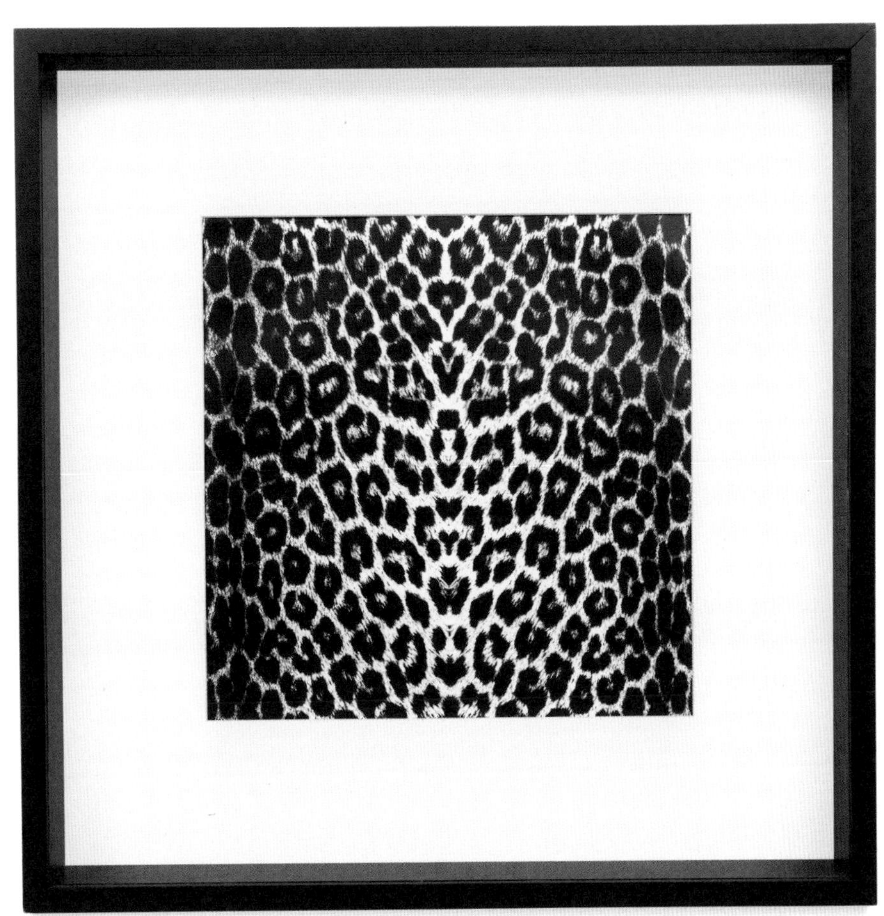

CHEATER

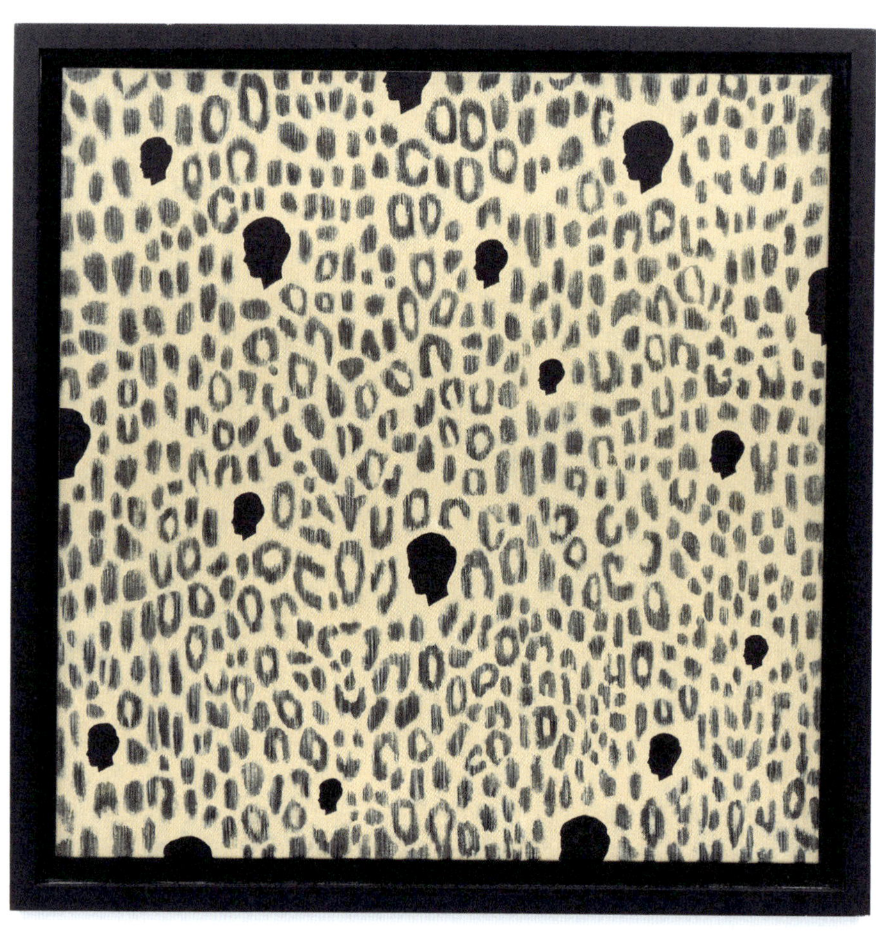

PAINTER

Without means to travel, she sought the exotic in the archive of the zoo, the botanical garden, and the museum. She was fascinated by the big cats, and the careful distinctions made among leopards, cheetahs and panthers.

Here may be mentioned the Mādigo of the Hausa women, a contrivance made in imitation of the male organ, which women strap on in order to gratify other women, and which is employed especially in very large harems. Before England took possession of the country a woman found with such an instrument was very severely punished: she was buried alive and her partner was sold into slavery. [For further details see Mischlich, "Bilder-Lexikon," I., p. 419; and for the same customs among the women of Lake Chad, see Bouillez.]

In classical antiquity, especially in Greece, as Knapp illustrated with various examples, the use of an instrument called "Olisbos," knowledge of which apparently came from Asia Minor, was for a time very widely spread so that even the authorities took severe measures against it. Passages in Aristophanes, Herondas, Lucian, as well as certain pictorial representations, which Knapp discusses in greater detail, give full particulars.

[The use of the *ὄλισβος* or *βαυβών* in antiquity is illustrated by a number of representations on Greek vases, of which Vorberg, Licht, Knight and the "Bilder-Lexikon" discuss and give selected examples. In Latin the term *fascinum scorteum* was employed, and the artificial phallus under the terms of *fascinum*, *godemiché*, *diletto*, *passo-tempo*, *dildo*, etc., was used and discussed up to the present day, as we shall see later.]

Apparently, too, such customs were not unknown to the ancient Israelites (*cf.* Ezek. xvi. 17). In the Midrash Schemot Rabba the following characteristic parable appears in this connection:

> "Like unto a king who, as he entered into his house, chanced upon his wife embracing a tripod toilet table (*mensa delphica*),* whereupon he fell into a rage. Then his bride's man stepped before him and said: 'If a child is born' (*i.e.*, if a child were to be expected from this intercourse) 'you would do right to be angered.' The King replied: 'Nothing is of importance in this matter but that she shall learn that she must not do such a thing'" (Wünsche [2]).

Very mischievous conditions must have prevailed in ancient India as a consequence of the hierarchy, as we can gather from the oft-quoted *Kāmasutrā* (see J. Kohler [2]). In both sexes we find sadistic tendencies, which are indicated as customs in certain neighbourhoods, as when it reads: "that one side strikes the other with the wedge on the breast, with the scissors on the head, with the piercing instrument on the cheeks, with the pinchers in the sides . . . certainly," says Vātsyāyana, "such doings are painful, barbarous and base. One may act according to the custom of the place, but, of course, only so that there is no danger to the other side. In connection with it, however, cases are cited that no more and no less, the King of the Panchalas making love to a courtesan, killed her with the wedge, that another lover, Naradeva, put out a dancer's eye with a needle prick" (*cf.* Fraxi,[2] p. 466).

Kohler also points out that masochism was not unrepresented among the women. Thus the *Kāmasutrā* states that some women were to be won by beating since by beating their lustfulness was aroused. Similarly, it is said of the women of other places that they enjoyed severe beatings. Moreover, the *Auparishtaka* (= *fellatio*) contemptuously designated "crows' love" was not unknown. [Artificial phalli were also well known. See Schmidt,[8] pp. 325, 334, 528, 540, 782, 783, 936.]

A form of abnormal intercourse which is not rare consists in so-called *tribadism*. This act is often found with *lesbianism*, because it is said to have been widespread among the women of Mytilene, the capital of the island of Lesbos. From here it is

* [*Cf.* Daremberg v. Saglio, Fig. 4908.]

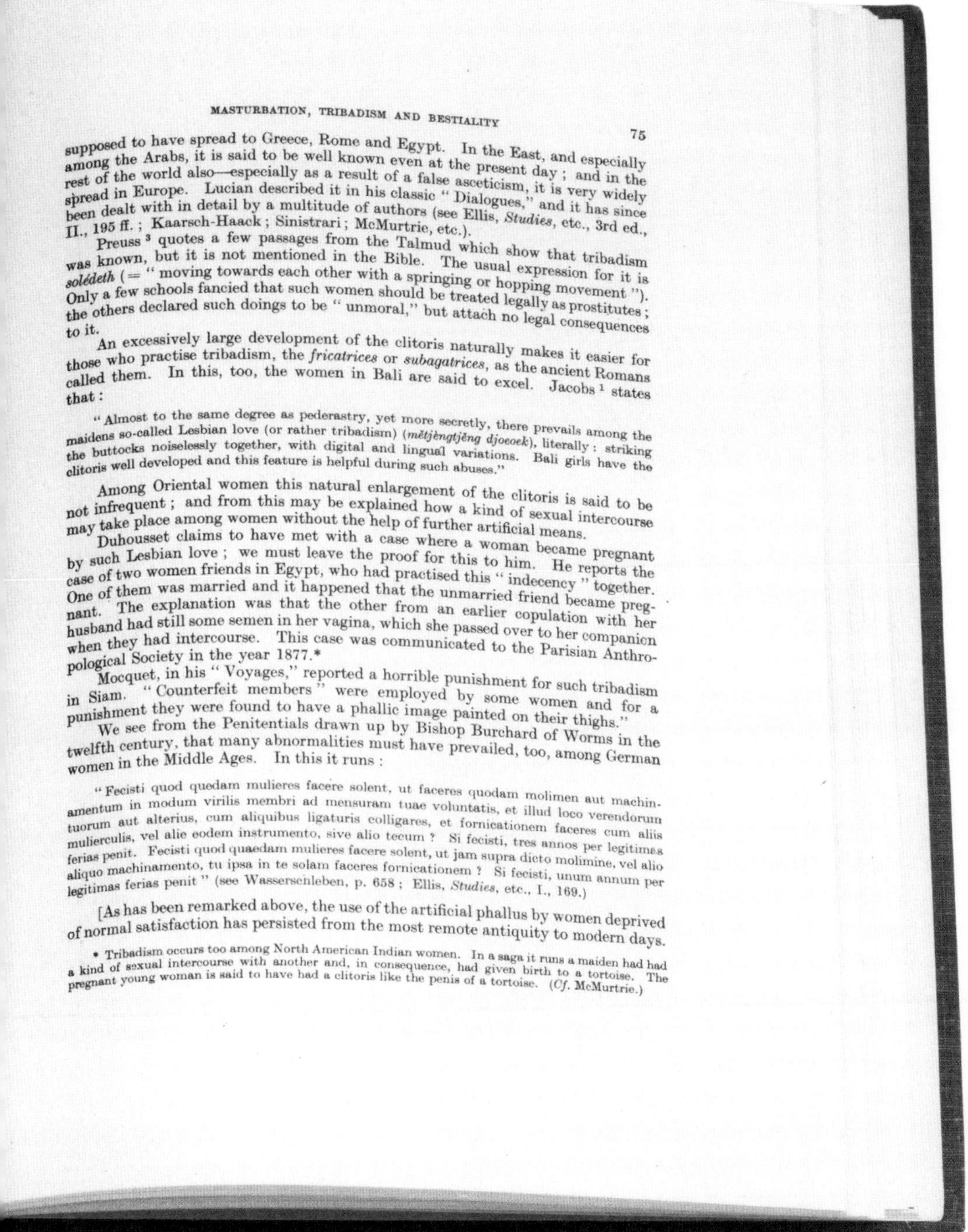

supposed to have spread to Greece, Rome and Egypt. In the East, and especially
among the Arabs, it is said to be well known even at the present day ; and in the
rest of the world also—especially as a result of a false asceticism, it is very widely
spread in Europe. Lucian described it in his classic " Dialogues," and it has since
been dealt with in detail by a multitude of authors (see Ellis, *Studies*, etc., 3rd ed.,
II., 195 ff. ; Kaarsch-Haack ; Sinistrari ; McMurtrie, etc.).

Preuss [3] quotes a few passages from the Talmud which show that tribadism
was known, but it is not mentioned in the Bible. The usual expression for it is
solédeth (= " moving towards each other with a springing or hopping movement ").
Only a few schools fancied that such women should be treated legally as prostitutes ;
the others declared such doings to be " unmoral," but attach no legal consequences
to it.

An excessively large development of the clitoris naturally makes it easier for
those who practise tribadism, the *fricatrices* or *subagatrices*, as the ancient Romans
called them. In this, too, the women in Bali are said to excel. Jacobs [1] states
that :

> " Almost to the same degree as pederastry, yet more secretly, there prevails among the
> maidens so-called Lesbian love (or rather tribadism) (*mĕtjèngtjĕng djoeoek*), literally : striking
> the buttocks noiselessly together, with digital and lingual variations. Bali girls have the
> clitoris well developed and this feature is helpful during such abuses."

Among Oriental women this natural enlargement of the clitoris is said to be
not infrequent ; and from this may be explained how a kind of sexual intercourse
may take place among women without the help of further artificial means.

Duhousset claims to have met with a case where a woman became pregnant
by such Lesbian love ; we must leave the proof for this to him. He reports the
case of two women friends in Egypt, who had practised this " indecency " together.
One of them was married and it happened that the unmarried friend became pregnant. The explanation was that the other from an earlier copulation with her
husband had still some semen in her vagina, which she passed over to her companion
when they had intercourse. This case was communicated to the Parisian Anthro-
pological Society in the year 1877.*

Mocquet, in his " Voyages," reported a horrible punishment for such tribadism
in Siam. " Counterfeit members " were employed by some women and for a
punishment they were found to have a phallic image painted on their thighs."

We see from the Penitentials drawn up by Bishop Burchard of Worms in the
twelfth century, that many abnormalities must have prevailed, too, among German
women in the Middle Ages. In this it runs :

> " Fecisti quod quedam mulieres facere solent, ut faceres quodam molimen aut machin-
> amentum in modum virilis membri ad mensuram tuae voluntatis, et illud loco verendorum
> tuorum aut alterius, cum aliquibus ligaturis colligares, et fornicationem faceres cum aliis
> mulierculis, vel alie eodem instrumento, sive alio tecum ? Si fecisti, tres annos per legitimas
> ferias penit. Fecisti quod quaedam mulieres facere solent, ut jam supra dicto molimine, vel alio
> aliquo machinamento, tu ipsa in te solam faceres fornicationem ? Si fecisti, unum annum per
> legitimas ferias penit " (see Wasserschleben, p. 658 ; Ellis, *Studies*, etc., I., 169.)

[As has been remarked above, the use of the artificial phallus by women deprived
of normal satisfaction has persisted from the most remote antiquity to modern days.

* Tribadism occurs too among North American Indian women. In a saga it runs a maiden had had
a kind of sexual intercourse with another and, in consequence, had given birth to a tortoise. The
pregnant young woman is said to have had a clitoris like the penis of a tortoise. (*Cf.* McMurtrie.)

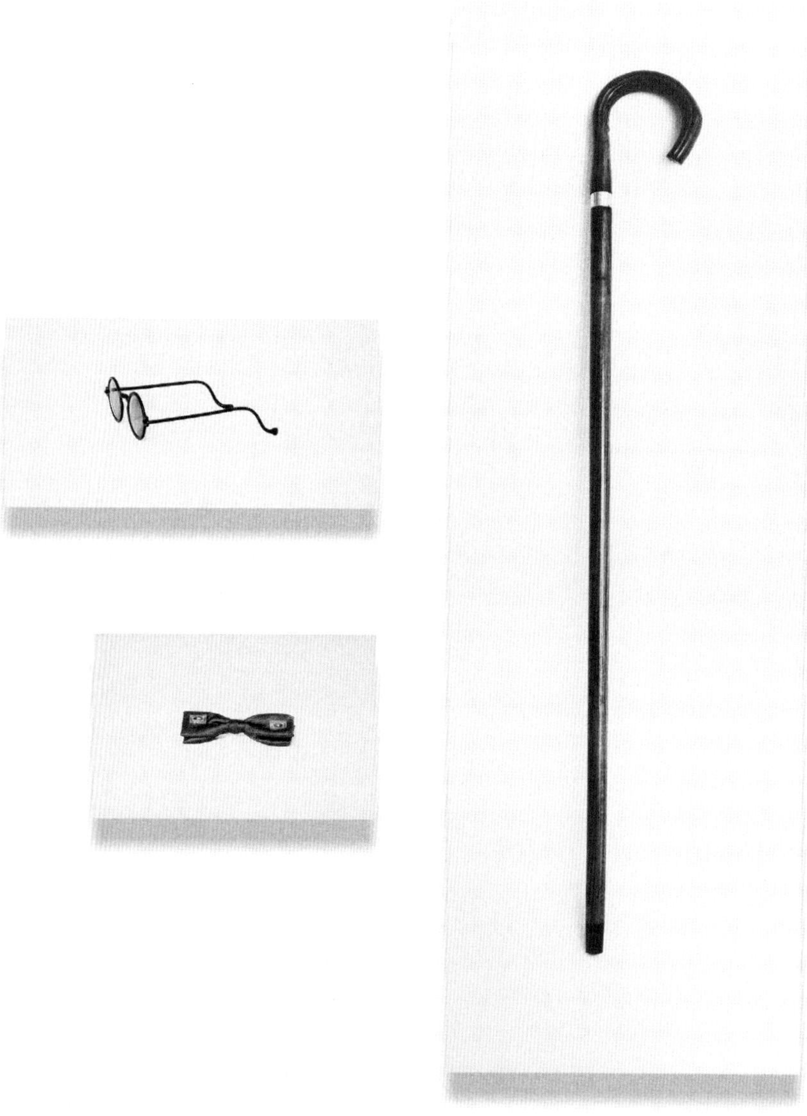

PAGES 80–83 *Cross-Dressing*, 1989. Six gelatin silver prints and two text panels mounted on Dibond

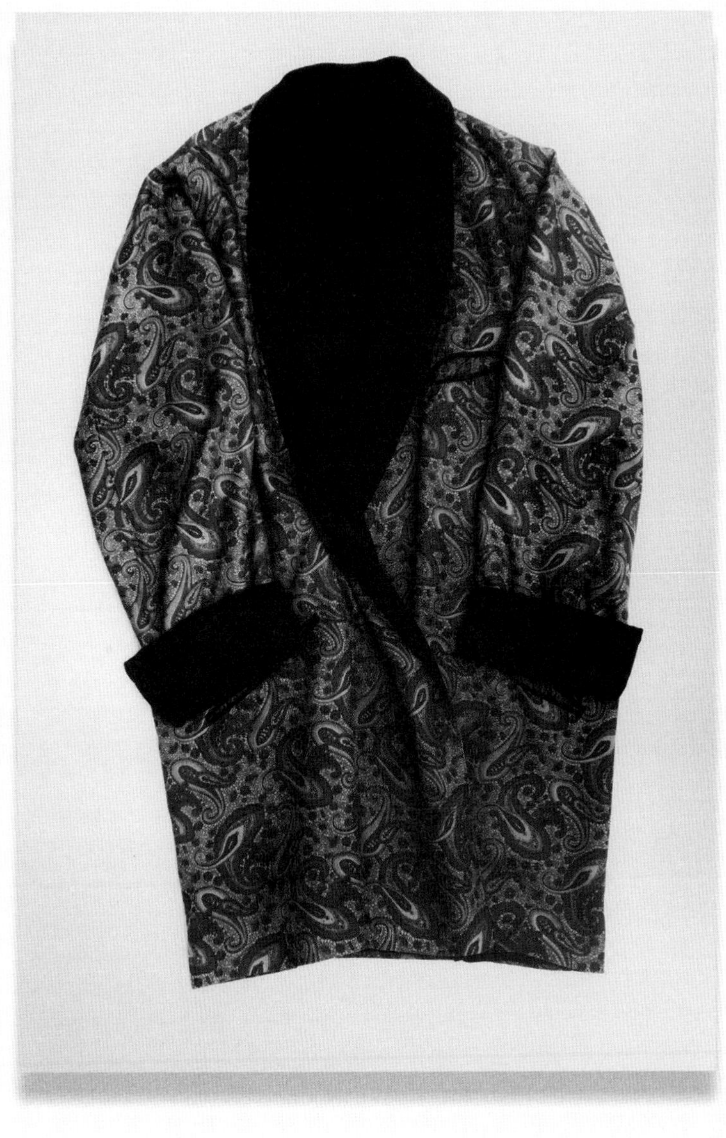

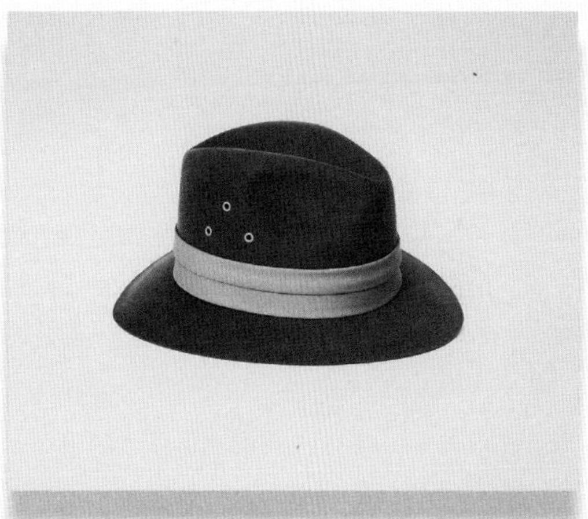

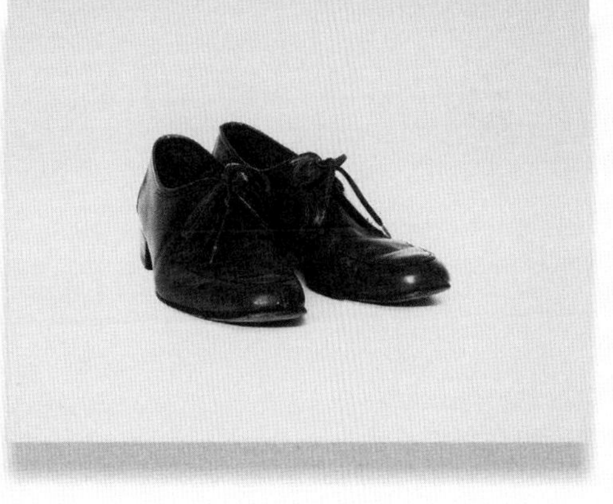

She came to believe that lesbianism could be detected in a baby's physical characteristics, and preserved only those photographs which confirmed her theories.

When questioned later about her cross-dressing, she would always stress the practical side. However, this was not the whole story. A strange malaise was behind both her cross-dressing and the decadence of her paintings.

Her Last Palette, 1989. Gelatin silver print, frame, and brass label

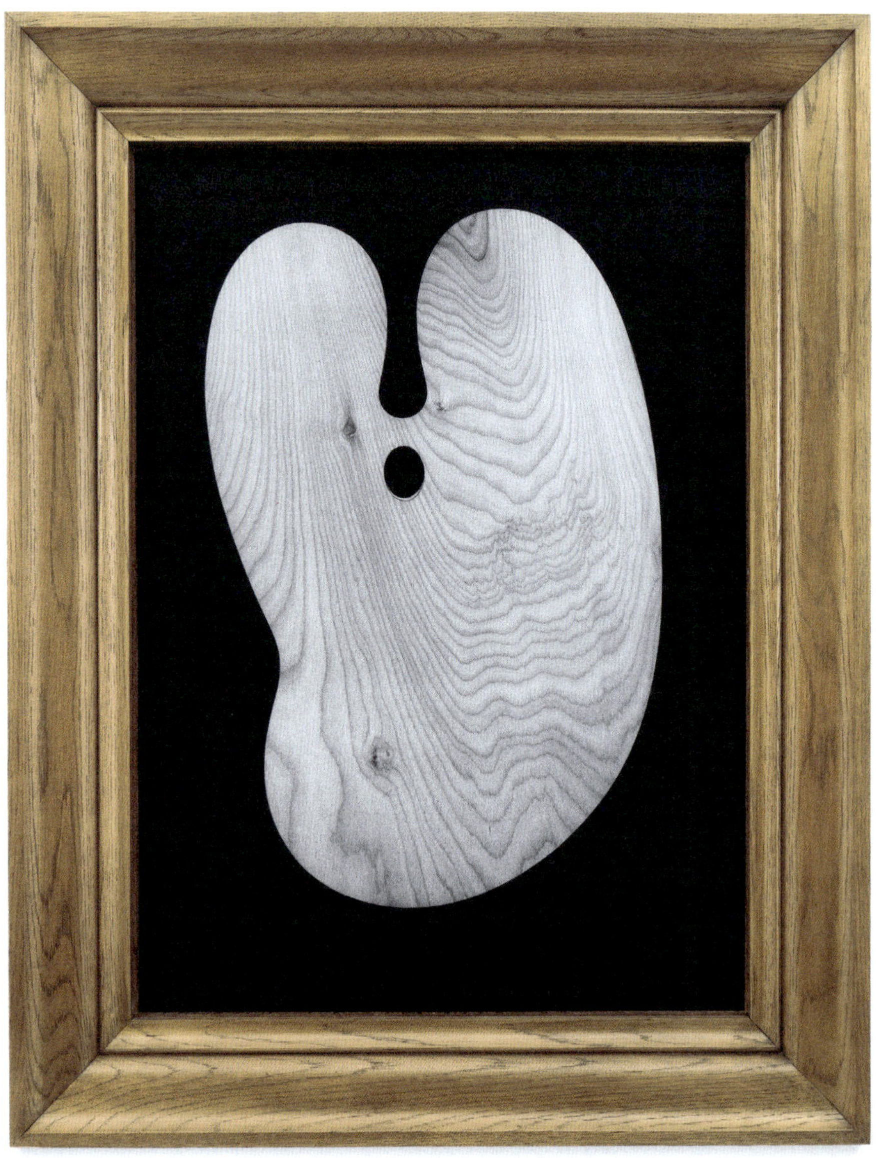

Proof prints for the portrait photograph in *Fauve Semblant*, 1989. Polaroid photographs. Photos by Catherine Opie

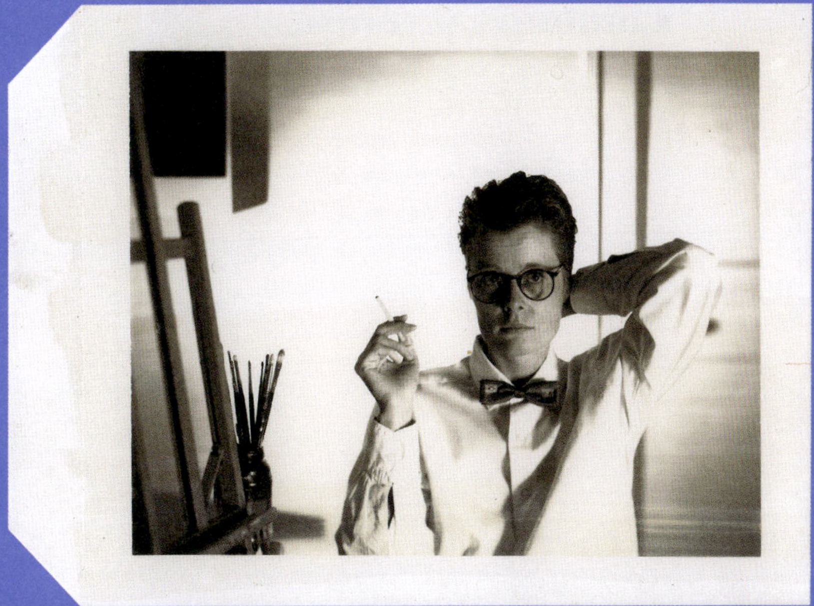

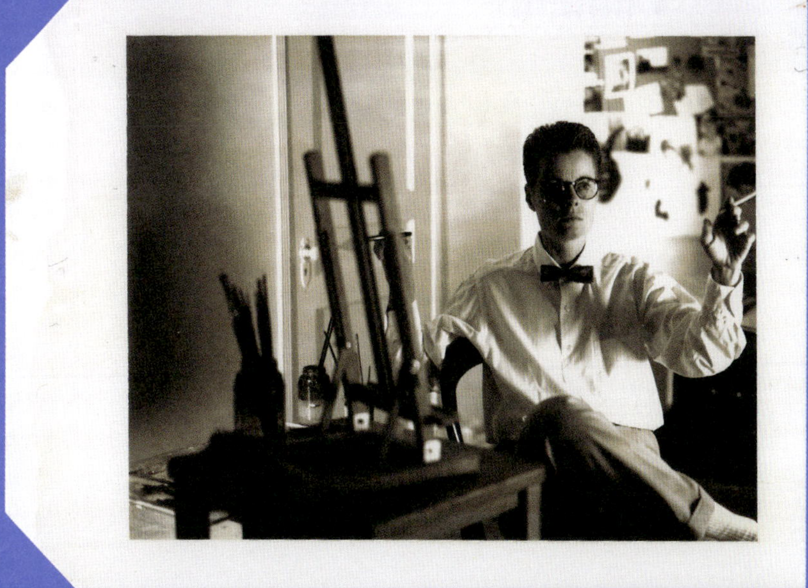

CLOCKWISE FROM LEFT Photograph of Matias Viegener and Millie Wilson at a CalArts drag ball, ca. early 1990. Photo by Connie Hatch; *Errors of Nature*, 1992. Artist's book. Published by New Langton Arts, San Francisco; Catherine Opie's *Dyke Deck* featuring Millie Wilson as the Queen of Spades, 1995. Set of playing cards. Published by the Museum of Contemporary Art, Los Angeles

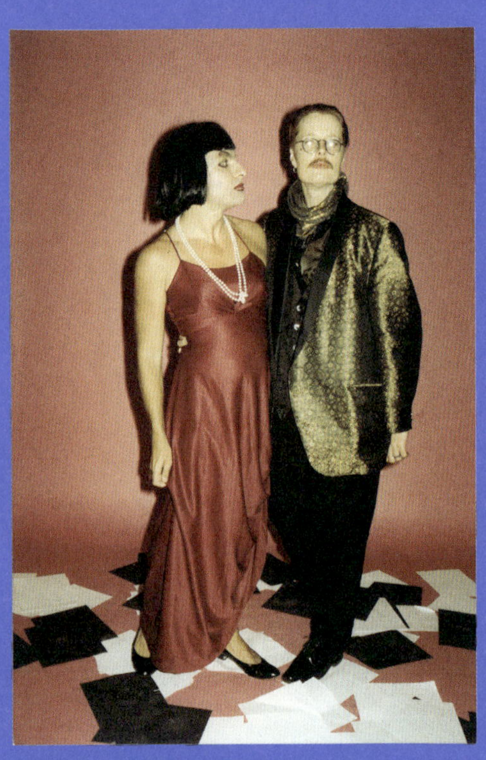

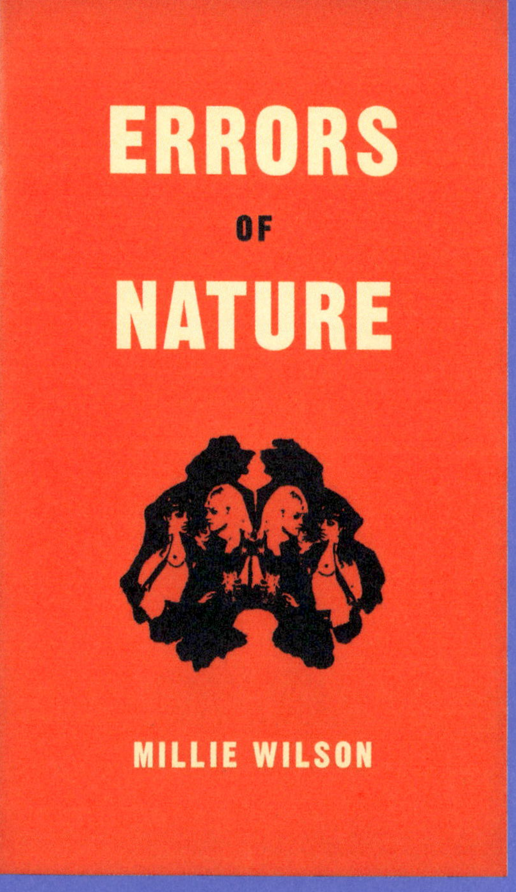

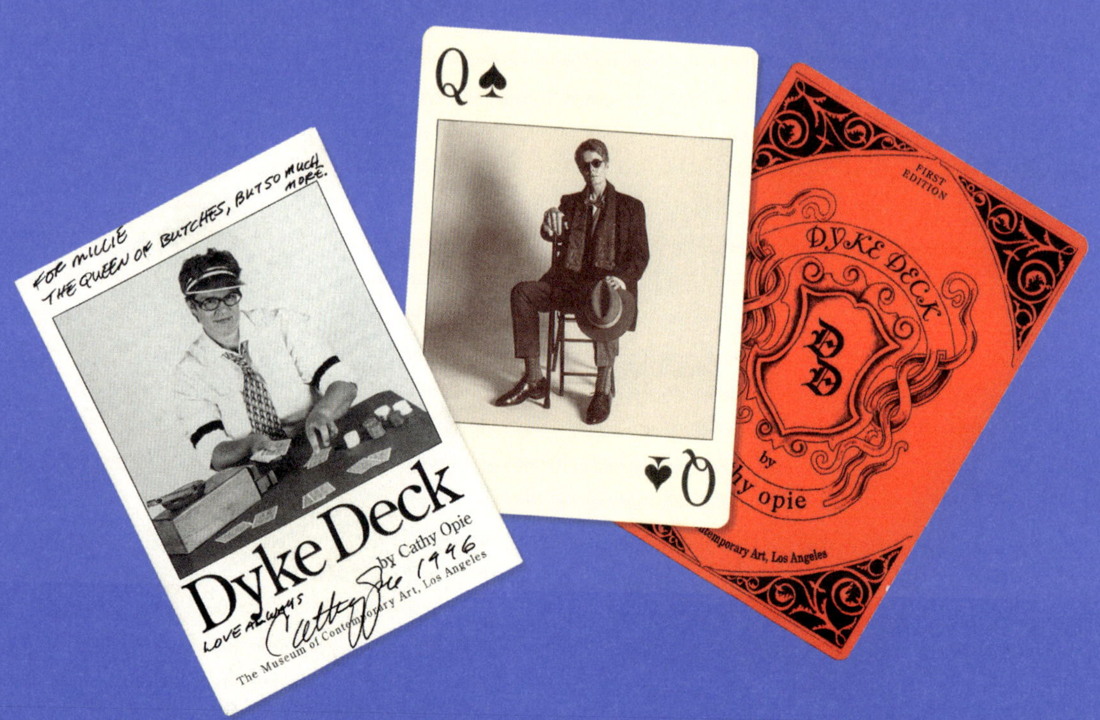

Course reader for Millie Wilson's "Dressing Up to Make the World: Transvestism as Cultural Practice," Spring 1992/Spring 1993

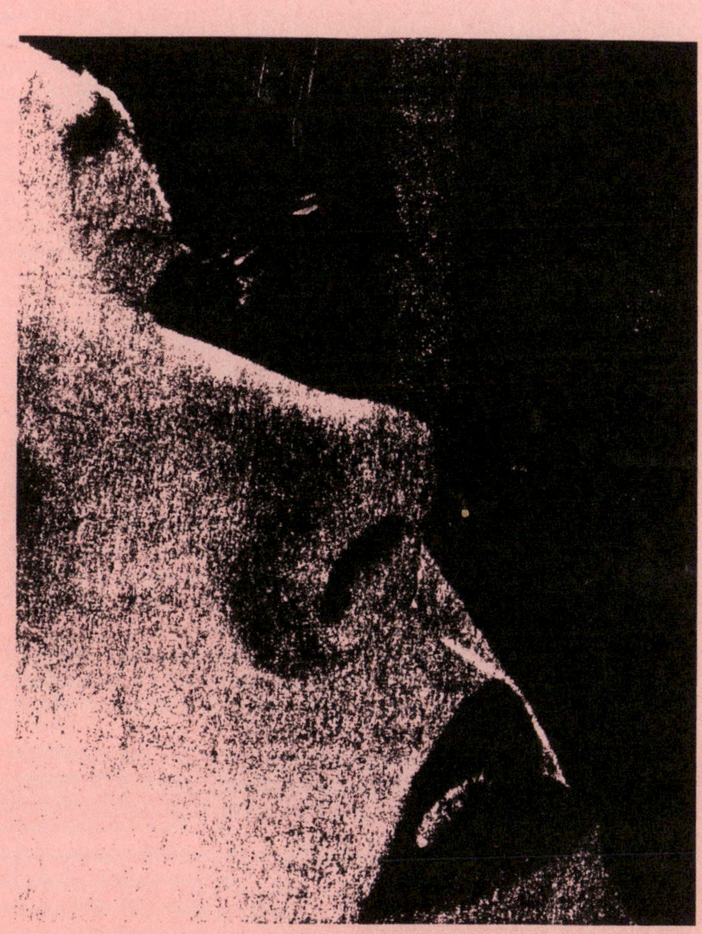

QUEER NATION

IF YOU'RE IN
CLOTHES
YOU'RE IN
DRAG

QUEER NATION

DRESSING UP etc M. WILSON SPR 93

LEFT TO RIGHT, TOP TO BOTTOM Selection of lesbian pulp novel covers that inspired works by Millie Wilson: Saxon Craig's *Student in Lesbos*, 1967. Published by Leisure Books; Donna Richards's *The Odd World*, 1965. Published by Domino Books; Lisa Robbins's *Lesbian Wives*, 1970. Published by Barclay House; and Frank G. Harris's *Lust Has No Mercy*, 1964. Published by Saber Books

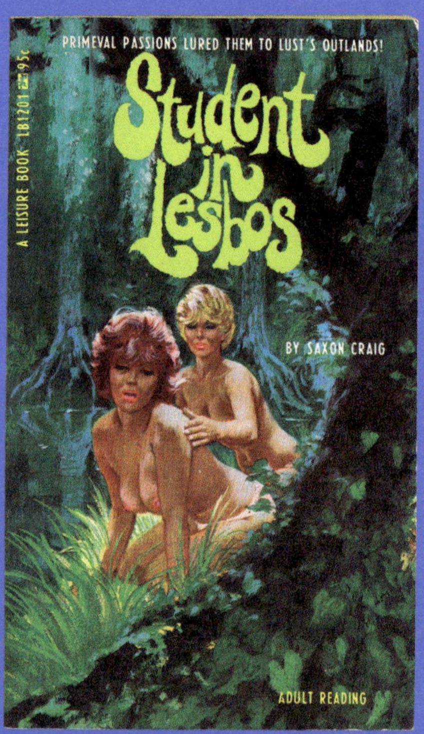

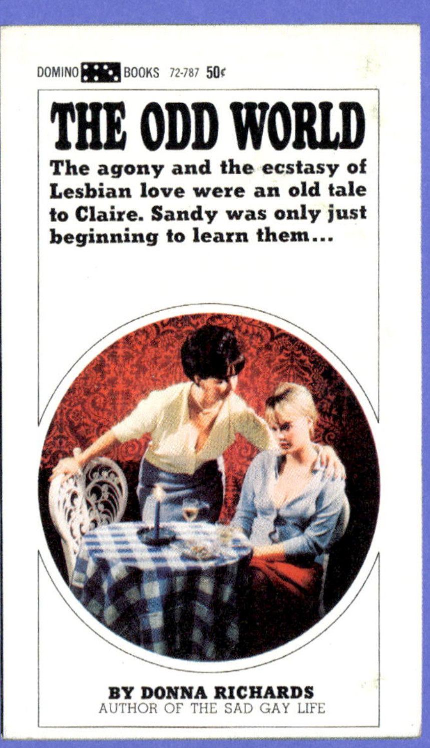

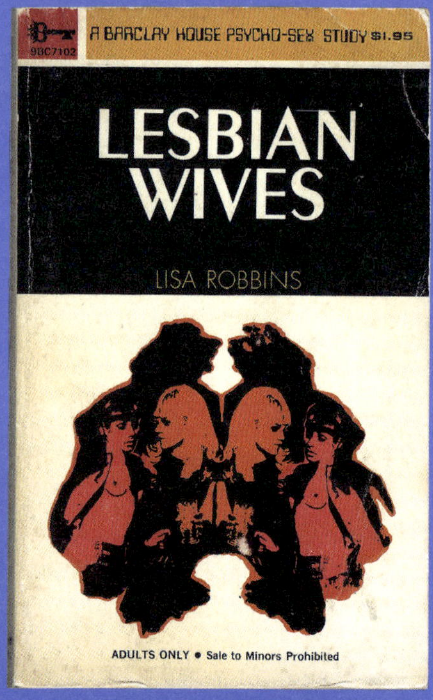

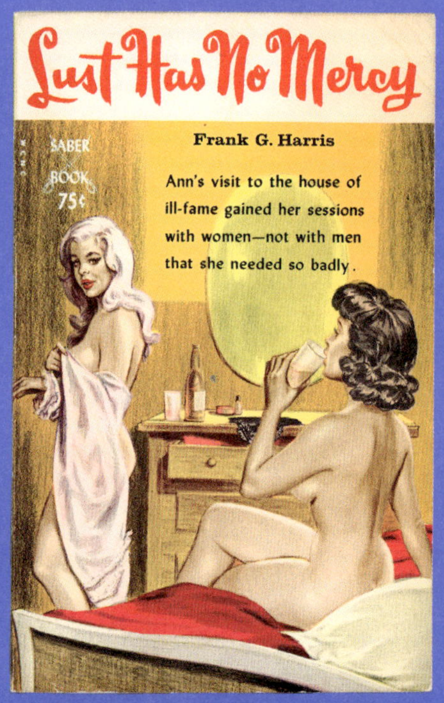

Lust Has No Mercy, 1992 (remade 2024).
Neon on aluminum

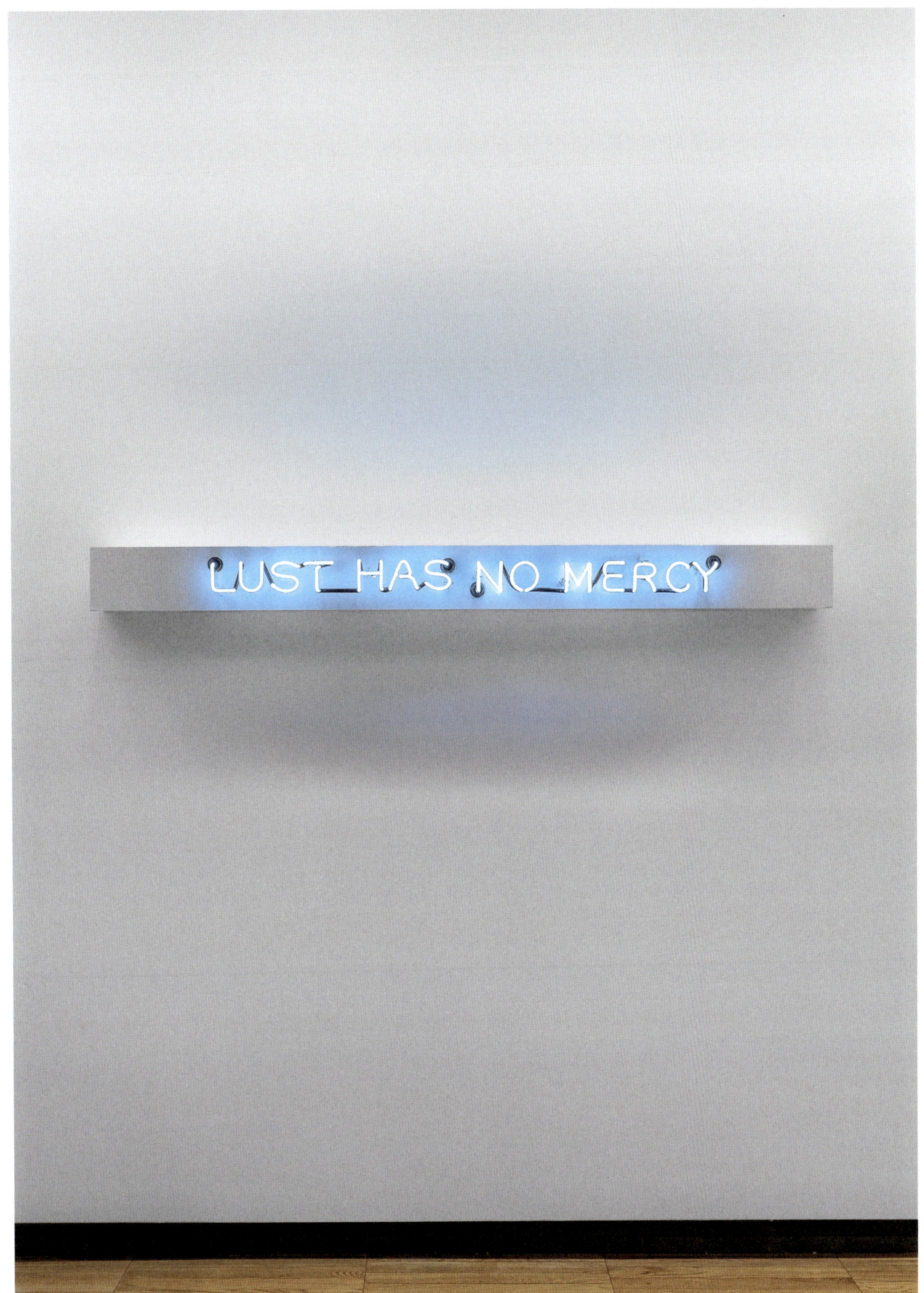

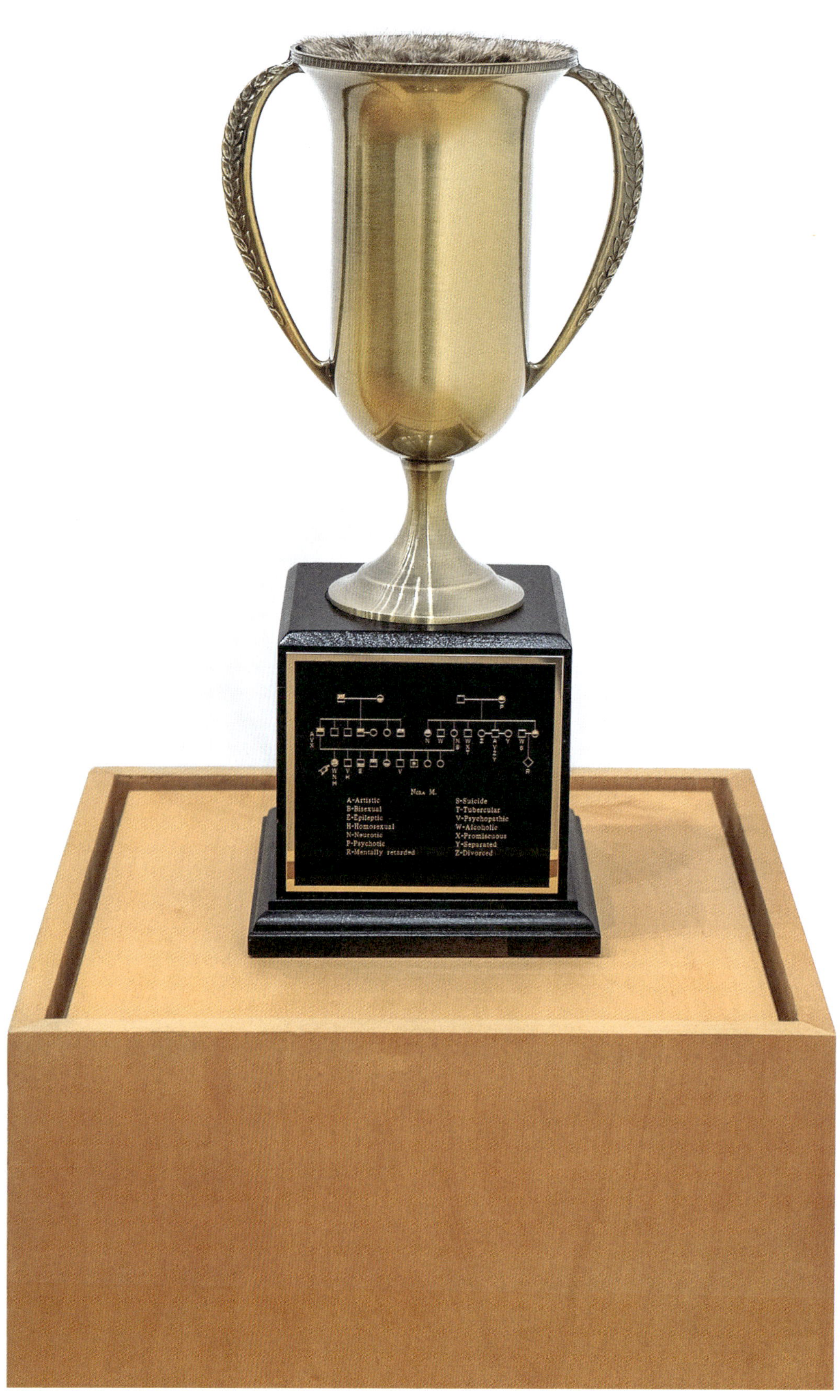
Nora M.
A-Artistic
B-Bisexual
E-Epileptic
H-Homosexual
N-Neurotic
P-Psychotic
R-Mentally retarded
S-Suicide
T-Tubercular
V-Psychopathic
W-Alcoholic
X-Promiscuous
Y-Separated
Z-Divorced

Trophy, 1990. Bronze trophy, fur, and wood-veneer pedestal

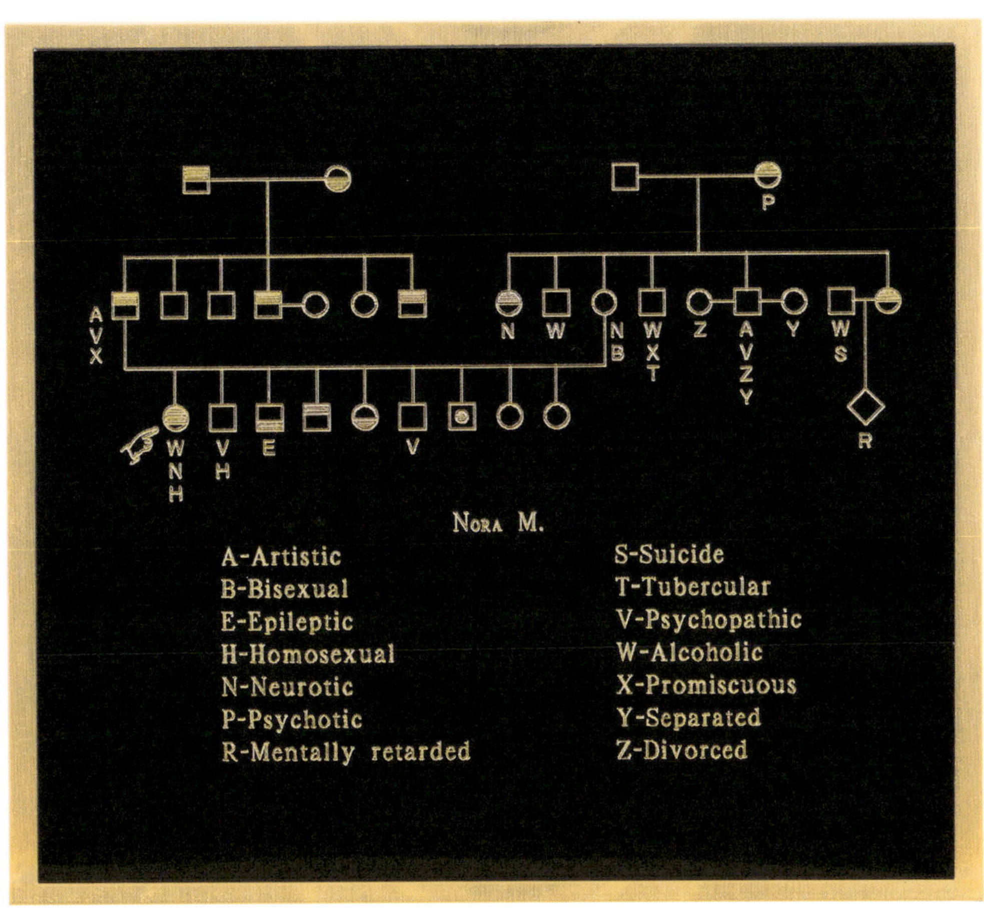

Turnip/Potato, 1991 (remade 2024). Brass, bronze, plexiglass, and walnut base

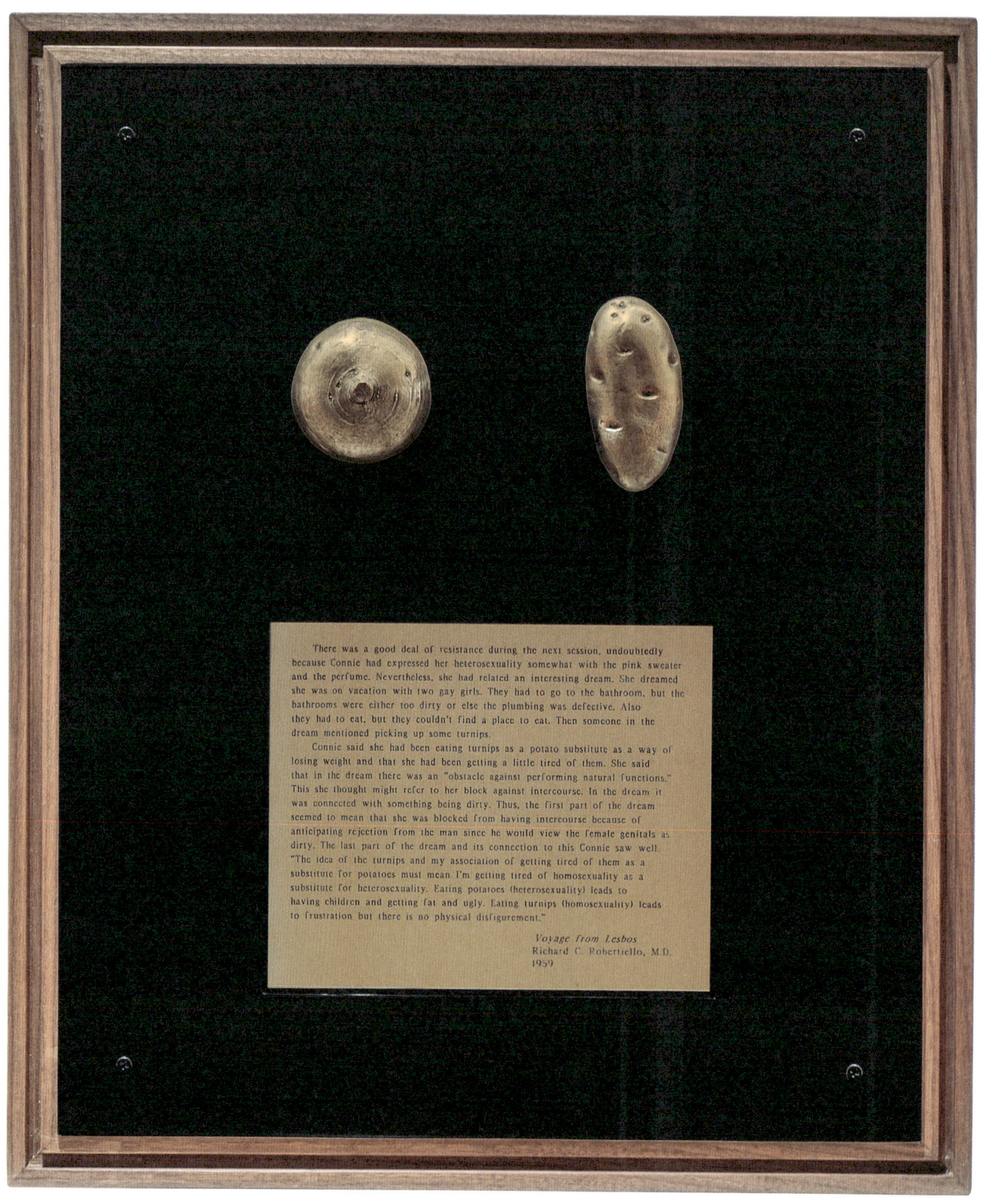

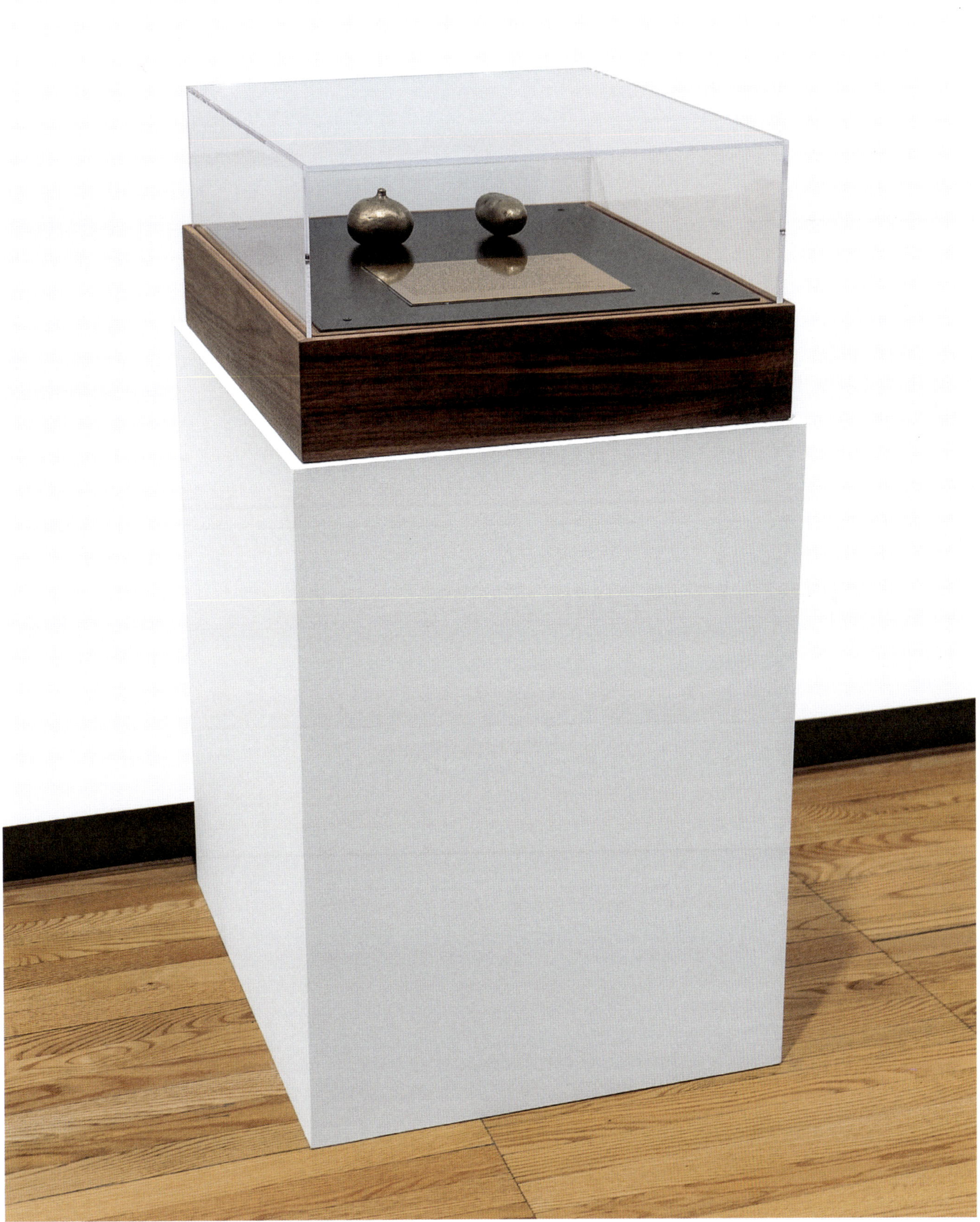

Merkins (Kathleen), 1992. Styled synthetic wig, wood shelf, enamel paint, and brass label

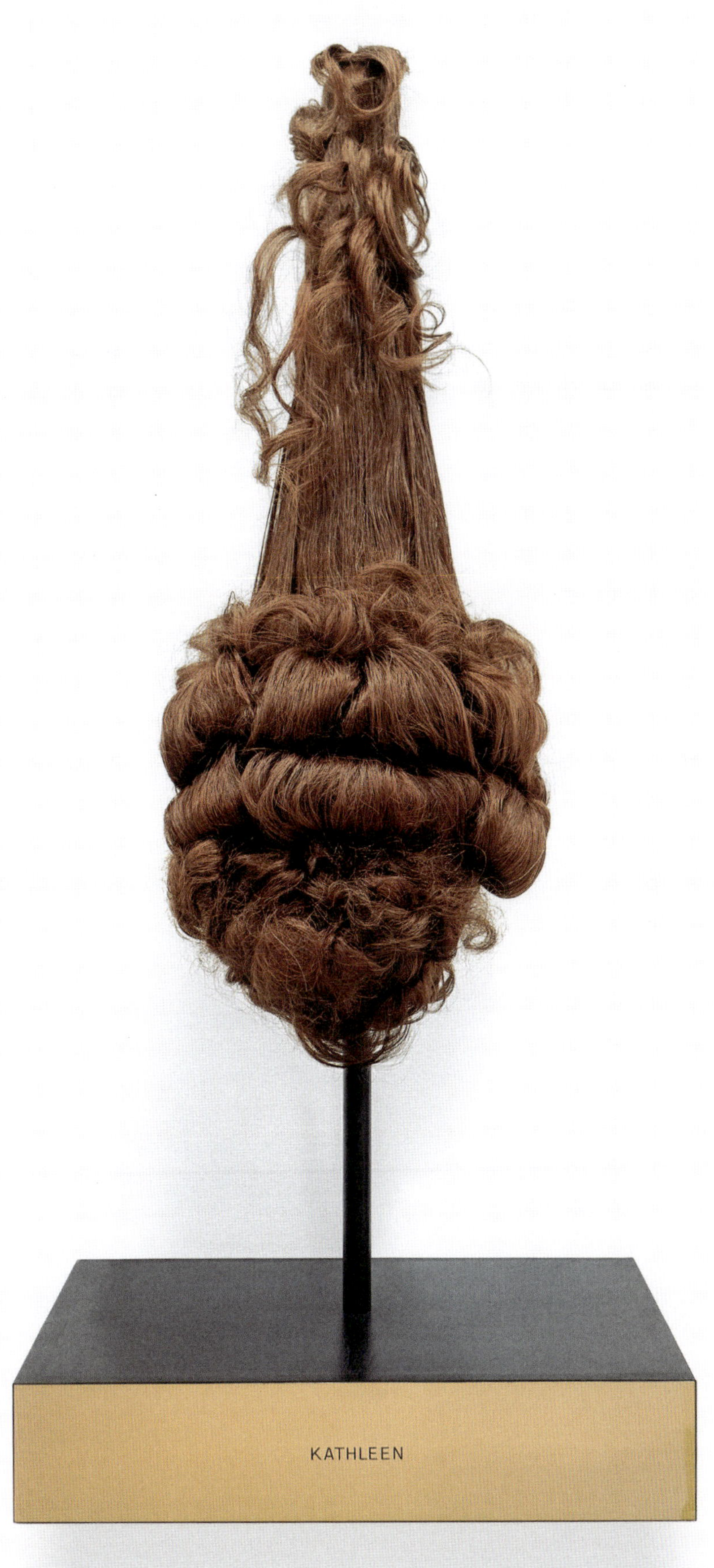

Merkins (Virginia), 1992. Styled synthetic wig, wood shelf, enamel paint, and brass label

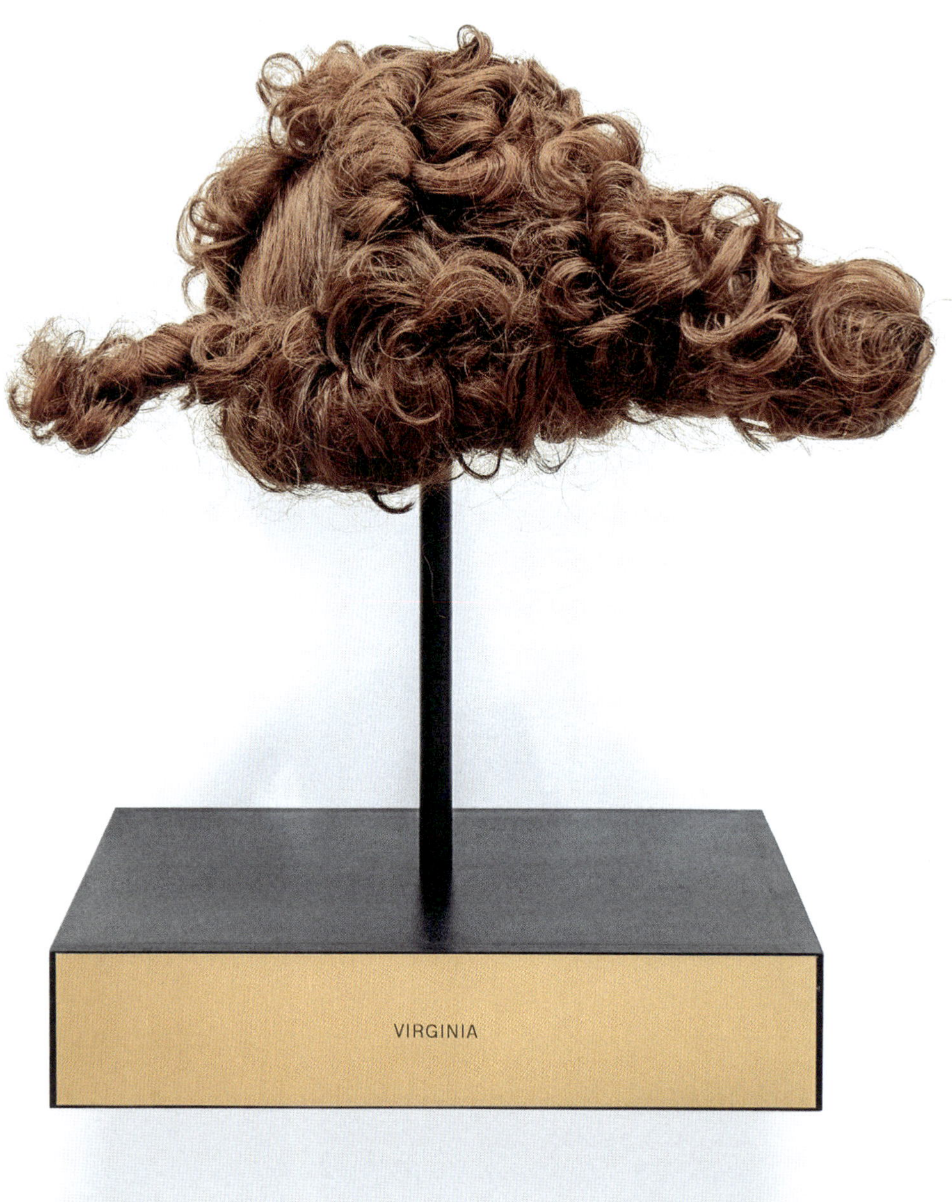

Merkins (Gladys), 1992. Styled synthetic wig, wood shelf, enamel paint, and brass label

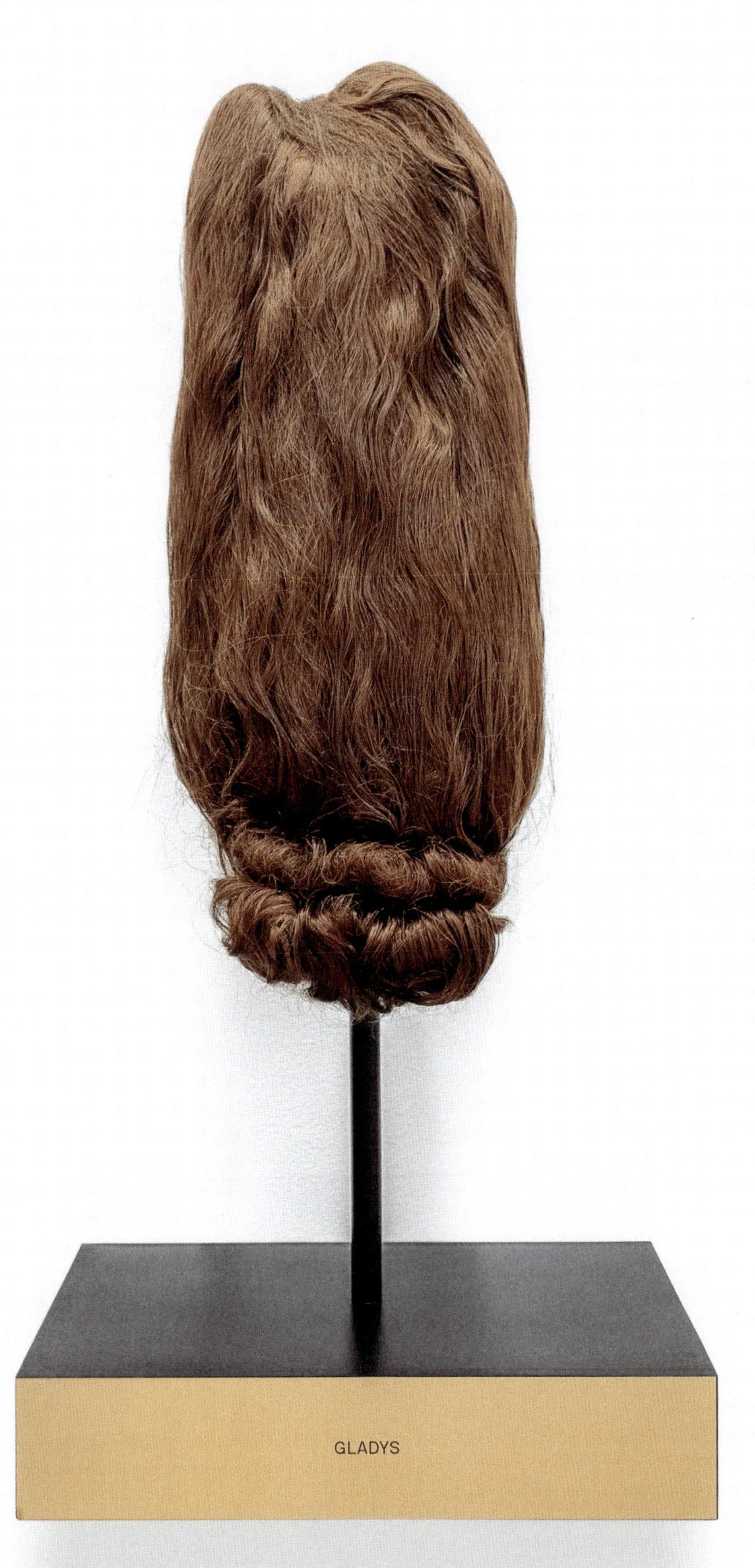

The Language of Dreams, 1991. Wood, ruler, plexiglass, and wood table

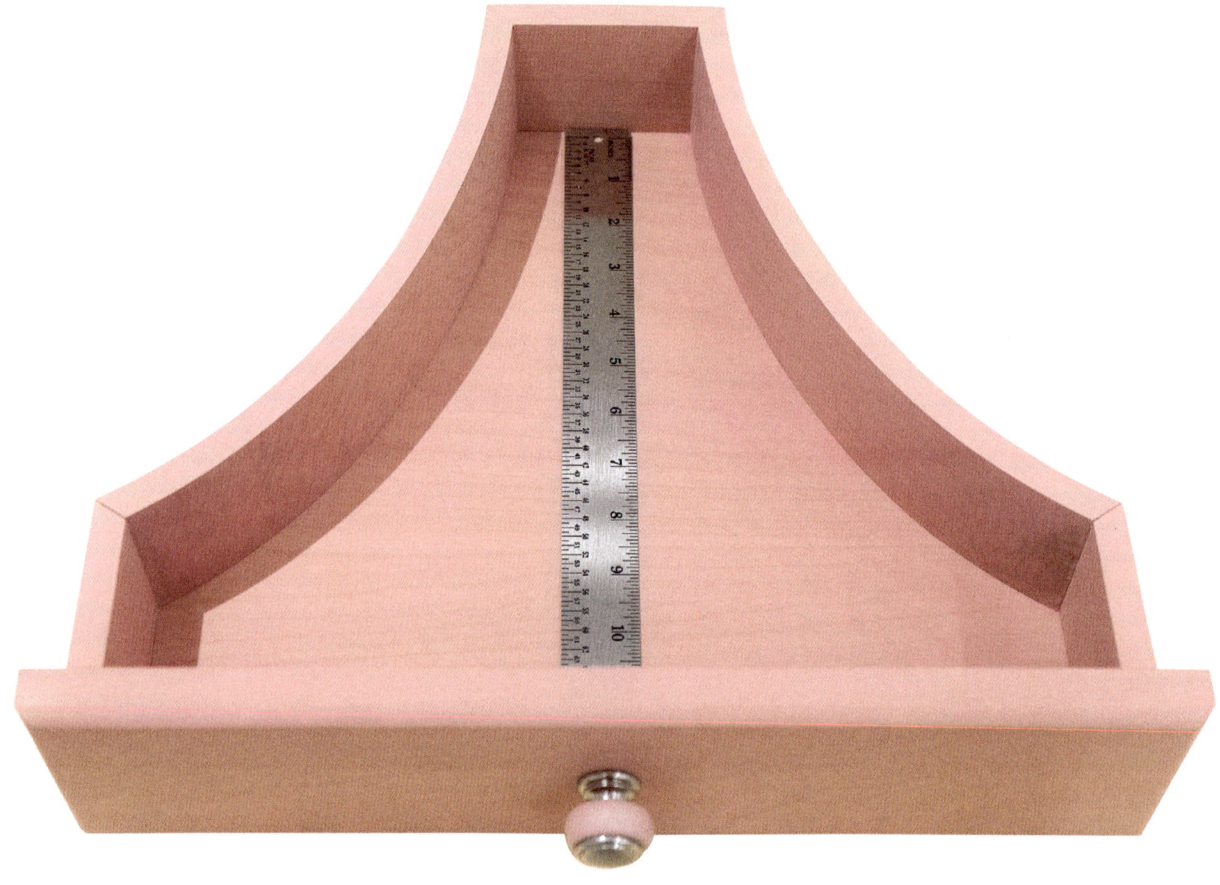

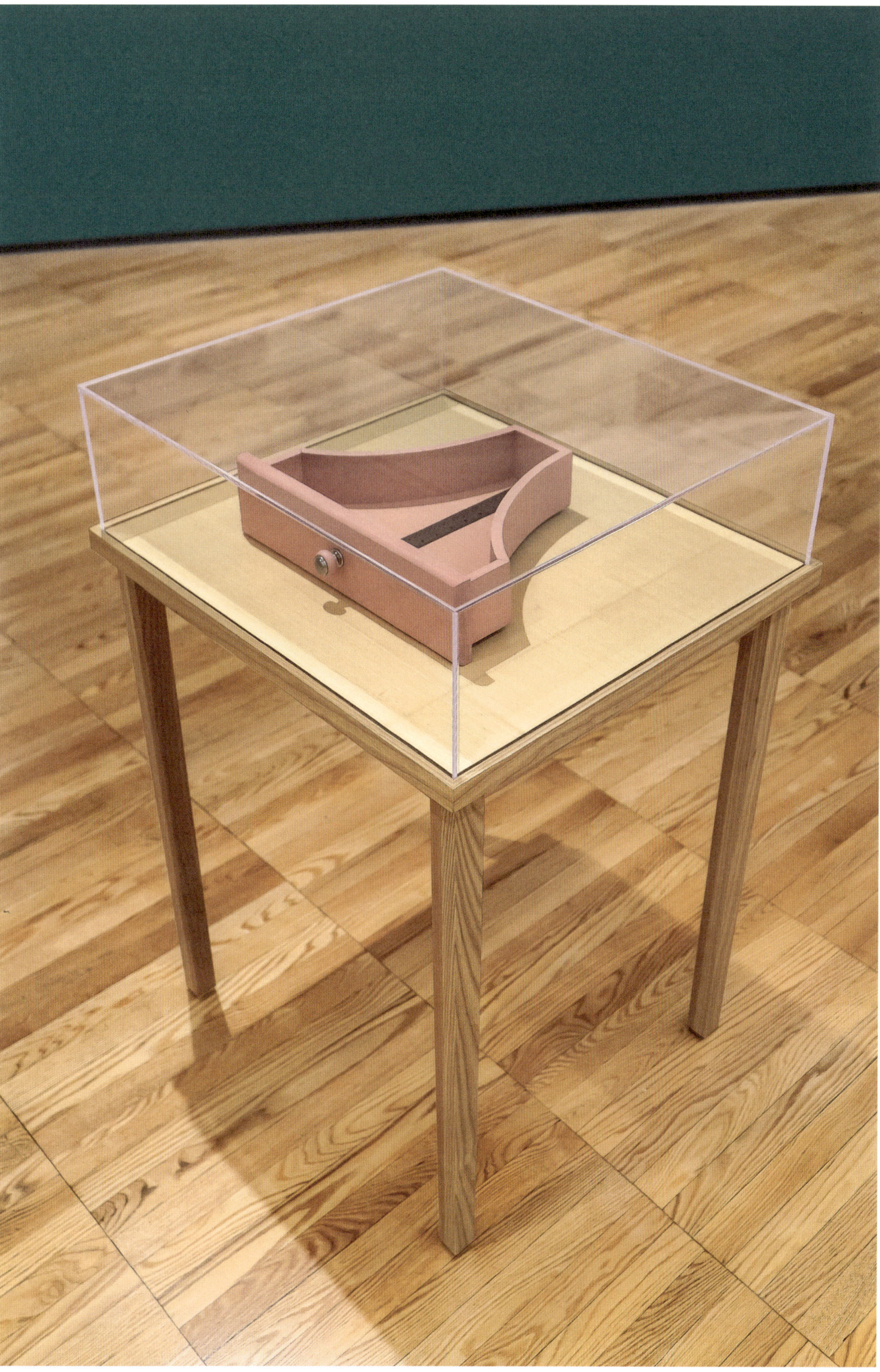

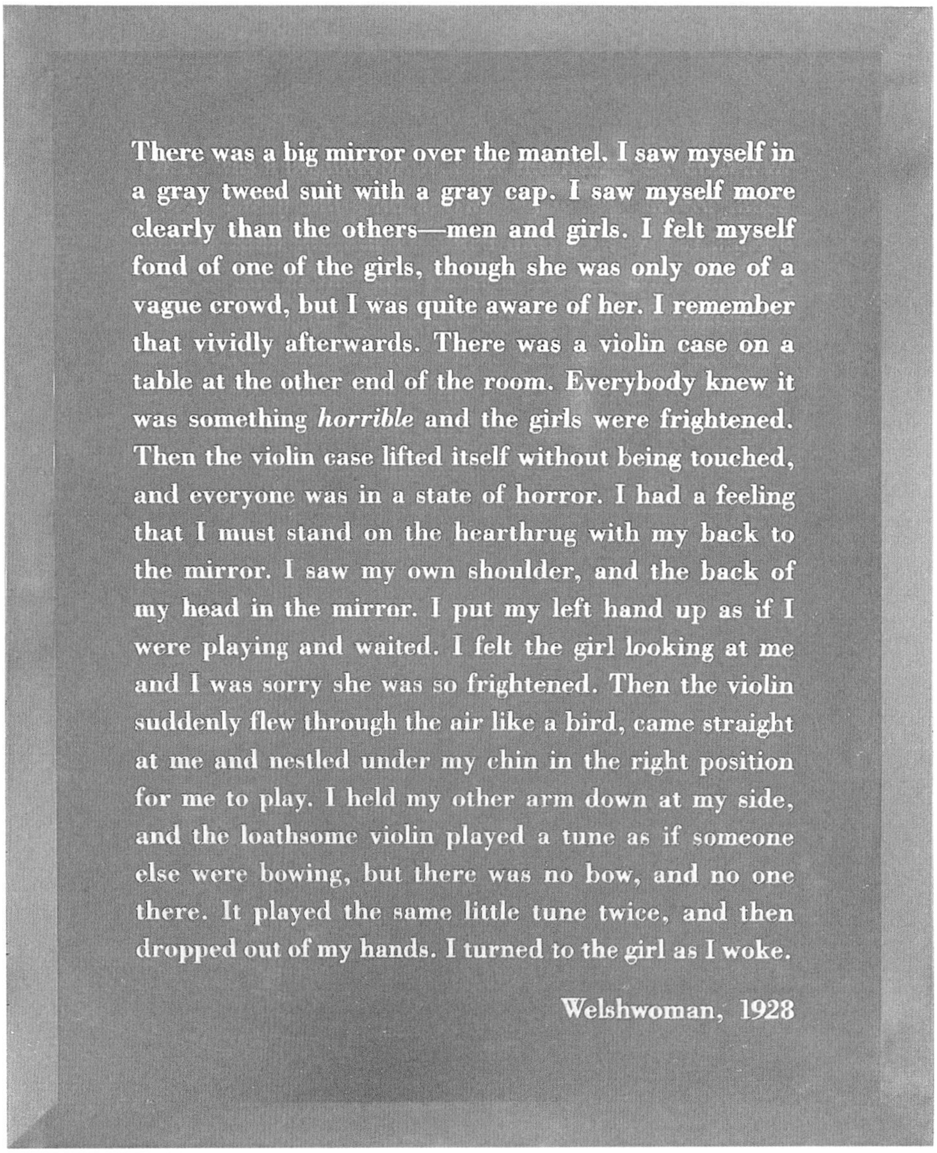

Easel/Mirrors, 1990. Etched mirror, hardwood easel, and framed hardwood mirror

There was a big mirror over the mantel. I saw myself in a gray tweed suit with a gray cap. I saw myself more clearly than the others—men and girls. I felt myself fond of one of the girls, though she was only one of a vague crowd, but I was quite aware of her. I remember that vividly afterwards. There was a violin case on a table at the other end of the room. Everybody knew it was something *horrible* and the girls were frightened. Then the violin case lifted itself without being touched, and everyone was in a state of horror. I had a feeling that I must stand on the hearthrug with my back to the mirror. I saw my own shoulder, and the back of my head in the mirror. I put my left hand up as if I were playing and waited. I felt the girl looking at me and I was sorry she was so frightened. Then the violin suddenly flew through the air like a bird, came straight at me and nestled under my chin in the right position for me to play. I held my other arm down at my side, and the loathsome violin played a tune as if someone else were bowing, but there was no bow, and no one there. It played the same little tune twice, and then dropped out of my hands. I turned to the girl as I woke.

Welshwoman, 1928

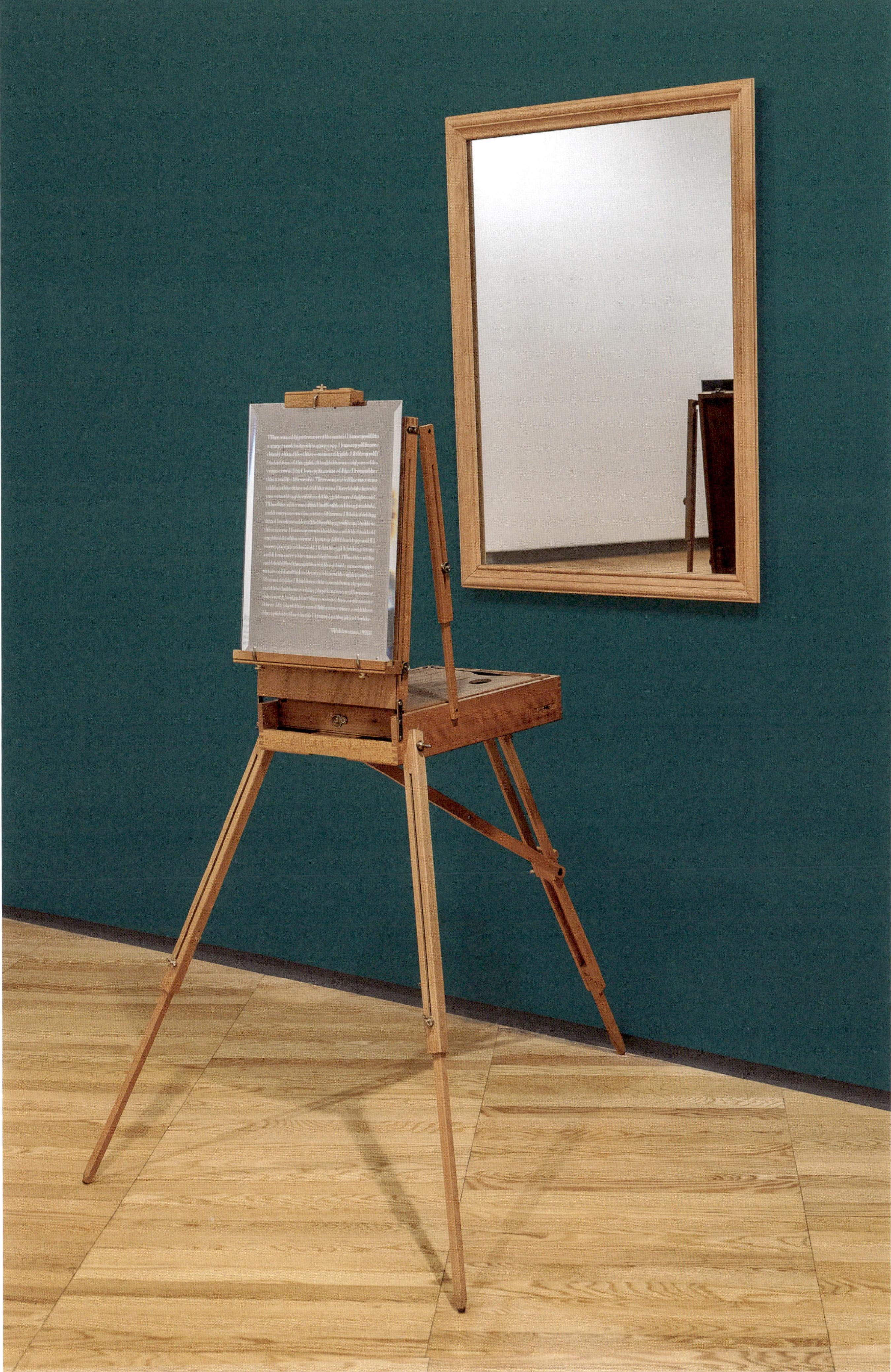

Beaded Tie, 1991. Beaded tie, velveteen on board, and frame

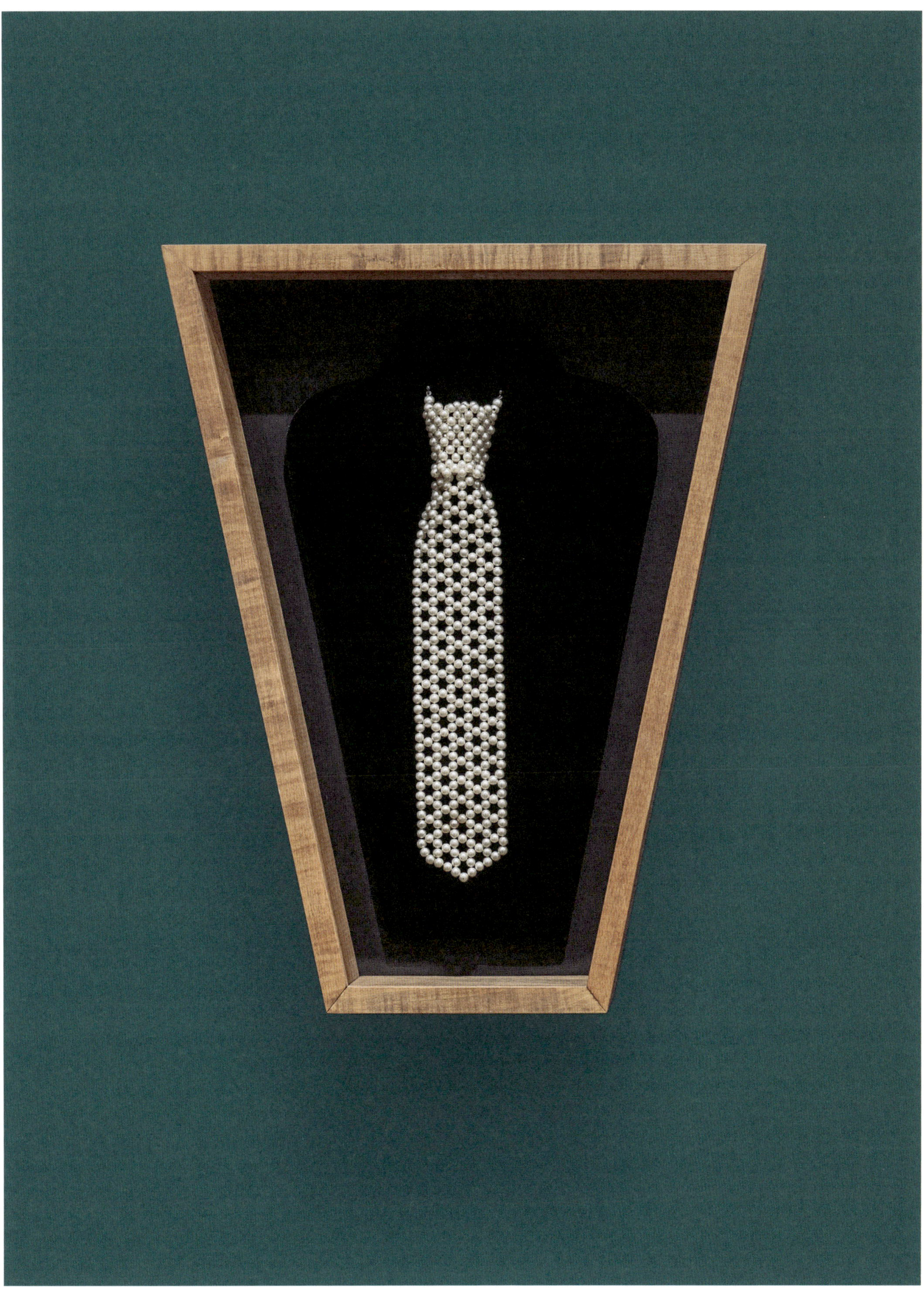

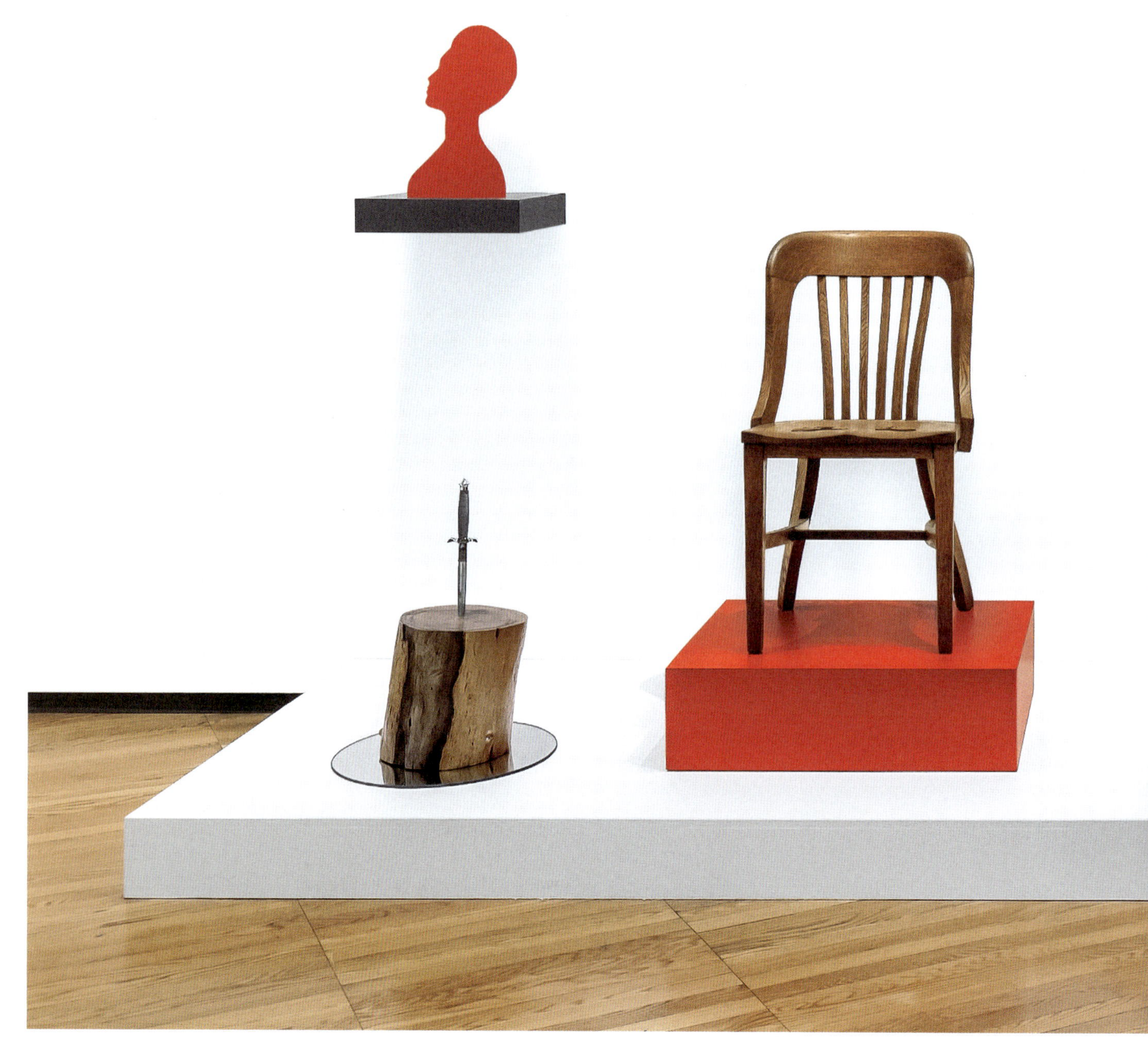

LEFT TO RIGHT Installation view with *Red Top*, *Fair Captive*, *Teacher*, *Rorschach Pillow*, *Urban Dyke*, *Token*, *Butterflies*, *Puddle*, and *Hair Fall* at Krannert Art Museum, 2024

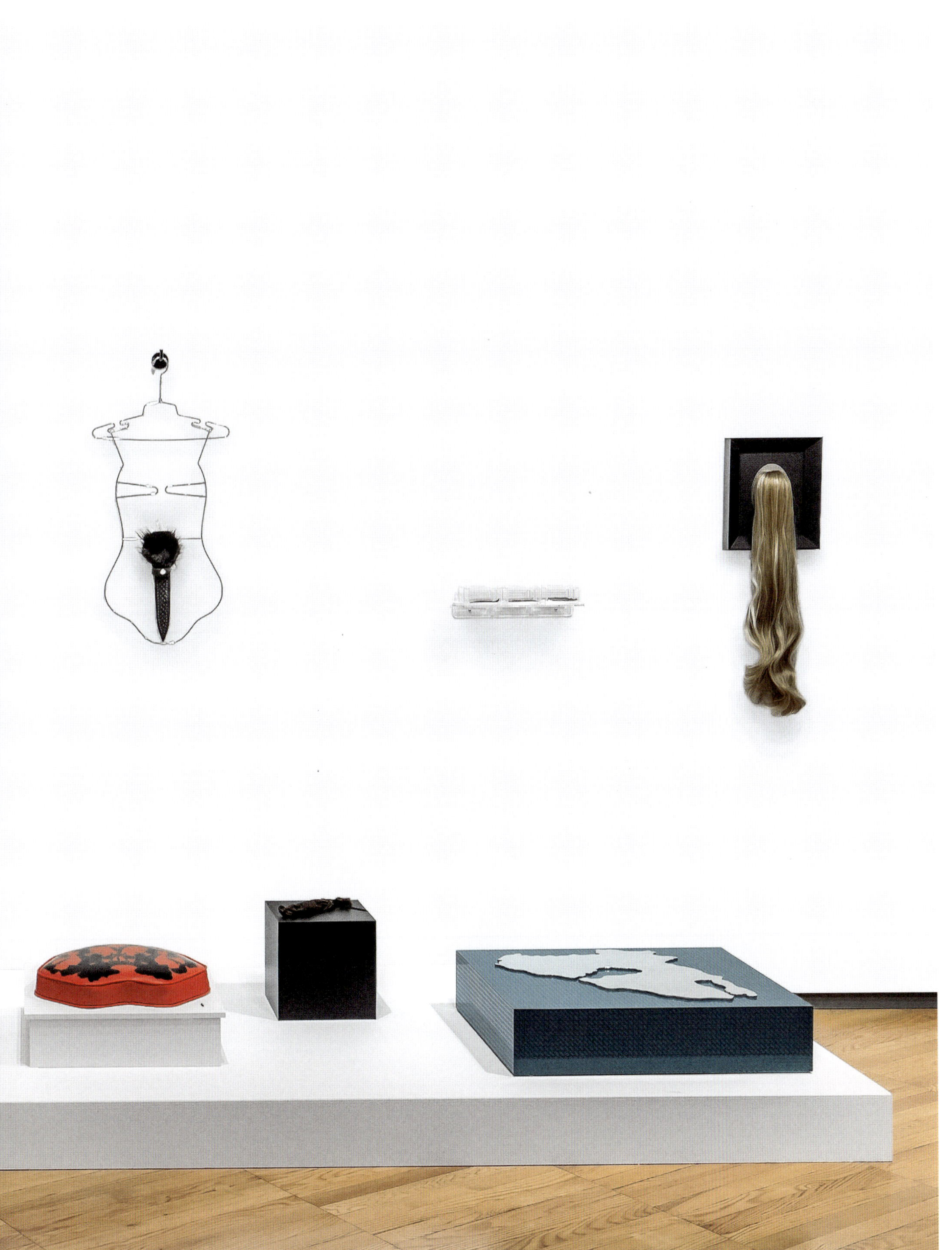

Red Top, 1992. Flocked cardboard profile, wood shelf, and enamel paint

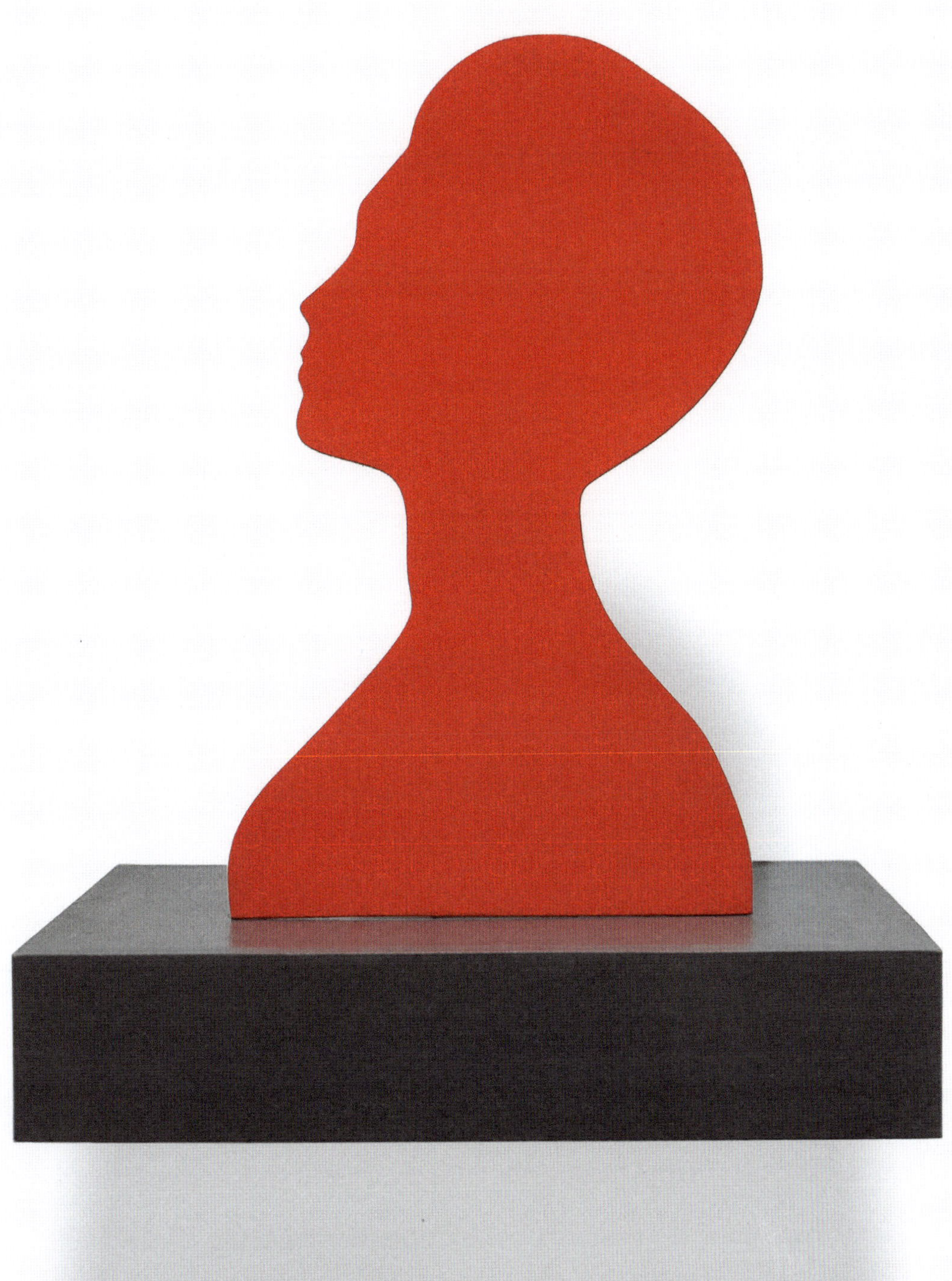

Urban Dyke, 1993. Steel frame, leather dagger case, and fur

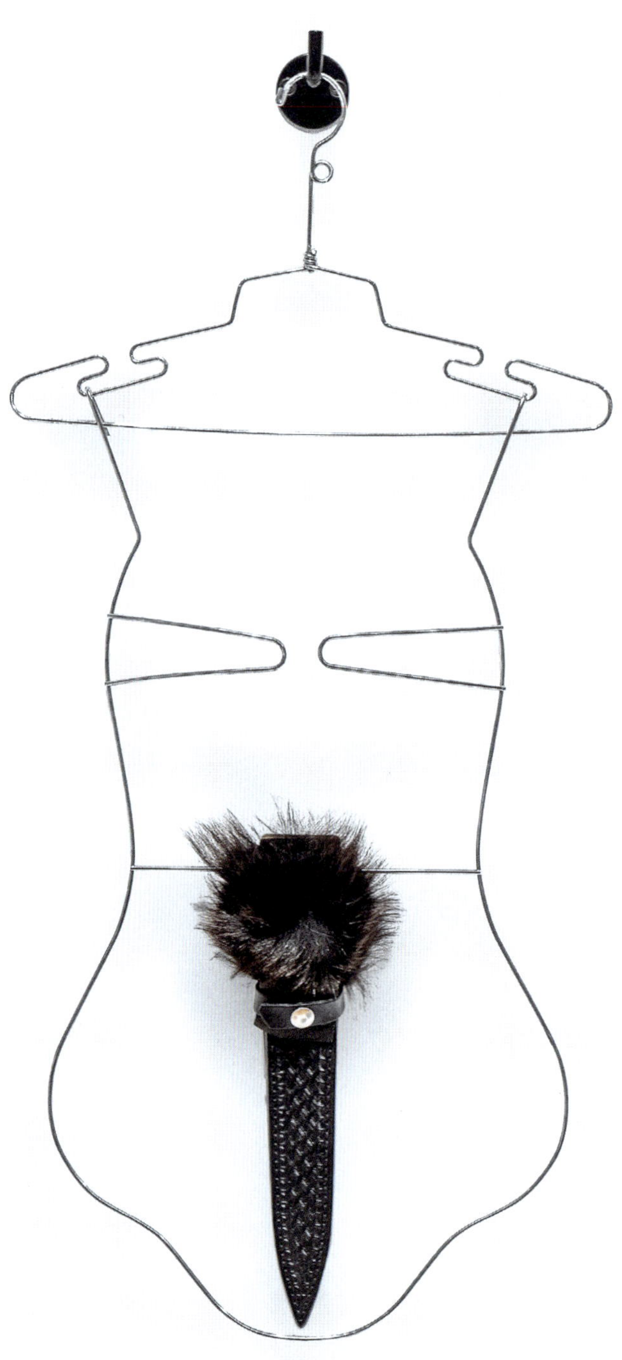

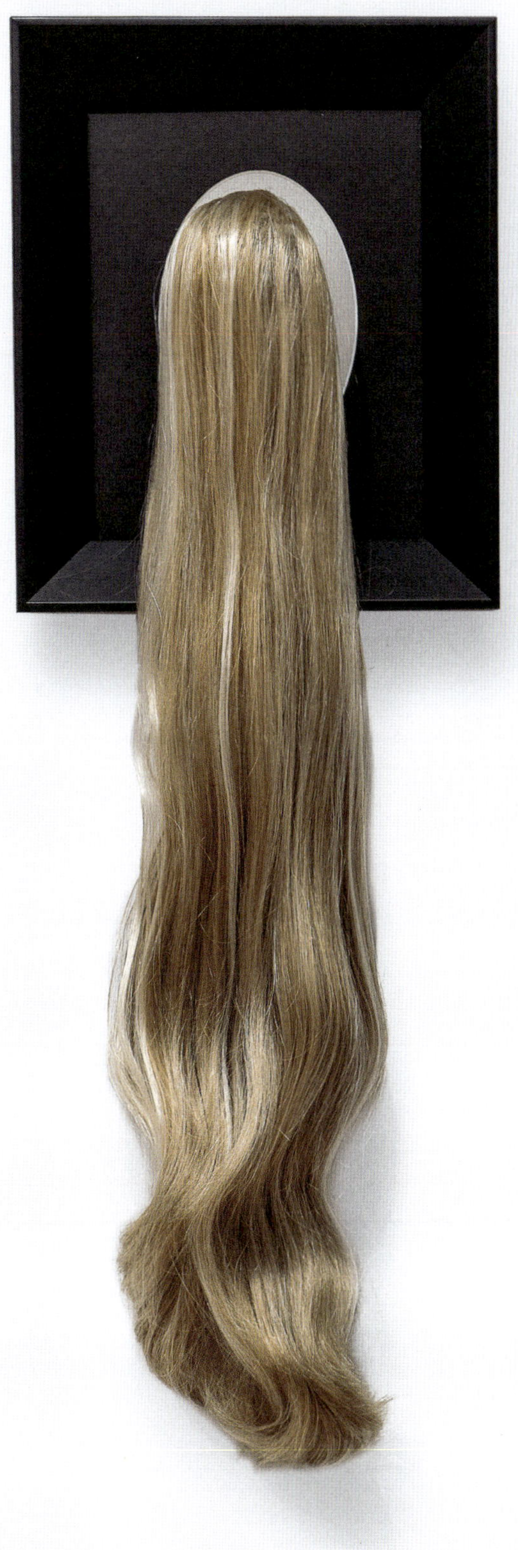

Fair Captive, 1993. Tree stump, steel dagger, and mirror

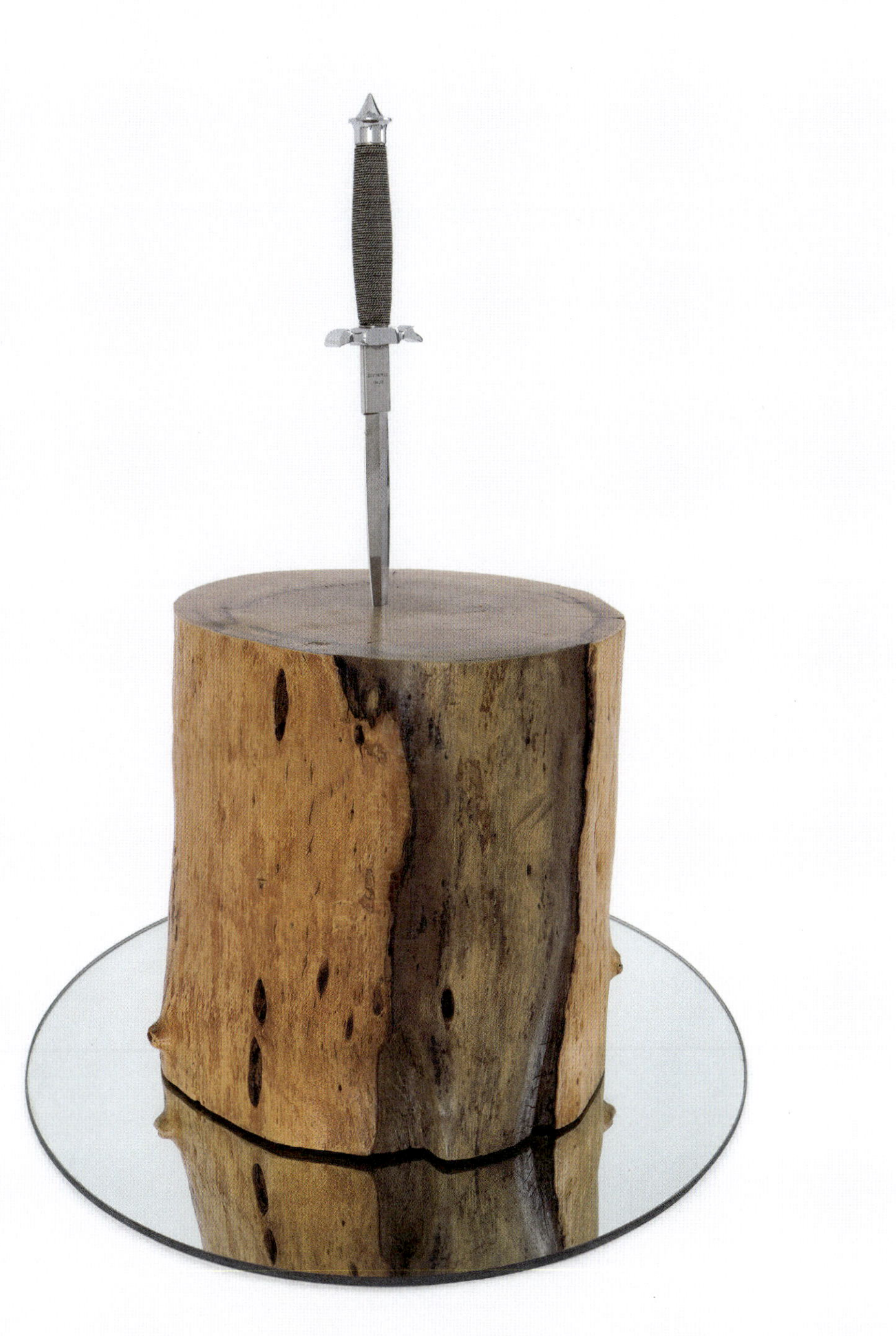

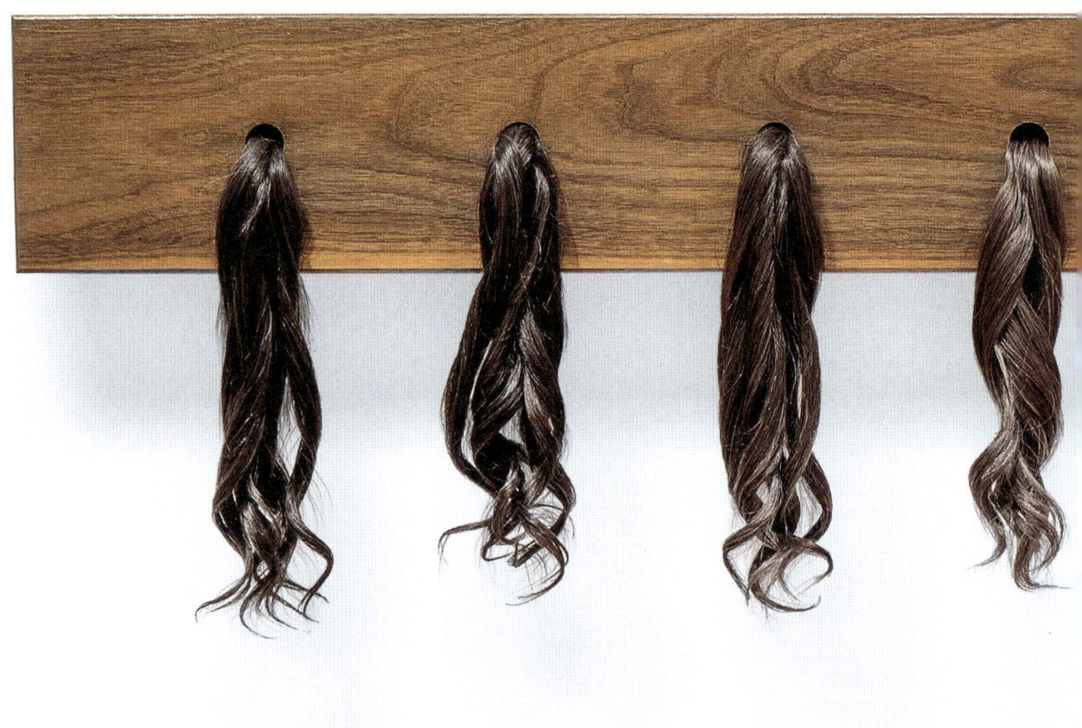

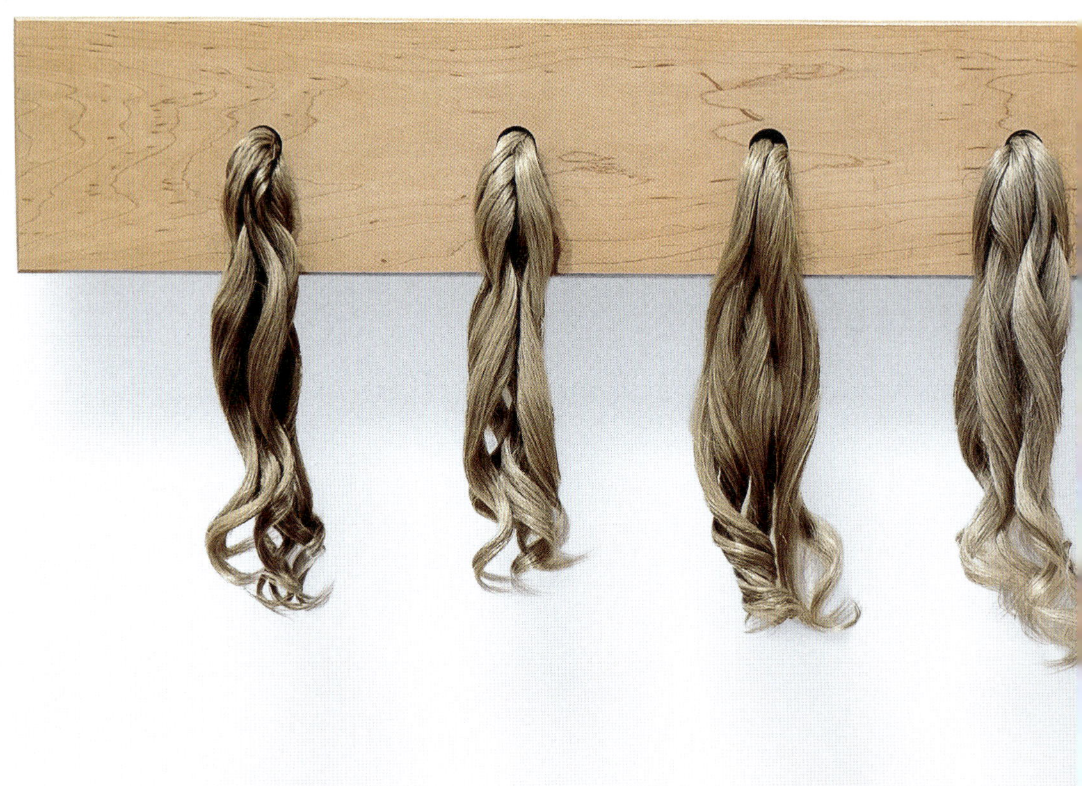

TOP *Ponies (Dark)*, 1992. Wood and human hair
BOTTOM *Ponies (Light)*, 1992. Wood and human hair

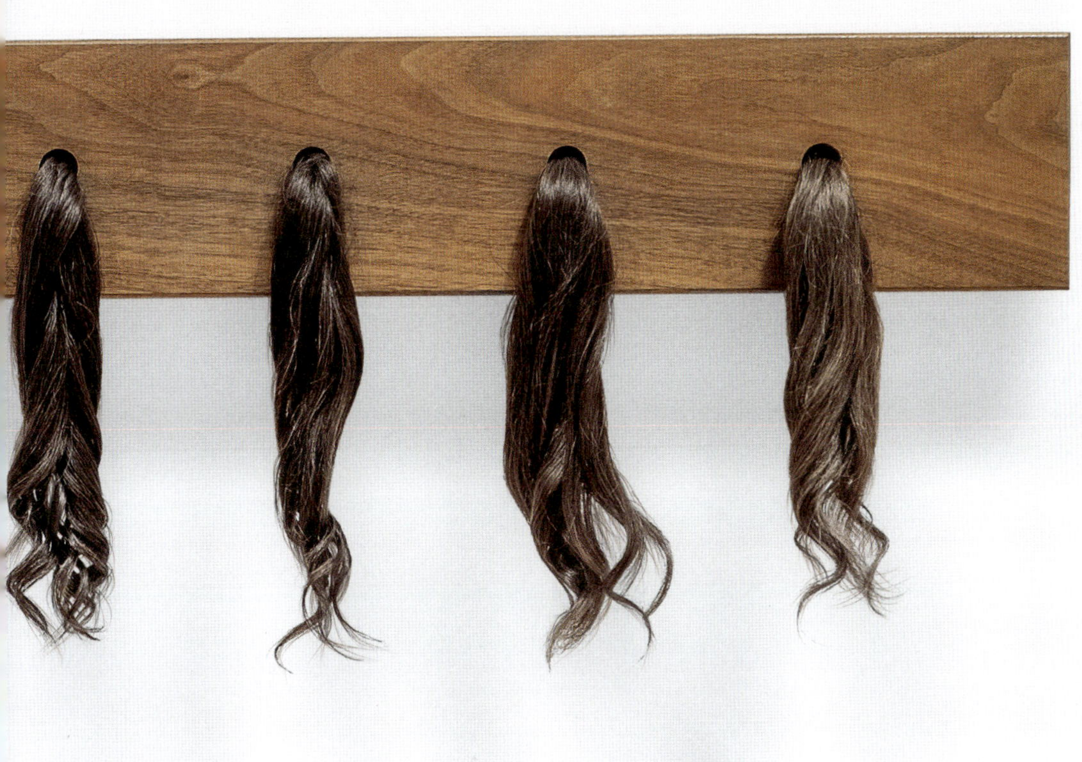

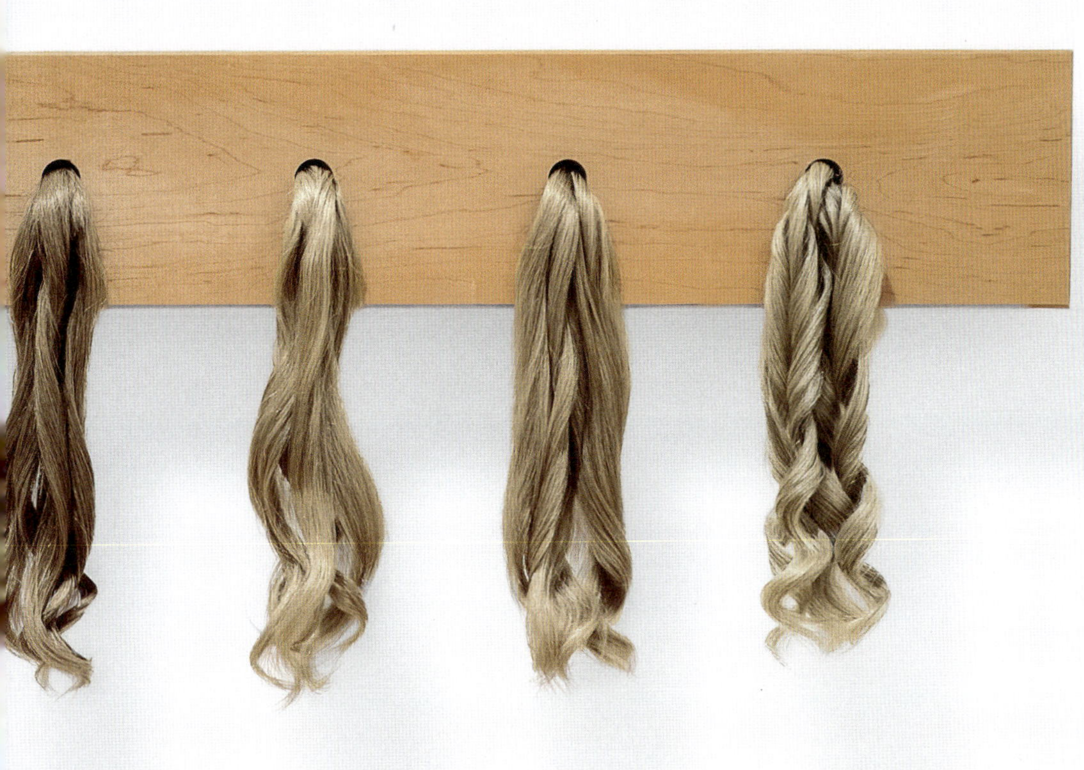

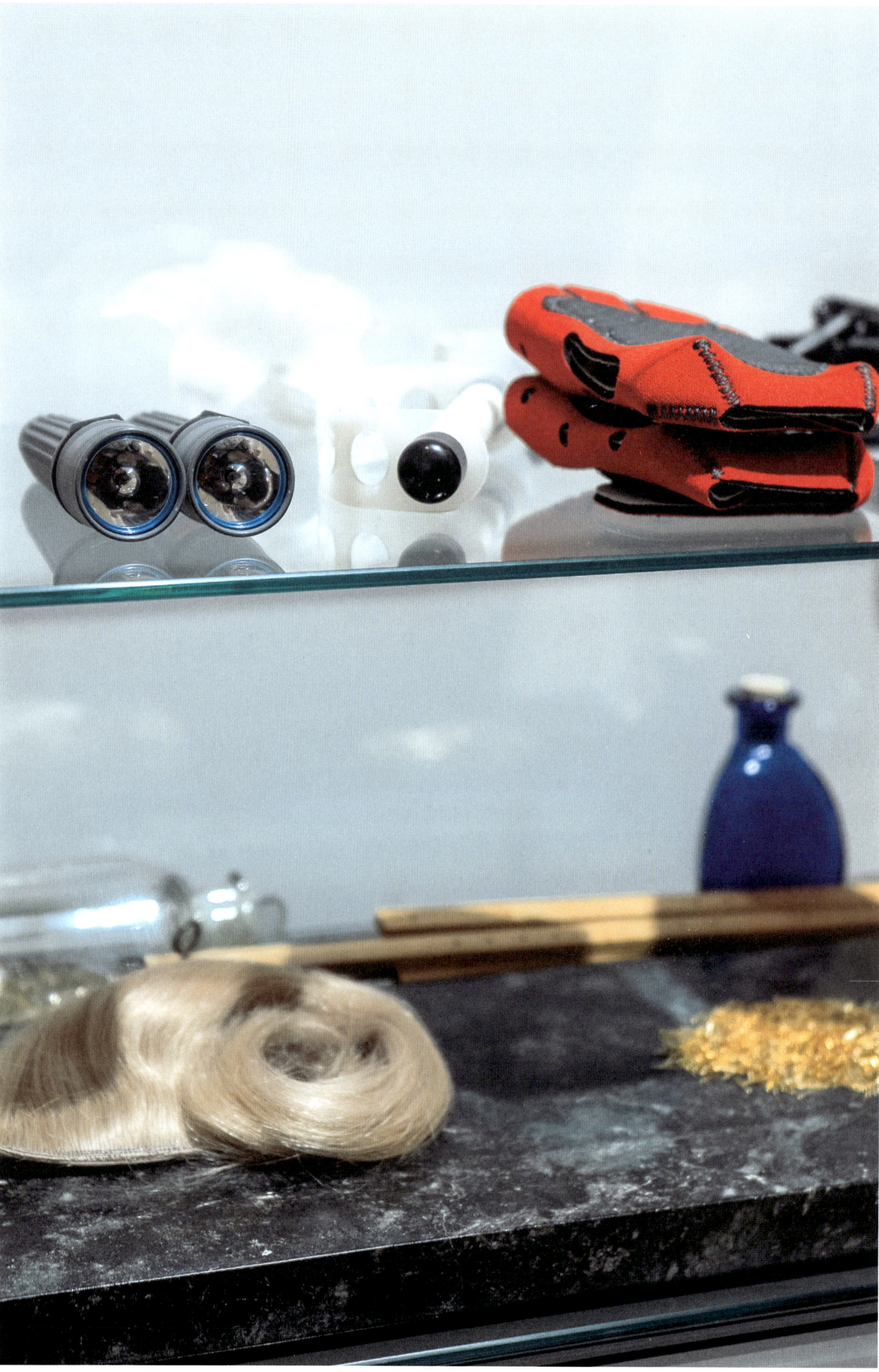

Deviant Cyborg F, 1992. Glass case, objects, vinyl type, and Formica-veneer pedestal

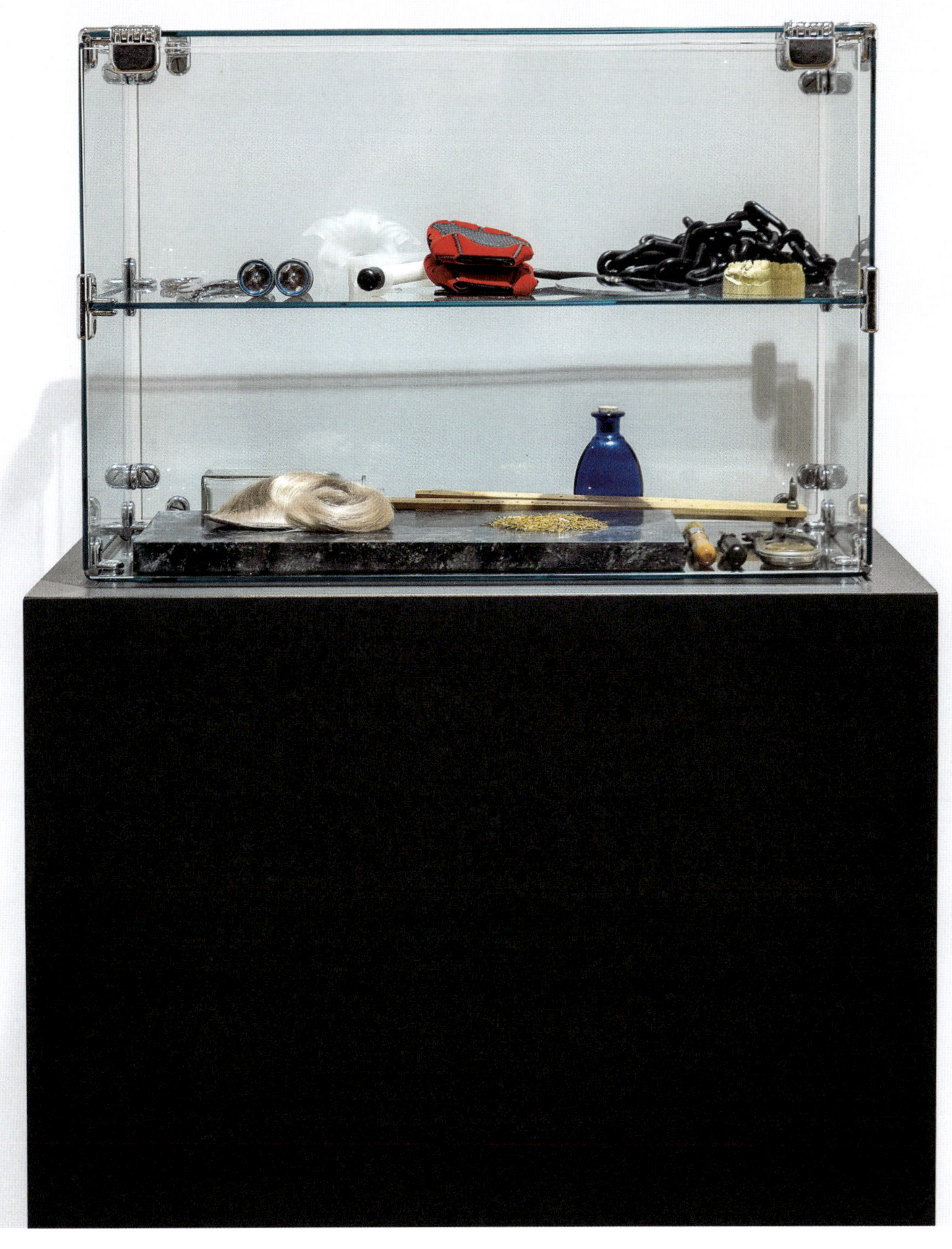

Butterflies, 1993. Human hair mustaches, vinyl type, plexiglass boxes, and plexiglass shelf

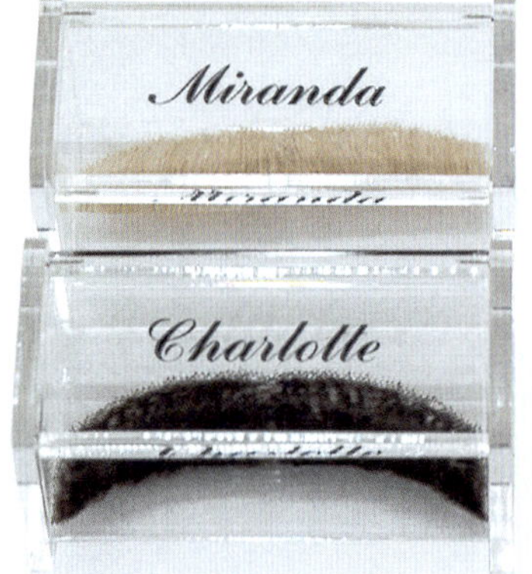

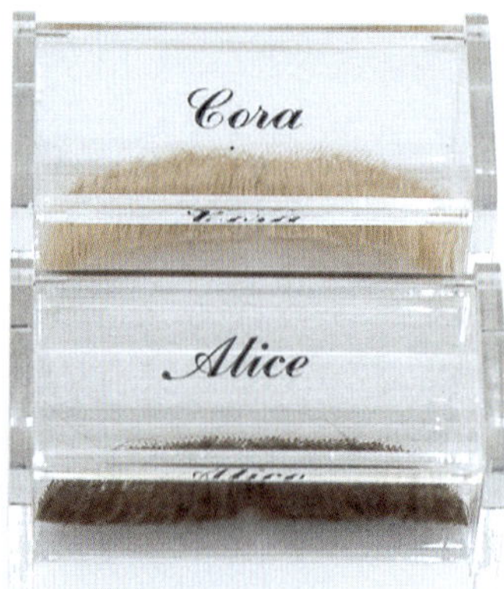

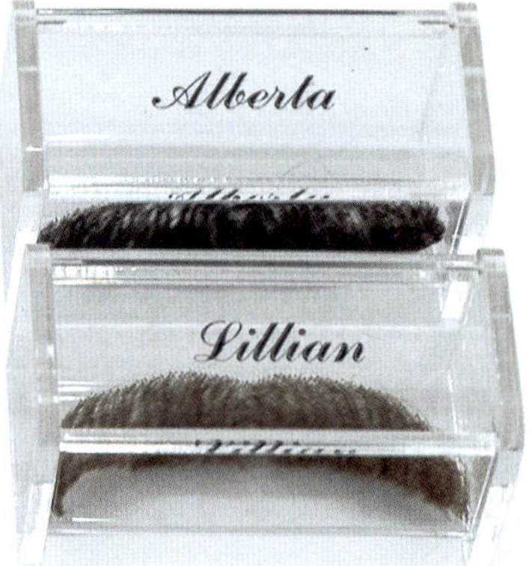

La Folle, 1991 (remade 2024). Postcard, pencil, and frame

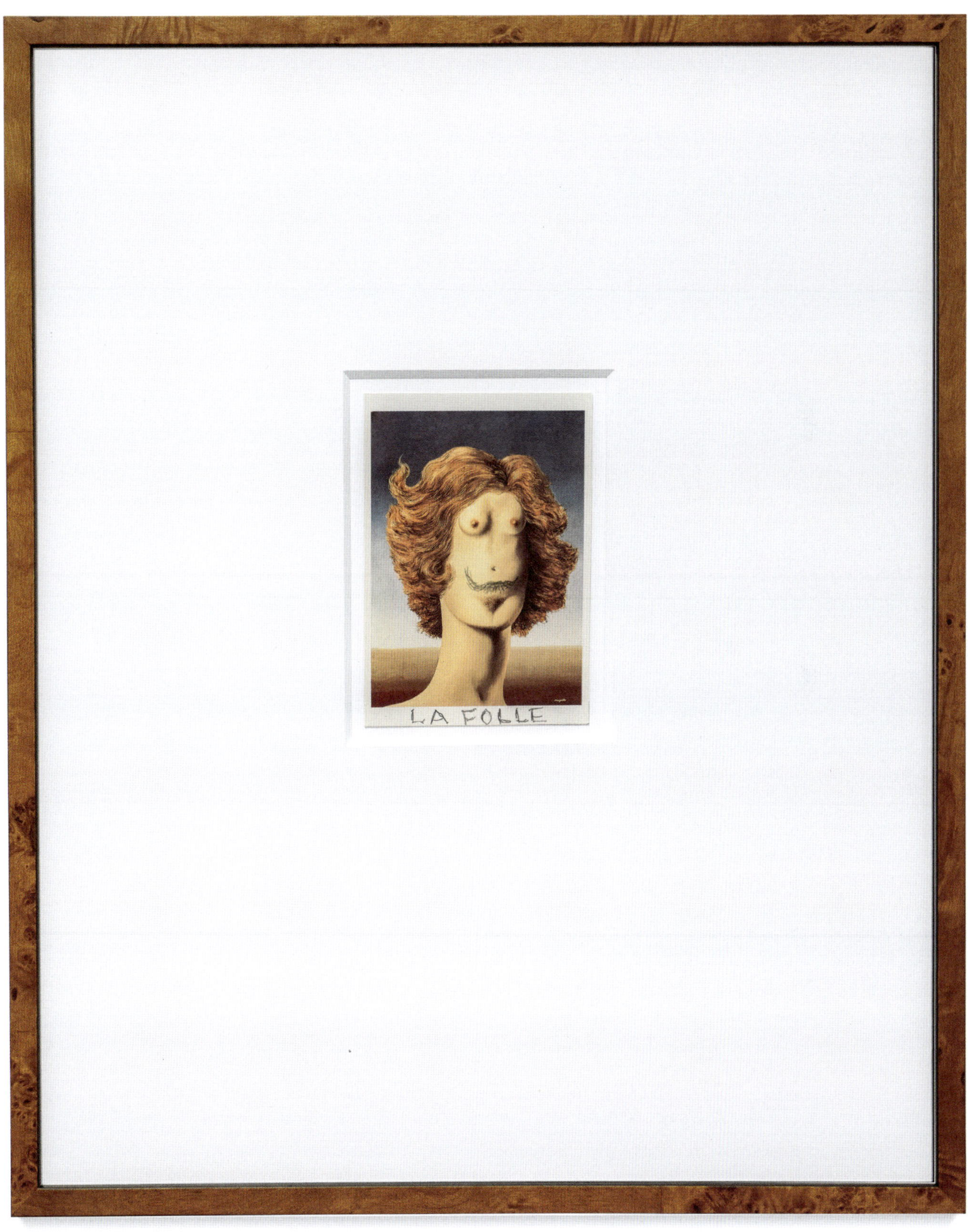

Odd Glove, 1990. Mirror, glove, brass, print, and oak table

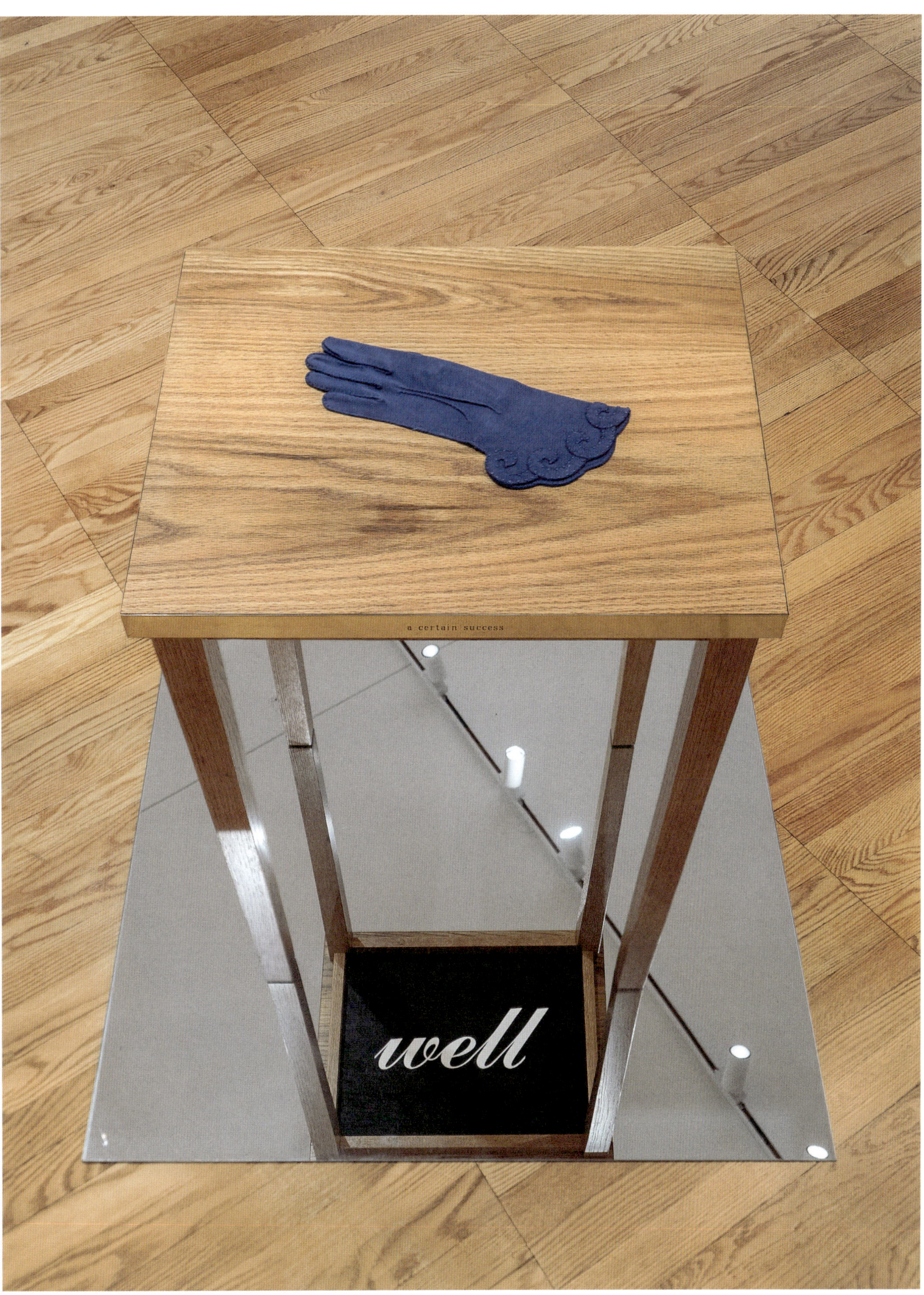

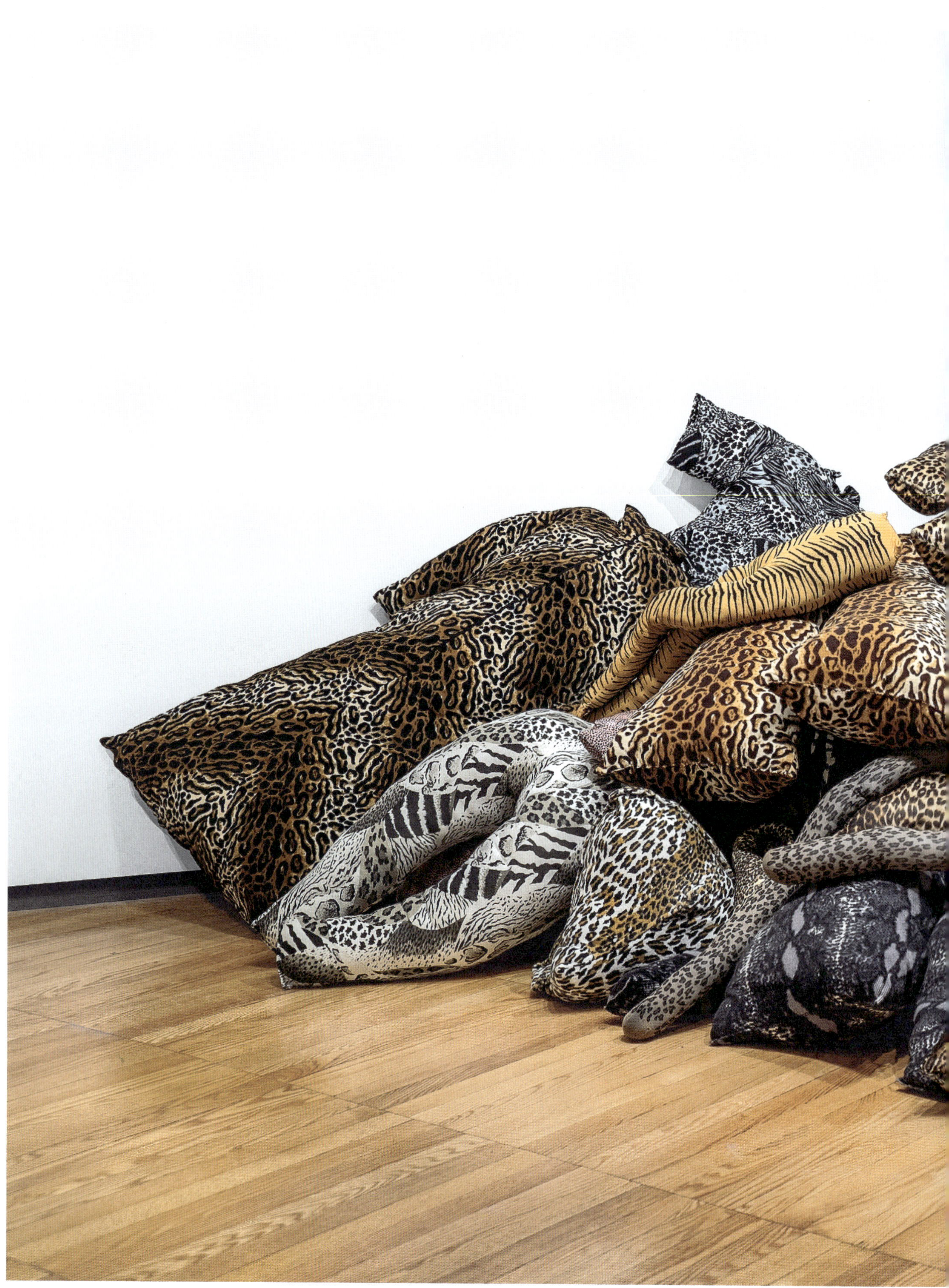

Monster Girls, 1994–95. Fabric and foam. Installation view at Krannert Art Museum, 2024

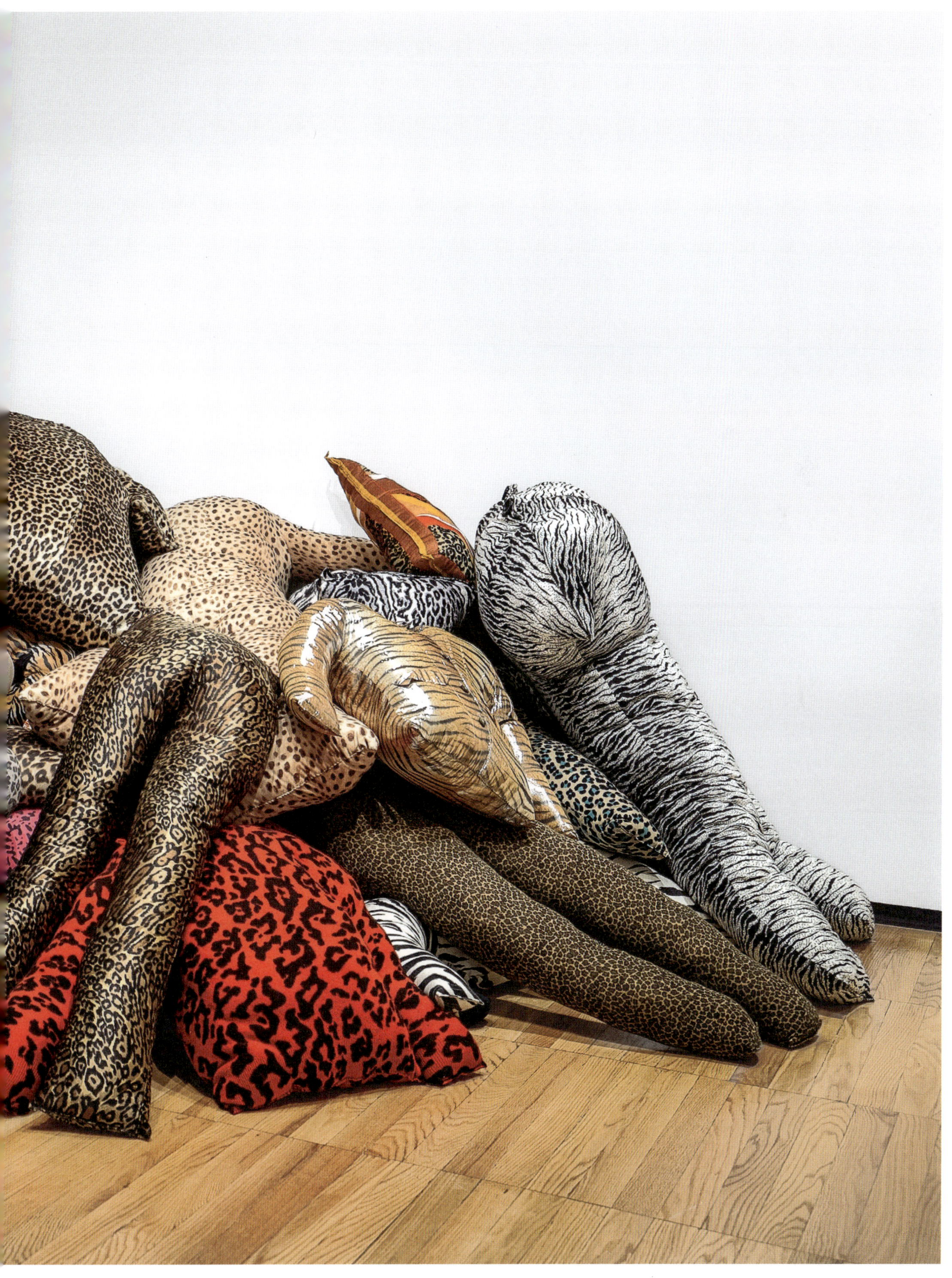

Lace Curtain Window, 1991. Custom French window with vinyl panes, brass hardware, lace curtains, and latex paint

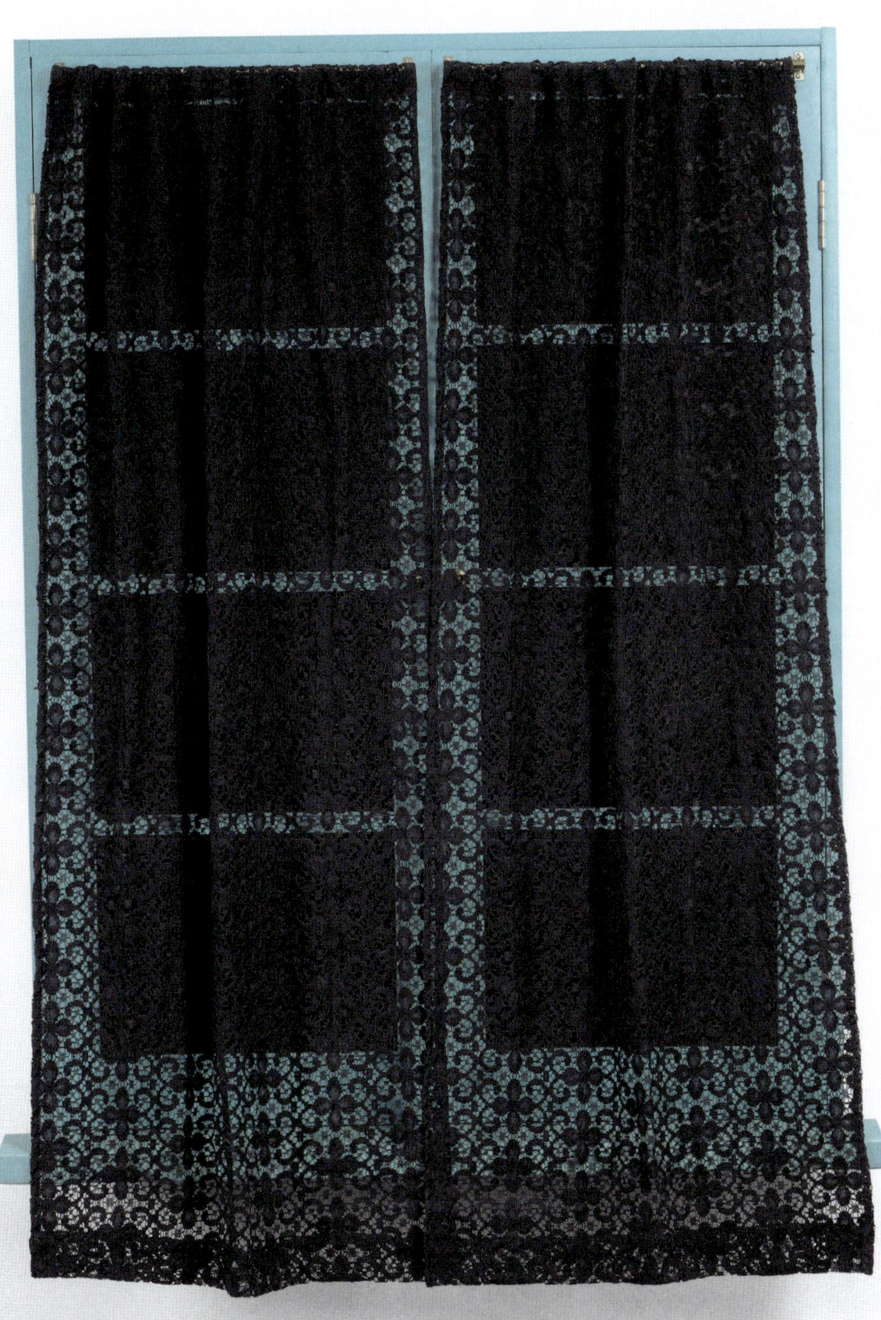

Witch's Cradle, 1994. Oak lectern and flocked fabric on wood

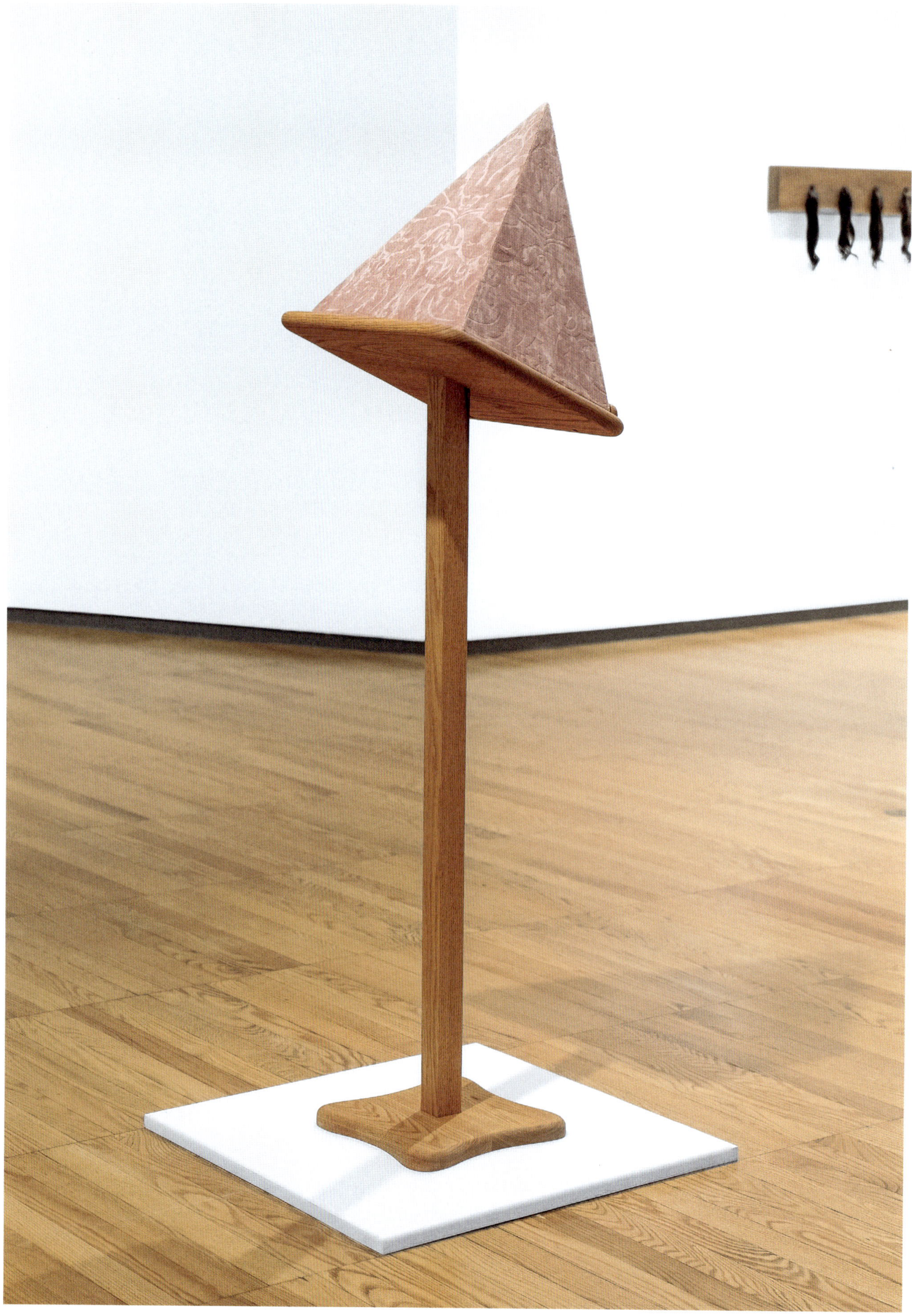

CLOCKWISE FROM TOP LEFT Brochure for *Bad Girls* and *Bad Girls West*, 1994. Co-published by the New Museum of Contemporary Art, New York, and the Frederick S. Wight Art Gallery, University of California, Los Angeles; Brochure for *The Monster Show*, 1995. Published by the Museum of Contemporary Art North Miami; Installation view of *Not A Serial Killer* at José Freire Fine Art, New York, 1994

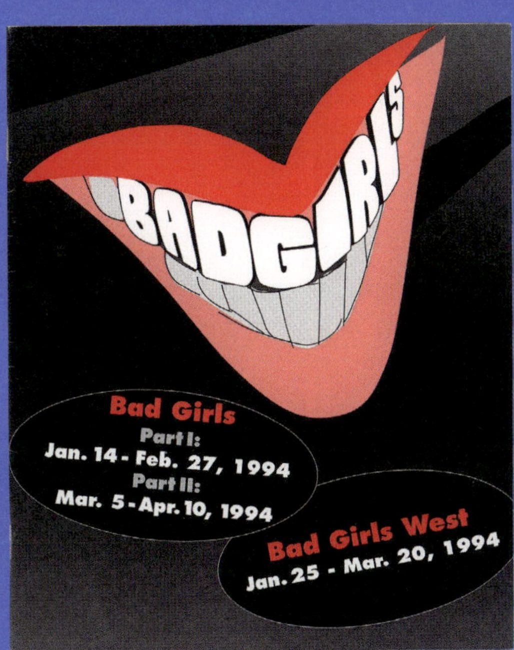

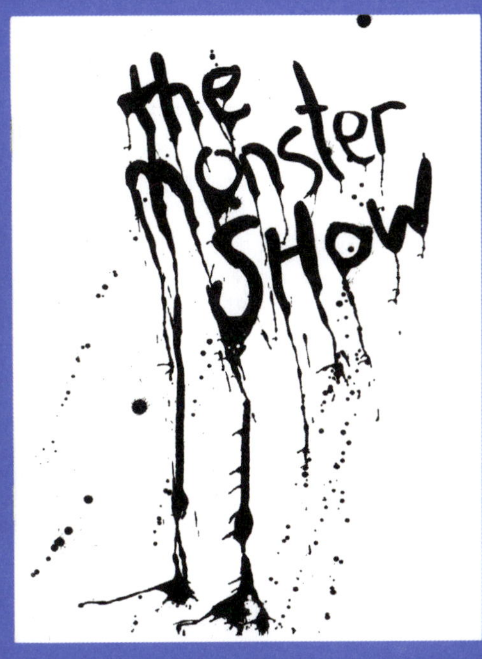

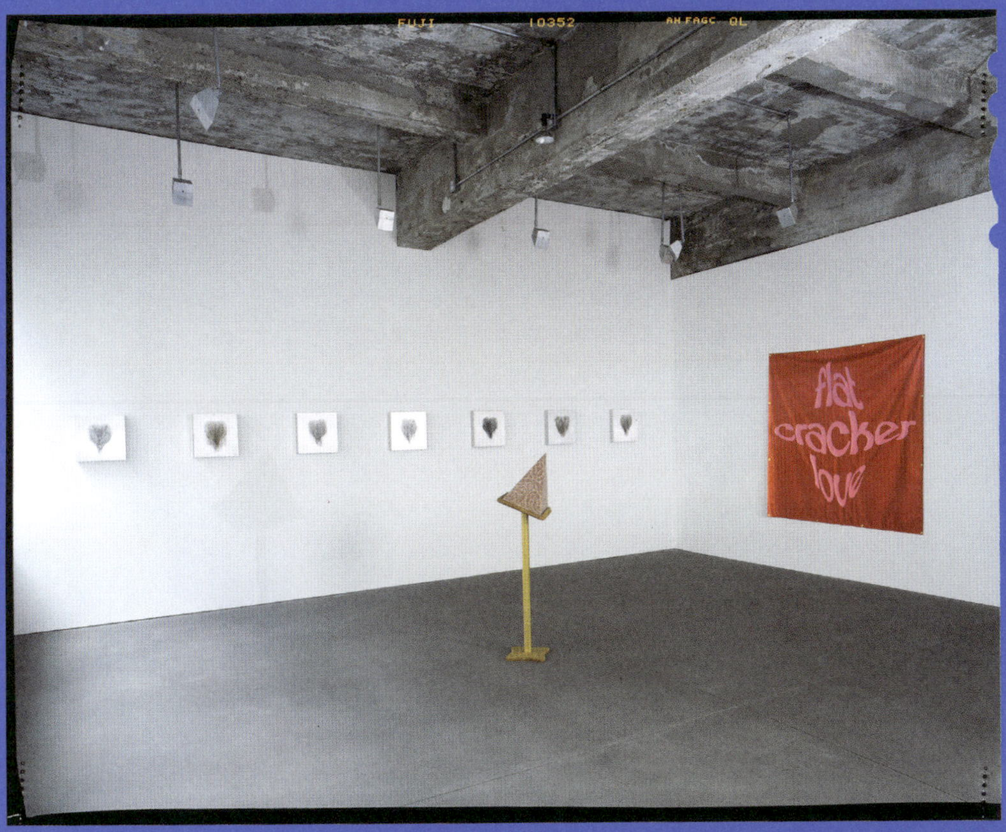

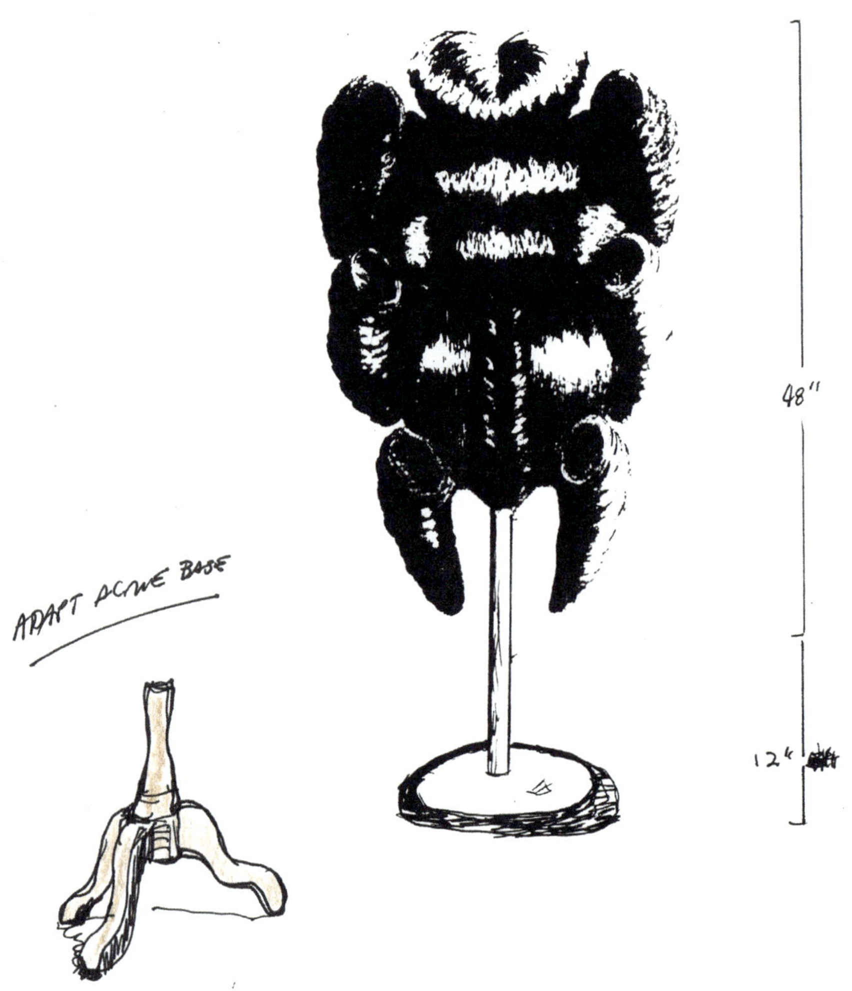

Sketch for *Mistress*, 1992. Ink and colored pencil on photocopy

TOP *Little Maids*, 1993. Ten flocked cardboard profiles
BOTTOM *Mistress*, 1993. Synthetic hair, fabric, and wood stand

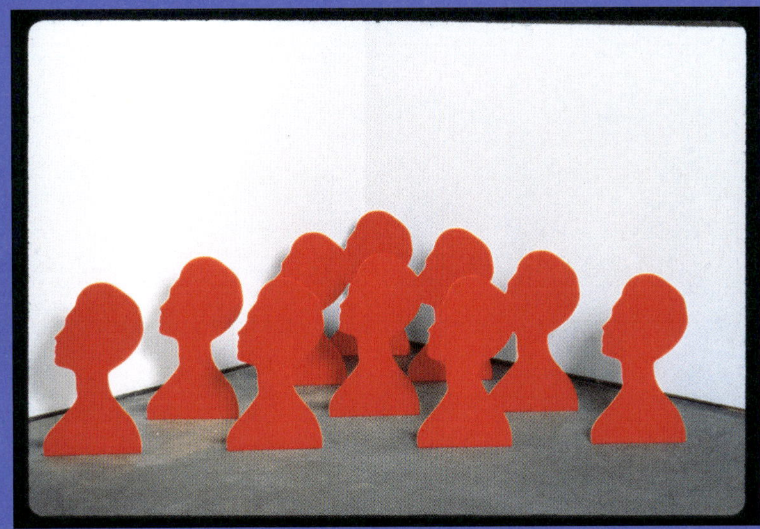

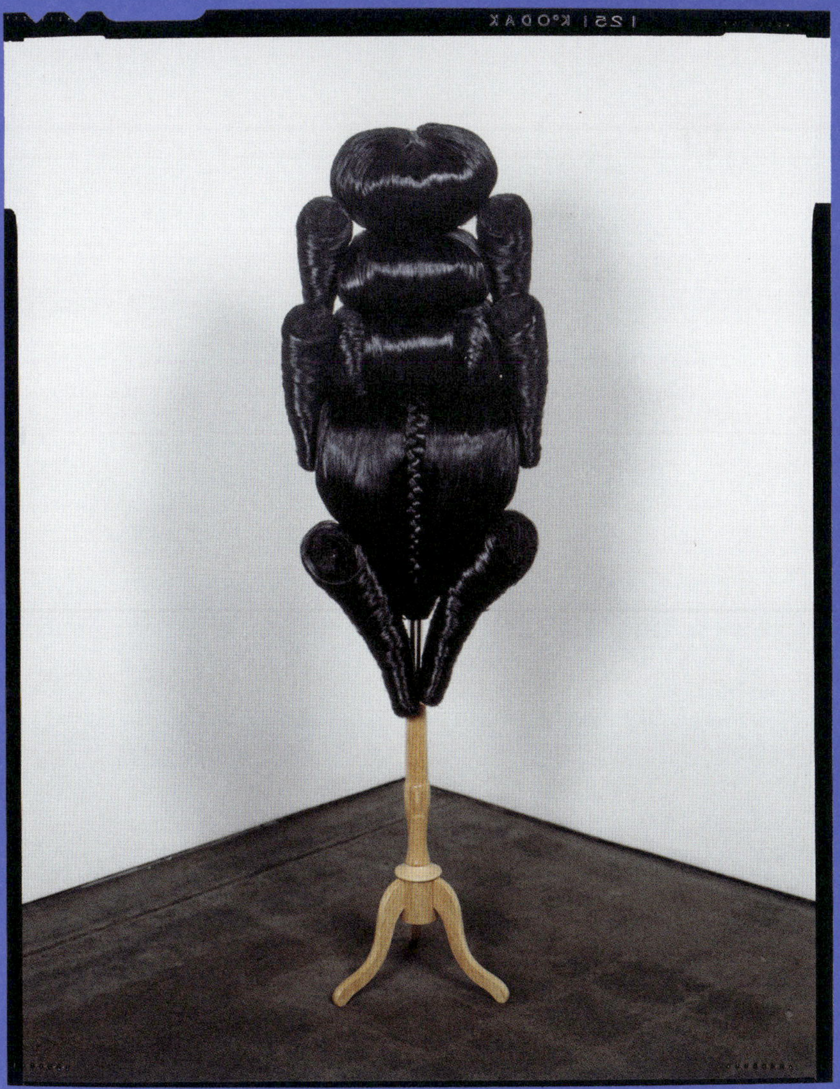

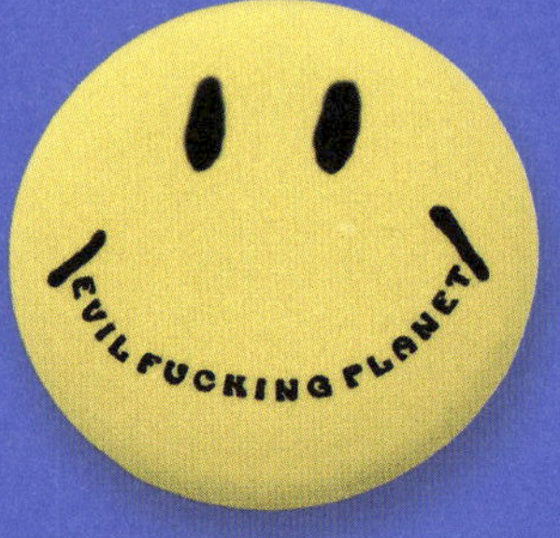
EVIL FUCKING PLANET

Door C, 1994. Solid-core door, latex paint, aluminum pull plate, and fur

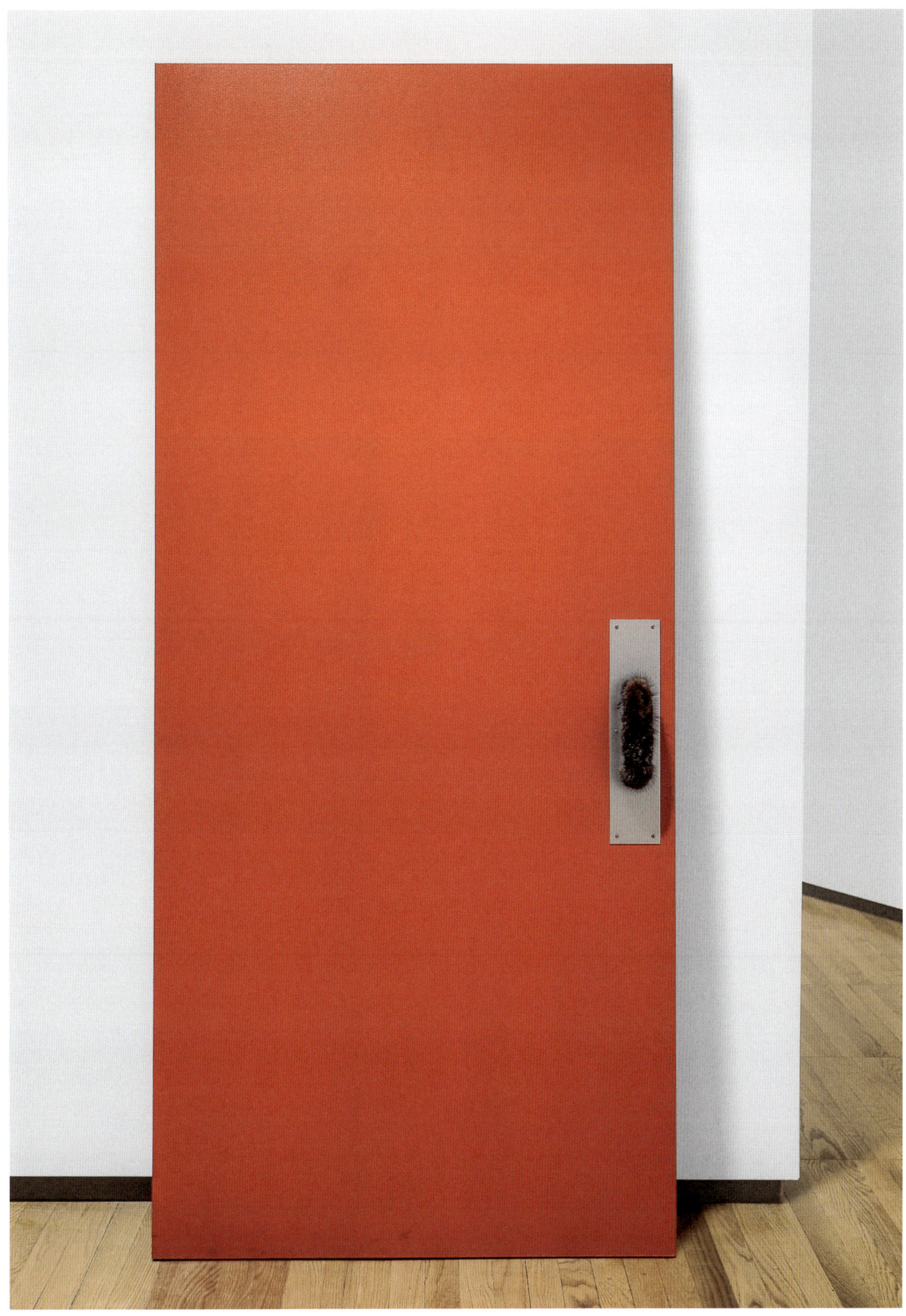

TOP TO BOTTOM *Sneakers*, 1994. Faux leopard boots, athletic laces, and plexiglass shelf; *Hair Shirt*, 1994. Flocked display busts with chest hair toupees and plexiglass shelf; *Bride*, 1994. Wood, plexiglass, rawhide, and faux fur

OPPOSITE *Lee's Locker (M.D./M.O./M.W.)*, 1994. Installation view at Krannert Art Museum, 2024

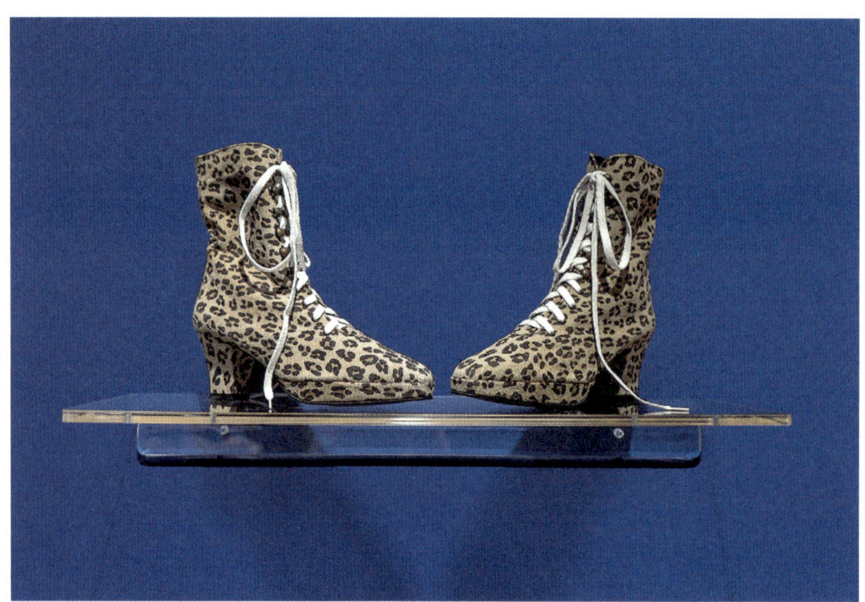

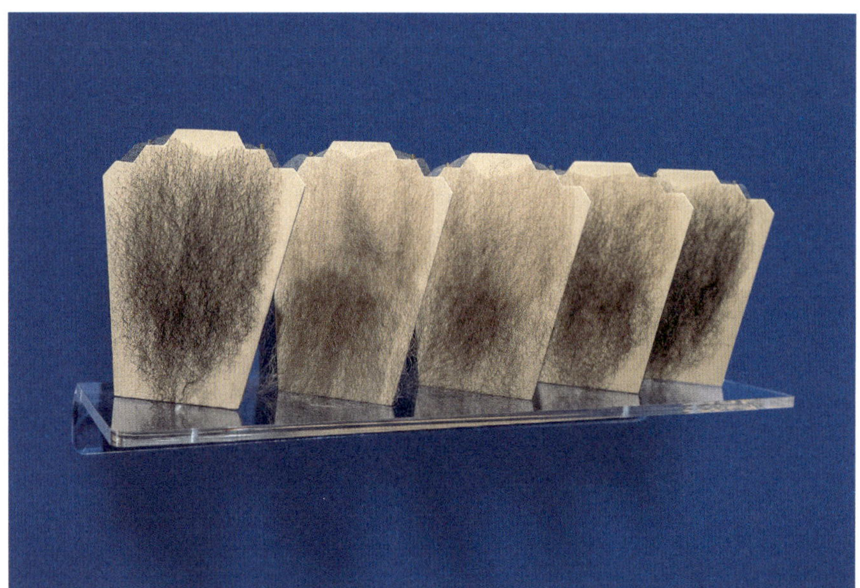

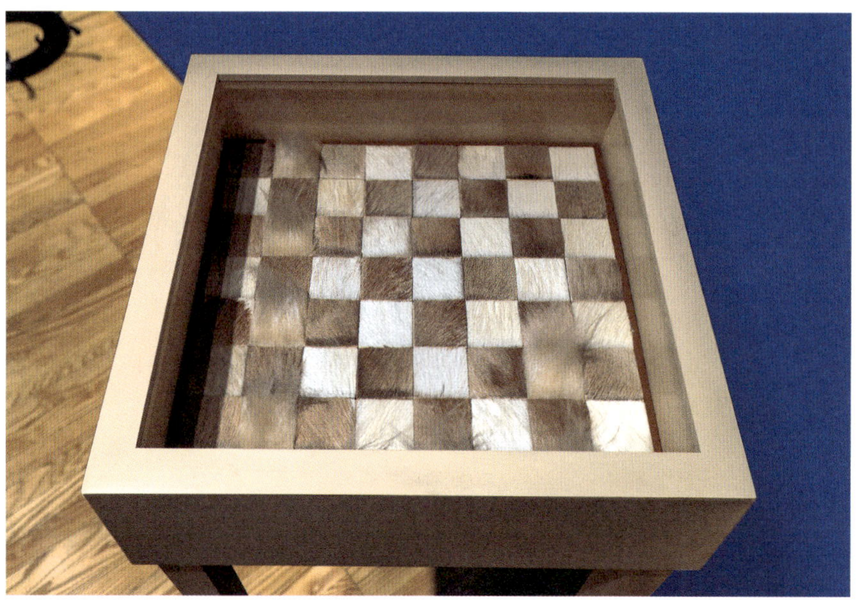

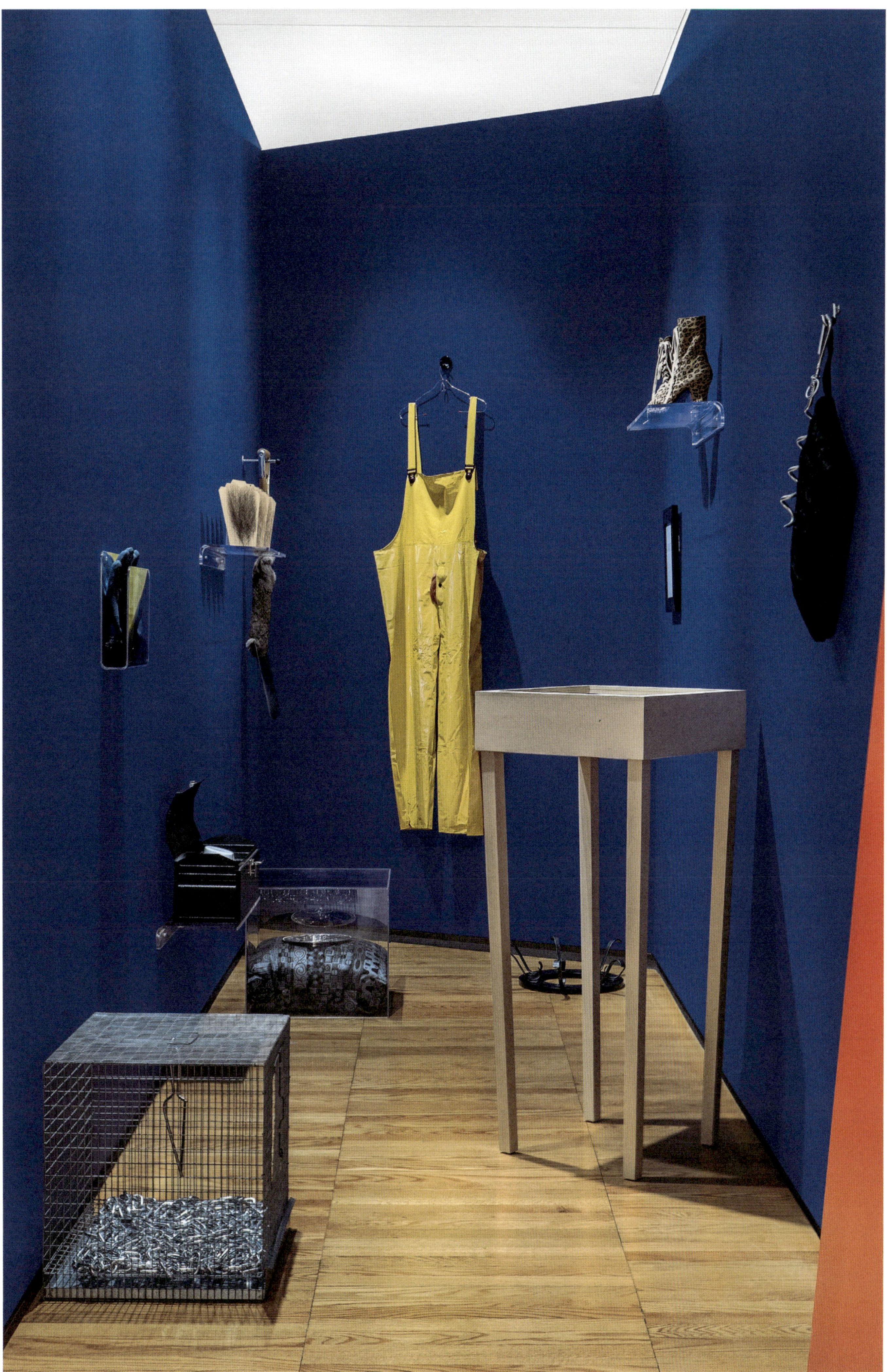

Detail of *Protection*, 1994. Vinyl and plastic overalls, fur, and steel hanger

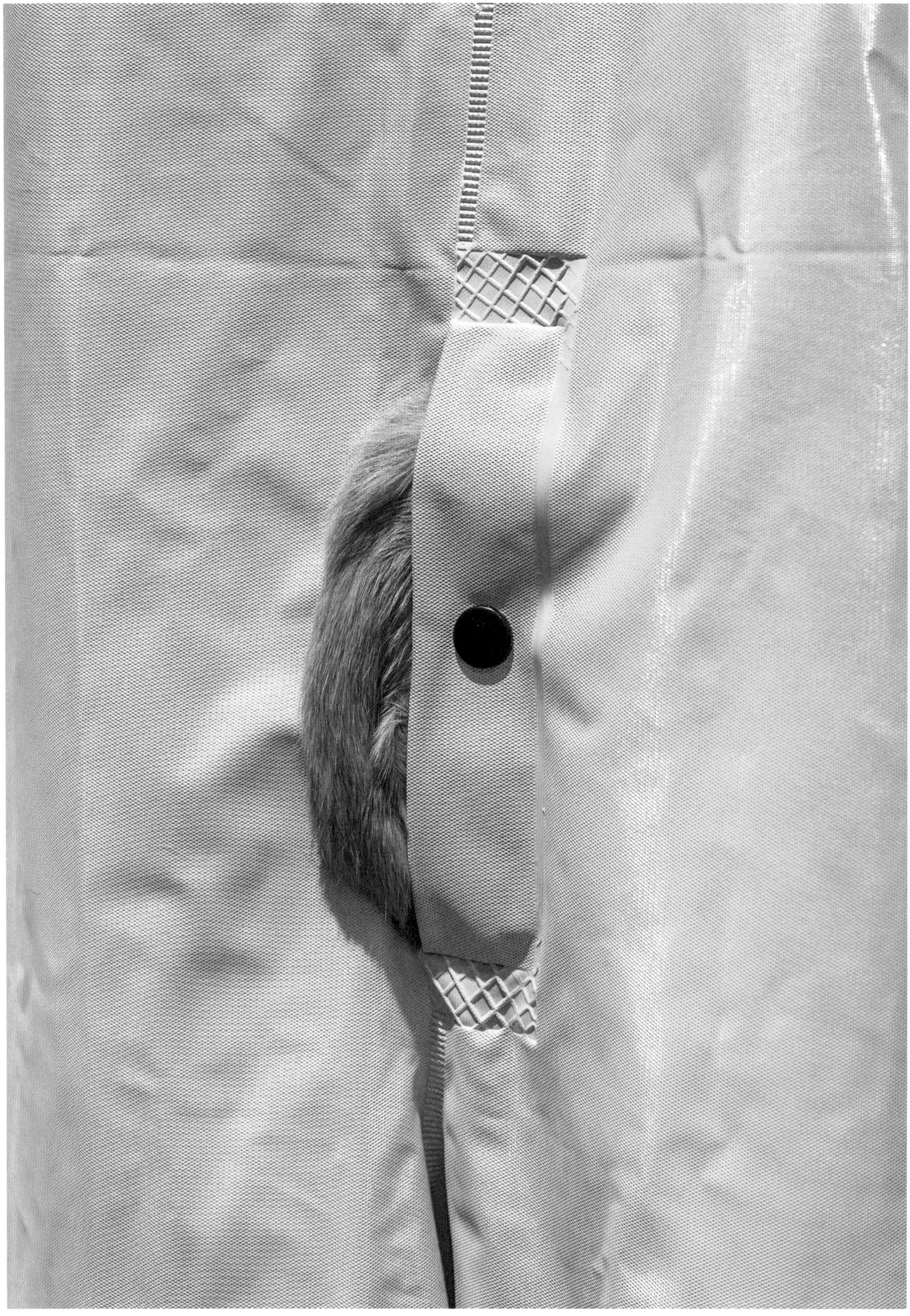

Witch's Spade, 1994. Steel and wood shovel, fur, steel and plastic hanger, and two screws

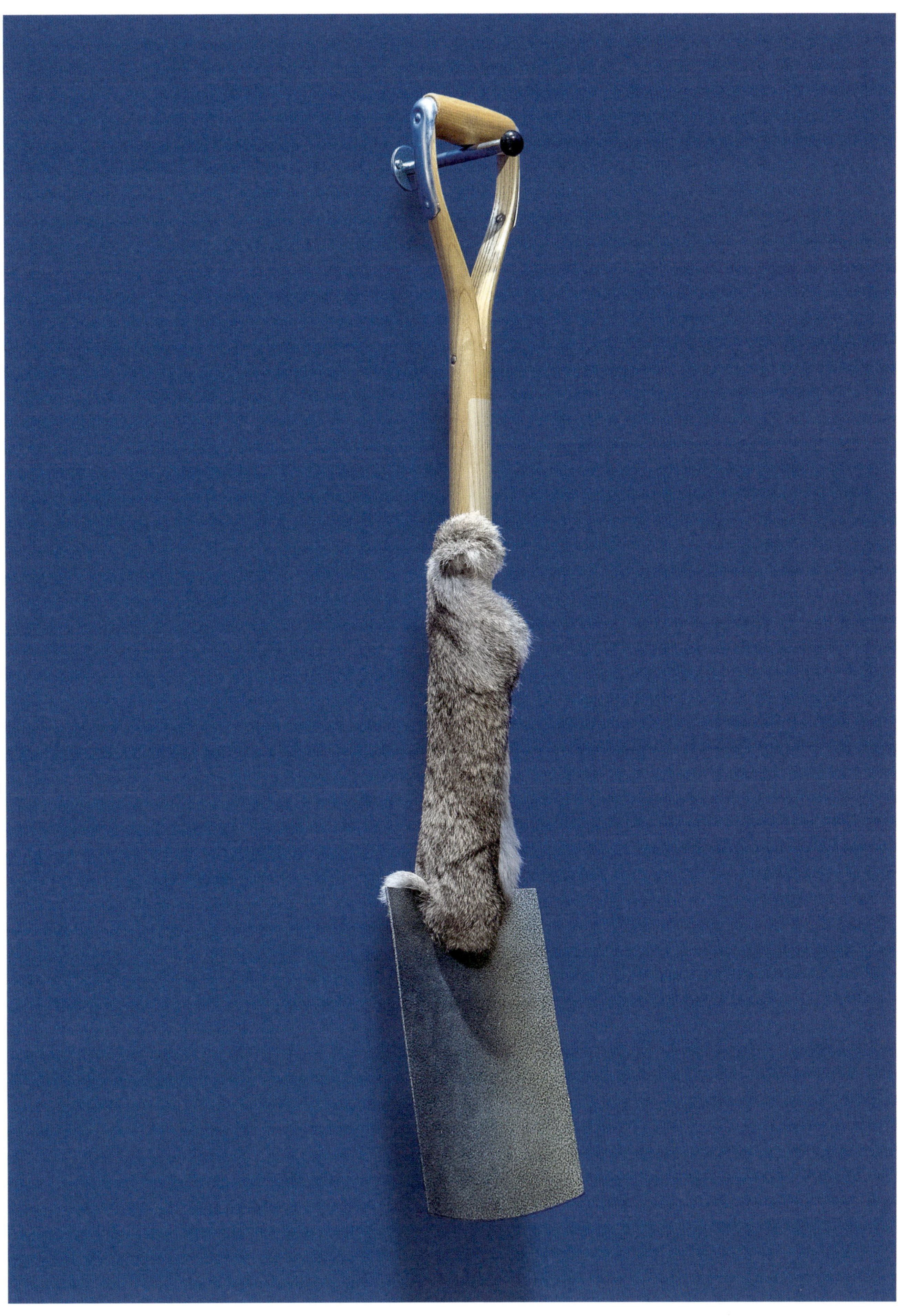

PAGES 135–37 *Daytona Death Angel*, 1994. Synthetic hair, fabric, and wood stand

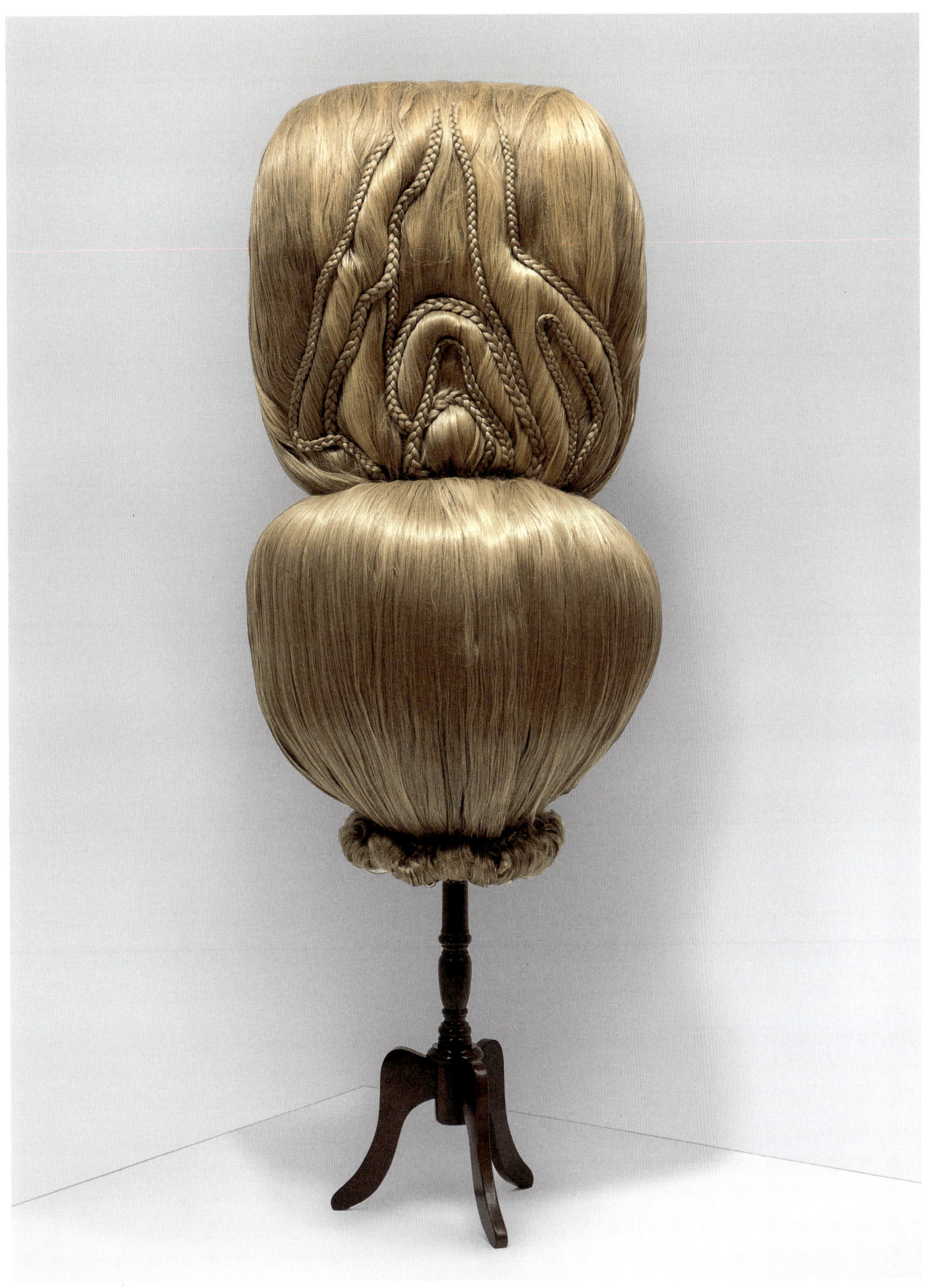

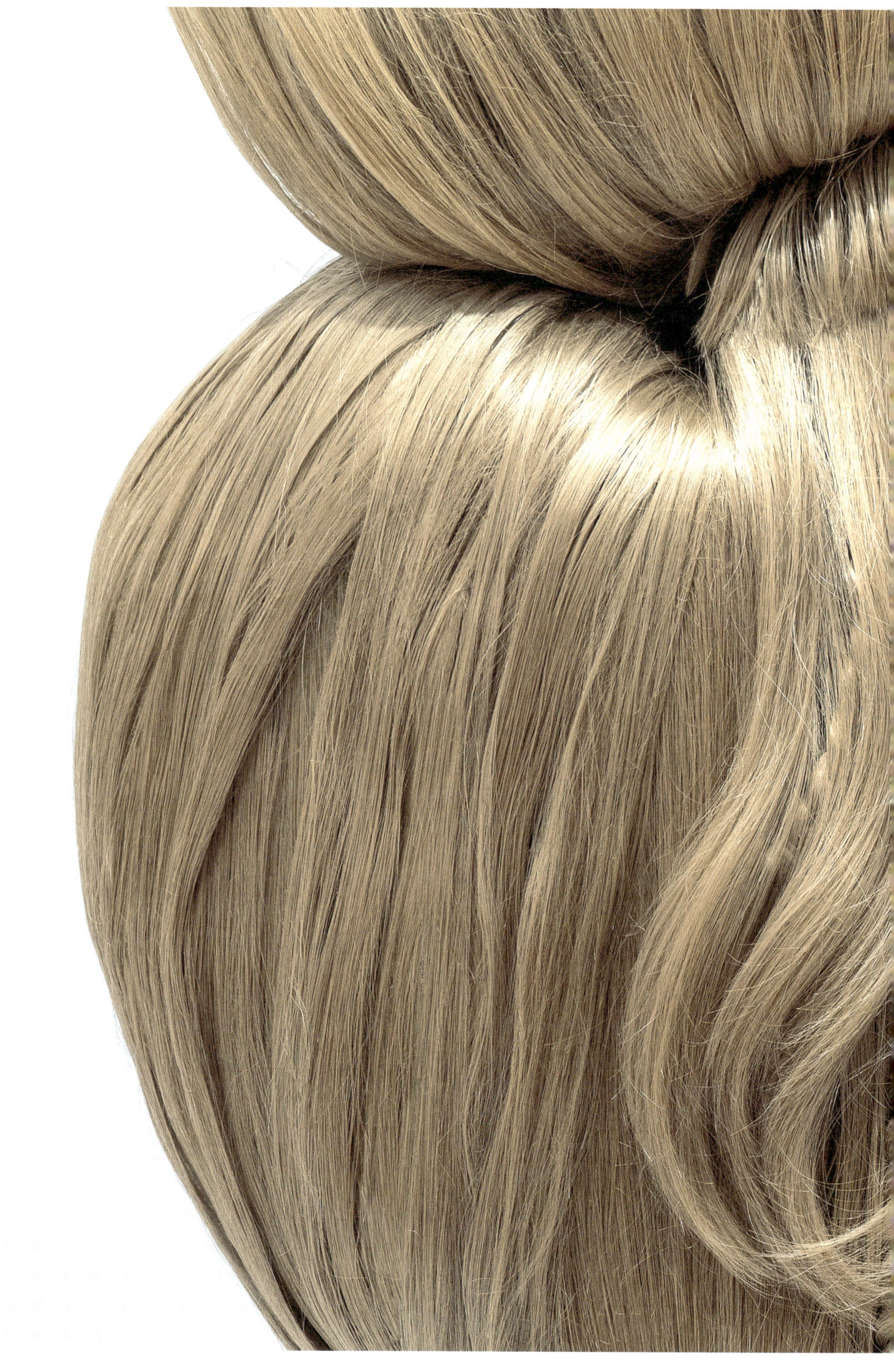

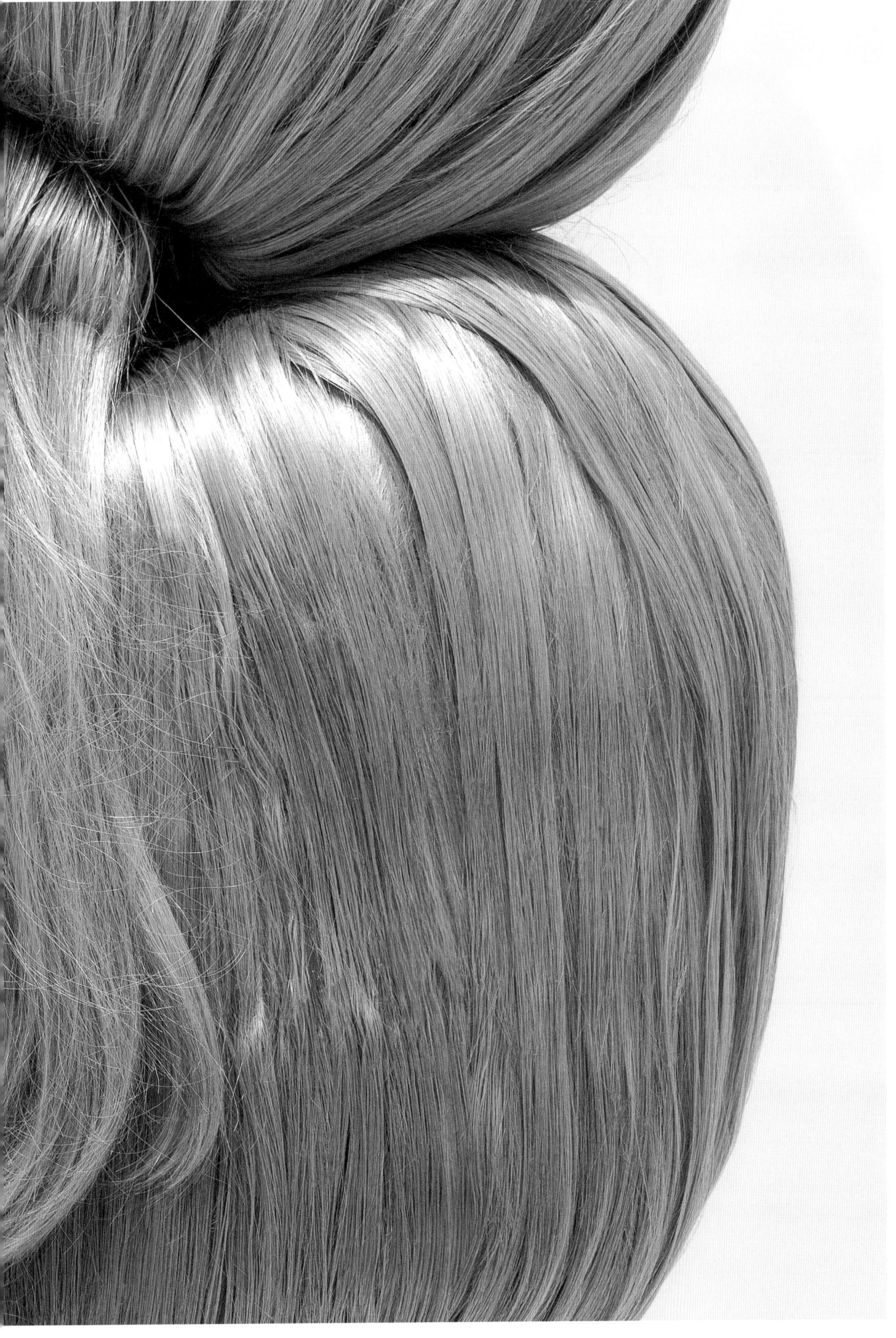

Beard, 1994. Motorcycle sissy bar, mixed media, and Formica-veneer pedestal

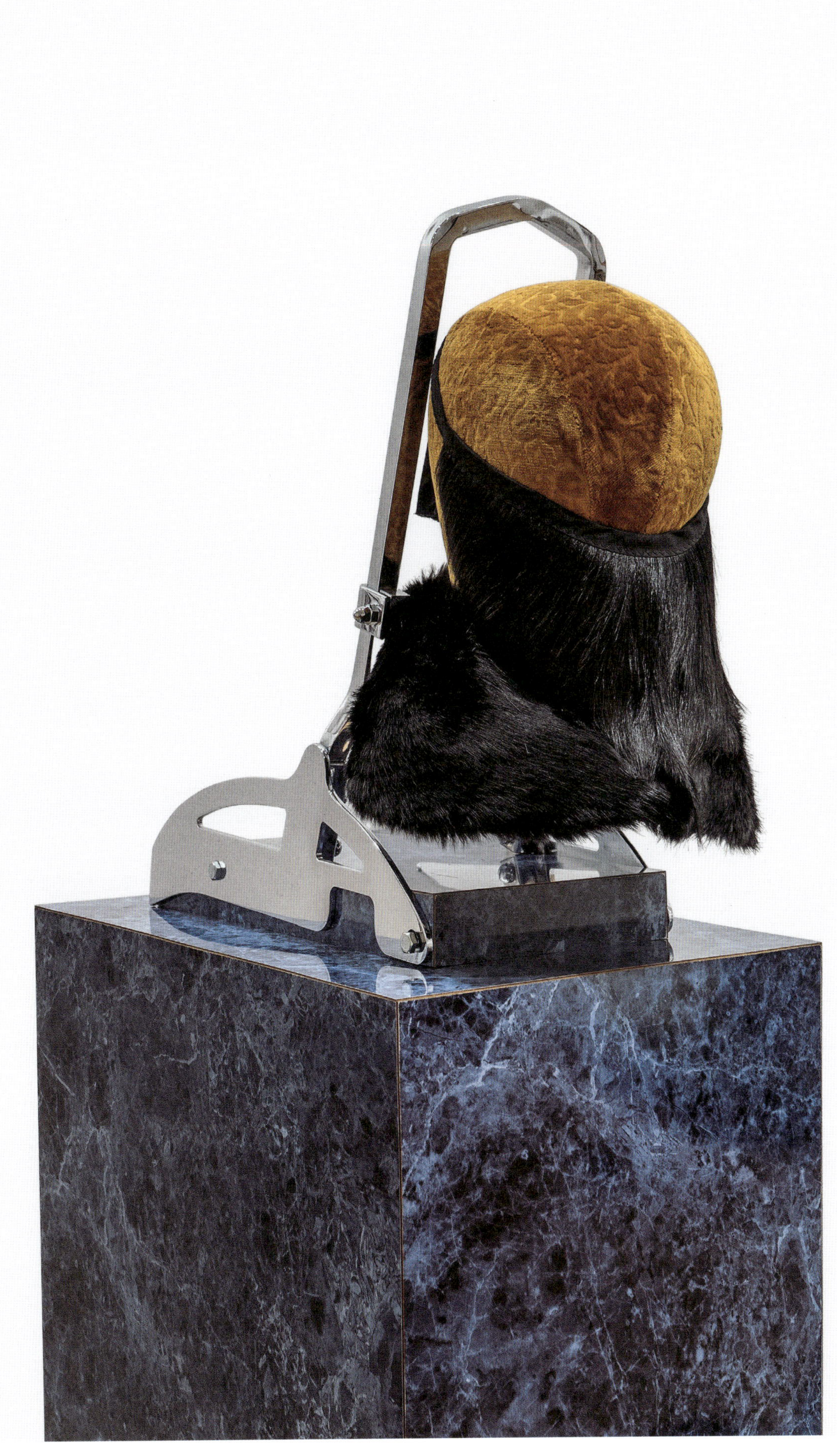

Family Room, 1994. Rug, fake wood paneling, motorcycle seats, and framed photograph. Installation view at Krannert Art Museum, 2024

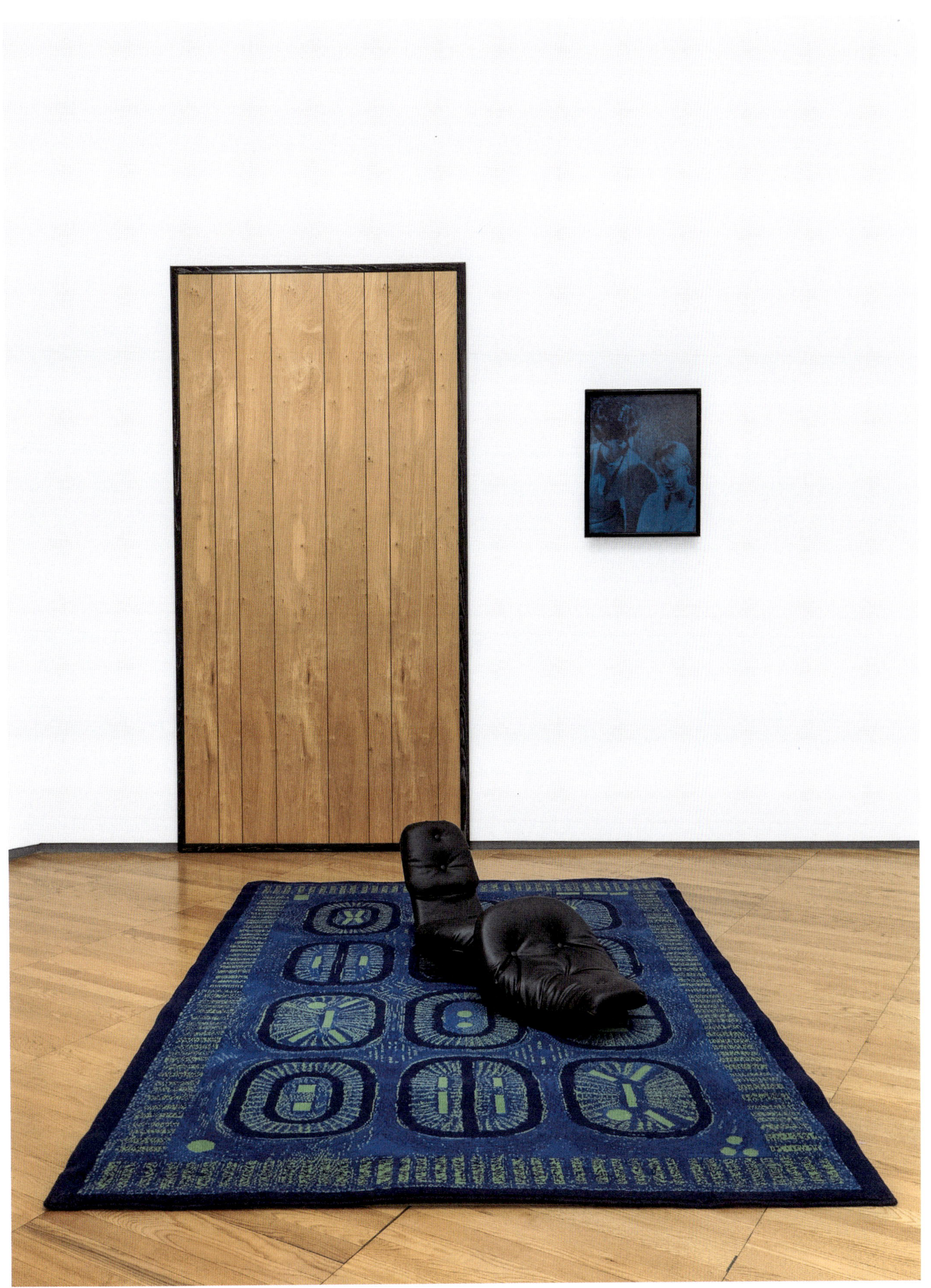

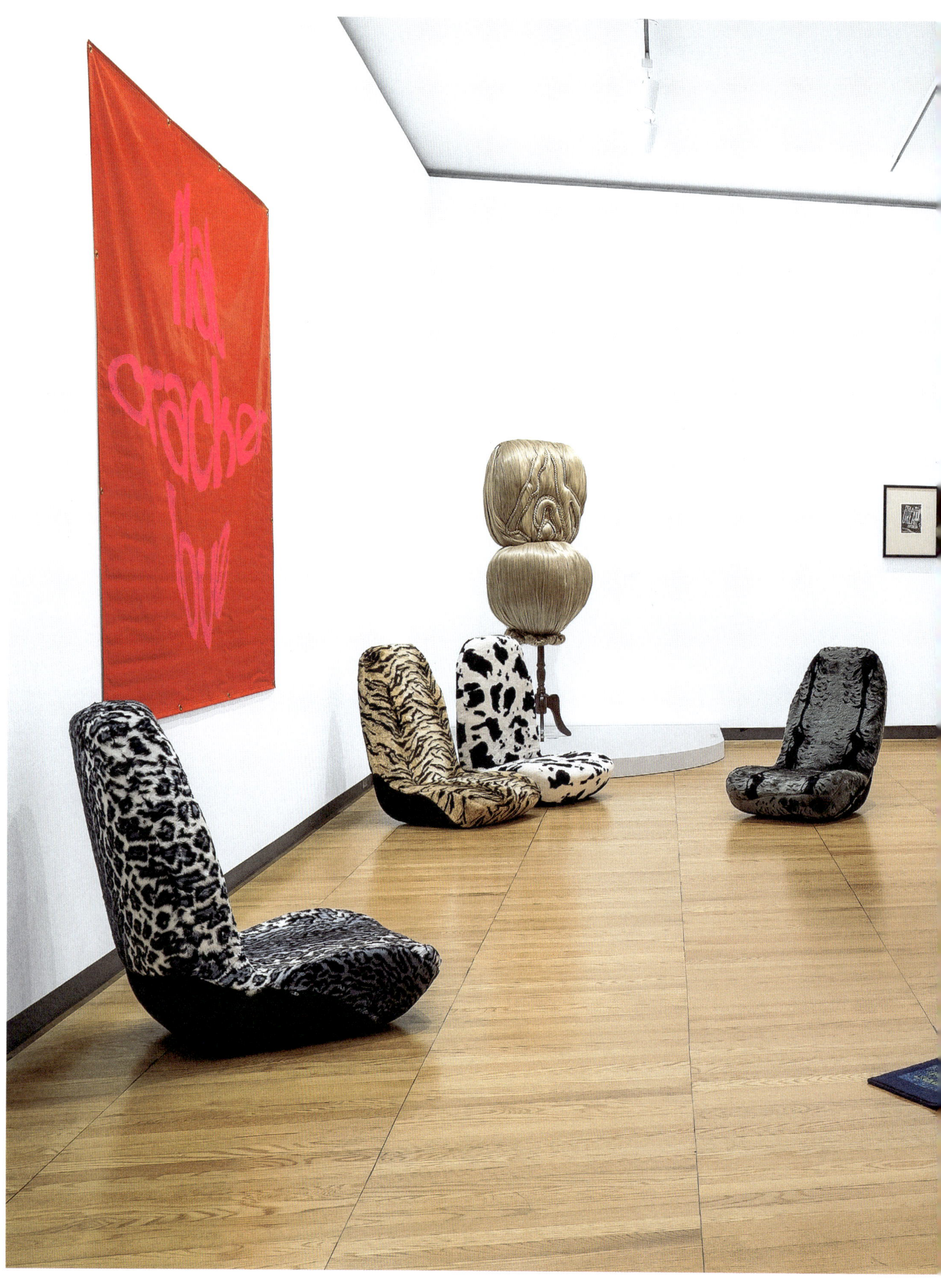
cracker

Autopsies, 1994. Seven bucket seats, fabric, and foam.
Installation view at Krannert Art Museum, 2024

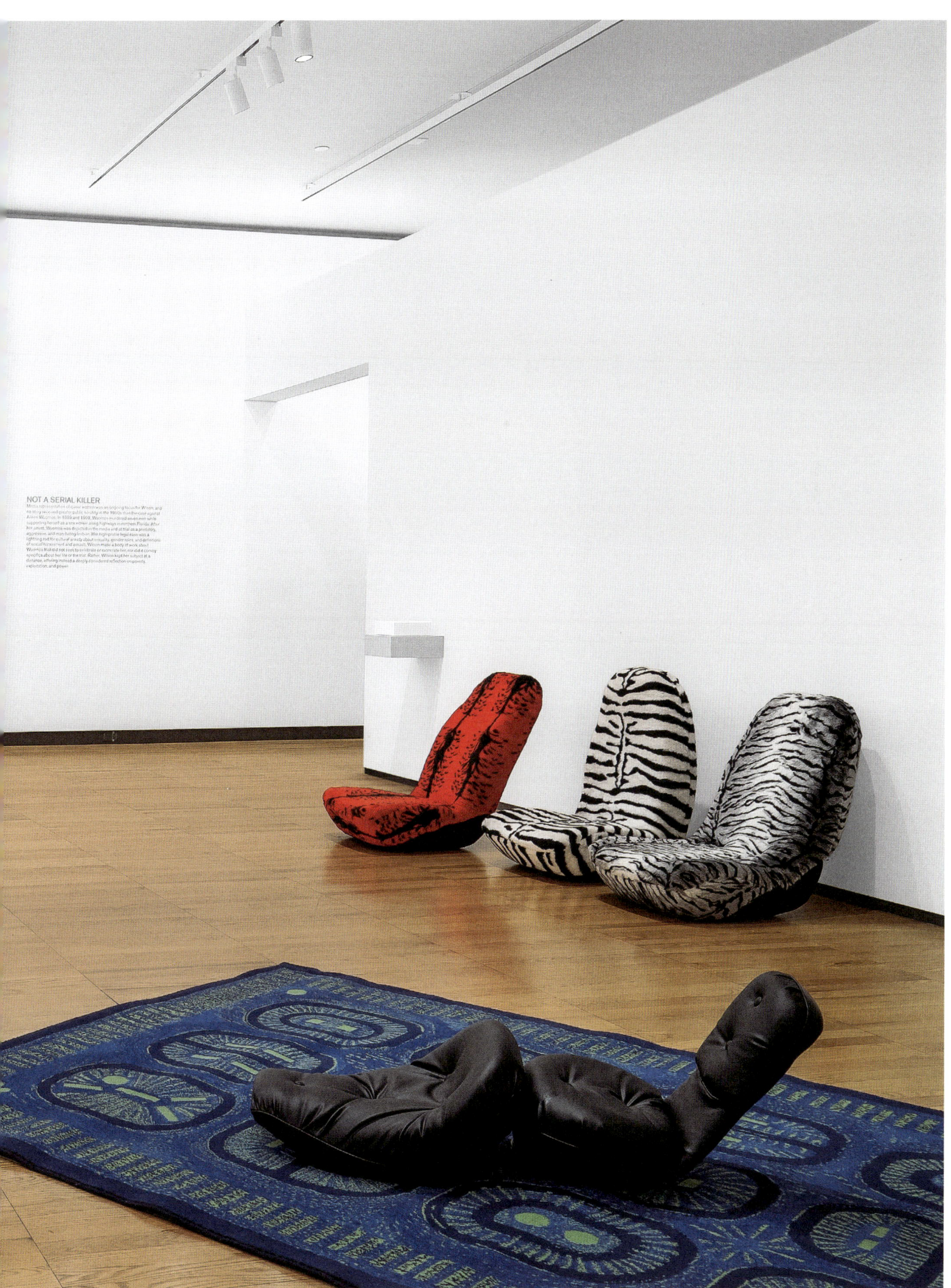

Chest Hair, 1994. Anodized aluminum and chest-hair toupee

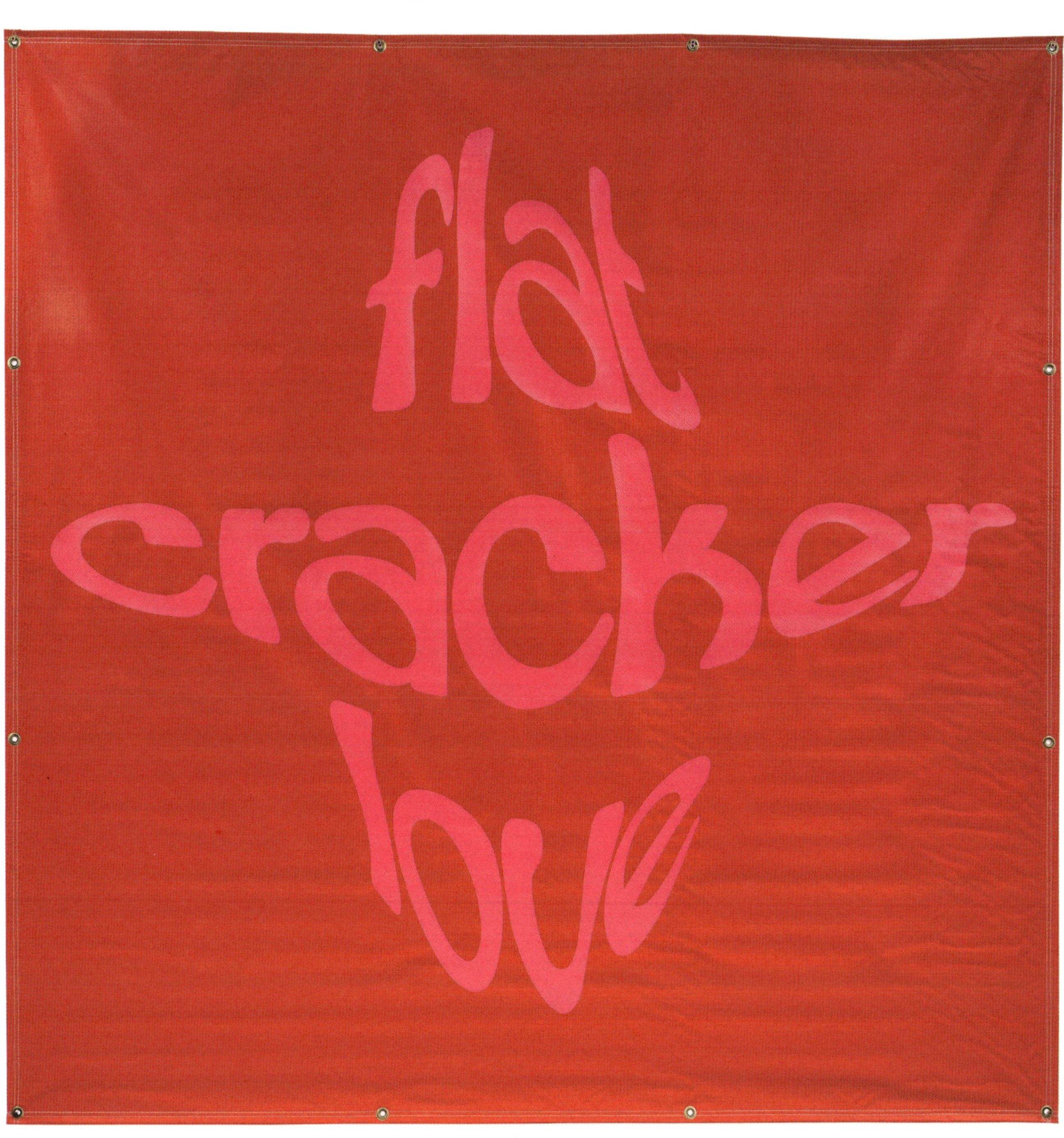
flat
cracker
love

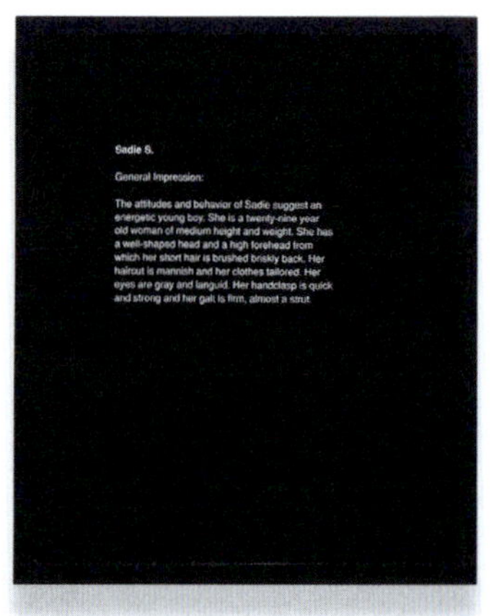
Sadie S.
General Impression:
The attitudes and behavior of Sadie suggest an energetic young boy. She is a twenty-nine year old woman of medium height and weight. She has a well-shaped head and a high forehead from which her short hair is brushed briskly back. Her haircut is mannish and her clothes tailored. Her eyes are gray and languid. Her handclasp is quick and strong and her gait is firm, almost a strut.

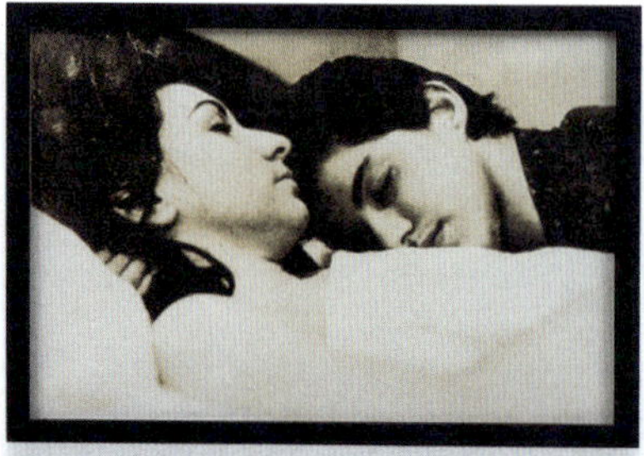

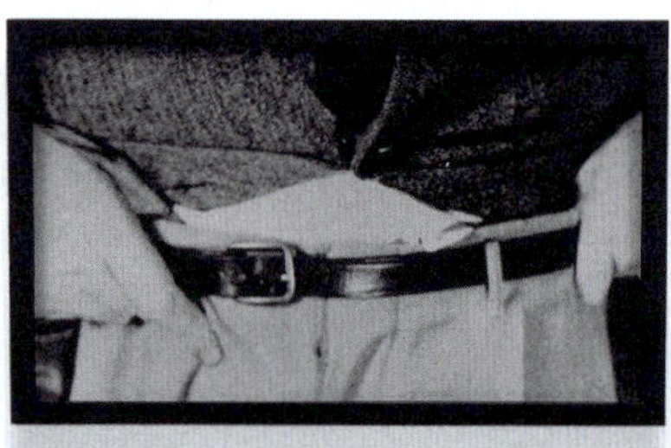

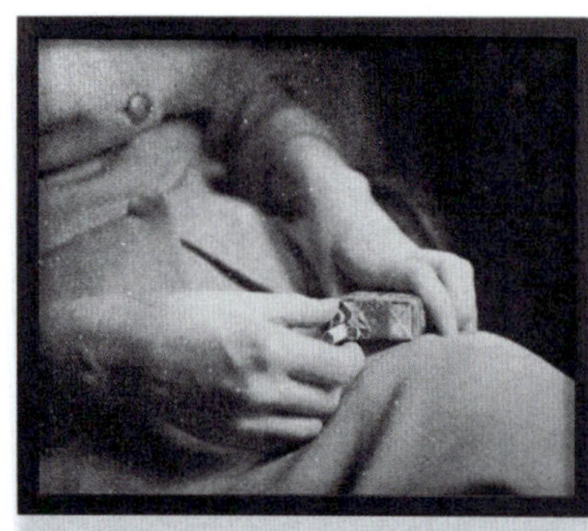

Swagger

Disturbances, 1990. Nine gelatin silver prints with silkscreen

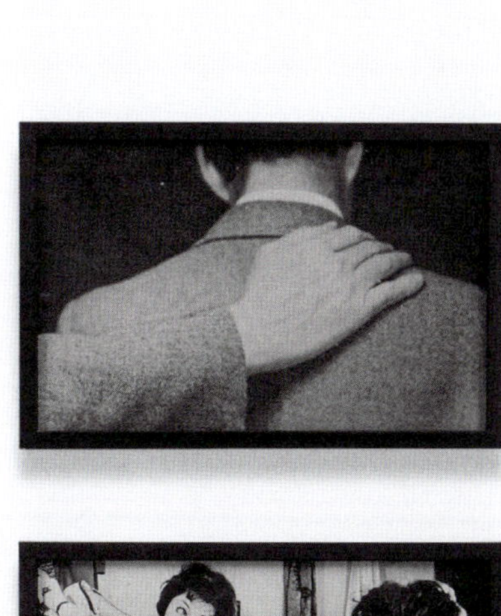

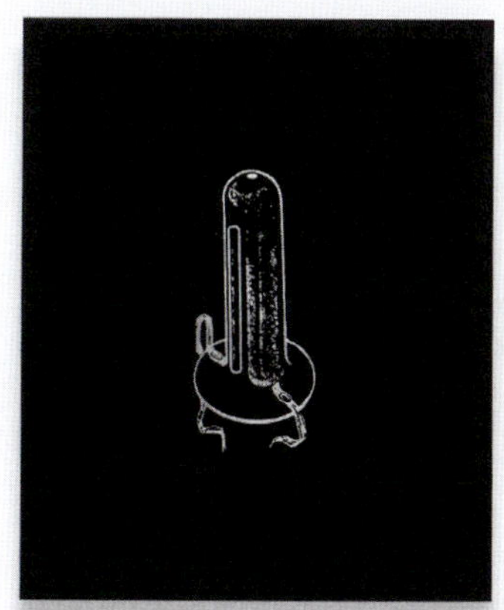

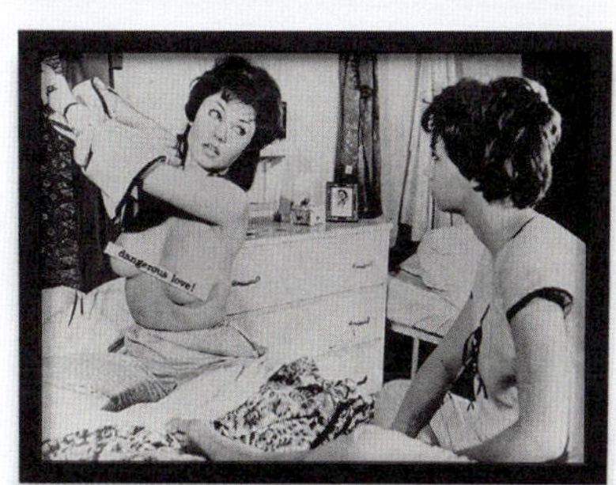

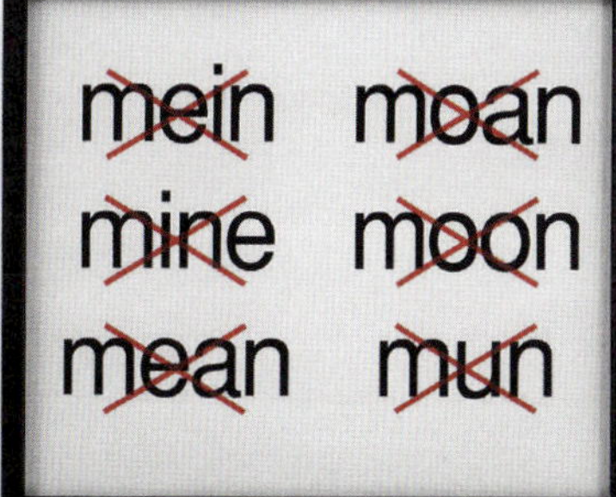

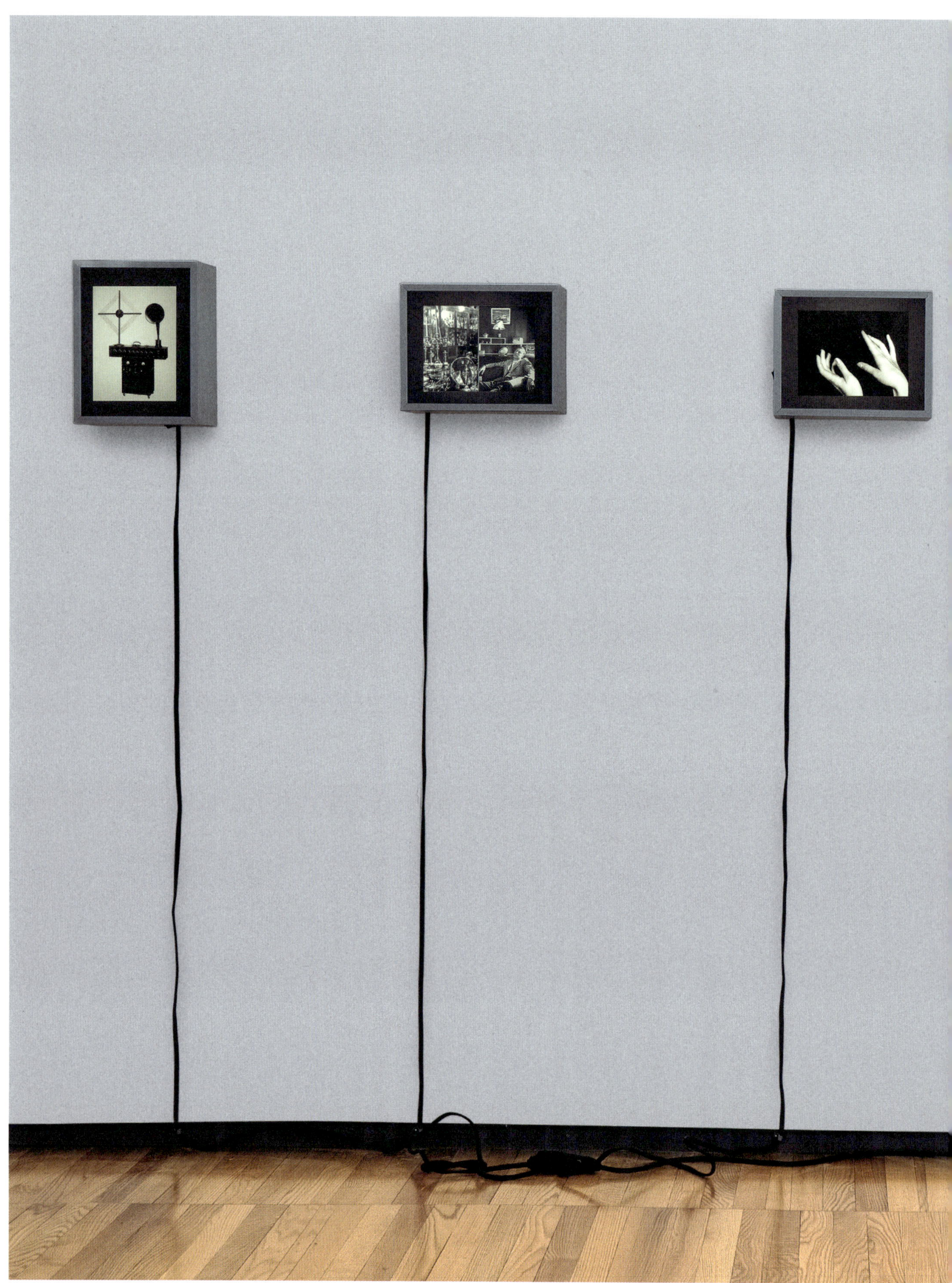

All works *Untitled*, 2010. FujiClear and aluminum lightboxes. Installation view at Krannert Art Museum, 2024

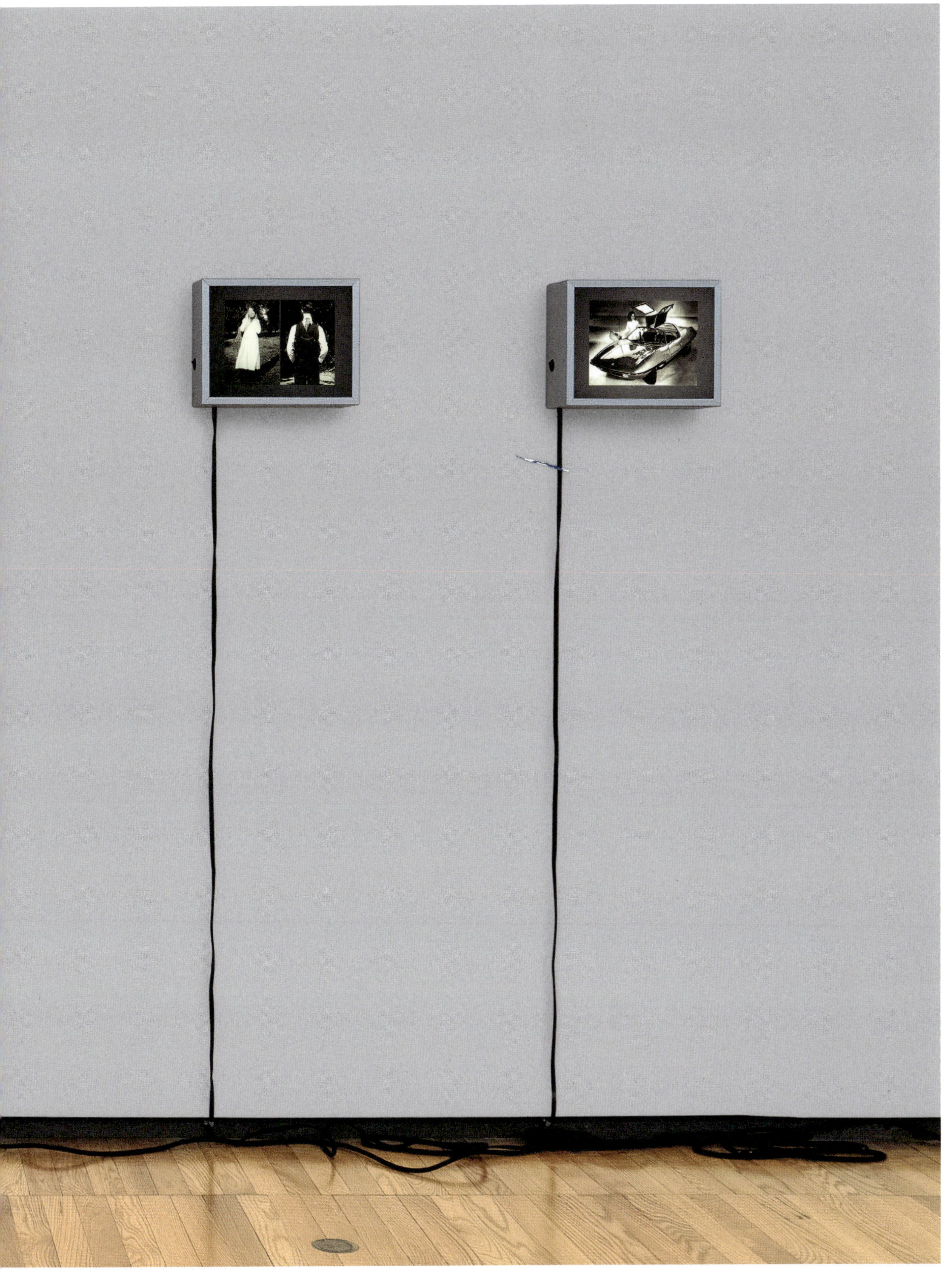

Untitled (pink girl), 2011. FujiClear and aluminum lightbox

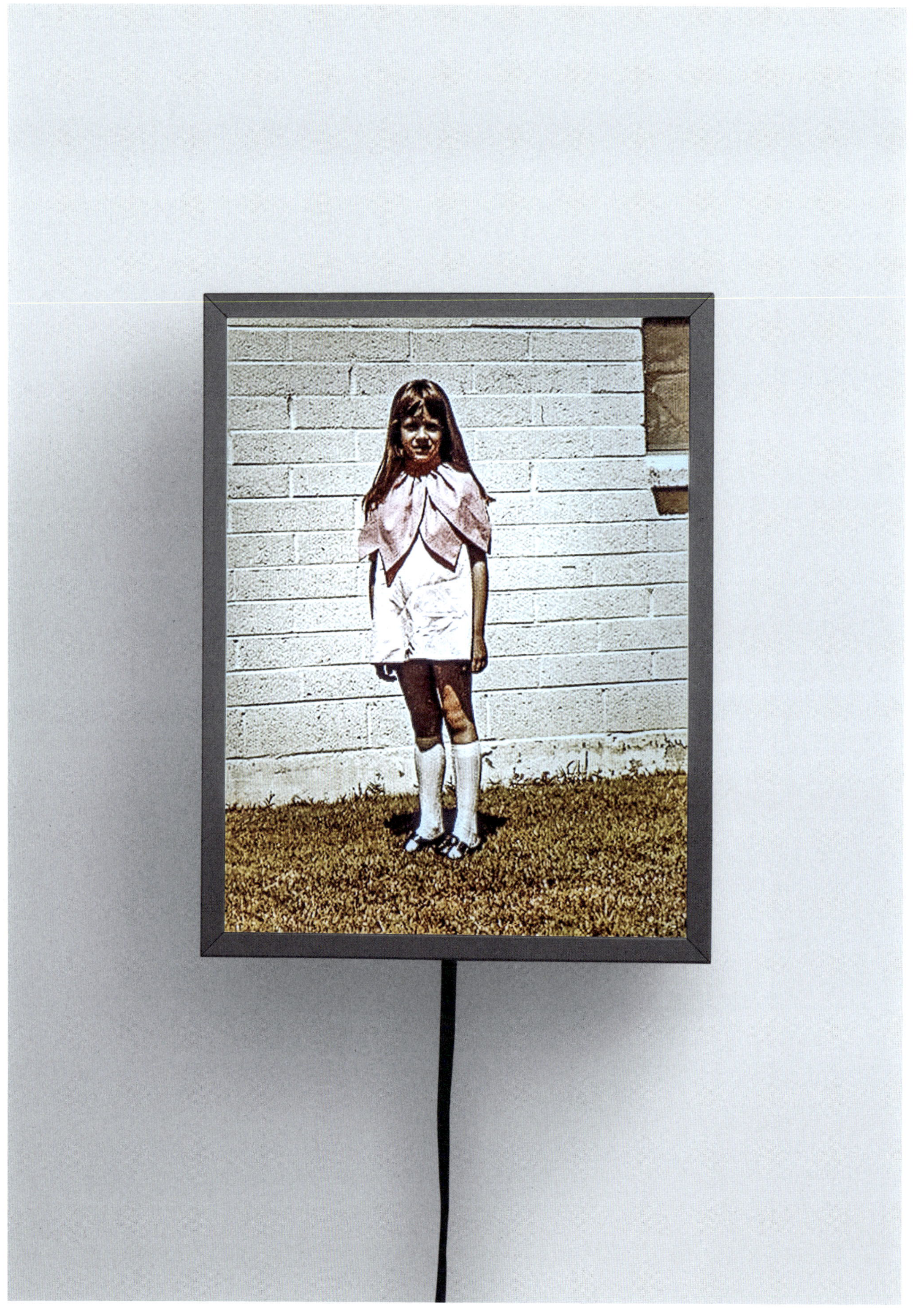

TOP Installation view of *Looks Bad*, Iceberg Projects, Chicago, 2011

BOTTOM Installation view of *I Am Not Here Anymore But I Am Fine*, Las Cienegas Projects, Los Angeles, 2010

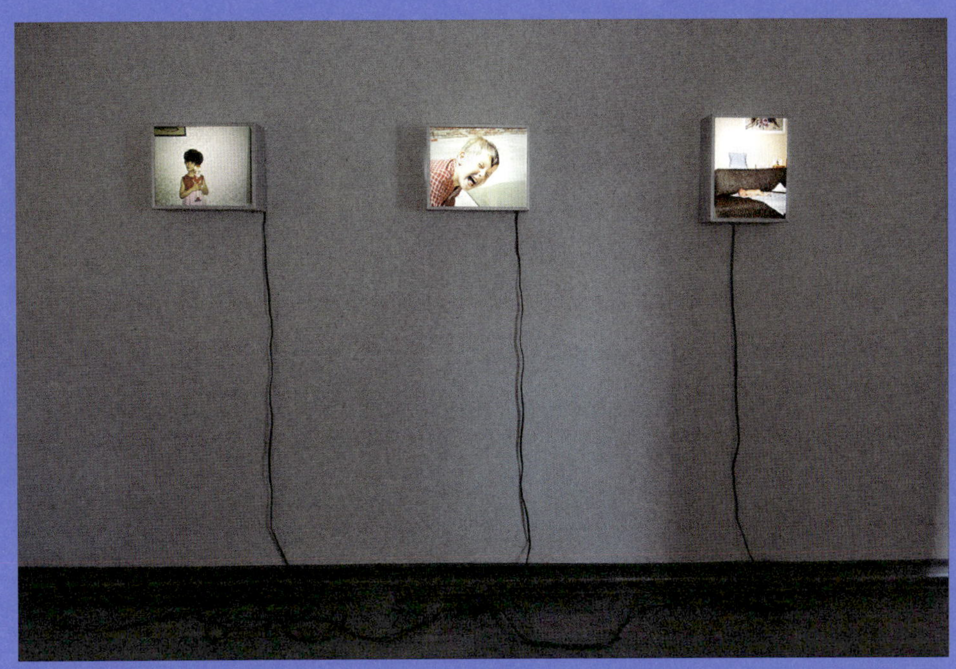

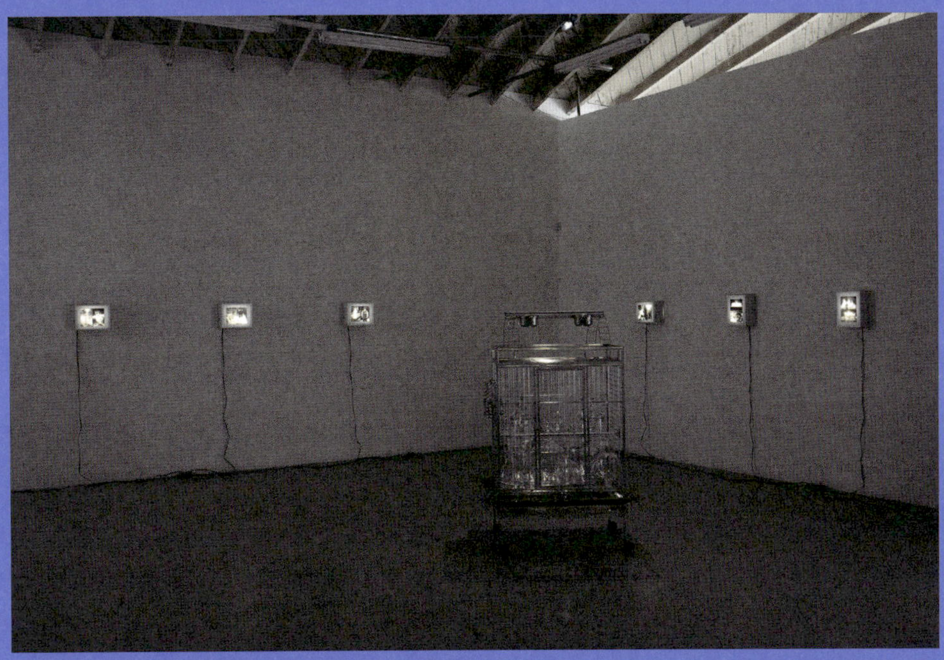

LEFT TO RIGHT, TOP TO BOTTOM Flyers for CalArts courses taught by Millie Wilson: "Horror & Humor: Hysterical Boys," Fall 1995; "Femme Fatales/2: Noir and Its Double," Spring 2004; "Not a Pretty Picture: Teen Cinema as Genre," ca. 1999; "Sex, Art and Critique," Fall 1990

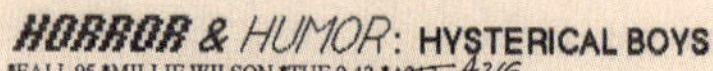

HORROR & HUMOR: HYSTERICAL BOYS
*FALL 95 *MILLIE WILSON *TUE 9-12 *~~A217~~ A216

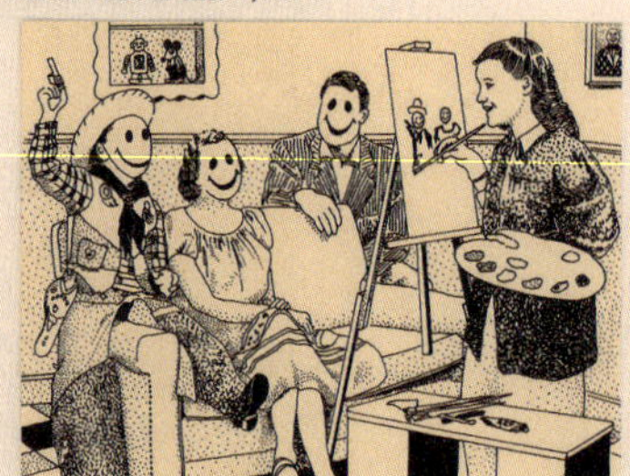

Readings:

Men, Women and Chain Saws: Gender in the Modern Horror Film by Carol J. Clover, 1992

Laughing Screaming: Modern Hollywood Horror & Comedy by William Paul, 1994

Films screened include *Night Life, Fast Times at Ridgemont High, Carrie, Texas Chain Saw Massacre II, Porky's, Blazing Saddles, Car Wash, Revenge of the Nerds, Poltergeist, The Exorcist, Don't Look Now* and others.

Roughly the last month of the semester will be used for student projects.

Jessica Rath is the Teaching Assistant for the class.

Books are available in the book store and are on reserve in the library.

Millie Wilson Art/Art Spring 2004 3.0 units
Femmes Fatales/2: Noir and Its Double AR231a

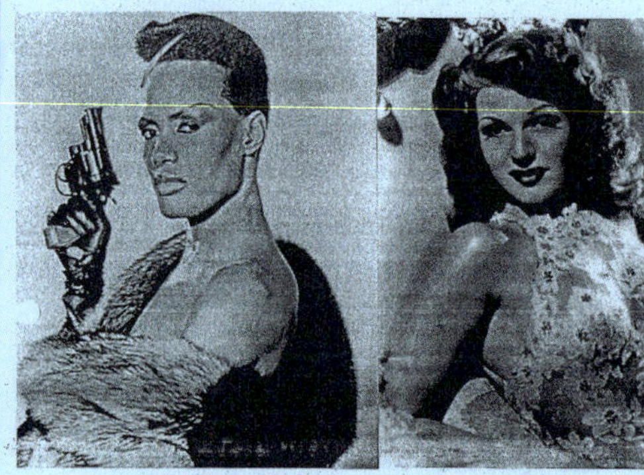

This seminar will investigate the construction of femininity as a significant, determining aspect of modernism and modernity. Topics will included evil women, mass culture, fashion, shopping, film and others. Readings and screenings of visual materials are required. Full participation as a seminar member is expected. Projects due during the latter half of the semester. Recommended for fourth year and graduate students. Permission of the instructor is required. Limited to 15 students. Most readings will be in the following books: **Women in Film Noir, Noir Anxiety**, and **Black & White & Noir.**

NOT A PRETTY PICTURE

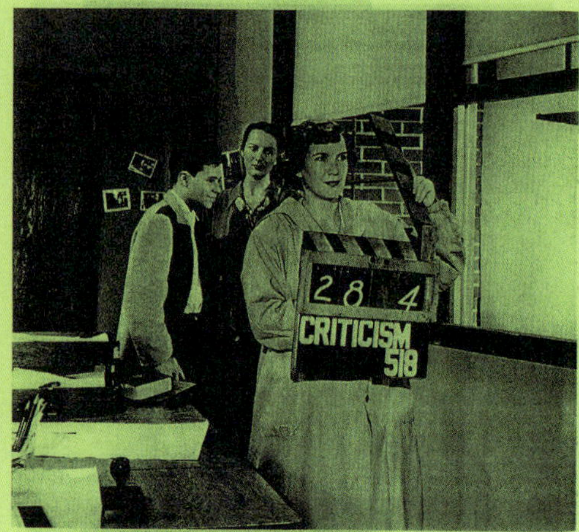

Filming the yearbook office scene for *Effective Criticism*, 1951.

TEEN CINEMA AS GENRE
AR230M Sem. I, II 3.0 units
Millie Wilson D214 Tue. 9-12

This seminar will investigate teen movies produced in the last two decades, films from the ridiculous to the ambitious, but having in common a target audience which has become significant to the print, film, and cyber industries. Each semester will engage different aspects of the genre. Screenings and readings will be the basis for class discussion, and projects in the form of seminar film selections will be expected. Enrollment limited to 20. Permission of instructor required.

SEX, ART AND CRITIQUE/M. WILSON, FALL, 1990

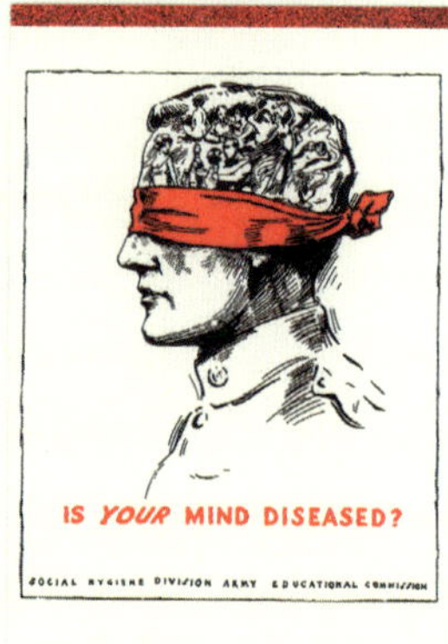

This course will address the prevalence of discourses of sexuality in recent art, as well the particular social and political significance of these practices. This will be done alternately through an examination of some of those works, critiques of work by students, and the reading of Passion and Power: Sexuality in History, edited by Kathy Peiss and Christina Simmons, with Robert A. Padgug.

A group exhibition (THE SEX SHOW??!!) has been scheduled for Nov. 25-Dec. 1 in D301.

For the first class on Tuesday, Sept. 11, please bring some representation (slide, tape, etc.) of a relevant work to be discussed by the group.

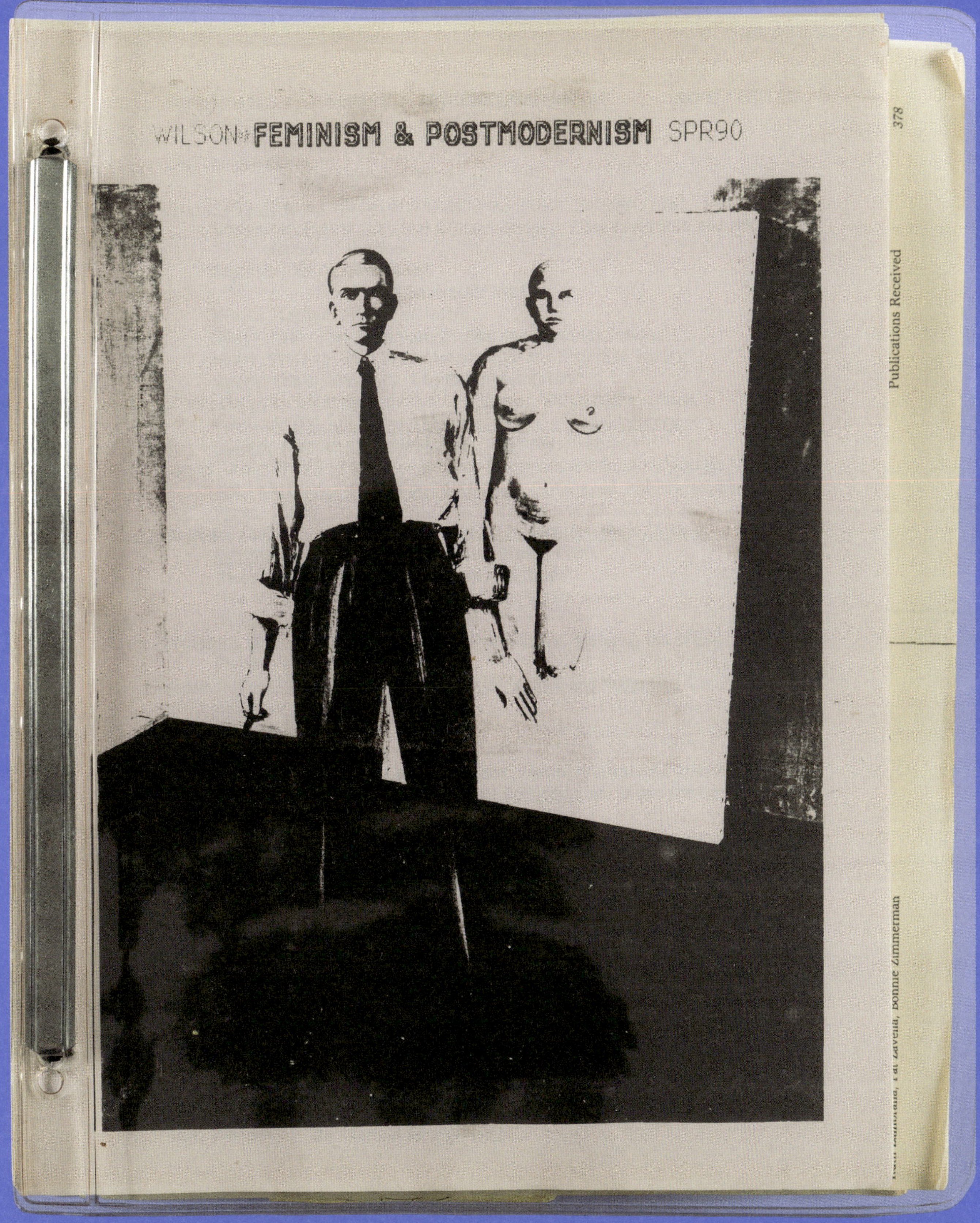
WILSON FEMINISM & POSTMODERNISM SPR90
378
Publications Received

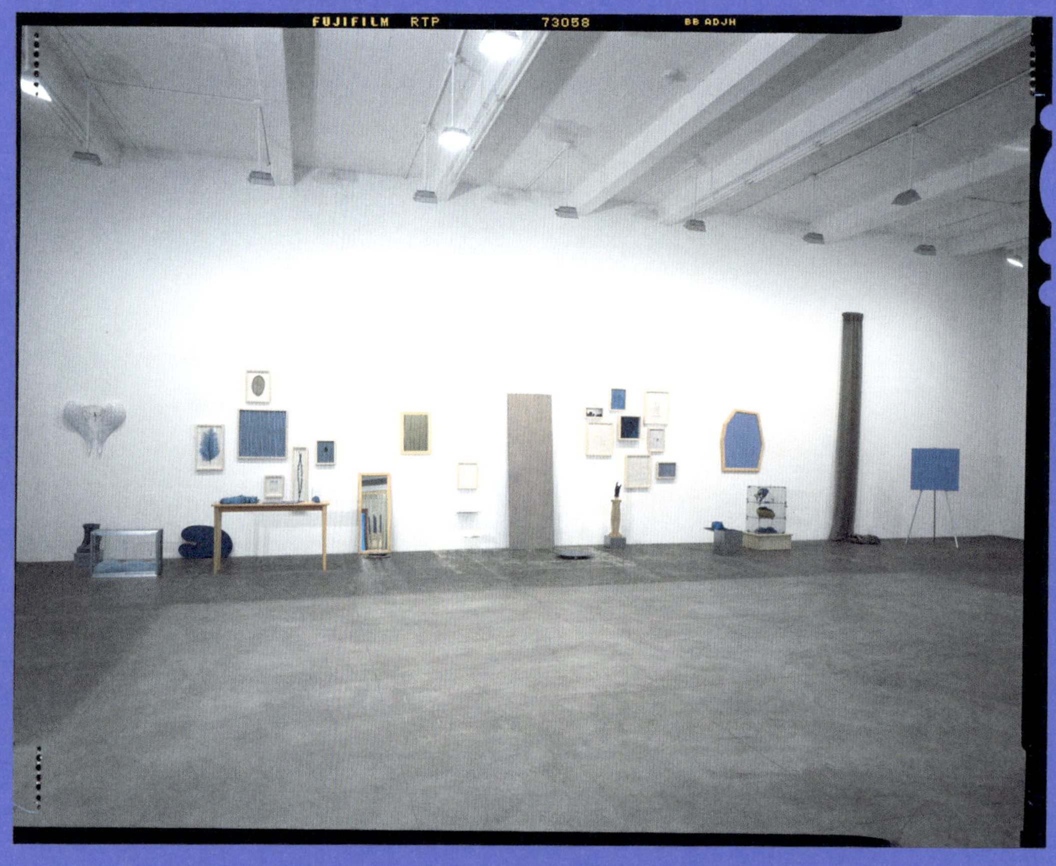

Installation view of *Something Blue* at Matthew Marks Gallery, New York, 1998

White Girl, 1995. Synthetic hair, fabric, and wood stand

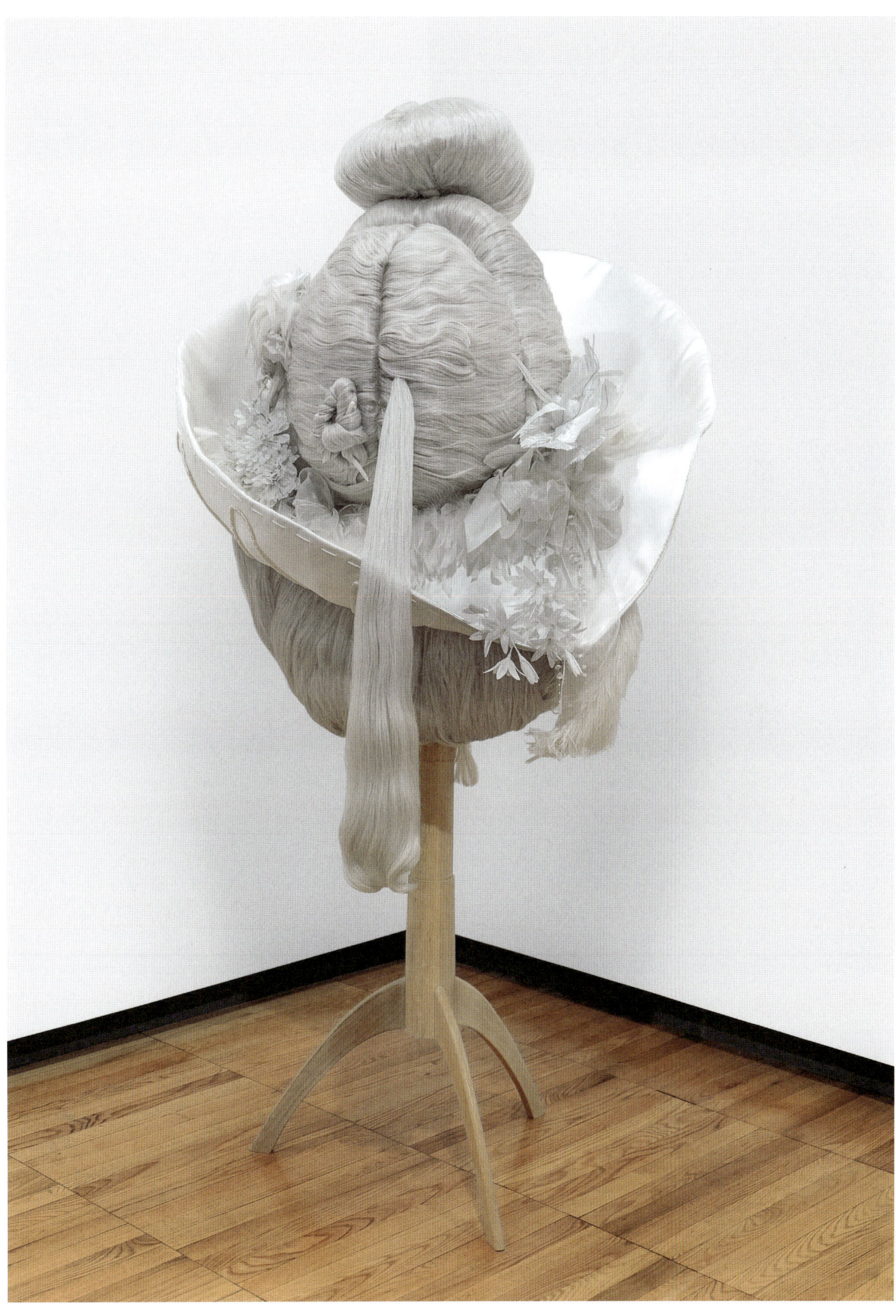

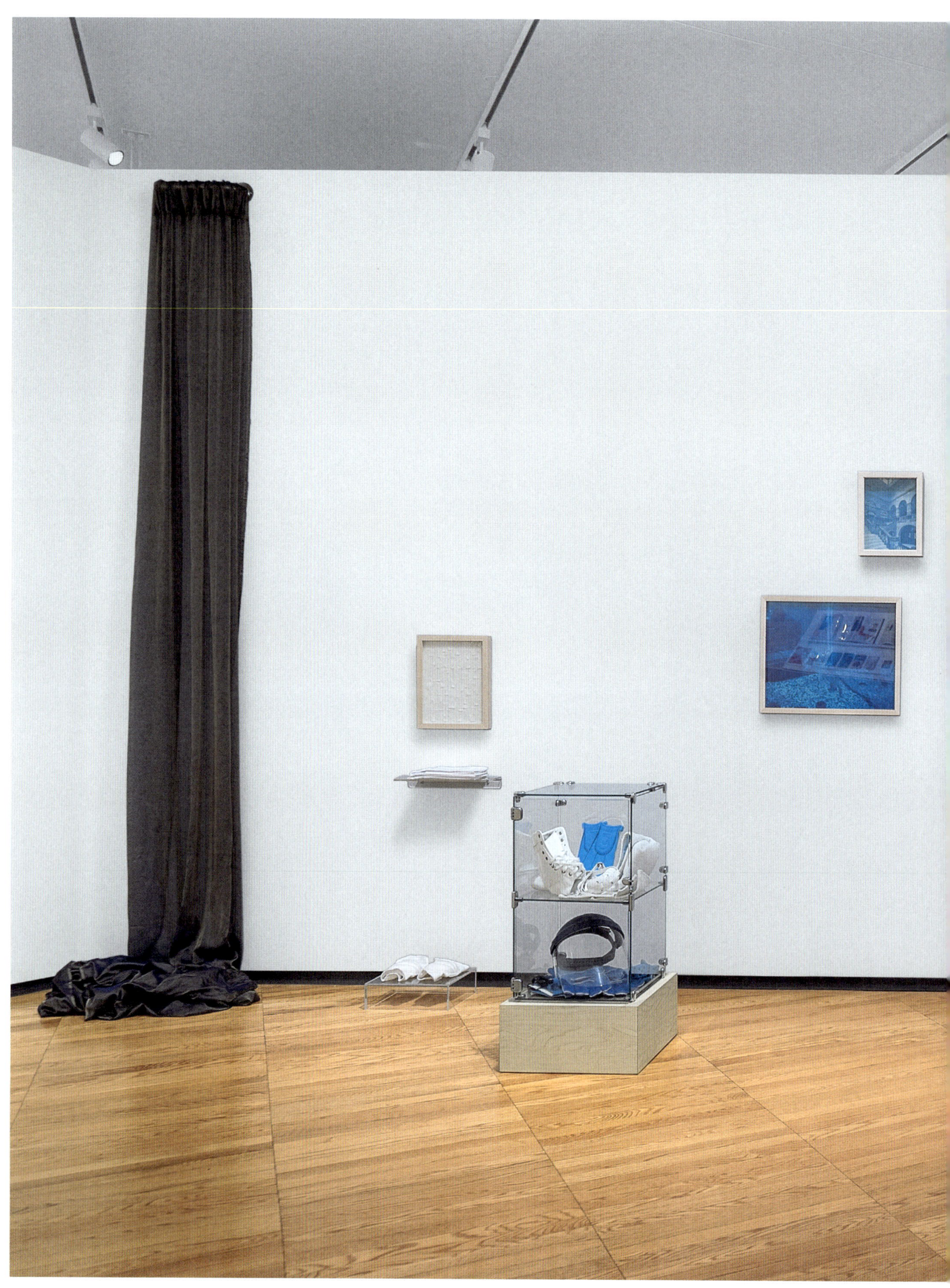

PAGES 156–58 *Something Blue*, 1998–2000. Installation views at Krannert Art Museum, 2024

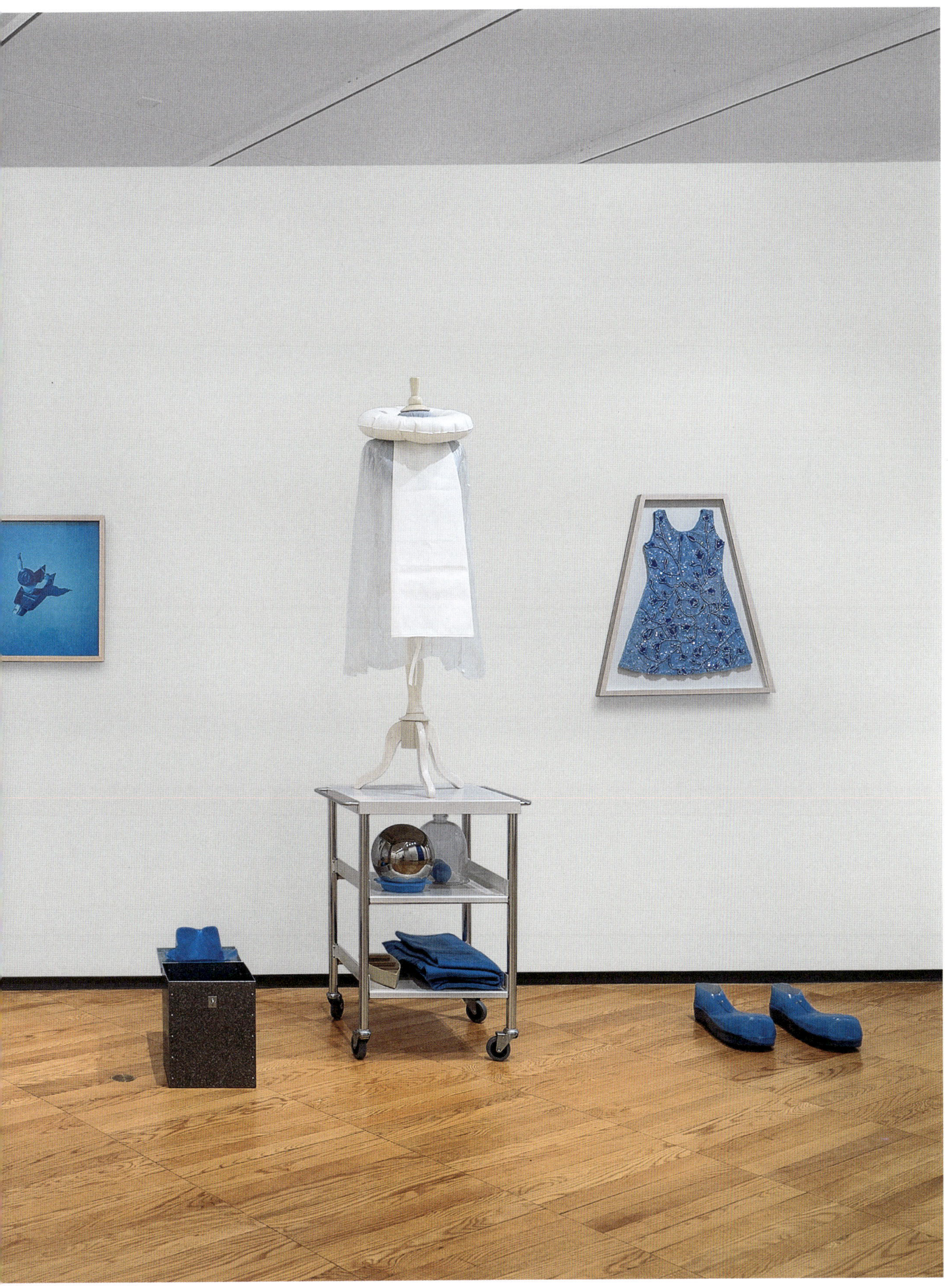

OPPOSITE Detail of *Deceit*, 1998. Wood hand, glove, latex brain, plaster pedestal, and aluminum box

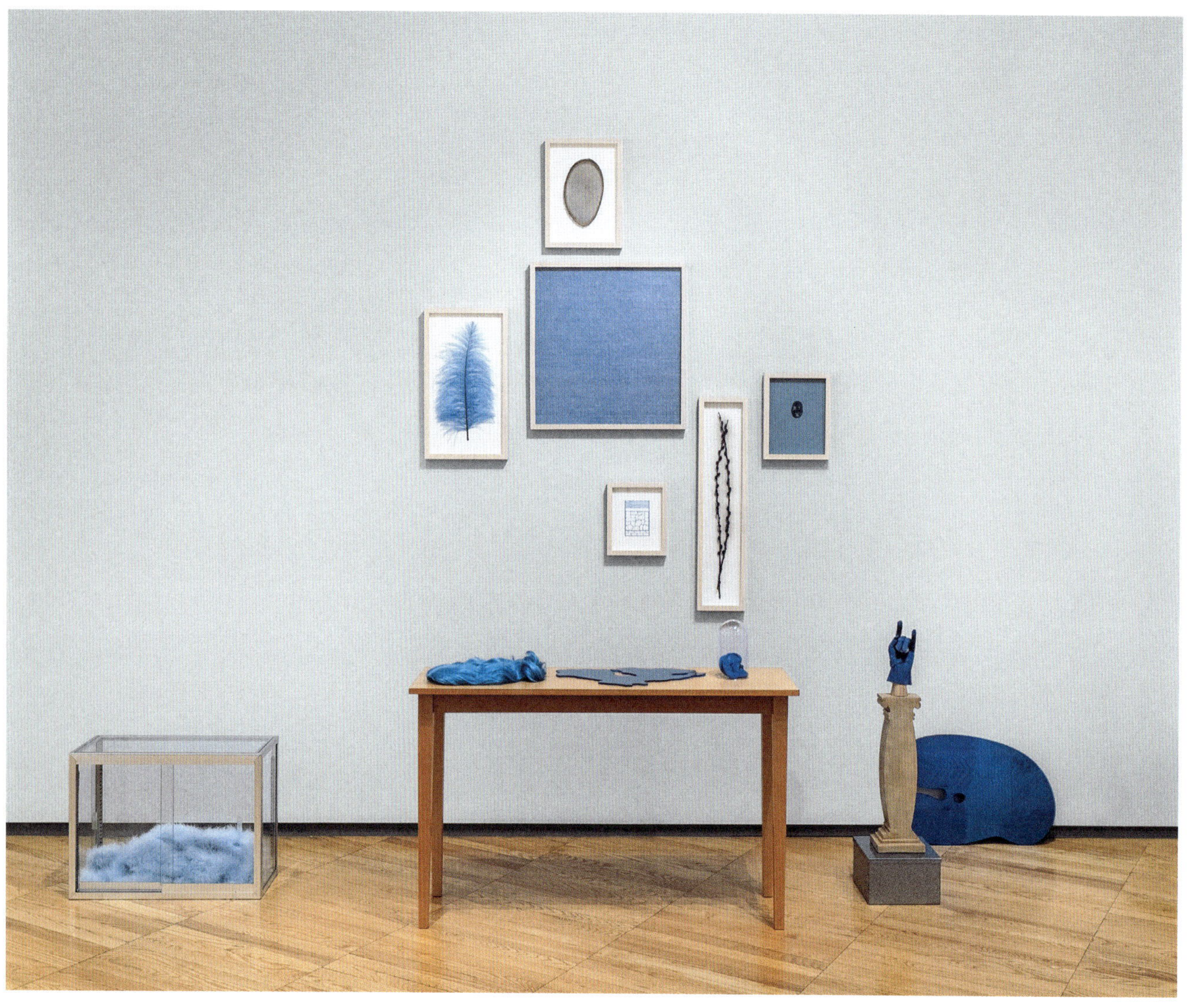

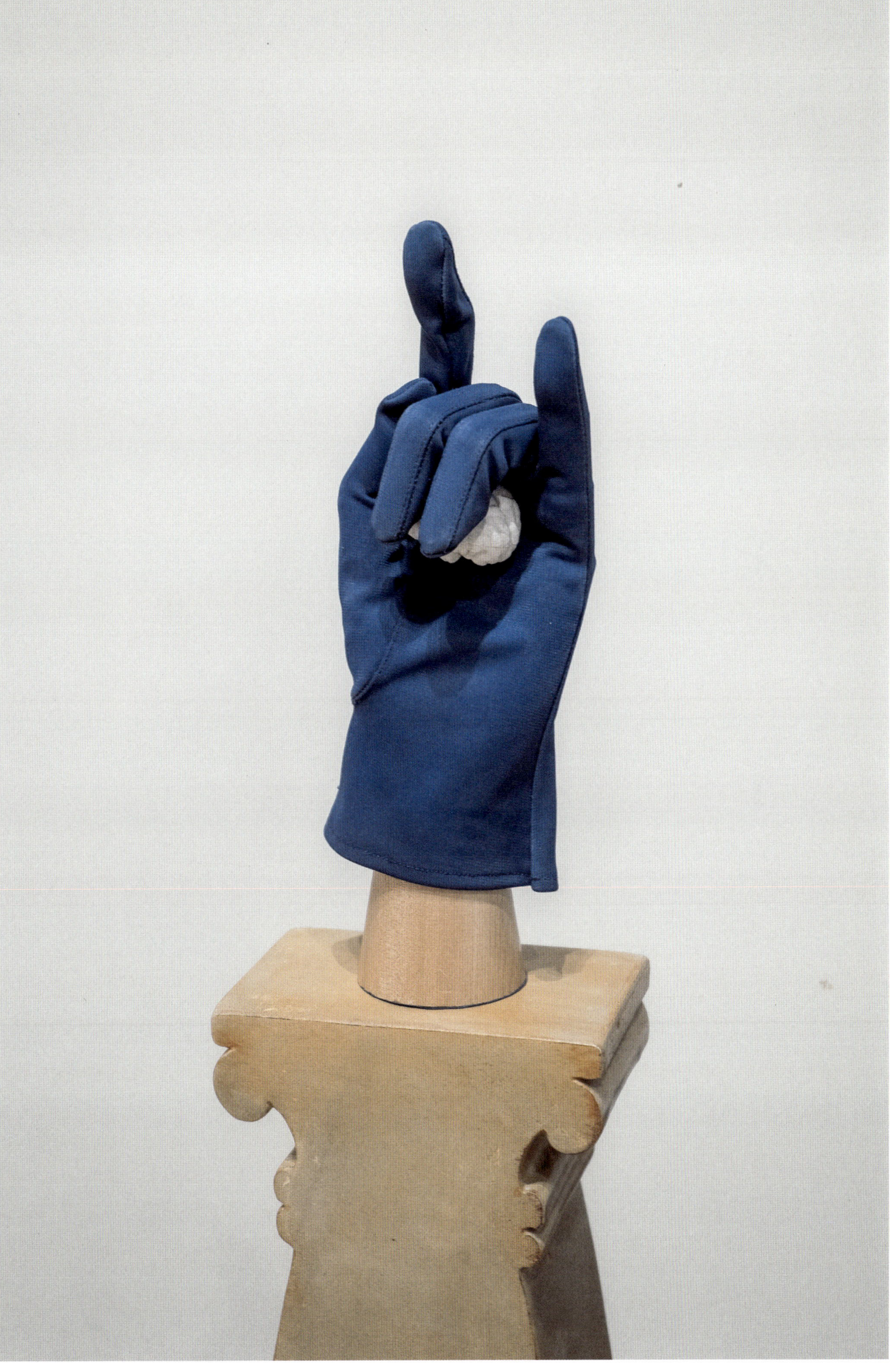

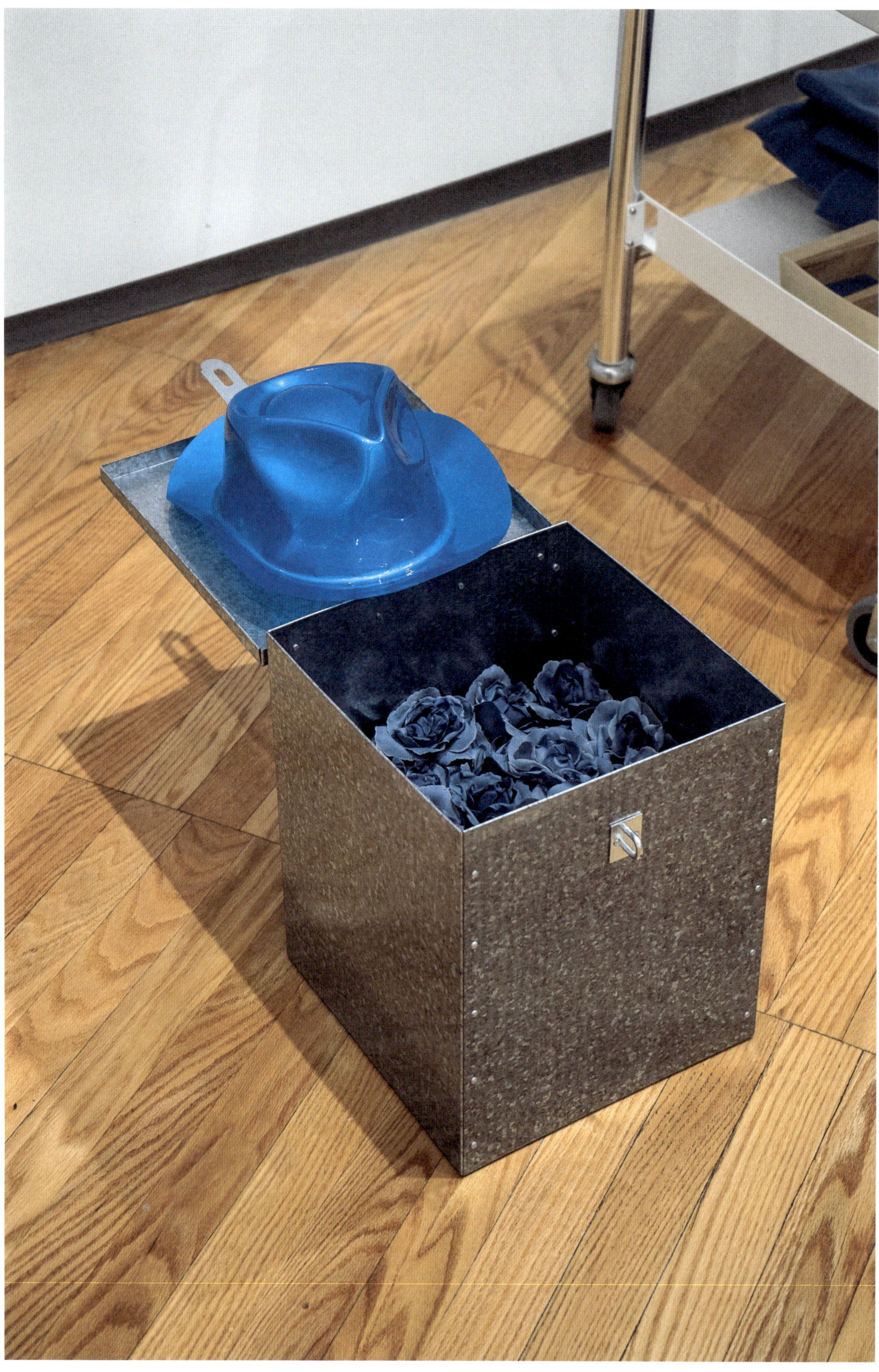

OPPOSITE *Archive*, 1998. Aluminum box, faux roses, and plastic fedora

TOP Detail from *Captive*, 1998. Wood table with blue wig, glass bell jar, rubber ears, and plexiglass

BOTTOM *Scuba*, 1999. Plastic shoes and sand

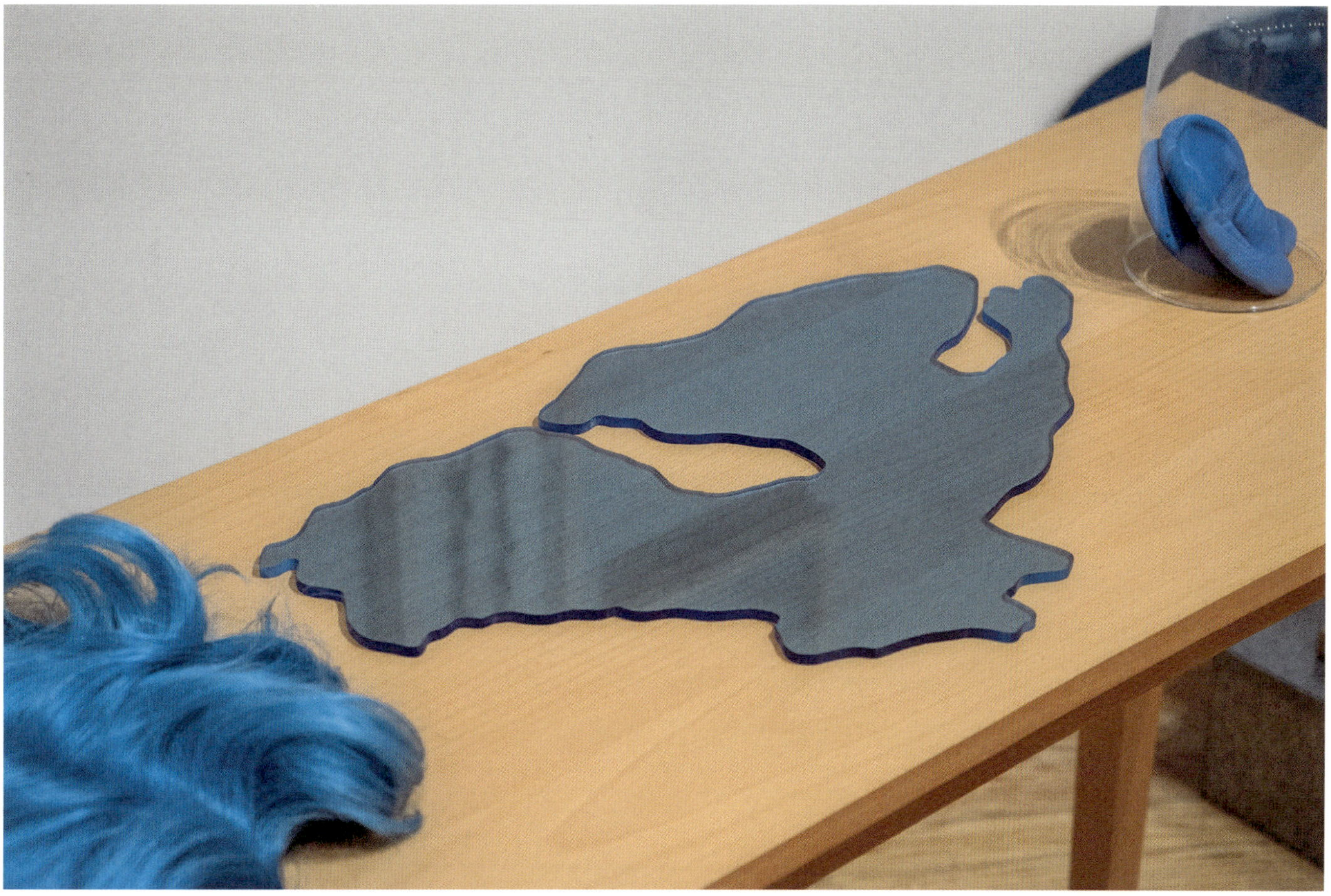

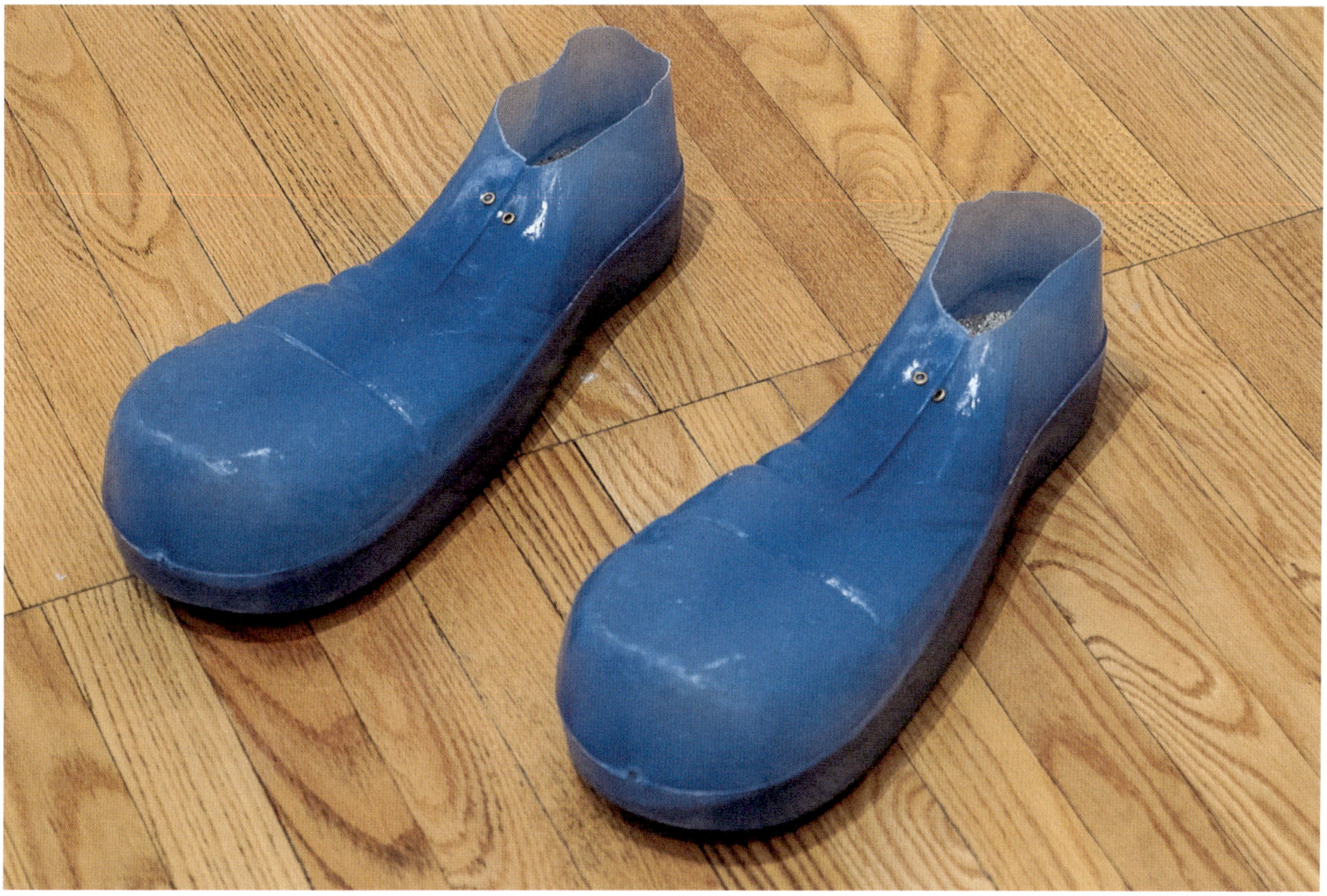

Her best friend died in the autumn. A few weeks later a thrift store run by an AIDS service organization opened in her neighborhood. She began to go there, sometimes as often as once a day, to check the racks of men's clothing. She had worn secondhand clothes for almost as long as she could remember. By ragpicking patiently and obsessively, she had eventually achieved the look of a privileged dandy.

The new store offered an unusual number of beautifully tailored jackets, shirts and trousers, and gradually it became the source of her entire wardrobe. Sometimes it seemed that the secrets and desires of her own body could be revealed in these acts of recuperation. At some point she realized that her shopping was an archaeology of thousands of lost lives. Like the chatty obituaries in gay newspapers, never had the details of gay men's lives been so carefully recorded. The more they vanished, the more they were represented. Her costumes, she came to understand, were evidence that what remained of beloved friends were garments scattered across the city, and beyond.

Trousers (for Tony), 1992. Incised bronze plaques and brilliant blue wall paint

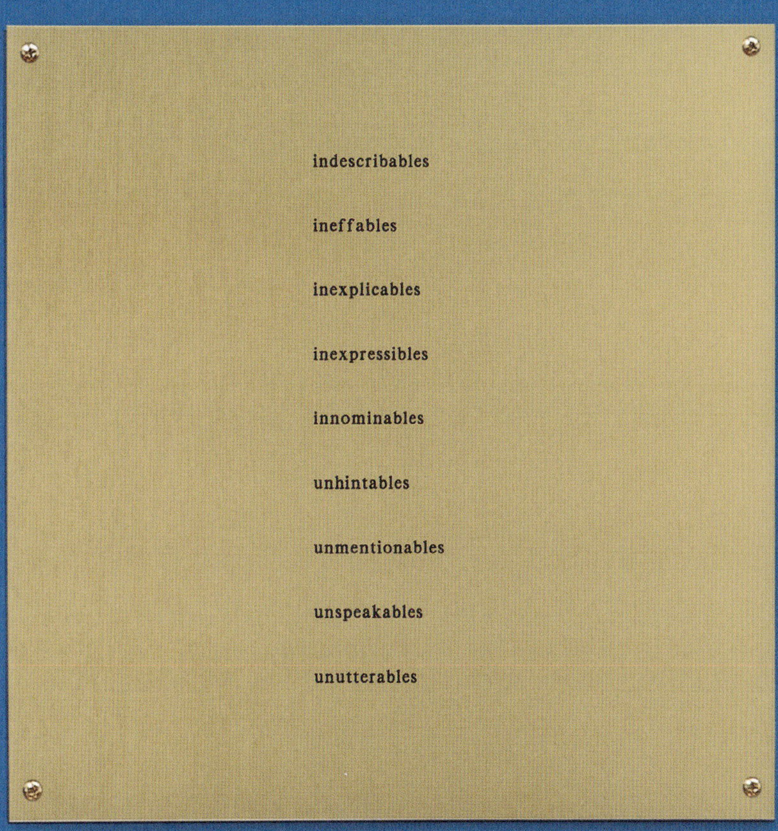

Student in Lesbos, 1992. Neon on aluminum

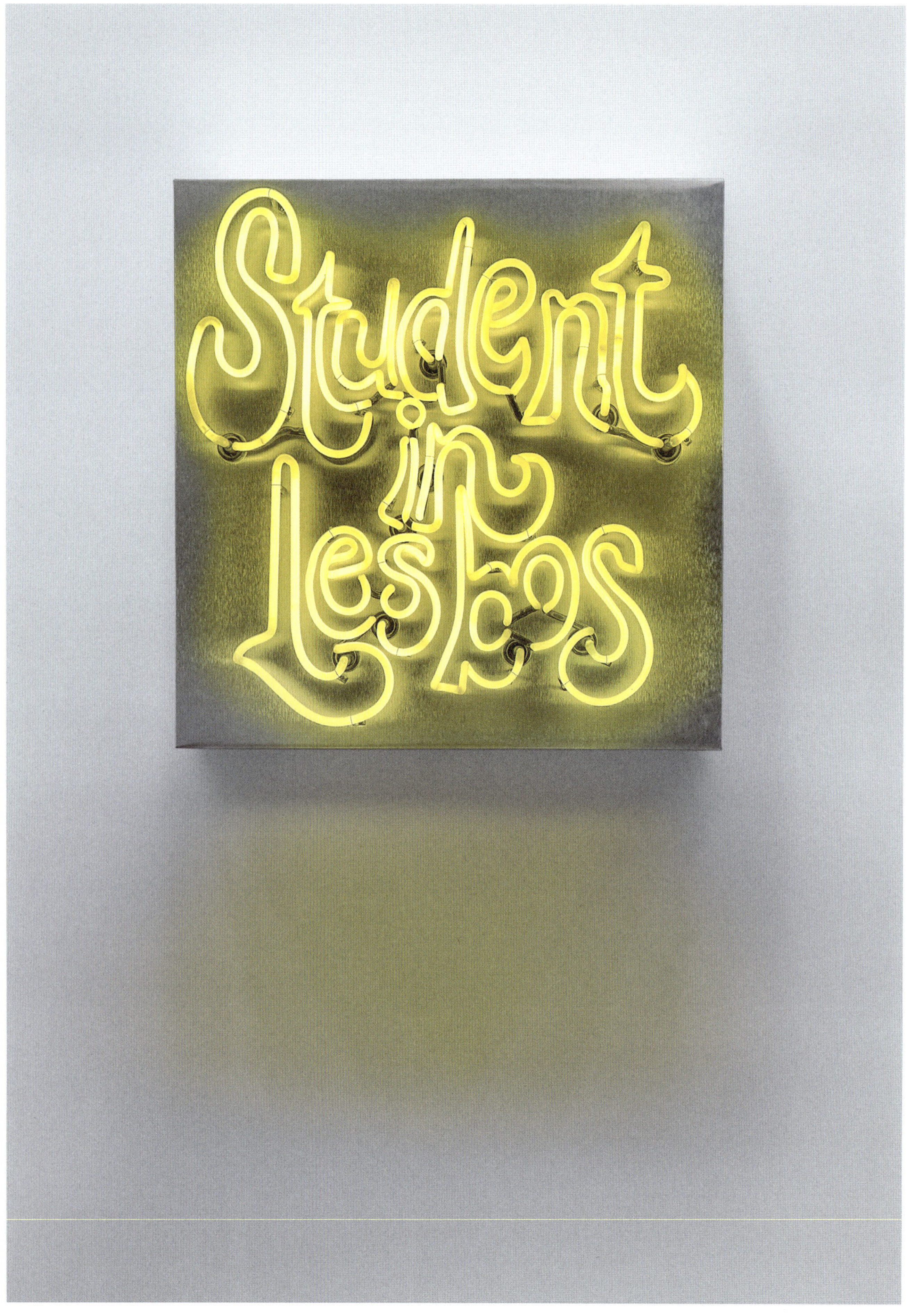

STUDENTS IN LESBOS: A CONVERSATION

Beatriz Cortez, Richard Hawkins,
Kang Seung Lee, and Jess Rath

Moderated by David Evans Frantz

Between 1985 and 2014, Millie Wilson taught in the Program in Art at the esteemed California Institute of the Arts, commonly known as CalArts, in Valencia, California, outside Los Angeles. Wilson came to CalArts from the University of Illinois Urbana-Champaign, where she taught for two years after completing her MFA at the University of Houston. During her twenty-nine years at CalArts, Wilson's pedagogy emphasized cultural theory, art history, and popular culture, via courses dedicated to queer cultural production, such as camp and drag; courses examining the cultural politics of the 1960s and 1970s; and numerous courses on cinema, including focused curricula on the genres of film noir, horror, and teen movies, among other topics. During her tenure, Wilson taught and mentored generations of artists, including the four artists in conversation here: Richard Hawkins (MFA 1988), Jess Rath (MFA 1996), Beatriz Cortez (MFA 2015), and Kang Seung Lee (MFA 2015). This conversation was recorded on Zoom and transcribed on May 6, 2024. It has been edited for length and clarity.

David Evans Frantz
Could you each introduce yourselves? Richard, do you want to start us off?

Richard Hawkins
Sure. I'm Richard Hawkins. I studied at CalArts with Millie from the fall of 1986 to the spring of 1988.

Jess Rath
I'm Jess Rath. I studied with Millie from the fall of 1994 through the spring of 1996.

Beatriz Cortez
I'm Beatriz Cortez. I was at CalArts between 2013 and 2015, and I met Millie through Kang. During my second semester at CalArts I was also Millie's teaching assistant.

Kang Seung Lee
I'm Kang Seung Lee and I was in the same class with Beatriz at CalArts between 2013 and 2015. Millie was my mentor, though she left at the end of fall 2014, so that was actually a short time. But we had a very special relationship.

David Thank you. I'm so excited you're all participating in the conversation! CalArts has an incredibly storied history of critical pedagogy, most often associated with Michael Asher's post-studio seminars and Judy Chicago and Miriam Schapiro's Feminist Art Program of the 1970s.[1] From your experience, how were Millie's pedagogical theory and practice aligned with those histories, and how did her teaching depart from them?

Richard Well, I would say, as the oldest person here, or the one who went to CalArts the earliest, I think you would also include in that history a kind of John Baldessarian ethos that was culturally critical yet somehow still a darling of the galleries. So it's not just Asher's institutional critique, it's also this kind of merging with a Baldessarian effect.

Millie was relatively new at CalArts, and she (among others) was instrumental in creating a context to be out and gay, but she also drew on Foucault, for example, as a beginning to talk about queerness. Catherine Opie and I arrived at the same time, Tony Greene and Doug Ischar a year earlier, William E. Jones, a year later. Millie was very involved, as well as Catherine Lord, in a focus on sexuality and representation. Millie was at the forefront of that. She was the kind of boots on the ground for that information, I think.

Jess By the time I got to CalArts, William E. Jones was teaching Asher's post-studio class, so having sexuality and gender as part of the critique was in the room, if not always welcome. I was coming from the Midwest, and even though I had worked with a couple of artists from California before I got to CalArts, the theoretical focus of teaching at the school was still really new to me. The ethos of Asher's class and the idea of approaching institutional critique as a sort of stripped-down model of thinking about things—getting to the bare bones of institutional structures, including architecture, language, and political systems—was still very prevalent. The idea was that anything that would exceed this process of intellectual unpacking could be discarded (e.g., class, race, sexuality, gender).

At the time, I was interested in ideas about the body and decoration, and how we could use those within institutional critique, and those ideas just didn't fly at that time in post-studio for some people. So we would be fighting for ground for different representations of gender and sexuality while doing institutional critique. This struggle was sort of constantly being shifted and negotiated in most classes, and Millie would hold the ground—within her own classes, studio visits with students, and more broadly within the program.

Millie was not there to gatekeep around sexuality or gender. Essentialism was out. We were dancing all night in glitter. I felt no connection to the feminism of Judy Chicago or Suzanne Lacy or the Feminist Art Program of before as I was doing both male (welding) and female (sewing) labor. The distinctions were meaningless as something to base art on by this time. Queer theory was there but very confined to those who qualified as gay or lesbian by sexual acts in the day-to-day at CalArts. If you fucked men and women, you were a traitor, and your approach was invalidated. It was like high school. But not with Millie. It was always fluid with Millie and that was something I really learned how to negotiate from her, especially as someone being gender fluid and bisexual before we had those terms.

Beatriz By the time I got to CalArts in 2013, this whole discourse of institutional critique had to be explained to me because the school had changed a lot. CalArts was a space where critical studies, critical theory, and philosophy were part of the conversation all the time, especially because Millie and Leslie Dick were there. CalArts had the presence of these two very strong artists who each had a particular way of doing things. For me, they complemented each other in many different ways, and it was a joy to see.

To me, Millie was so important. I loved how Millie brought a critique of queerness as a construction that was often presumed to be solely male. When we would discuss queer theory, for Millie, it was always fluid and playful, and it included monsters and vampires and films, and I remember being her assistant and laying on the carpet in the room watching movies because we had a class that was all films, many vampire films, that we would discuss. I remember thinking that part of criticality was to have fun, to have a moment of fun and joy with others, and to have a community where you would feel comfortable, and enjoy having a conversation about the films that you were watching. The figure of the monster has been theorized in nonhuman schools of thinking and also in that fantastic talk "Can the Monster Speak?" by Paul B. Preciado.[2] When I read these things today, I always think of Millie's class discussions about the monster.

I also had the opportunity to be Millie's teaching assistant. And that was really fun, too, because I was able to sit down with Millie, think about what she was going to do in the class, and how I could assist her—I didn't need to do much, I could bring the projector or whatever—but having access to her thinking was really special for me.

Kang Like Beatriz, by the time I got to CalArts, Asher had already passed and the legacy of the school as a place for a certain type of institutional critique and California conceptualism still existed, but it was also not that special anymore, because those ideas were already shared by many professors teaching in other schools. That way of looking at art was part of the mainstream, in my opinion. To me, the scope of CalArts's pedagogy was not as diverse or international as I expected, especially for me as an international student originally from South Korea who moved to Los Angeles from Mexico City and lived in many different places in between.

To be honest, during my time at the school, Millie was withdrawn and quite fed up with the institutional bureaucracy. As a queer woman and teacher, Millie often mentored the queer and trans students, female students, and students of color, because the faculty wasn't actually that diverse. She took on a lot more work compared to her peers. Millie was still really willing to mentor all these students, and I was obviously one of the lucky ones to have her, and she understood my perspective coming from a more international experience rather than the identity politics of the United States or Europe.

Beatriz To follow up on what Kang was saying, CalArts was a place where I experienced so much joy, and I learned so much, and I took a break to read so many things, and to have so many conversations. But at the same time, it was a place that was not very diverse. I didn't know many people from El Salvador. I had to constantly speak about an art world that was foreign to me, and this was not the art world that I was always interested in talking about, or the one I knew. I constantly had to explain and translate things. In the years I was there, Kang's company and conversation were really important for my sanity, because Kang also came from elsewhere. I had to constantly remind people what my name was, constantly explain how to pronounce it, constantly tell them where El Salvador is, constantly explain so many things.

Millie's classes were amazing, and I loved them, but what I recall the most about Millie was what she signified for us, which was a place where we could talk about diversity, and about the world, and about the things that were missing in the library, the things that were missing in the classes, and the issues that were not discussed in the other classes. Millie was fed up with a lot of things within the institution, but she was not tired of us. She was not tired of her students. She had energy for that, and she had fun. And she made time to do things with us. I remember when she retired, she didn't want a party, but we gave her a party, and she partied with us for a long time. Millie had time to have the conversations that we felt were not always present in other classes. That was beautiful and important.

It's really significant what Kang is saying, that supporting students from different backgrounds and positionalities ended up falling on the shoulders of women professors. Those conversations and Millie's philosophical framework were not aligned with the Feminist Art Program, for example, nor with essentializing, identity-based ideas about how to be a woman, or what it meant to be a woman, or the concept of "woman." It was completely open-minded.

What I now miss, or feel kind of shortchanged by, was that I didn't get a chance to see Millie's work installed in galleries or museums. I was able to see it on occasions when Kang and I assisted Millie with moving her work in storage, or when it appeared in small group installations. But to me, what's exciting is to see this other part of Millie through the exhibition you're organizing now, David. When we were at CalArts, Millie was really generous and took the time to have the conversations that we needed to have. But we didn't have a chance to talk about her work, and that's something that I think I would have loved to do.

Richard When I was a teaching assistant for a foundation class with Millie and John Mandel (or it may have been Stephen Prina), there was a student from Somalia who wanted to make work around their culture. The class was having a hard time getting their minds out of a Western canon, and I remember it was specifically Millie who pushed for a kind of open-mindedness. This was around 1986, and Millie was only three years into teaching. It took me years to learn those qualities of an educator that she seemed to have from the start.

The late 1980s were a strange but incredibly interesting time at CalArts. Millie was working to integrate some of the newest theory into class and was very supportive of discussions around sexual difference. And at the same time, we were at the height of the AIDS epidemic. Numerous thinkers and activists were coming through the school, at the invitation of folks like Millie as well as Catherine Lord, the dean of the School of Art. Simon Watney spoke at CalArts about his writing and activism, most notably addressed in his influential essay "The Spectacle of AIDS."[3] And Douglas Crimp was there pretty consistently, and there as an activist rather than as a representative of his more art historical interests—you know, with *October*, on the Wunderkammer, commodity critique, institutional critique. John Greyson, the Toronto-based video artist, was also around, and if anybody was using the word "queer," it would have been John.

David Richard, thank you for talking about the late 1980s at CalArts. Jess, how did the campus context shift in the 1990s, with the rising culture wars?

Jess I came to CalArts having been the lead project coordinator for the public art exhibition *Culture in Action* curated by Mary Jane Jacob in Chicago. I oversaw the projects of Mark Dion, Suzanne Lacy, Daniel J. Martinez, among others. When I arrived at CalArts, I had rejected much of the legacy of the Feminist Art Program for myself. All the identity politics, both internally and externally, didn't make for an expansive way of thinking or making new meaning. And I thought my job as an artist was to make new meaning and new connections, and I didn't find anybody who was doing that because everybody, mostly faculty members, were gatekeeping. But Millie had this way of cutting right through everything. I mean some of the things that she would say like, "You love who you love when you love them." That enabled me to say, "Just fuck off. I don't need to be labeled, ever."

I had this experience of working with artists in Chicago, like Lacy and Martinez, that felt like community resource extraction, that these were not genuine relationships going on. I was pissed, and when I came to CalArts I didn't know who to study with. That doesn't mean that I knew very much, right, I was twenty-three years old. But when I was working with Millie it felt absolutely genuine, and it felt like she was really showing up in a way that was meant to encourage us to think that we had visions of the future and ways of making meaning that needed to be explored. There were some things that Mike Kelley would say, too, about not being afraid of what your interests were, that you could be very involved in whatever your thing is that you really love. Go ahead and go deep into it because you will find a whole world in there that will start to change meaning culturally for other people. Like, just go in.

Richard That's what I remember, that kind of focus on the individual, despite what cultural expectations might be, even when it comes to identity. It seems very Millie to me.

Jess And I don't want to erase what I hear from Kang and Beatriz, that Millie was also holding space for what elsewhere was being culturally erased—she wasn't letting that happen either. There's space for all that's here and there's responsibility for other people to engage. And she was able to do both. In the studio you would have these long meetings that were like gold. There was nothing like them.

Richard Subjectivity is valid. Subjectivity is not only valid but cherished.

Jess Yeah.

Kang I came to CalArts as an older student. I had already had a full-time corporate job for nine years while also doing other things. I didn't major in art as an undergraduate. CalArts was also my first time going to an American school (much less a private art school), and I had a hard time, especially the first semester. One big reason was that I didn't have much interest in the American-centric art, history, or art history that was being discussed. I was a lot more into fashion and design history. Millie and Leslie Dick were the two people who understood this and how I was trying to incorporate these other histories into my artistic practice and trying to make something out of that. Millie was very into fashion history. I don't know if you all knew that. She introduced me to Valerie Steele's writings and gave me some catalogues, looking at this fashion history from queer women's perspectives. I think she was very interested in that. Millie had an extensive collection of teapots, and so you know, she was very interested in objects, and the history of industrial design, and all of that. Millie actually gave me two Thierry Mugler jackets with 1980s power shoulders. She has a wide range of interests outside fine art or contemporary art history. And we can really see that in her work. She was encouraging students to pay more attention to things going on outside of contemporary art and the art world, and I think that was really important for me. Millie was the person who introduced me to Simon Watney's writings, because I was just learning the history of AIDS activism in the United States and Europe. She gave me several recommendations of books and readings, which would go on to profoundly impact my artistic practice.

Jess The importance of fashion and adornment have a long, if under-recognized, history at CalArts. In the spring of 1995, for instance, Kimberli Meyer put on a big fashion show. It featured a raised ramp with a dozen cars. The car headlights were pointed at the stage, and we all had made clothing for this very large, extensive evening fashion show, and Millie was a part of that. I remember Mark Bradford wore this hoop dress and Leslie Dick emceed. This was Kimberli's production, yet it was born out of the community that Leslie and Millie had created. There were no other faculty participating.

There was this feeling that there was this power within fashion and within our bodies, that we could express other versions of what was going on in the studio, and Millie was the one who held space for that idea, regardless of whether it was in the studio, the gallery, or on the street, you could disrupt through fashion.

David And you certainly get that. All those ideas come through in Millie's practice and how her work disrupts the body. And relies on a less assimilationist kind of queerness or femininity.

Richard There are aspects of Millie's work I am only truly understanding now. In the late 1980s, I was put off by references to Duchamp. And that's only because my ass was sitting in so many fucking classes at CalArts and the idiot po-mo anti-painters would always uncritically bring up the readymade tube of paint, and it became just a frustrating piece of BS. But Millie's take on the readymade and Duchamp, it's only literally in the past few days of going back through the work that I've been able to get a sense of it. To Millie, I think all those references to Duchamp were already overplayed; like just another male mythmaker misusing vital things like drag and sexuality in the service of yet another jerk-off conceptual pun.

David Millie's art imagines ways to function within institutions of art, such as museums or schools, or political and social orders, that are playful and imaginative.

I wonder if there's anything from either her work or from her pedagogy that has been instructive in this regard?

Jess I was thinking of the role of the hysterical male in Millie's pedagogy. Especially in her teaching of horror films. I was the teaching assistant for the course "Horror & Humor: Hysterical Boys" taught by Millie in the fall of 1995. Then I got to go out into the world, and you know there's always that sort of idea or prompt that you go into a large group, and you imagine everyone nude. And then somehow, you're more comfortable. When I would go into places of power, instead of imagining people without clothing, I would just imagine all the men as hysterical. And that was very helpful for me, to remember that mostly they were acting out of fear, especially of loss of control, and that allowed me to sit in the middle of fearlessness. When I would walk into institutions, I would imagine a very different place in which men were hysterically holding power, and that was what I needed to disrupt.

Eventually, I was no longer interested in doing that within the art world, but realized I could do that in biology. That's what led me into ecology, to be a disruptor and create a new curriculum that was not necessarily wanted in scientific fields, and which was really a kind of reimagining of who has power and why they have it. My reasoning went, if I could think about individuals in power differently, maybe I could move in and start to shift meaning in other disciplines.

Beatriz When I got to CalArts, I had already been fighting the imposition of gendered and racialized and ethnicized identities on me and on my work. And I shared that with Millie, and she was a great interlocutor for that, and I really appreciated that. She influenced me both by being at CalArts and by her way of being at CalArts. It made a difference knowing that Millie paid attention to how the labor was distributed among the faculty and who did what kind of labor, and who didn't. And also, in her way of leaving an institution where she'd been for twenty-nine years. All those things have stayed with me as a way to think of institutions as spaces that can enable conversations and relationships, but also as spaces that are not our end goal. And that we have to sacrifice our work for them. And so there came a moment when being in the space of CalArts was no longer yielding what Millie wanted, and she was able to walk away, and at that moment I remember thinking, well, she has so much ahead of her, and she has so much to give, and I wonder why she's leaving. But I understand now, and I understand that it's as important to know when to go as it is to know how to remain. And so, for me, her institutional critique was her way of being in that place, and also her way of leaving.

Kang Yeah, I remember her leaving in 2014. And a couple of years later, Leslie Dick and I were talking about Millie's departure from CalArts and how badass that was, that in some ways she really didn't give a fuck. She didn't want this grand gesture of farewell or anything like that, she just basically said, like, my time's up here, and I'm leaving. And goodbye. Which, in retrospect, I think was really amazing. And her making that decision without making any fuss.

Looking over the checklist of the show, I can see even more how much of a renegade Millie is and has been. For example, the images of the 1989 installation *Fauve Semblant*—I had never seen that before. And it's just really amazing, given the strategies that installation shares with Cheryl Dunye's 1996 film *The Watermelon Woman*. For that film Dunye and Zoe Leonard produced a fictional archive of a forgotten Black lesbian actress. But Millie made this huge project imagining a lost early twentieth-century lesbian artist in the late 1980s, with very similar ideas but more humor. Now I understand more about how Millie was pushing me to explore my interest in archives. Not traditional forms of archive but more the nature and the construction of the archive itself, to trigger the archive and make something outside of that idea. I think I understand a lot more about Millie and where she was coming from through this work, particularly.

Richard I've remembered one slightly humorous anecdote. It must've been in a foundation class that, out of a combination of ignorance and pompousness, I had come up with the word "transvestiture." The state of being a transvestite is how I was interpreting it, and Millie corrected me and said, why do you need that when there's already a word: "transvestism?" That's just to say, if she wasn't teaching a class on drag yet, that's already where her interests were, and this would have surely had an impact on her other students, like Lyle Ashton Harris and Catherine Opie. And this was all happening prior to the publication of what would become the formative texts of the era on sexual identity, gender, and drag, such as the writings of Judith Butler and Elaine Showalter, and maybe Camille Paglia in a more pop way. But the most important one, I think, with the most resonance with the *Fauve Semblant* installation, is an early text by Eve Kosofsky Sedgwick called "Jane Austen and the Masturbating Girl."[4] It compares a woman in a Jane Austen novel who's being punished for masturbating with a contemporary case study of hysteria. Yet Millie's *Fauve Semblant* preceded Kosofsky's text by two years. So, she was very much ahead of her time in this discourse, not just talking about the ideas, but making her work. I'm saying for me it's been kind of a shock, reviewing the work over the last few days, comparing dates with what else related was going on, and coming to the conclusion that—really—the current renewed interest in Millie's work has been far too long overdue.

David Millie's a badass.

Richard She is. I think that's been said already.

David It has been said, I'm repeating for emphasis.

Richard Let's reiterate.

Jess I've been close to Millie since I was in school with her. I remember the way she made us all feel like family when we were in her presence. That we felt like whatever queerness was, and however it was shifting and changing, we were a part of this group of students who understood each other. And so, without really having family, I felt, with the sometimes bitter art world around me, that feeling of her having, you know, parented me in these early stages, which really, for a lot of us, kept us going, and feeling seen, for decades. Really feeling seen, and all the complexity of our projects being seen—which very few teachers could handle. Millie's amazing brain could hold all of what we were bringing to our work, which enabled us to use that moving forward. That's a pretty special gift. I really haven't seen it replicated in another teacher.

Kang I did a collaboration with Millie ten years ago. At the time, I didn't realize how generous she was in agreeing to do it. She didn't wait two seconds to say yes when I asked her to collaborate with me on the *Untitled (Artspeak?)* series (2014–15; p. 61), which was part of my MFA thesis at CalArts. I've taught at several schools since graduating from CalArts, and after experiencing what it means to be a teacher and the challenges from the other side, I appreciate more and more how generous she was with her time, not just as a teacher, but also as a friend. She didn't have any hang-ups about collaborating with a student, she only cared about the work itself. She thought that was interesting enough, which now when I look at the work, I see I was being very didactic, like perhaps intentionally didactic. I needed to do that work, and she understood that immediately. You know that desire! Millie was willing to do something with me, and it still means just so much to me, and I try to be that way with others as well. That's Millie for me.

1. Michael Asher's post-studio course, begun in 1976, is legendary in the mythos of CalArts. Held on Fridays beginning at 10 a.m., two students presented work that would be rigorously critiqued until consensus determined a conclusion of discussion. This resulted in the seminar sometimes lasting into the evening. Numerous artists who went through Asher's course (either with Asher or an acolyte) would adapt this model of teaching at other schools in Southern California, fostering a style of critical dialogue that has dominated art schools throughout the region.

The Feminist Art Program (FAP) was launched in fall 1970 at Fresno State College by artist Judy Chicago. Artist Miriam Schapiro invited Chicago to reestablish and expand the program at CalArts in 1971. The program emphasized collaboration, performance, consciousness-raising, and feminist pedagogical methods, and is most associated with the *Womanhouse* installation in November 1971. FAP dissolved in 1974 following Chicago's departure in 1973; Shapiro left CalArts in 1975.

2. Paul B. Preciado, *Can the Monster Speak?: Report to an Academy of Psychoanalysts*, trans. Frank Wynne (Los Angeles: Semiotext(e), 2021).

3. Simon Watney, "The Spectacle of AIDS," *October* 43, "AIDS: Cultural Analysis/ Cultural Activism" (Winter 1987): 71–86.

4. Eve Kosofsky Sedgwick, "Jane Austen and the Masturbating Girl," *Critical Inquiry* 17, no. 4 (Summer 1991): 818–37.

Catherine Opie, *Millie*, 1994. C-print

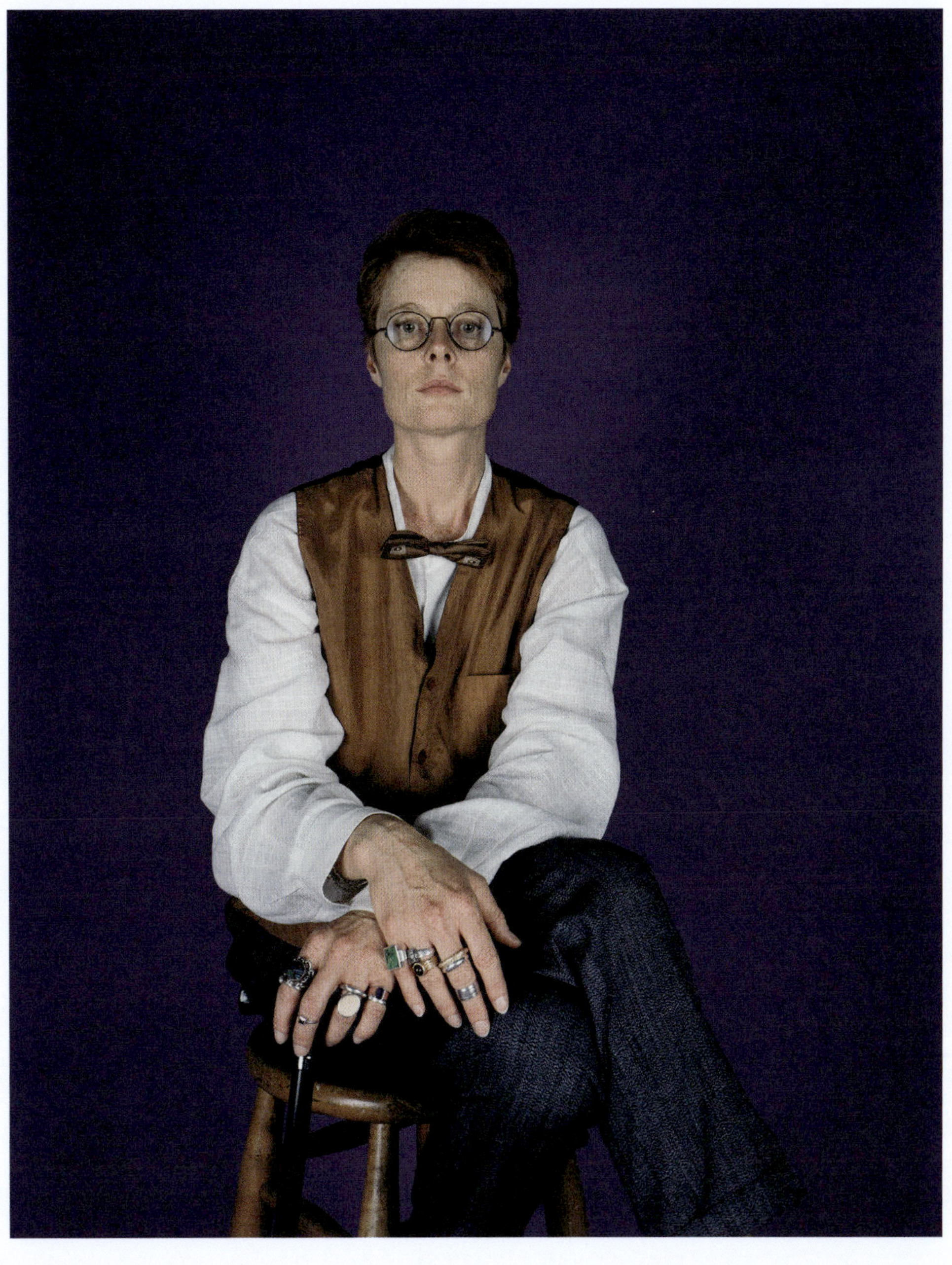

ACKNOWLEDGMENTS

IN 2019 MY FRIENDS Kimberly Varella and Robby Herbst invited me to organize a show for their self-described micro-gallery, Reading Ours, which they founded in their backyard garage a year prior. Dedicated to alternative print media and artists' books and magazines, Reading Ours was DIY in spirit, a purposefully social enterprise meant to bring art-book lovers together for a few Saturdays over a show's short run. I had long wanted to work with Millie Wilson, and my friends' invitation offered an excuse to initiate a project with her; I hoped it could also serve as a stepping stone to a more expansive exhibition. While I was introduced to Millie's work as an undergraduate, when interning at the Orange County Museum of Art, I first met her in 2014 when I curated *Tony Greene: Amid Voluptuous Calm*, a show-within-a-show for the 2014 iteration of the Hammer Museum's *Made in L.A.* biennial. Part of a series of projects masterminded by artist Richard Hawkins about the late artist Tony Greene, a student and close friend of Millie's, the show placed Greene's work alongside that of friends and peers. Millie's beguiling *Daytona Death Angel* (1994) commanded the room.

In preparation for the Reading Ours show, I traveled to Austin to meet with Millie and peruse her archives. Millie was generous with her time and supportive of my interest in her work for this admittedly modest project. At Reading Ours we showcased her artist's book *Errors of Nature* (1992) and realized the first presentation of the installation *Twisted Love*, which Millie had initially envisioned in 1990. The project was warmly received in Los Angeles by many friends, curators, and former students of Millie, and as a headstrong (some may say stubborn) individual, I was now thoroughly committed to realizing a major survey exhibition, even in the face of delays caused by the global COVID-19 pandemic. Once museums began slowly reopening in late 2020, I started sharing a proposal with like-minded museum curators and directors. Thank you to everyone who reviewed this proposal (you know who you are).

In April 2022 I met Amy L. Powell, curator of modern and contemporary art at Krannert Art Museum (KAM) and curator of campus arts research at the University of Illinois Urbana-Champaign, while participating in the 2022 Curatorial Forum organized by Independent Curators International (ICI) at EXPO Chicago. Amy's recent exhibition of Louise Fishman's drawings attested to a shared commitment to highlighting under-recognized queer and feminist artists, and she was receptive to reviewing my proposal, especially given Millie's history with the university. I am supremely grateful for her interest in and advocacy for the exhibition, this publication, and Millie's work more broadly. It has been a thrill to work with and learn from Amy.

Realizing *Millie Wilson: The Museum of Lesbian Dreams* at KAM has been a privilege. The dedication, enthusiasm, and professionalism of its mighty team have made this ambitious show possible. I thank Director Jon L. Seydl for his interest in the project and trust in my curatorial practice. This publication would not have been possible without the managerial brilliance and attentive care of Kathryn Koca Polite, assistant curator and publications specialist. Christine Saniat, museum registrar and exhibitions director, masterfully oversaw the logistics of bringing together the numerous works in the exhibition, and Tim Fox, design and installation specialist, expertly directed the mounting of the show, unfazed by its many idiosyncratic requirements. Walter Wilson, design and installation specialist, was similarly a vital and enthusiastic collaborator in installing the artist's work at KAM. Diane Gutenkauf, senior assistant director, operations and strategy, coordinated the budgetary and administrative needs of the exhibition and publication, and Brenda Nardi, senior director of advancement, secured support via grants and fundraising. Last but not least, Hannah Brown, KAM graduate curatorial intern, provided vital logistical assistance.

Since the Reading Ours show, Kimberly Varella has been a steadfast champion of this project, and it has been a joy to work with her again on this catalogue. Her design responds beautifully to the conceptual rigor and aesthetic panache of Millie's work. On behalf of KAM and myself, we thank her and Gabrielle Pulgar for their work at Content Object. In addition to being a visually seductive object, this publication also seeks to illuminate the historical importance of Millie's art and the impact of her teaching. Jill H. Casid's essay—as insightful as it is playful—asutely examines Millie's work via the core ideas that have animated her practice, and I extend my appreciation to Jill for her enthusiasm and profound support for this project. Acknowledgment is due as well to Beatriz Cortez, Richard Hawkins, Kang Seung Lee, and Jess Rath—talented artists, thinkers, and Millie's former students—for their reflections on Millie's significance and her mentorship at the California Institute of the Arts. This publication required an abundance of new documentation of Millie's work, which was professionally made by Taryn Mills-Drummond (of individual artworks in the artist's own holdings) and Mikey Mosher (of the exhibition at KAM). Tony Manzella and his team at Echelon Color did a terrific job preparing images for print. The texts in this book were expertly copyedited by Amy R. Peltz and attentively proofread by Eugenia Bell. It has been delightful to collaborate with Inventory Press to publish this book; Zoe Kauder Nalebuff and Shannon Harvey's oversight of the project was invaluable.

The exhibition was fortunate to bring together many of Millie's numerous noteworthy works held in institutional collections. For their care and enthusiastic support, we thank the Hammer Museum, especially Shira Abramsohn, Portland McCormick, and Emma Rudman; The Luckman Fine Arts Complex at Cal State LA, especially Aaron Gomez and Nicholas A. Mestas; ONE National Gay & Lesbian Archives at the USC Libraries, especially Joseph Hawkins, Alexis Bard Johnson, and Loni Shibuyama; the Orange County Museum of Art, especially Ziying Duan, Courtenay Finn, and Amanda Seadler; the Palm Springs Art Museum, especially Matthew Clouse, Rachel Faust, Christine Giles, Julie Hoogland, Sharrissa Iqbal, and Adam Lerner; The Frances Young Tang Teaching Museum and Art Gallery, Skidmore College, especially Ian Berry, Evan Little, Rebecca McNamara, Rachel Seligman, and Elizabeth Karp; and Video Data Bank at the School of the Art Institute of Chicago, especially Tom Colley and Emily Martin. We are grateful as well to Madeleine Craig and Sage Sommer at the Henry Art Gallery. Sophia Belsheim and Gwen Hill Russakis facilitated loans from significant private collections with care. The exhibition also had the good fortune to include works graciously loaned from the personal collections of Allison Acken, Penny Cooper and Rena Rosenwasser, Kang Seung Lee, and Tom Patchett (with special thanks to Sean Meredith).

It was a unique challenge assembling works for the exhibition, most of which have been seen only rarely since the 1990s. For the objects coming directly from Millie, we worked with the team at Vault Fine Art Services in Austin, Texas, who transported, condition checked, and packed art for shipment to KAM. I extend a special thanks to Graeme Durant, Katherine McKerley, and the entire staff at Vault. In June 2022 I made a rudimentary inventory of art in Millie's storage with the assistance of artist Austin Swearengin, who made this arduous task significantly more manageable. For the exhibition, KAM remade two critically important works by Millie with the assistance of gifted art fabricators: the team at Artscape Sculpture Studio in Los Angeles remade *Turnip/Potato* (special thanks to Nick Petronzio), and the team at Lite Brite Neon Studio in Brooklyn remade *Lust Has No Mercy* (special thanks to matteline devries-dilling). Special thanks to Paige Stewart-Rankins, hair and makeup supervisor at the Krannert Center for the Performing Arts, for her expert attention in bringing Wilson's works made with hair back to their original glory.

Numerous friends, supporters, and coconspirators have provided encouragement, insight, and assistance throughout the process. I acknowledge Julia Bryan-Wilson, C. Ondine Chavoya, Stuart Comer, Lisa Dorin, Richard Hawkins, Michael Ned Holte, Claire Howard, Sara Frier, Adriene Jenik, Denise M. Johnson, Alex Klein, Thomas Lawson, Kang Seung Lee, Christina Linden, Catherine Lord, Susan Morgan, Karen Moss, Becky Nahom, John Neff, Catherine Opie, Renaud Proch, LJ Roberts, Veronica Roberts, MacKenzie Stevens, Chris E. Vargas, and Matias Viegener. I am grateful especially to Jon-erik Méndez for his continued love and support.

Finally, and most importantly, I thank Millie for her warmth, wit, guidance, patience, and trust. Her love and friendship have been the most rewarding aspect of this journey, and I thank her for welcoming me into her life and her *Museum of Lesbian Dreams*.

DAVID EVANS FRANTZ

FIRST AND FOREMOST, I thank curator David Evans Frantz, without whom this exhibition would not have been realized. His vision, tenacity, and vast labor over several years has been steadfast and sustaining. David's understanding of my work is the most informed and sympathetic in my experience. I am truly fortunate.

Thanks to all of the numerous individuals who have made this survey of my work possible. Working with Amy L. Powell and the attentive staff at Krannert Art Museum has been a privilege. Thank you for your care, attention, brilliance, and willingness to take on a challenging project. Thanks as well to Kimberly Varella for designing this gorgeous catalogue and for your continued interest in and support of my work. The thoughtful contributions from Jill H. Casid, Beatriz Cortez, Richard Hawkins, Kang Seung Lee, and Jess Rath are a welcome addition to this beautiful book. Finally, I would like to thank Martha Boethel and Cathy Warren for their friendship and generous support.

MILLIE WILSON

SELECTED EXHIBITION HISTORY

Millie Wilson
Born 1948, Hot Springs, Arkansas
Resides in Austin, Texas

SOLO EXHIBITIONS

2019
Errors of Nature, Reading Ours, Los Angeles

2013
Some People, Maloney Fine Art, Culver City, CA

2011
Looks Bad, Iceberg Projects, Chicago (exh. cat.)

2010
I Am Not Here Anymore But I Am Fine, Las Cienegas Projects, Los Angeles

1998
Something Blue, Matthew Marks Gallery, New York

1995
Monster Girls, Ruth Bloom Gallery, Santa Monica, CA

1994
Not A Serial Killer, José Freire Fine Art, New York

1993
Wolf in the Garden, Ruth Bloom Gallery, Santa Monica, CA

1992
Living in Someone Else's Paradise, New Langton Arts, San Francisco

A Disturbing Emotional Coloring, White Columns, New York

1991
Sweet Thursday, Meyers/Bloom Gallery, Santa Monica, CA

1990
Fauve Semblant: Peter (A Young English Girl), SF Camerawork, San Francisco

1989
Fauve Semblant: Peter (A Young English Girl), LACE (Los Angeles Contemporary Exhibitions)

The Los Angeles Times Series, University Art Museum, State University of New York at Binghamton (exh. cat.)

SELECTED GROUP EXHIBITIONS

2024
Scientia Sexualis, Institute of Contemporary Art, Los Angeles (exh. cat.)

2020
Never Done: 100 Years of Women in Politics and Beyond, The Frances Young Tang Teaching Museum and Art Gallery, Skidmore College, Saratoga Springs, NY

2018
Rose Ocean: Living With Duchamp, The Frances Young Tang Teaching Museum and Art Gallery, Skidmore College, Saratoga Springs, NY

2015
Home/Office, Track 16, Santa Monica, CA

2014
Tony Greene: Amid Voluptuous Calm, part of *Made in L.A. 2014*, Hammer Museum, Los Angeles (exh. cat.)

2007
Beauty and the Blonde: An Exploration of American Art and Popular Culture, Mildred Lane Kemper Art Museum, Washington University in St. Louis, MO

Girly Show: Pin-Ups, Zines & the So-Called Third Wave, Wignall Museum of Contemporary Art, Chaffey College, Rancho Cucamonga, CA

2004
Hair: Untangling a Social History, The Frances Young Tang Teaching Museum and Art Gallery, Skidmore College, Saratoga Springs, NY (exh. cat.)

SHOWDOWN! at the Schindler House (with Jess Rath), MAK Center for Art and Architecture at the Schindler House, West Hollywood, CA

2003
Whiteness, A Wayward Construction, Laguna Art Museum, Laguna Beach, CA (exh. cat.)

2002
Parallels and Intersections: Art/Women/California, 1950–2000, San José Museum of Art, San Jose, CA (exh. cat.)

Song Poems, Rosamund Felsen Gallery, Santa Monica, CA

2000
COLA 2000, Hammer Museum, Los Angeles (exh. cat.)

1998
Addressing the Century: 100 Years of Art and Fashion, Hayward Gallery, London (exh. cat.)

1997
Some Lust, Patricia Faure Gallery, Santa Monica, CA

1996
Sexual Politics: Judy Chicago's Dinner Party in Feminist Art History, Hammer Museum, Los Angeles (exh. cat.)

1995
In a Different Light, University Art Museum and Pacific Film Archive, University of California, Berkeley (exh. cat.)

Longing and Belonging: From the Faraway Nearby, SITE Santa Fe and Museum of Fine Arts, Santa Fe, NM (exh. cat.)

Pervert, University Art Gallery, University of California, Irvine (exh. cat.)

Piece: Nine Artists Consider Yoko Ono, Kiki Gallery, San Francisco (exh. cat.)

LIMIARES: Dez escultores americanos (THRESHOLD: Ten American Sculptors), Fundação de Serralves, Porto, Portugal (exh. cat.)

1994
Absence, Activism and the Body Politic, Fischbach Gallery, New York

Addressing Herself, The Lab, San Francisco

Altered Egos, Santa Monica Museum of Art, Santa Monica, CA (exh. cat.)

Bad Girls, New Museum of Contemporary Art, New York (exh. cat.)

Bad Girls West, Frederick S. Wight Art Gallery, University of California, Los Angeles (exh. cat.)

Duchamp's Leg, Walker Art Center, Minneapolis (traveled)

Monsters, Miami Art Center, Miami

Persona Cognita, Museum of Modern Art at Heide, Melbourne (exh. cat.)

Trophies, Fine Arts Gallery, California State University, Los Angeles

1993
2 Much: The Gay & Lesbian Experience, University of Colorado, Boulder

Fourth Newport Biennial: Southern California 1993, Newport Harbor Art Museum, Newport Beach, CA (exh. cat.)

Backtalk: Women's Voices in the 90's, Santa Barbara Contemporary Arts Forum, Santa Barbara, CA (exh. cat.)

Currents '93: Dress Codes, Institute of Contemporary Art, Boston

Different Strokes, Guggenheim Gallery, Chapman University, Orange, CA

Disrupted Borders: An Intervention in Definitions of Boundaries, Arnolfini Gallery, Bristol, UK, and The Photographer's Gallery, London

Empty Dress: Clothing as Surrogate in Recent Art, Independent Curators, Inc. (traveled; exh. cat.)

Everyday Life, Kim Light Gallery, Los Angeles

I Am the Enunciator, Thread Waxing Space, New York (exh. cat.)

Remapping Tales of Desire: Writing Across the Abyss, A Space, Toronto

Tema AIDS, Henie-Onstad Art Centre, Høvikodden, Norway (exh. cat.)

The Return of the Cadavre Exquis, The Drawing Center, New York

1992
Rosamund Felsen Clinic and Recovery Center, Rosamund Felsen Gallery, Los Angeles

Counterweight: Alienation, Assimilation, Resistance, Santa Barbara Contemporary Arts Forum, Santa Barbara, CA (traveled; exh. cat.)

Effected Desire, Carnegie Museum of Art, Pittsburgh

Facing the Finish: Some Recent California Art, San Francisco Museum of Modern Art (traveled; exh. cat.)

Hair, John Michael Kohler Arts Center, Sheboygan, WI

Re-Visions, Randolph Street Gallery, Chicago

The Politics of Difference: Artists Explore Issues of Identity, University Art Gallery, University of California, Riverside

We Interrupt Your Regularly Scheduled Programming . . ., White Columns, New York

1991
AIDS Timeline (New York City 1991), an installation by Group Material for the Whitney Biennial 1991, Whitney Museum of American Art, New York (exh. cat.)

Gender and Representation, Zoller Gallery, Pennsylvania State University, University Park

(Dis)Member, Museum of Traditional Values, New York

Making Sense: Kaucyila Brooke, Diane Neumaier, Michael Tidmus, Millie Wilson, Allegheny College Art Galleries, Meadville, PA

Situation: Perspectives on Work by Lesbian and Gay Artists, New Langton Arts, San Francisco (exh. cat.)

Someone or Somebody, Meyers Bloom Gallery, Santa Monica, CA

1990
All But the Obvious, LACE (Los Angeles Contemporary Exhibitions) (exh. cat.)

Post-Boys & Girls: Nine Painters, Artists Space, New York (exh. cat.)

Queer, Wessel O'Connor, New York

1989
Loaded, Richard Kuhlenschmidt Gallery, Los Angeles (exh. cat.)

The Body You Want, Southern Exposure, San Francisco

Thick and Thin: Photographically Inspired Paintings, Fahey Klein Gallery, Los Angeles

Self-Evidence, LACE (Los Angeles Contemporary Exhibitions) (exh. cat.)

1988
Drawings by Ten, Mandeville Gallery, University of California, San Diego, La Jolla

Omnibus Exhibition, Herron Gallery, University of Indiana, Indianapolis

That's Progress, Los Angeles Center for Photographic Studies (LACPS) at Beyond Baroque, Venice, CA

1987
Selections, DiverseWorks, Houston

1986
Just 4, Krannert Art Museum, Champaign-Urbana (traveled; exh. cat.)

1985
Millie Wilson/Lisa Ginzel, Contemporary Art Workshop, Chicago

1984
Discovery, Lawndale Alternative, Houston

Introspectives, Pyramid Arts Center, Rochester, NY

1983
Eleven Artists, Blaffer Art Gallery, University of Houston

1978
Works on Paper: Southwest, 1978, Dallas Museum of Fine Arts, Dallas

1977
Women in Sight, Women & Their Work at the Laguna Gloria Art Museum, Austin

2024
Frantz, David Evans. "Sick Jokes, Blasphemous Rumors, and Fabulous Antics: West Coast Artists Respond to AIDS." In *For Dear Life: Art, Medicine, and Disability*, edited by Isabel Casso and Jill Dawsey, 232–40. San Diego, CA: Museum of Contemporary Art San Diego; Seattle: Marquand Books, 2024.

Lubin, Joan. "Sex by the Book." In *Scientia Sexualis*, edited by Jennifer Doyle and Jeanne Vaccaro, 108–20. Los Angeles: Institute of Contemporary Art, Los Angeles; Los Angeles: Inventory Press, 2024.

2023
Flavelle, Genevieve. "Once Upon a Queer Time: A Study of Reparative and Speculative Histories in the Work of 2SLGBTQ+ Contemporary Artists." PhD diss., Queen's University, 2023.

2021
Bryan-Wilson, Julia. "Impermanent Collections." *Artforum* 60, no. 1 (September 2021), 228–33.

2019
Soboleva, Ksenia M. "The Need for More Complex Exhibitions on Lesbian Visual Culture." *Hyperallergic*. March 21, 2019. https://hyperallergic.com/491036/lesbian-matters-trestle-gallery/.

2016
Schwendener, Alyssa E. "The Most Fantastic Lie: The Invention of Lesbian Histories." Master's thesis, California State University, Long Beach, 2016.

Latimer, Tirza True. "Improper Objects: Performing Queer/Feminist Art/History. In *Otherwise: Imagining Queer Feminist Art Histories*, edited by Amelia Jones and Erin Silver, 93–109. Manchester, UK: Manchester University Press, 2016.

2015
Lee, Kang Seung. *Untitled (Artspeak?)*. Claremont, CA: Pitzer College Art Galleries, 2015.

Hull, Steven, and Amy Thoner, eds. *Las Cienegas Projects: Time Runs Out*. Los Angeles: Nothing Moments, 2015.

2014
Frantz, David Evans. "Tony Greene: Amid Voluptuous Calm." In *Made in L.A. 2014*, edited by Connie Butler and Michael Ned Holte, 165–66. Los Angeles: Hammer Museum; New York: DelMonico Books; Munich: Prestel, 2014.

Lawson, Thomas. "On Site: Made in L.A. 2014." *Artforum* 53, no. 2 (October 2014), 117.

Johnson, Denise. "Millie Wilson: On Both Sides and in Between." *Make/Shift*, no. 14 (Fall/Winter 2013–14), 11.

Miranda, Carolina. "'Made in L.A.' Best in Show: 5 Must-See Pieces at the Hammer Biennial." *Los Angeles Times*. June 16, 2014. https://www.latimes.com/entertainment/arts/miranda/la-et-cam-5-best-pieces-at-hammer-made-in-la-biennial-20140614-column.html.

2013
Dowing, Lisa. *The Subject of Murder: Gender, Exceptionality, and the Modern Killer*. Chicago: University of Chicago Press, 2013.

2011
Wolverton, Terry. "Lesbian Art: A Partial Inventory." In *From Site to Vision: The Woman's Building in Contemporary Culture*, edited by Sondra Hale and Terry Wolverton, 353–83. Los Angeles: Ben Maltz Gallery, Otis College of Art and Design, 2011.

2008
Joyce, Susan. "Picturing Lesbian, Informing Art Therapy: A Postmodern Feminist Autobiographical Investigation." Master's thesis, Southern Cross University, Lismore, Australia, 2008.

2006
Myers, Holly. "Around the Galleries; Making a Collective Statement." *Los Angeles Times*. February 3, 2006.

2005
Molina, Margot. "El proyecto 'Copilandia' reune a 300 artistas contra la propiedad intelectual." *Andalucia*. December 29, 2005.

Sanchez, Immaculada. "'Copilandia' un barco pirato para propagar la obra de 300 artistas." *Diario de Sevilla*. December 29, 2005.

2003
Haldane, David. "'Whiteness' Exhibit and Exercise in Identity." *Los Angeles Times*. April 28, 2003.

Lancaster, Roger N. *The Trouble with Nature: Sex in Popular Science and Mass Culture*. Berkeley, CA: University of California Press, 2003.

Meyers, Holly. "White Noise." *LA Weekly*. April 25–31, 2003.

2002
Dove, Amy. "Ideas in Practice." *ARTlies*, no. 36 (Fall 2002), 4–7.

Wolverton, Terry. *Insurgent Muse: Life and Art at the Woman's Building*. San Francisco: City Lights, 2002.

2000
Hammond, Harmony. *Lesbian Art in America: A Contemporary History*. New York: Rizzoli International, 2000.

1999
Saslow, James J. *Pictures and Passions: A History of Homosexuality in the Visual Arts*. New York: Viking Penguin, 1999.

1998
Morgan, Margaret A. "A Box, a Pipe, and a Piece of Plumbing." In *Women in Dada: Essays on Sex, Gender, and Identity*, edited by Naomi Sawleson-Gorse, 48–74. Cambridge, MA: MIT Press, 1998.

Schlager, Neil, ed. *Gay and Lesbian Almanac*. New York: St. James Press, 1998.

1997
Joselit, David. "Exhibiting Gender." *Art in America* 85, no. 1 (January 1997), 36–39.

1996
Atkins, Robert. "Goodbye Lesbian/Gay History; Hello Queer Sensibility: Meditating on Curatorial Practice." *Art Journal* 55, no. 4 (Winter 1996): 80–85.

Basilio, Miriam. "Corporal Evidence: Representations of Aileen Wuornos." *Art Journal* 55, no. 4 (Winter 1996): 56–61.

Chadwick, Whitney. *Women, Art and Society*. 2nd ed. London: Thames and Hudson, 1996.

Hammond, Harmony. "The Ups and Downs of SITE Santa Fe." *Sculpture* 15, no. 3 (March 1996), 26–29.

Petry, Michael, ed. "Abstract Eroticism." Special issue, *Art and Design Profile* 2, no. 3–4 (March/April 1996), 103.

1995

Atkins, Robert. "Very Queer Indeed." *Village Voice*. January 31, 1995.

Bonetti, David, "Looking at Art 'In a Different Light.'" *San Francisco Examiner*. January 11, 1995.

Brea, José Luis. "Reviews: Threshold." *Artforum* 34, no. 3 (November 1995), 97–98.

Corrin, Lisa. "Installing History." In *Redefining American History Painting*, edited by Patricia Burnham and Lucretia Giese. Cambridge, UK: Cambridge University Press, 1995.

Duncan, Michael. "Queering the Discourse." *Art in America* 83, no. 7 (July 1995), 27–31.

Mitchell, Charles Dee. "Introducing SITE Santa Fe." *Art in America* 83, no. 10 (October 1995), 44–47.

Pagel, David. "Women's View." *Los Angeles Times*. April 17, 1995.

Pedrosa, Adriano. "Longing and Belonging: From the Faraway Nearby." *Frieze*, no. 25 (November/December 1995), 73–74.

Smyth, Cherry. *Damn Fine Art by New Lesbian Artists*. London: Cassell, 1995.

Solnit, Rebecca. "Santa Fe Fax." *Art Issues*, no. 39 (September/October 1995), 34–35.

Van de Walle, Mark. "SITE Santa Fe." *Artforum* 34, no. 3 (November 1995), 96.

1994

Baker, Kenneth, "Bad Girls in New York." *San Francisco Chronicle*. February 27, 1994.

Benjamin, Marina. "Artists on the Edge: A New Exhibition Using Art as a Political Weapon Seeks to Explode the Practice of Cultural Marginalisation. Marina Benjamin Takes a Look." *The Independent* (UK). July 15, 1994.

Drohojowska-Philp, Hunter. "And When They Were Bad." *Los Angeles Times*. January 16, 1994.

Greene, David A. "A Feast for the Eyes." *Los Angeles Reader*. July 29, 1994.

Hammond, Harmony. "A Space of Infinite and Pleasurable Possibilities: Lesbian Self-Representation in Visual Art." In *New Feminist Criticism: Art, Identity, Action*, edited by Joanna Frueh, Cassanova Langer, and Arlene Raven, 97–131. New York: Icon, 1994.

Helfand, Glen. "Transformer." *San Francisco Weekly*. February 2, 1994.

Hess, Elizabeth. "Flat Cracker Love." *Village Voice*. May 31, 1994.

Hugo, Joan. "San Francisco Fax." *Art Issues*, no. 33 (May/June 1994), 34–35.

Matthews, Lydia. "The Illustrated Woman: The Second Annual Feminist Activism and Art Conference." *Camerawork: A Journal of Photographic Arts* 21, no. 1 (Spring/Summer 1994): 34–36.

Saltz, Jerry. "L.A. Rising." *Art & Auction Magazine* 16, no. 9 (April 1994), 88–91, 122.

Smith, P.C., "Millie Wilson at Jose Freire." *Art in America* 82, no. 9 (September 1994), 119.

Smith, Roberta. "A Raucous Caucus of Feminists Being Bad." *New York Times*. January 21, 1994.

Tamblyn, Christine. "The Hair of the Dog that Bit Us: Theory in Recent Feminist Art." In *New Feminist Criticism: Art, Identity, Action*, edited by Joanna Frueh, Cassanova Langer, and Arlene Raven, 289–305. New York: Icon, 1994.

Wells, Liz. "Drowning in Numbers: Disrupting Borders at Arnolfini." *Creative Camera*, no. 326 (February/March 1994), 46–47.

Weissman, Benjamin. "[Sigh]." *Artforum* 32, no. 9 (May 1994), 87–89, 125.

Wilson, William. "Santa Monica's Exquisite Deceptions 'Altered Egos' and 'Return of the 'Cadavre Exquis'' Present Works with Their Hearts in Surrealist-Era Paris." *Los Angeles Times*. July 16, 1994.

Wilson, William. "Enjoyable, Endearing Paean to 'Romance.'" *Los Angeles Times*. December 15, 1994.

1993

Blowen, Michael. "A Wild Mixer." *Boston Globe*. March 12, 1993.

Creery, Janet. "Remapping Tales of Desire." *Fuse Magazine* 17, no. 2 (Winter 1993–94), 31–32.

Curtis, Cathy. "Painting Pictures: Newport Harbor's Fourth Biennial Draws on Style, Sense, Tastes of Its Chief Curator." *Los Angeles Times*. October 14, 1993.

Darling, Michael. "Voices Carry." *Santa Barbara News Press*. September 24, 1993.

Fee, Gayle. "ICA Dresses Up New Exhibit." *Boston Herald*. March 10, 1993.

Hess, Elizabeth. "Body Triple: An Old Art Game, New Art Tricks." *Village Voice*. November 30, 1993.

Magdalena, Kathairein. "Art for Art's Sake' Blasts Open New Orleans' Social and Art Season." *The New Voice*, no. 676 (October 8–14, 1993), 3.

Martin, Victoria. "Talking Back." *Artweek* 24, no. 3 (February 4, 1993), 22–23.

Miller, Francine Koslow. "Currents '93: Dress Codes." *Artforum* 32, no. 3 (November 1993), 110–11.

Sherman, Mary. "Clothes Call." *Boston Herald*. March 12, 1993.

Stapen, Nancy. "At the ICA, It's Guys as Dolls." *Boston Globe*. March 7, 1993.

Temin, Christine. "ICA's Provocative Dress Codes." *Boston Globe*. March 7, 1993.

Wilson, William. "Biennial Uses Humorous Paradox to Tackle Issues." *Los Angeles Times*. October 9, 1993.

1992

Bakargiev, Carolyn Christov, and Ludovico Pratesi. *Molteplici culture: Itinerari dell'arte contemporanea in un mondo che cambia*. Rome: Museo del Folklore, 1992.

Bleckner, Ross. "Independents: Emerging Artists." *Out Magazine* 1, no. 2 (Fall 1992), 41–49.

Bonetti, David. "Things Are Not What They Seem." *San Francisco Chronicle*. February 28, 1992.

Cunningham, Michael. "After AIDS, Gay Art Aims for a New Reality." *New York Times*. April 26, 1992.

De Sanctis, Linda. "Quei cento artisti nell'epoca della complessita." *La Repubblica*. May 21, 1992.

Helfand, Glen. "Millie Wilson." *SF Weekly*. February 12, 1992.

Hirsch, David. "Lesbian Dreams." *New York Native* 11, no. 19 (April 20, 1992), 45.

Kandel, Susan. "L.A. in Review." *Arts Magazine* 66, no. 5 (January 1992), 90–92.

Knight, Christopher. "Art Review: 10 California Artists 'Facing the Finish.'" *Los Angeles Times*. May 1, 1992.

Linwood, Elliot. "New Additions to Millie's Museum." *Bay Area Reporter* 22, no. 7 (February 13, 1992), 32.

Pagel, David. "The Doctor's In." *Los Angeles Times*. August 7, 1992.

Paine, Janice. "Hair Pieces." *Milwaukee Sentinel*. January 8, 1992.

Porges, Maria. "On the Scene: San Francisco." *Artspace* 16, no. 3 (May/June 1992), 84–85.

1991

Baker, Kenneth. "Modernism Goes International." *San Francisco Chronicle*. September 20, 1991.

Bonetti, David. "Reviews: Facing the Finish." *ArtNews* 90, no. 10 (December 1991), 139.

Bonetti, David. "In Search of a Gay Sensibility." *San Francisco Examiner*. July 4, 1991.

Crowder, Joan. "And in the End." *Santa Barbara News Press*. July 19, 1991.

Grigsby, Darcy Grimaldo. "Dilemmas of Visibility: Contemporary Women Artists' Representations of Female Bodies." In *The Female Body: Figures, Styles, Speculations*, edited by Laurence Goldstein, 83–102. Ann Arbor: University of Michigan Press, 1991.

Helfand, Glen, "San Francisco." *Art Issues*, no. 19 (September/October 1991), 30–31.

Hess, Elizabeth. "Upstairs, Downstairs." *Village Voice*. April 30, 1991.

Hirch, David. "Millie Wilson at SFMOMA: Seducing the Viewer." *Bay Area Reporter* 21, no. 39 (September 26, 1991), 40, 42.

Kandel, Susan. "L.A. in Review" *Arts Magazine* 65, no. 6 (February 1991), 108–10.

Langer, Cassandra L. "The Queer Show." *Women Artists Newsletter* 15, no. 4 (Winter 1991), 6–7.

Linwood, Elliot. "Every Story Tells a Picture Don't It?" *San Francisco Sentinel* 19, no. 27 (July 4, 1991), 18.

Meyer, Richard and Liz Kotz. "Situation." *Out/Look* 4, no. 2 (Fall 1991), 8–13.

Rugoff, Ralph. "World Under Glass." *LA Weekly*. November 29–December 5, 1991.

Samaras, Connie. "Look Who's Talking." *Artforum* 30, no. 3 (November 1991), 102–6.

Sonbert, Warren. "Playful Pushing." *Bay Area Reporter* 21, no. 39 (September 26, 1991), 33, 40.

Wolverton, Terry. "Portraying Sexuality." *The Advocate*, no. 574 (April 9, 1991), 70–73.

1990

Bonnetti, David. "Explosion of Gay, AIDS Art." *San Francisco Examiner*. June 22, 1990.

Gipe, Lawrence. "The Photograph as Verisimilitude: Millie Wilson and Doug Ischar." *Visions* 4, no. 4 (Fall 1990), 22–23.

Grigsby, Darcy Grimaldo. "Dilemmas of Visibility: Contemporary Women Artists' Representations of Female Bodies." *Michigan Quarterly Review* 29, no. 4 (Fall 1990): 584–619.

Kotz, Liz. "The Body You Want." *Afterimage* 17, no. 6 (January 1990): 12.

Kotz, Liz. "Images of Women." *Artweek* 21, no. 3 (January 25, 1990), 16.

Oberlander, Wendy. "Fauve Semblant: Peter (A Young English Girl)." *Camerawork: A Journal of Photographic Arts* 17, no. 2 (Summer 1990): 28.

Wolverton, Terry. "Thoroughly Postmodern Millie." *The Advocate*, no. 564 (November 20, 1990), 70–71.

Zellen, Jody. "Millie Wilson at LACE." *Art Issues*, no. 10 (March/April 1990), 26.

1989

Curtis, Cathy. "LACE's 'Self-Evidence' Exhibit Takes Viewer for a Spin." *Los Angeles Times*. June 2, 1989.

Curtis, Cathy. "The Galleries: Santa Monica." *Los Angeles Times*. August 18, 1989.

Donohue, Marlena. "The Galleries: Wilshire Center." *Los Angeles Times*. September 29, 1989.

Helfand, Glenn. "Liberating the Sexual Viewpoint." *Artweek* 20, no. 28 (August 26, 1989), 7.

Knight, Christopher. "Loaded." *Los Angeles Herald Examiner*. August 4, 1989.

Lazzari, Margaret. "Contemplating the Self." *Artweek* 20, no. 21 (May 27, 1989), 5.

Rugoff, Ralph. "Circumstantial Evidence." *LA Weekly*. June 9–15, 1989.

1988

Raczka, Robert. "Millie Wilson." In "3rd Annual Critics' Picks: Ten Rising LA Artists." *LA Weekly*. December 9–15, 1988.

WILSON'S WRITINGS AND PROJECTS FOR PRINT

2023

"Fauve Semblant (Peter a Young English Girl)." Entry in *Trans Hirstory in 99 Objects*, edited by David Evans Frantz, Christina Linden, and Chris E. Vargas, 256–57. Pasadena, CA: Museum of Trans Hirstory & Art; Munich: Hirmer, 2023.

2007

Pipe, Pulp, Pony. With drawings by Marcos Rosales and design by Brian Roettinger. Los Angeles: Nothing Moments, 2007.

2005
"Regarding a Boy." With drawings by Marcos Rosales. In *AB OVO*, edited by Steven Hull, 31–36. Los Angeles: Nothing Moments, 2005.

1998
"Colorful Girls." In *Blind Date*, edited by Steven Hull, 97. Los Angeles: Nothing Moments, 1998.

1997
With Nicky Hirst. "Inferno." In *Errant Bodies: Flowers*, edited by Brandon LaBelle and Matias Viegener, 30–32. Los Angeles: B. LaBelle and Louise Sandhaus, 1997.

Wanted. Poster. New York: Us Girls, 1997.

1996
"A Fiction of M. (An Excerpt)." In *Things That Quicken the Heart*, edited by Soo Jin Kim, 161–63. Los Angeles: Soo Jin Kim, 1996.

"Wild Rooms." In *Cookin' with Honey: What Literary Lesbians Eat*, edited by Amy Scholder, 140–41. Ithaca, NY: Firebrand, 1996.

1995
"Dandy." Part of "Artists' Pages: Tailor-Made." In "Clothing as Subject," edited by Nina Felshin. Special issue, *Art Journal* 54, no. 1 (Spring 1995): 7–9.

"A Fiction of Masculinity" and "Trousers (for Tony)." In *The New Fuck You: Adventures in Lesbian Reading*, edited by Liz Kotz and Eileen Myles, 217–23 and 283–84. New York: Semiotext(e), 1995.

[Untitled]. In *This Is Not Her*, edited by Rick Jacobson and Wayne Smith, n.p. San Francisco: Kiki Gallery, 1995.

1994
Artist statement in "Memory & Time." *Artweek* 25, no. 7 (April 7, 1994), 18–22.

"Colorful Girls." In *Color This! A Collection of Los Angeles Artist's Drawings*, n.p. Los Angeles: Foundation for Art Resources, 1994.

"Excerpt (A Fiction of M.)" In *Some Weird Sin II*, edited by Rex Ray and Wayne Smith, n.p. San Francisco: Some Weird Sin, 1994.

[Untitled]. In "Wretch Like Me," edited by Robert Blanchon. Special issue, *Whitewalls: A Journal of Language and Art*, no. 35 (Fall/Winter 1994): 44–45.

1993
"Anomaly." In *Promotional Copy*, edited by Robin Kahn, 24–25. New York: S.O.S. Int'l and B.R.A.T., an Arts Organization, 1993.

"Disturbances: From *The Museum of Lesbian Dreams*." In *Disrupted Borders: An Intervention in Definitions of Boundaries*, edited by Sunil Gupta, 159–65. London: Rivers Oram, 1993.

1992
Errors of Nature. Artist's book. San Francisco: New Langton Arts, 1992.

1991
"Dear Tony." In *Exhausted Autumn*, edited by Richard Hawkins, 51–53. Los Angeles: LACE (Los Angeles Contemporary Exhibitions), 1991.

[Untitled]. In *Dear World: Queer Art & Lit*, edited by Nayland Blake and Camille Roy, 18–19. San Francisco: Nayland Blake and Camille Roy, 1991.

[Untitled]. In *FRAME-WORK* 3, no. 2/3 (May 1991): 38–29.

1990
"The Theoretical Closet." In *All But the Obvious*, edited by Pam Gregg and Catherine Lord, 16. Los Angeles: LACE (Los Angeles Contemporary Exhibitions), 1990.

[Untitled]. In *ZYZZYVA* 6, no. 2 (Summer 1990), 88–89.

1989
"Family." *Lucky*, no. 3 (Fall/Winter 1989), n.p.

"The *Los Angeles Times* Series." *Exposure* 27, no. 1 (1989): 16–23.

1988
"The *Los Angeles Times* Series." *Real Life Magazine* no. 19 (Winter 1988–89), 10–13.

COLLECTIONS

Berkeley Art Museum and Pacific Film Archive, Berkeley, CA

Escalette Permanent Collection of Art, Chapman University, Orange, CA

Hammer Museum, Los Angeles

Henry Art Gallery, University of Washington, Seattle

The Luckman Fine Arts Complex at Cal State LA, Los Angeles

ONE National Gay & Lesbian Archives at the USC Libraries, Los Angeles

Orange County Museum of Art, Costa Mesa, CA

Palm Springs Art Museum, Palm Springs, CA

San Francisco Museum of Modern Art, San Francisco

The Frances Young Tang Teaching Museum and Art Gallery, Skidmore College, Saratoga Springs, NY

The Walt Disney Company, Burbank, CA

TEACHING

California Institute of the Arts, Program in Art, Faculty Emeritus
- Professor, 1985–2014
- Director, Program in Art, 1990–93
- Acting Director, Program in Art, 1988–89

University of Illinois Urbana-Champaign
- Assistant Professor, 1983–85

EDUCATION

University of Texas at Austin
- Bachelor of Fine Arts, 1971

University of Houston
- Master of Fine Arts, 1983

CHECKLIST OF THE EXHIBITION

All artworks are by Millie Wilson, are in the collection of the artist, and appear courtesy of the artist unless otherwise noted.

SHE WAS FRAMED

The Los Angeles Times Series, 1988–89

Part 1, page 7, Friday, January 15, 1988, "Kim Hyon Hui as she confessed to blowing up plane." 115 DIED IN NOV. 29 CRASH: N. KOREA AGENT CONFESSES, SAYS SHE PUT BOMB ON JET SAVE 20% TO 40% ON NEWBORN, INFANT AND TODDLER ESSENTIALS. Acrylic on four canvases, 42 × 24¾ in. (106.7 × 62.9 cm) overall.

Part 1, page 12, Sunday, January 31, 1988, "Carolina Garcia Salas displays giant molar of a mammoth that her son found in their yard." BONES: OFFICIALS ARE SHOWING SCANT INTEREST IN TOWN'S NEW 'TREASURE' BALI SUPPORT BRAS, 30% OFF. *Lowest prices this season! Plus, meet a Bali fitting specialist at a May Company listed below.* Acrylic on four canvases, 35⅝ × 22⅝ in. (90.5 × 57.5 cm) overall.

Part 1, page 2, Tuesday, February 9, 1988, "Simmering—Kilauea volcano in Hawaii and, right, a worshiper of the volcano goddess Pele gathering ferns for an offering to her. An effort to tap the mountain for geothermal energy has brought Pele followers out of the shadows and into a battle." (Story on page 1). Acrylic on four canvases, 35⅝ × 22⅝ in. (90.5 × 57.5 cm) overall.

Part 3, page 6, Wednesday, February 17, 1988, "Bonny Warner of the United States zips around luge run Tuesday at Calgary. Warner is in eighth position as East Germans hold the top three places after first two runs." WOMEN'S LUGE: BONNY WARNER MAY BE IN EIGHTH PLACE, BUT SHE IS RELAXED. Acrylic on three canvases, 26⅝ × 30⅛ in. (67.6 × 76.5 cm) overall.

Part 1, page 9, Saturday, February 20, 1988, "Israeli troops use clubs to strike the legs of protesting Palestinian women in Ramallah, on West Bank. Using violence against civilians can leave emotional scars on soldiers, experts say." TROOPS: EFFECT OF RIOTS. Acrylic on three canvases, 27⅝ × 25½ in. (70.2 × 64.8 cm) overall.

Part 1, page 26, Thursday, February 2, 1989, "Musician Billy Tipton shown in the 1950s." DEATH REVEALS MUSICIAN WHO LIVED AS MAN TO BE WOMAN. *High rates. No anxiety.* Acrylic on five canvases, 26⅝ × 25 in. (67.6 × 63.5 cm) overall.

The Painter Who Is Not One: Millie Wilson/Romaine Brooks, 1990. Acrylic on three canvases, periwinkle wall paint, color photographs and text panels mounted on Dibond. 98 × 198 in. (248.9 × 502.9 cm) overall.

Elektra, 1991. Upholstered torso and head forms and two Formica-veneer pedestals, dimensions variable, torso and pedestal: 64 × 18 × 4 in. (162.6 × 45.7 × 10.2 cm), head and pedestal: 73 × 12 × 12 in. (185.4 × 30.5 × 30.5 cm).

Kang Seung Lee in collaboration with Millie Wilson, *Millie*, from the series *Untitled (Artspeak)*, 2014–15. Ink, watercolor, colored pencil, acrylic, gouache, pen, pencil, and collage on paper, 52 × 38 in. (132.1 × 96.5 cm). Courtesy of Kang Seung Lee, Los Angeles.

FAUVE SEMBLANT

Fauve Semblant: Peter (A Young English Girl), 1989

Baby on Tractor, 1989. Gelatin silver print and text panel mounted on Dibond, photograph: 20⅞ × 13¾ in. (53 × 34.9 cm), text panel: 14 × 9 in. (35.6 × 22.9 cm).

Book, 1989. Gelatin silver print mounted on Dibond, 16 × 23 in. (40.6 × 58.4 cm).

Bulldagger/Painter, 1989. Teal wall paint and two plexiglass panels with vinyl text, plexiglass panels: 4¾ × 12 in. (12.1 × 30.5 cm) each.

Cross-Dressing, 1989. Six gelatin silver prints and two text panels mounted on Dibond, photographs: dimensions variable, text panels: 14 × 9 in. (35.6 × 22.9 cm) each.

Her Last Palette, 1989. Gelatin silver print, frame, and brass label, framed photograph: 36⅞ × 28¾ × 3⅛ in. (93.7 × 73 × 7.9 cm), brass label: 1¾ × 7⅞ in. (4.4 × 20 cm).

Leotard, Cheater, Painter, 1989. Stretched fabric, gelatin silver print, acrylic on canvas, frame, vinyl type, and text panel mounted on Dibond, 26 × 26 in. (66 × 66 cm) each framed.

Mirror, 1989. Mirror, frame, and text panel mounted on Dibond, mirror: 43⅞ × 42⅛ in. (111.4 × 107 cm), text panel: 14 × 9 in. (35.6 × 22.9 cm) framed.

Photograph, 1989. Gelatin silver print and text panel mounted on Dibond, photograph: 58½ × 46 in. (148.6 × 116.8 cm), text panel: 17 × 11 in. (43.2 × 27.9 cm).

Two Women, 1989. Gelatin silver print mounted on Dibond, 20 × 12 in. (50.8 × 30.5 cm).

We Two in Solitude Were Wandering There (Sphinx and Wild Lilies), 1989. Acrylic on linen, frame, wood, plexiglass, burlap, and brass label, framed painting: 38½ × 48½ × 5 in. (97.8 × 123.2 × 12.7 cm), brass label: 3½ × 12 in. (8.9 × 30.5 cm). Collection of Allison Acken.

ERRORS OF NATURE

Easel/Mirrors, 1990. Etched mirror, hardwood easel, and framed hardwood mirror, 70 × 35 × 45 in. (177.8 × 88.9 × 114.3 cm).

Trophy, 1990. Bronze trophy, fur, plexiglass, and wood-veneer pedestal, trophy: 24 × 10 × 10 in. (61 × 25.4 × 25.4 cm), plexiglass and pedestal: 62½ × 12 × 12 in. (158.8 × 30.5 × 30.5 cm).

Beaded Tie, 1991. Beaded tie, velveteen on board, and frame, 18 × 14½ × 3 in. (45.7 × 36.8 × 7.6 cm). Courtesy of Tom Patchett.

The Language of Dreams, 1991. Wood, ruler, plexiglass, and wood table, 42 × 28 × 25 in. (106.7 × 71.1 × 63.5 cm). ONE National Gay & Lesbian Archives at the USC Libraries.

Turnip/Potato, 1991 (remade 2024). Brass, bronze, plexiglass, and walnut base, 47 × 23 × 27 in. (119.4 × 58.4 × 68.6 cm).

Errors of Nature, 1992. Artist's book, 6⅞ × 4⅛ in. (17.5 × 10.5 cm) closed.

Lust Has No Mercy, 1992 (remade 2024). Neon on aluminum, 6 × 72 × 7 in. (15.2 × 182.9 × 17.8 cm).

Merkins (Gladys), 1992. Styled synthetic wig, wood shelf, enamel paint, and brass label, 33 × 15 × 15 in. (83.8 × 38.1 × 38.1 cm). Orange County Museum of Art, Gift of the artist.

Merkins (Kathleen), 1992. Styled synthetic wig, wood shelf, enamel paint, and brass label, 36 × 15 × 15 in. (91.4 × 38.1 × 38.1 cm). Collection of Penny Cooper and Rena Rosenwasser.

Merkins (Virginia), 1992. Styled synthetic wig, wood shelf, enamel paint, and brass label, 21 × 15 × 15 in. (53.3 × 38.1 × 38.1 cm). Orange County Museum of Art, Gift of the artist.

Student in Lesbos, 1992. Neon on aluminum, 28 × 28 × 8 in. (71.1 × 71.1 × 20.3 cm).

LIVING IN SOMEONE ELSE'S PARADISE

Odd Glove, 1990. Mirror, glove, brass, print, and oak table, 30½ × 34 × 30 in. (77.5 × 86.4 × 76.2 cm). The Luckman Fine Arts Complex at Cal State LA, Gift of Gwen and Peter Norton.

Hair Fall, 1991. Hair, mixed media, and frame, 12 × 9 × 2½ in. (30.5 × 22.9 × 6.4 cm).

La Folle, 1991 (remade 2024). Postcard, pencil, and frame, 21¼ × 17⅜ in. (54 × 44.1 cm) framed.

Lace Curtain Window, 1991. Custom French window with vinyl panes, brass hardware, lace curtains, and latex paint, 48 × 36 × 8 in. (121.9 × 91.4 × 20.3 cm). The Frances Young Tang Teaching Museum and Art Gallery, Skidmore College, Gift of Peter Norton.

Miss Meret, 1991. Iron frame, mirror, chiffon, plexiglass, and Formica-veneer pedestal, 66 × 13 × 20 in. (167.6 × 33 × 50.8 cm). Collection of Gwen and Peter Norton, New York.

Rorschach Pillow, 1991 (remade 2024). Vinyl, screenprint, and upholstery filling, 17¼ × 15½ × 2½ in. (43.8 × 39.4 × 6.4 cm).

Teacher, 1991. Oak chair, wood motifs, and Formica-veneer base, 41½ × 24 × 28 in. (105.4 × 61 × 71.1 cm).

Deviant Cyborg F, 1992. Glass case, objects, vinyl type, and Formica-veneer pedestal, 60 × 28 × 16 in. (152.4 × 71.1 × 40.6 cm) overall.

Ponies (Dark), 1992. Wood and human hair, 12 × 54 × 3 in. (30.5 × 137.2 × 7.6 cm). Orange County Museum of Art, Gift of the artist.

Ponies (Light), 1992. Wood and human hair, 12 × 54 × 3 in. (30.5 × 137.2 × 7.6 cm). Orange County Museum of Art, Gift of the artist.

Red Top, 1992. Flocked cardboard profile, wood shelf, and enamel paint, 19 × 15 × 15 in. (48.3 × 38.1 × 38.1 cm).

Token, 1992. Human hair, ribbon, and Formica-veneer base, 10 × 10 × 10½ in. (25.4 × 25.4 × 26.7 cm).

Butterflies, 1993. Human hair mustaches, vinyl type, plexiglass boxes, and plexiglass shelf, 2½ × 15 × 5¼ in. (6.4 × 38.1 × 13.3 cm). The Luckman Fine Arts Complex at Cal State LA, Gift of Gwen and Peter Norton.

Fair Captive, 1993. Tree stump, steel dagger, and mirror, 22 × 19 × 19 in. (55.9 × 48.3 × 48.3 cm).

Puddle, 1993. Aluminum and Formica-veneer base, 22 × 28 × 6½ in. (55.9 × 71.1 × 16.5 cm).

Urban Dyke, 1993. Steel frame, leather dagger case, and fur, 32 × 15½ in. (81.3 × 39.4 cm). The Luckman Fine Arts Complex at Cal State LA, Gift of Gwen and Peter Norton.

Lee's Locker (M.D./M.O./M.W.), 1994

Bachelors, 1994. Metal toolbox, ceramic busts, and plexiglass shelf, 16 × 24 × 10 in. (40.6 × 61 × 25.4 cm). The Luckman Fine Arts Complex at Cal State LA, Gift of Gwen and Peter Norton.

Bride, 1994. Wood, plexiglass, rawhide, and faux fur, 3⅝ × 38¾ × 9¼ in. (9.2 × 98.4 × 23.5 cm). Private collection.

Chastity, 1994. Silver-plated platter, lock and key, polyester pillow, and plexiglass, 16 × 18 × 18 in. (40.6 × 45.7 × 45.7 cm). The Luckman Fine Arts Complex at Cal State LA, Gift of Gwen and Peter Norton.

Door C, 1994. Solid-core door, latex paint, aluminum pull plate, and fur, 78¼ × 31¾ × 2¾ in. (198.8 × 80.6 × 7 cm). The Frances Young Tang Teaching Museum and Art Gallery, Skidmore College, Gift of Peter Norton.

For Any Job, 1994. Rubber gloves, fur, and plexiglass holder, 12 × 12 × 3 in. (30.5 × 30.5 × 7.6 cm). The Luckman Fine Arts Complex at Cal State LA, Gift of Gwen and Peter Norton.

Hair Shirt, 1994. Five flocked display busts with chest-hair toupees and plexiglass shelf, 6¾ × 8 × 3½ in. (17.1 × 20.3 × 8.9 cm). The Luckman Fine Arts Complex at Cal State LA, Gift of Gwen and Peter Norton.

Hooker, 1994. Fur muff, steel tie-down stake, and steel hanger, 26½ × 16 × 4 in. (67.3 × 40.6 × 10.2 cm). The Luckman Fine Arts Complex at Cal State LA, Gift of Gwen and Peter Norton.

Protection, 1994. Vinyl and plastic overalls, fur, and steel hanger, 72 × 26 × 4 in. (182.9 × 66 × 10.2 cm). The Luckman Fine Arts Complex at Cal State LA, Gift of Gwen and Peter Norton.

Question, 1994. Metal birdcage, hacksaw, and heavy chain, 17 × 18 × 16 in. (43.2 × 45.7 × 40.6 cm). The Luckman Fine Arts Complex at Cal State LA, Gift of Gwen and Peter Norton.

Sneakers, 1994. Faux leopard boots, athletic laces, and plexiglass shelf, 12½ × 24 × 8¼ in. (31.8 × 61 × 21 cm). The Luckman Fine Arts Complex at Cal State LA, Gift of Gwen and Peter Norton.

Trap, 1994. Wood, coat hooks, and latex paint, 22 × 22 × 5 in. (55.9 × 55.9 × 12.7 cm). The Luckman Fine Arts Complex at Cal State LA, Gift of Gwen and Peter Norton.

Wanted, 1994 (remade 2024). Framed laser print, 13⅛ × 11 in. (33.3 × 27.9 cm) framed.

Witch's Spade, 1994. Steel and wood shovel, fur, steel and plastic hanger, and two screws, 38¾ × 7⅜ × 4 in. (98.4 × 18.7 × 10.2 cm). The Frances Young Tang Teaching Museum and Art Gallery, Skidmore College, Gift of Peter Norton.

Witch's Cradle, 1994. Oak lectern and flocked fabric on wood, 60 × 14 × 15½ in. (152.4 × 35.6 × 39.4 cm). The Luckman Fine Arts Complex at Cal State LA, Gift of Gwen and Peter Norton.

Monster Girls, 1994–95. Fabric and foam, dimensions variable.

Robert Blanchon, *Millie Wilson: An Interview*, 1998. Digital video, 41:16 minutes. Video Data Bank at the School of the Art Institute of Chicago.

NOT A SERIAL KILLER

Pick a Dream, 1991. Gelatin silver print of appropriated photograph of a drawing by Aileen Wuornos, 19¼ × 16 in. (48.9 × 40.6 cm) framed.

Autopsies, 1994. Seven bucket seats made of fabric and foam, 36 × 17 × 17 in. (91.4 × 43.2 × 43.2 cm) each.

Beard, 1994. Motorcycle sissy bar, upholstered head form, synthetic beard, fur, and Formica-veneer pedestal, 74 × 18⅞ × 12½ in. (188 × 47.9 × 31.8 cm). Private collection.

Chest Hair, 1994. Anodized aluminum and chest-hair toupee, 15 × 15 × 3 in. (38.1 × 38.1 × 7.6 cm).

Daytona Death Angel, 1994. Synthetic hair, fabric, and wood stand, 66 × 36 × 24 in. (167.6 × 91.4 × 61 cm). Hammer Museum, Los Angeles, Gift of the artist.

Evil Fucking Planet, 1994. Pinback buttons for public distribution, 1¼ in. (3.2 cm) diam. each.

Family Room, 1994. Rug, fake wood paneling, motorcycle seats, and framed photograph, dimensions variable.

Flat Cracker Love, 1994. Vinyl banner, 72 × 72 in. (182.9 × 182.9 cm).

DISTURBANCES

Disturbances, 1990. Nine gelatin silver prints with silkscreen, 196 × 48 in. (243.8 × 121.9 cm) overall.

Untitled, 2010. FujiClear and aluminum lightbox, 14 × 11 × 5 in. (35.6 × 27.9 × 12.7 cm).

Untitled, 2010. FujiClear and aluminum lightbox, 11 × 14 × 5 in. (27.9 × 35.6 × 12.7 cm).

Untitled, 2010. FujiClear and aluminum lightbox, 11 × 14 × 5 in. (27.9 × 35.6 × 12.7 cm).

Untitled, 2010. FujiClear and aluminum lightbox, 11 × 14 × 5 in. (27.9 × 35.6 × 12.7 cm).

Untitled, 2010. FujiClear and aluminum lightbox, 11 × 14 × 5 in. (27.9 × 35.6 × 12.7 cm).

Untitled (pink girl), 2011. FujiClear and aluminum lightbox, 14 × 11 × 5 in. (35.6 × 27.9 × 12.7 cm).

Untitled (nude with paneling), 2011. FujiClear and aluminum lightbox, 11 × 14 × 5 in. (27.9 × 35.6 × 12.7 cm).

Untitled (shopping cart), 2011. FujiClear and aluminum lightbox, 11 × 14 × 5 in. (27.9 × 35.6 × 12.7 cm).

SOMETHING BLUE

Trousers (for Tony), 1992. Two incised bronze plaques and brilliant blue wall paint, plaques: 12 × 12 in. (30.5 × 30.5 cm) each.

White Girl, 1995. Synthetic hair, fabric, and wood stand, 84 × 30 × 30 in. (213.4 × 76.2 × 76.2 cm). Palm Springs Museum of Art, Gift of the artist.

Something Blue, 1998–2000

Archive, 1998. Aluminum box, faux roses, and plastic fedora. 12 × 10¼ × 23¼ in. (30.5 × 26 × 59.1 cm).

Captive, 1998. Wood table with blue wig, glass bell jar, rubber ears, and plexiglass, 37 × 46 × 15 in. (94 × 116.8 × 38.1 cm) overall.

Cascade, 1998. Silk chiffon and steel grab bar, dimension variable.

Deceit, 1998. Wooden hand, glove, latex brain, plaster pedestal, and aluminum box, 35 × 9 × 9 in. (88.9 × 22.9 × 22.9 cm) overall.

Device, 1998. Feather, 21 × 12 in. (53.3 × 30.5 cm) framed.

Domain, 1998. Paper mesh, 23⅜ × 10⅜ in. (59.4 × 26.4 cm) framed.

Drought, 1998. Wood and paint, 15⅛ × 11⅛ in. (38.4 × 28.3 cm) framed.

Emblem, 1998. Pussywillows, 30½ × 7⅛ in. (77.5 × 18.1 cm) framed.

Inquest, 1998. Inkjet print, 12⅛ × 9½ in. (30.8 x 24.1 cm) framed.

Labyrinth, 1998. Framed piece of felt, cotton knee pads, plexiglass pedestal, men's handkerchiefs, and plexiglass shelf, dimensions variable.

Model, 1998. Aluminum and glass case and feather boas, case: 24 × 18 × 10 in. (61 × 45.7 × 25.4 cm), five boas: 72 in. (182.9 cm) long each.

Phoenix, 1998. Seven-sided painting on wood. 34 × 28 in. (86.4 × 71.1 cm) framed.

Puddle, 1998. Wood and plexiglass palettes, 15½ × 23 × ¼ in. (39.4 × 58.4 × 0.6 cm).

Schema, 1998. Plastic cutout, 10⅜ × 8⅝ in. (26.4 × 21.8 cm) framed.

Vault, 1998. Cyanotype, 12 × 9½ in. (30.5 × 24.1 cm) framed.

Conundrum, 1999. Cibachrome print. 21⅛ × 17⅛ in. (53.7 × 43.5 cm) framed.

Mirabilia, 1999. Cibachrome print, 17 × 21 in. (43.2 × 53.3 cm) framed.

Scuba, 1999. Plastic shoes and sand, 4½ × 16 × 6 in. (11.4 × 40.6 × 15.2 cm).

Asylum, 2000. Glass and steel case, waterproof underpad, ankle braces, children's swim fins, cowhide work gloves, chin guard, mouth guards, foam dice, face shield, arm protectors, swim goggles, and Formica-veneer base, 33 × 17 × 17 in. (83.8 x 43.2 x 43.2 cm).

Caryatid, 2000. Fabric and sequins, 29 × 26½ in. (73.7 × 67.3 cm) framed.

Clinic, 2000. Aluminum and steel cart, steel ball, coat display form, plastic pillow, plastic raincoat, cotton apron, felt, wood boat, miniature brain, and sand, 84 × 23¾ × 19¾ in. (213.4 × 60.3 × 50.2 cm).

EPHEMERA

Proof prints for the portrait photograph in *Fauve Semblant*, 1989. Polaroid photographs. Photos by Catherine Opie.

Fauve Semblant: Peter (A Young English Girl) 1989. Brochure. LACE (Los Angeles Contemporary Exhibitions).

Terry Wolverton, "Thoroughly Postmodern Millie." *The Advocate*, no. 564 (November 20, 1990).

Ross Bleckner, "Independents: Emerging Artists." *Out Magazine*, no. 2 (Fall 1992). Private collection.

Millie Wilson, "Dressing Up to Make the World: Transvestism as Cultural Practice," Spring 1992/Spring 1993. Course reader. California Institute of the Arts.

Catherine Opie, *Dyke Deck*, 1995. Set of playing cards. Museum of Contemporary Art, Los Angeles.

Millie Wilson and Marcos Rosales, *Pipe, Pulp, Pony*, 2007. Nothing Moments Publishing.

Selection of lesbian pulp novels that inspired works by Millie Wilson:

Frank G. Harris, *Lust Has No Mercy*, 1964. Saber Books. Private collection.

Donna Richards, *The Odd World*, 1965. Domino Books. Private collection.

Saxon Craig, *Student in Lesbos*, 1967. Leisure Books. Private collection

Lisa Robbins, *Lesbian Wives*, 1970. Barclay House. Private collection.

JILL H. CASID is an artist-theorist and historian and Professor of Visual Studies in the Departments of Art History and Gender and Women's Studies at the University of Wisconsin–Madison. Casid is completing *Doing Things with Being Undone in the Necrocene*, the first volume of a two-book project titled *Form at the Edges of Life*. Casid is the author of *Sowing Empire: Landscape and Colonization* (University of Minnesota Press, 2005) and *Scenes of Projection: Recasting the Enlightenment Subject* (University of Minnesota Press, 2015), which has been translated into Spanish (Metales Pesados, 2022), and a co-editor of the collection *Art History in the Wake of the Global Turn* (Yale University Press, 2014). Casid's artwork has been exhibited nationally and internationally, most recently at the Ford Foundation Gallery, New York; documenta fifteen, Kassel, Germany; and steirischerherbst '23, Graz, Austria.

BEATRIZ CORTEZ is a multidisciplinary artist born in El Salvador and based in Los Angeles and Davis, California. Her work explores simultaneity, multiple temporalities, the untimely, and speculative imaginaries of the future. Recent solo exhibition venues include Storm King Art Center, Windsor, New York (2023); Williams College Museum of Art, Williamstown, Massachusetts (2023); Commonwealth and Council, Los Angeles (2022); and Pitzer College Art Galleries, Claremont, California (2022). Her work was included in the 60th International Exhibition at the Venice Biennale, *Foreigners Everywhere* (2024), and the 14th Shanghai Biennial, *Cosmos Cinema* (2023–24). Cortez has received the Latinx Artist Fellowship (2023); the Borderlands Fellowship at the Vera List Center for Art and Politics (2022–24); the Atelier Calder Artist Residence in Saché, France (2022); the California Studio: Manetti Shrem Artist Residence at University of California Davis (2022); the Longenecker-Roth Artist in Residence at the University of California San Diego (2021); the Artadia Los Angeles Award (2020); and the inaugural Frieze LIFEWTR Sculpture Prize (2019); among others. She teaches sculpture and theory at the University of California, Davis.

DAVID EVANS FRANTZ is a curator based in Los Angeles. He is currently Executive Director of the Claire Falkenstein Foundation and Curator-at-Large for the Q+ initiative at the Palm Springs Art Museum. Frantz has previously held curatorial positions at ONE National Gay & Lesbian Archives at the USC Libraries, the Palm Springs Art Museum, and the Lucas Museum of Narrative Art. With Christina Linden and Chris E. Vargas, he is co-editor of *Trans Hirstory in 99 Objects*, a publication of the Museum of Trans Hirstory & Art (MOTHA), and he recently organized, with C. Ondine Chavoya, the exhibition *Teddy Sandoval and the Butch Gardens School of Art*, a collaboration among Independent Curators International (ICI); the Vincent Price Art Museum, Monterey Park, California; and the Williams College Museum of Art, Williamstown, Massachusetts.

RICHARD HAWKINS is an American artist known for his collages, paintings, and sculptures, which explore themes ranging from pop culture to desire, and encompass research-based work on Antonin Artaud, Forrest Bess, and Tatsumi Hijikata. Born in 1961 in Mexia, Texas, he graduated with a BFA from the University of Texas, Austin, in 1984 and went on to receive his MFA from the California Institute of the Arts in 1988. Today Hawkins lives and works in Los Angeles. His work is in the collections of the Museum of Modern Art, New York; the Stedelijk Museum, Amsterdam; the Art Institute of Chicago; and the Museum of Contemporary Art, Los Angeles, among others.

KANG SEUNG LEE is a multidisciplinary artist who was born in South Korea and now lives and works in Los Angeles. His work frequently engages the legacy of transnational queer histories, particularly as they intersect with art history. Lee's work has been included in international exhibitions such as the 60th International Exhibition at the Venice Biennale, *Foreigners Everywhere* (2024); *Made in LA: Acts of Living* at the Hammer Museum, Los Angeles (2023); documenta fifteen, Kassel, Germany (invited by Jatiwangi Art Factory; 2022); the New Museum Triennial, New York (2021); and the Gwangju Biennale, South Korea (2021). Recent solo exhibitions have been mounted at MASP, São Paulo (2024); the National Museum of Modern and Contemporary Art, Seoul (2023–24); and the Vincent Price Art Museum, Monterey Park, California (2023). His work is in the collections of the Hammer Museum, Los Angeles; the Los Angeles County Museum of Art; the Solomon R. Guggenheim Museum, New York; the National Museum of Modern and Contemporary Art, Korea; the Getty Research Institute, Los Angeles; the RISD Museum, Providence, Rhode Island; and the Cantor Arts Center at Stanford University, Stanford, California; among others.

AMY L. POWELL is curator of modern and contemporary art at Krannert Art Museum and curator of campus arts research in the Office for Arts Integration at the University of Illinois. Her exhibitions have included solo presentations by Jen Everett (co-curated with Blair Ebony Smith), Louise Fishman, Kennedy Browne, Basel Abbas and Ruanne Abou-Rahme, Autumn Knight, and Zina Saro-Wiwa, and and the group exhibitions *Time/Image* and *Attachment*. Previously Cynthia Woods Mitchell Postdoctoral Curatorial Fellow at Blaffer Art Museum at the University of Houston, she organized projects with Zineb Sedira, Clarissa Tossin, Anna Campbell, and Antena (Jen/Eleana Hofer and JD Pluecker). Her research has been supported by The Andy Warhol Foundation for the Visual Arts, the Smithsonian Institution, and the Institute for Research in the Humanities at the University of Wisconsin-Madison, where she completed her PhD in art history.

JESS RATH is an artist, ecologist, and educator based on Tongva homelands in the Los Angeles basin. In their twenty-five-year career as an environmental artist, Rath has created multimedia installations about plants and ecosystems that have garnered press coverage from *Smithsonian Magazine*, *Artforum*, and *Art in America*. They currently work as an environmental scientist and teach at ArtCenter College of Design, Pasadena, California, and in Ecology and Evolutionary Biology at the University of California, Irvine. Ongoing projects include Block Stewards for Native Parkways and the Farm Unfixed Science and Design Internship in the Ozarks. Rath holds an MFA from California Institute of the Arts (1996) and an MSc from the University of California, Irvine (2022).

IMAGE PERMISSIONS

p. 15, fig. 4: © 2024 Artists Rights Society (ARS), New York/DACS, London; p. 15, fig. 5: Courtesy of the artist, Galerie Gisela Capitain, Cologne, and Hauser & Wirth © Zoe Leonard; p. 16, fig. 6: © Association Marcel Duchamp/ADAGP, Paris/Artists Rights Society (ARS), New York 2024; p. 18, fig. 9: © 2024 Artists Rights Society (ARS), New York/ProLitteris, Zurich; p. 22, fig. 13: © 2024 C. Herscovici/Artists Rights Society (ARS), New York; p. 61: © Kang Seung Lee; pp. 86 and 175: © Catherine Opie, Courtesy of Regen Projects Los Angeles and Lehmann Maupin, New York, Seoul, and Hong Kong

PHOTOGRAPHY CREDITS

Front and back cover images, inside cover and flaps, and pp. 32, 64–68, 71, 74–79, 82–84, 91, 111, 144, 162–63: Taryn Mills-Drummond; pp. 8, 33 (fig. 1), 44 (fig. 6), 53–63, 69–73, 80–81, 89–90, 92–109, 112–121, 124, 130–33, 135–37, 139, 141–43, 145–150, 155–161, 164: Mikey Mosher; pp. 12 (fig. 2), 17 (fig. 8), 49 (right), 87, 153: Ian Byers-Gamber; p. 13, fig. 3: Smithsonian American Art Museum, Washington, DC/ Art Resource, NY; p. 20, fig. 11: Photo: Jeff McLane/ICA LA

COVER

Inspired by *Red Top*, 1992. Flocked cardboard profile, wood shelf, and enamel paint

BACK COVER

Pick a Dream, 1991. Gelatin silver print of appropriated photograph of a drawing by Aileen Wuornos

INSIDE COVER AND FLAPS

Detail of *Leotard, Cheater, Painter*, 1989. Stretched fabric, gelatin silver print, acrylic on canvas, and vinyl type

GUTTER THROUGHOUT BOOK

Text from *Errors of Nature*, 1992. Artist's book

ILLUSTRATIONS ON PAGES 1 AND 192

Anonymous, figures 49 and 50 in the chapter "Transvestism," in Bernard S. Talmey's *Love: A Treatise on the Science of Sex-Attraction*, 3rd ed. (New York: Eugenics Publishing Company, 1939).

Wilson reproduced these illustrations in her brochure for *Fauve Semblant: Peter (A Young English Girl)* (Los Angeles: LACE [Los Angeles Contemporary Exhibitions], 1989), n.p.; and as her entry, "Anomaly," in *Promotional Copy*, ed. Robin Kahn (New York: S.O.S. Int'l and B.R.A.T., an Arts Organization, 1993), 24–25.

Published by

Inventory Press
2305 Hyperion Avenue
Los Angeles, CA 90027
inventorypress.com

Krannert Art Museum
University of Illinois
Urbana-Champaign
College of Fine and Applied Arts
500 East Peabody Drive
Champaign, IL 61820
kam.illinois.edu

Edited by David Evans Frantz and Amy L. Powell

Copyedited by Amy R. Peltz

Proofread by Eugenia Bell

Publication managed by Kathryn Koca Polite

Designed by Content Object (Kimberly Varella, art direction and design; Gabrielle Pulgar, production designer)

Color Separations by Echelon, Los Angeles

Printed and bound by Ofset Yapımevi in Turkey on Ege Paper (cover) and Amber Graphic (interior)

Typefaces used are BB Modern Pro SemiCondensed, GT Super, and Romie Italic

LCCN: 2024945800
ISBN: 978-1-941753-75-0

Distributed by
ARTBOOK | D.A.P.
75 Broad Street, Suite 630
New York, NY 10004
artbook.com

This publication accompanied the exhibition *Millie Wilson: The Museum of Lesbian Dreams*, curated by David Evans Frantz and organized by Krannert Art Museum, University of Illinois Urbana-Champaign, on view from August 29, 2024 to March 1, 2025, and touring to The Luckman Fine Arts Complex at Cal State LA, on view from October 2025 to May 2026.

Curated by David Evans Frantz

Organized at Krannert Art Museum by Amy L. Powell

This exhibition is made possible through support from the Terra Foundation for American Art. Major support is provided by the Henry Luce Foundation and The Andy Warhol Foundation for the Visual Arts. Additional support comes from the Michael Asher Foundation, the Eileen Harris Norton Foundation, the Richard M. and Rosann Gelvin Noel Krannert Art Museum Fund, the KAM Exhibition Fund, the Art and Design Visitors Series, the Francis P. Rohlen Fund, the Humanities Research Institute Supplemental Event Fund, and the Lorado Taft Lectureship on Art courtesy of the College of Fine and Applied Arts. The program is partially supported by a grant from the Illinois Arts Council Agency. Additional support from Jerry Carden and Tim Temple, Nancy Davidson and Greg Drasler, Brice Hutchcraft, Tim Hutchison and Michael Lambert, Steven Incontro and David Joselit, Dirk Mol and Jerry Wray, Ingrid Nyeboe/President of the Louise Fishman Foundation, Mary Parker, Julie Rundell, and an anonymous donor.

TERRA
FOUNDATION FOR AMERICAN ART

LUCE HENRY LUCE FOUNDATION

Andy Warhol
The Andy Warhol Foundation for the Visual Arts

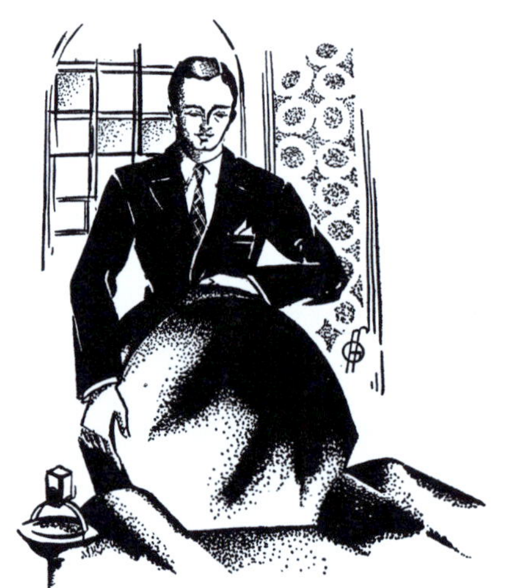